Bruce and Sharon Asakawa's

CALIFORNIA

Gardener's Guide

Dedication

For our parents, Moto and Florence Asakawa and Harry and Elsie Hashimoto, who not only passed on their love of nature to us, but who raised us to believe that dreams become realities through education and perseverance. For our children, Tasia and Eric Asakawa, and their spouses, Claudio and Stephanie, who gently nudged us to continue writing by asking, "Have you finished the book yet?" Last, but certainly not least, for our "Ya-Ya" friends, who intuitively knew when to take us on long hikes to renew our spirits and sweep away the mental cobwebs.

Acknowledgments

Although the title of our book is *Bruce and Sharon Asakawa's California Gardener's Guide,* credit for its completion is due to many people.

We gratefully acknowledge Bert Wahlen Jr. and his family for offering our West Coast gardening forums in their magazine and radio, television, and webcast programs. With their vision and enthusiastic support, we have come in contact with countless garden professionals and hobbyists and, as a result, have expanded our knowledge.

Thanks to Dori Peterson and Acacia Travel for making our garden-tour wishes come true, along with providing a wellspring of inspirational horticultural ideas.

We are also very appreciative of Roger Waynick and Hank McBride of Cool Springs Press for their leap of faith in signing us up and giving us this opportunity of a lifetime by publishing our maiden-effort book. Bouquets of gratitude to our editors, Billie Brownell and Jan Keeling, who worked tirelessly through the arduous process of reading, suggesting, editing, and coordinating with patience, grace, and tact. We also value the expertise of the entire Cool Springs Press staff. Thanks to Dee Maranhao, our Horticulture Editor, for her painstaking review and thoughtful corrections.

A special thank you to our faithful listeners who have supported our radio and webcast shows, attended our public speaking engagements, and toured with us to wondrous garden sights around the world.

Without all of you, we could not have written this book . . . *good growing, everyone.*

Bruce and Sharon Asakawa

Bruce and Sharon Asakawa's

CALIFORNIA

Gardener's Guide

COOL
SPRINGS
PRESS

Published by Cool Springs Press, a Division of Thomas Nelson, Inc., P.O. Box 141000, Nashville, Tennessee 37214.

Asakawa, Bruce and Sharon.
  California gardener's guide
  Bruce and Sharon Asakawa's California gardener's guide.
    p. cm.
  Includes bibliographical references (p.).
  ISBN 1-930604-47-5
  1. Gardening—California. I. Title: Bruce and Sharon Asakawa's
    California Gardener's Guide. II. Title.
SB453.2.C3 A82 2000
635'.09794—dc21

                                    00-045177

First printing 2000
Printed in the United States of America
10 9 8 7 6 5 4 3

Managing Editor: Billie Brownell
Horticultural Editor: Diana Maranhao
Copyeditor: Jan Keeling
Designer: Sheri Ferguson
Production Artist: S. E. Anderson

On the Cover: California Poppies, photographed by Thomas Eltzroth

Table of Contents

Welcome to Gardening
in California

One would have to travel through a number of nations to find the enormous variety of plants, climate, and topography that exist in our 800-mile-long state. Gardeners who have moved here from another part of the United States, or from another country, may be at a bit of a loss when confronted with California's diversity. To begin gardening here, they must first learn about the microclimates, soil conditions, and plant materials of their areas.

Not only do growing conditions change dramatically from region to region, but they also change within these regions. The United States Department of Agriculture (USDA) cold-hardiness zone map on page 17 shows the approximate zones of average minimum temperatures. A zone assigned to an individual plant indicates the lowest temperature at which the plant can be expected to survive. California has eight of the twelve cold-hardiness zones (4 to 11) across its 160,000 square miles . . . more than any other state. The Preferred Zone range assigned to each plant in this book is based partly on the USDA data, but mostly on our many years of experience, taking into account factors such as humidity, wind conditions, soil conditions, and salt tolerance. They represent the area in which a plant will grow best, not the only area in which the plant can grow. (Under the proper conditions, one could grow a Lemon tree in the mountains. It certainly would not be the plant's preferred area, however, nor would it be practical.)

In addition to these climate zones, every landscape has microclimates that will enhance or diminish a plant's ability to grow. We recommend that gardeners record the temperature variations in their yards in order to help them make the best plant selections. Consult page 400 to learn how to do this.

A Land of Tremendous Diversity

California is a land of astonishing geologic formations. These land forms influence regional climate, soil development, and flora and fauna diversification.

Southern California, for example, is more than Hollywood stars and surfers. It is a geologic area formed by the north-south Peninsular mountain ranges to the east and the east-west

Transverse mountain ranges to the north, offering a Mediterranean climate with subtropical temperatures and lavish vegetation. The Pacific Ocean moderates potential temperature extremes, resulting in an ideal environment for growing both native and imported plants.

To the east of the Peninsular ranges is the western portion of the Colorado Desert, known as the low desert, where California's sole endemic palm, the California Fan Palm, flourishes. Travel north of the Peninsular ranges, across the Transverse ranges, and you enter the Mojave Desert, known as the high desert, home of the unique Joshua Trees and the California Poppy Reserve. This area is subject to severe temperature fluctuations, freezing in the winter and broiling in the summer.

The Coastal mountain ranges extend northward from the western end of the Transverse ranges and parallel to the Pacific Ocean. This is where stands of California Live Oaks and Monterey Pines anchor the sky to the earth. Continuing northward along the coast to the San Francisco Bay area, the influence of the Pacific pushes farther inland as the ocean moisture moves through the delta regions and moderates the extreme temperatures of the vineyard-filled Napa Valley. Farther north, along the coast, grows the majestic Redwood Forest, filled with California's treasured state trees. An unusual process called *fog drip* means that coastal moisture condenses on the mighty trees, then accumulates and rains to the ground, creating a moist home for native plants. As you move farther inland towards Redding, on the eastern side of the Coastal range of the mountains, the geography is dominated by the southern end of the Cascade Mountain ranges, whose soils are of volcanic origin.

The Great Central Valley, which includes Sacramento and the San Joaquin Valleys, is one of the most intense agricultural growing regions in the world, with alluvial soils that make it the most fertile land in California. The Central Valley is bounded on the east by the Sierra Nevada, and on the west by Coastal mountain ranges.

California Gardening: Rewards

A tremendous reward of gardening throughout most of California is the year-long growing season. The nursery industry does not shut down in the fall as it does in other states. This year-long growing season, coupled with the continuously growing population, has allowed California to become one of the world's leaders in the nursery industry.

Our chapters on Annuals, Berries, Bulbs, Citrus, Fruit Trees, Ground Covers, Houseplants, Lawns, Nut Trees, Palms, Perennials, Roses, Shrubs, Trees, and Vines include indigenous plants as well as many others from around the world that thrive in California. Our state may be known for its native plant diversity, but we estimate that at least ninety percent of the plant material used for landscaping comes from other parts of the world. Some of the exotic plants have actually displaced some of California's native plants. As you will read in many of our plant entries, we have taken horticultural trips all over the world to view a large number of these plants in their native habitats.

You will always find a great variety of succulents, herbaceous plants, and tropical trees in our state, often growing in the same location without any problem. In many parts of California you may observe fascinating plant combinations while driving down neighborhood streets. You might see a Hibiscus from China, a Bird of Paradise from South Africa, an Amaryllis from South America, and a Persian Buttercup from Europe, all coexisting in the same landscape.

California Gardening: Challenges

Every entry in this book describes the particular needs of a particular plant. Consulting these pages is the answer to the question: How does a gardener deal with California's horticultural diversity? The Planting Techniques information section in the back of the book presents past, present, and future knowledge to make you less frustrated and more successful in your own garden.

The countless variations in California's climates and soils bring their share of challenges. There are periods of drought, dry winds, and a scarcity of chill hours in the coastal climates, all conditions that could limit the varieties that can be grown in certain areas. Desert gardeners, in the Mojave, for example, have to be particularly mindful that they select plant materials that tolerate drought, intense heat, and day-to-night temperature extremes.

Tomorrow, perhaps even today, limited natural resources, overpopulation, and minimum recycling will temper the state's abundance. As the population increases, the space available for gardening diminishes, and the scale of gardening will become smaller. You will find we address all of these challenges in this book.

Innovations and Trends

In the 1930s, gardeners in California began growing trees in used fruit cans, earning the derisive nickname "Tin Can Growers." Before too long, however, the trend caught on, and today you cannot visit any state where people don't have ornamental landscape plants growing in containers.

After World War II and during the population explosion, Californians popularized indoor/outdoor living with patios and barbecues under sunny skies. In the 1960s, California horticulturists developed what was then called "spaghetti irrigation," an innovative process further improved by the Israelis and now known as "drip irrigation."

Gardeners like color. It may be hard to believe today, but there was a time when plants sold in nurseries were all green. When nurseries began stocking plants in bloom in the late seventies, parades of flowers appeared in public areas and private gardens. "Selling color" was a major trend that had its beginnings in the Golden State. California was also one of the first states to plant highways and freeways, beginning a trend of beautifying businesses, neighborhoods and communities that spread across the country.

The most recent innovation is the development of the webcast as a tool for the dissemination of gardening information, communicating directly with folks online. Today, interactive webcasts connect California experts with gardeners all over the world. But although the use of technology to transmit valuable gardening information is an exciting development, it is still your own garden that matters most to you.

Welcome to Our Garden —*Bruce*

I remember the moment, many years ago, when Sharon commented to me, "Today is the day that we have known each other longer than we have not known each other!" Diplomatically, I scratched my head and uttered distinctly, "Yes dear, I was just thinking about the very same thing." Even though we were both born in the month of August, she is a Virgo and I am a Leo. Her college degrees are in Political Science and American History, while mine is in Landscape Architecture. Her thoughts are more linear and mine are more "outside the box." She is an organized, artistic, musical, goal-oriented, compassionate, no-nonsense kind of person—a perfect match for Mr. Laissez-Faire, who prefers a spontaneous approach to life. After thirty-seven years of marriage, our differences complement rather than separate us.

What does all this have to do with gardening? Well, it goes a long way to explain why our yard is the way it is, as well as our uniquely blended approach to landscapes. We live in an unincorporated east-to-west stretch of coastal valley in California's southernmost county. Tucked in between three established municipalities, we are about ten minutes north of the U.S.-Mexican border. This is about as rural as a community can be and still be only fifteen minutes from the center of California's third largest city. Each time our community is asked if we would like to be annexed, annexation is voted down. I suppose we like country roads, big trees, and wide open spaces, open enough to raise chickens, ducks, goats, and horses, as well as the more exotic peacocks, ostriches, and buffalo.

A Haven for Wildlife

You've probably guessed by now that our yard is not a manicured landscape—it is more like a habitat we share with Mother Nature's critters, large and small, furry, scaled, and feathered.

On a steep southeast-facing slope in our backyard is a stand of enormous sixty-year-old Eucalyptus trees. The tallest tree towers one hundred twenty-five feet above the surrounding landscape, dominating the garden, but five years ago it unfortunately succumbed to an infestation of the Eucalyptus Longhorned Borer. Since it posed no danger to any nearby structure, we let it remain, and the insect infestation attracted a tremendous population of woodpeckers and sapsuckers who have set up housekeeping in our tall sentry, feasting on the insects' larvae.

Over the past several years, another welcome manifestation has been the continuing presence of two magnificent red-tailed hawks. They reside in one of our younger Eucalyptus trees, a tall one that reaches skyward as if in anticipation of replacing the canopy of its neighboring dead sentinel. When we look out our dining-room window every morning, there they are, perched on the tallest, barest branch, awaiting the early warmth of the sun's rays. Later in the day they gracefully dip and soar, riding the thermal air currents with the greatest of ease. During the early spring months for the past four years, we have seen them flying back and forth, carrying various-sized sticks that they use to carefully build a huge nest in one of the more protected branches of another of our Eucalyptus trees. After about sixty days we hear the insistent calling of their offspring and know that once again they have successfully hatched a youngster. Every summer, just when the fledgling is almost mature, he or she swoops down and lands on our deck or in our vegetable garden and spends thirty minutes or more inspecting us. We like to believe this is the fledgling's way of saying farewell to all that is familiar before it soars away in the next day or two to establish its own home.

This year was particularly special, because the hawks were the proud parents of twins. But this year the hawks also changed their routine—this time the parents bade us farewell and the twins remained behind. While it is sad to see the parents leave, we find comfort in the fact that the twins remain in our backyard habitat and that all the young hawks successfully raised by those remarkable parents have established their own homes in and around our area. Sharon believes that some of them follow her when she calls out during her long hikes. Perhaps the next time she calls out during one of our walks, the parents will fly overhead to greet us.

In addition to our stand of Eucalyptus trees, we have a very old, gnarled Cork Oak tree cantilevered over the driveway, and in our front yard we have an aggressive, fruiting Mulberry tree with an ever-spreading root system lifting the adjacent asphalt driveway. Each spring the Mulberry's light-green foliage emerges from barren branches, announcing the arrival of the vernal equinox. At the same time its berries begin to form, attracting scouting parties of glossy black phainopeplas, buff-colored crested waxwings, jabbering scrub jays, and the brilliant golden-orange-and-black hooded orioles. The birds test the fruit daily until the berries are sweet enough, then as if there were a public announcement, hundreds of their closest friends descend on the tree for a feast. It is amusing to watch sometimes—as the berries mature past their prime, they ferment, and as the insatiable birds continue to consume them, they become inebriated and fly off a little tipsy.

More diminutive pollinators such as the iridescent Anna's hummingbirds, brightly painted swallowtail butterflies, fuzzy bumblebees, and industrious honeybees hover around our Butterfly Bush, Pride of Madeira, blossoming fruit trees, and cut-flower garden. Families of coyotes, gray foxes, and an occasional bobcat also traverse our slopes. Resident skunks and opossums use their keen olfactory senses to ferret out tasty morsels like grubs and insects in our garden. Gophers, squirrels, and rabbits tunnel, scurry, and hop by; alligator lizards and rosy boas sunbathe during the warm days; and frogs serenade us at night. We are on the visitation path of a trio of juvenile-delinquent raccoons who peek in on us on our back deck, scaring the stripes off our usually mellow fat cat, Hobie. In addition to our resident red-tailed hawks, other raptors frequent our trees: kestrels, Cooper's hawks, and the great horned and western screech owls. As well as being home to a varied assortment of citrus,

avocado, fruit, and Eucalyptus trees and drought-tolerant plants such as Rock Rose, Pride of Madeira, and European Olive, the lower portion of our back-yard is truly a haven for wildlife.

Understanding the Not-So-Perfect Environment

Over the years we have traveled with other garden lovers to horticulturally significant destinations like South Africa, Botswana, Costa Rica, China, Hawaii, England, France, Canada, the Galapagos, and others, a practice that has increased our tolerance for and heightened our understanding of the "not-so-perfect" environment. One of our most memorable excursions was to the ancient Monteverde Cloud Forest in Costa Rica. Each morning the cloud forest is shrouded in a mystical mist that gently deposits beads of glistening condensation on outstretched leaves reaching towards the shafts of light. As we walked along on the floor of the forest, we were actually strolling through a living laboratory, teeming with wildlife. There were screeching raptors high in the forest canopy, moss-laden two-toed sloths living their slow-motion lives upside-down on borrowed branches, and armies of chewing insects feeding on every leaf, in and out of sight. In fact, there wasn't a single undamaged leaf along the entire walk—and yet every plant seemed perfectly beautiful. In our own gardens, we may fret when we see a single leaf being devoured by a beastly beetle, but in the forest, there is an understanding between provider and consumer.

The Organized Areas of Our Landscape

As is our marriage, our garden is a blend of careful design and carefree habitat, a blend of two different styles that works for us. While allowing a large portion of our yard to be more "natural," we have designated smaller areas for more intensified and organized landscapes. Sharon appreciates her cut-flower garden sprinkled with a few of her favorite roses, bulbs, annuals, and orchids as well as a collection of assorted greenery suitable for flower arrangements. We also enjoy our freshly picked herbs and seasonal fruits and vegetables, and although our resident birds and other wildlife "steal" much of our bounty, it is a small price to pay for their company. In fact, it nudges us to improve the productivity of our harvest so there will be plenty to share with everyone, critters and friends alike. Our love of gardening is based on the observation of such activities as the red-tailed hawks' daily routines and the seasonal changes in our landscape. Gardening slows down our lives so that we can appreciate all the small and large miracles going on in our yard, which brings us to the question: "Why do we need another California gardening book?"

Why Another California Gardening Book

There have been hundreds of books published on all aspects of gardening, landscaping, and horticulture. So why do we need another publication tilling the same soil that has nurtured our interest in the wonders of the natural world?

We believe the answer lies in the personal involvement we all experience as we tend our gardens. We are individuals, with different personalities and different life experiences that form our individuality, and our gardens reflect this uniqueness. Many, like my wife, have moved from elsewhere and initially did not know where to begin when it comes to California gardening or even what questions to ask. Others, like myself, are native Californians but still have a lot to learn about our diverse state. After fifty years in the retail nursery and florist business, twenty years on the radio, and now, most recently, on the webcast program, we hope this book will enable you to use our knowledge gathered over these many years from personal and learned experience.

Many Ways to Garden

As with life, there are many ways to be successful in gardening. Gardens are eclectic, they are expressions of our unique personalities. I hope the format of this book will enable you to use the knowledge that is a distilled collection of our life experiences. May it provide you with the information and inspiration to spend more time in your garden. *Good growing, everyone.*

How To Use This Book

Each entry in this guide provides you with information about a plant's characteristics, habits, and basic requirements for active growth, as well as our personal experience and knowledge of the plant. We have tried to include the information you need to know about each plant to help you further appreciate California's plants, and to help you be a successful gardener. You will find such pertinent information as the plant's mature height and spread, bloom period and colors (if any), sun and soil preferences, water requirements, fertilizing needs, pruning and care, and pest information. To help you achieve striking and personal results, we offer suggestions for landscape design and companion plants.

Sun Preferences

The range of sunlight suitable for each plant is represented by icons:

Full Sun   **Partial Sun/Shade**   **Full Shade**

Additional Benefits

Many plants offer benefits that further enhance their appeal. The following icons indicate some of the more important additional benefits:

Attracts Butterflies

Attracts Hummingbirds

Produces Edible Fruit

Has Fragrance

Produces Food for Birds and Wildlife

Drought Resistant

Suitable for Cut Flowers or Arrangements

Long Bloom Period

Supports Bees

Provides Shelter for Birds

Good Fall Color

Personal Favorites

An "Our Personal Favorites" box lists specific varieties of plants that we have found particularly noteworthy. In some cases, we do not have a specific Personal Favorite, as none is particularly noteworthy. Perhaps you will find your own personal favorites.

USDA Cold-Hardiness Zones

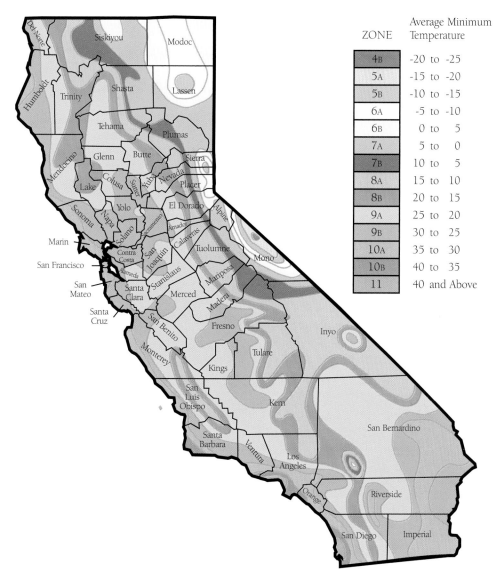

ZONE	Average Minimum Temperature
4B	-20 to -25
5A	-15 to -20
5B	-10 to -15
6A	-5 to -10
6B	0 to 5
7A	5 to 0
7B	10 to 5
8A	15 to 10
8B	20 to 15
9A	25 to 20
9B	30 to 25
10A	35 to 30
10B	40 to 35
11	40 and Above

Preferred Zones

Cold-hardiness zone designations were developed by the United States Department of Agriculture (USDA) to indicate the minimum average temperature for an area. A zone assigned to an individual plant indicates the lowest temperature at which the plant can be expected to survive over the winter. California has an extremely wide zone range, from zone 4 to zone 11. The Preferred Zone range assigned to each plant in this book is based partly on the USDA cold-hardiness zone range, but mostly on our many years of experience. Our Preferred Zone recommendations take into account factors such as humidity, wind conditions, soil conditions, and salt tolerance. They represent the area in which a plant will grow best, not the only area in which the plant can grow.

Now, let's get started. Have a great day, and good growing!

Annuals *for California*

A mixture of annuals with perennials, shrubs, ground covers, and even fruits and vegetables creates an interplay of texture and color, a living orchestra. Permanent plants may require far less care than annuals and they may bloom quite heavily during certain seasons, but most annuals "bloom their heads off" over a very long period of time.

The Merits of Annuals

Cool-weather annuals such as Icelandic Poppy, Pansy, Wood Violets, and Phlox grow and blossom during winter and spring. When planted in warmer regions in the fall, many cool-weather annuals continue to bloom until the heat and humidity of summer peaks. When they fade, you can replace them with hot-weather lovers such as Cosmos, Ageratum, and Alyssum. Many are already in flower when you plant them in early spring and they continue to bloom until the first frost in fall.

Some annuals, like California Poppy and Nasturtiums, are excellent when planted *en masse* for spectacular splashes of garden color. Others, like Alyssum, Ageratum, and

Pansies, are well suited for borders and low edging around beds and walkways. Climbing Sweet Peas can be used as quick-growing screens. Many annuals are sources of cut, dried, or edible flowers.

If flower color is the *fortissimo* in your garden symphony, the *diminuendo* is the more muted qualities of annual foliage. The fresh, green, rounded leaves of Nasturtiums and the variegated foliage of some California Poppies make beautiful ornamentals by themselves.

When and How to Plant Annuals

Annuals can be started by seed or from containers. The most economical way is to start from seeds, and it can be very rewarding to see those tiny leaves popping up in flats. Seeds sown indoors are safe from being washed out by torrential rains, eaten by birds, nipped in the bud by frost, or choked to death by weeds.

As a general rule, delay sowing seeds outdoors or setting out starter plants until the soil warms to about 60 degrees Fahrenheit—although Phlox, Poppies, Alyssum, and

Sweet Pea may be set out sooner. Start seed indoors about eight weeks prior to the last frost in your area, or anytime if winters are mild. By setting starter plants in your garden you can get a jump-start on flowers, which will appear several weeks earlier than if you sow seeds directly in the beds.

For the highest rate of germination for annuals sown from seed, use a starter flat indoors or cold frame outdoors and create half-inch furrows filled with potting soil. Sprinkle with water, make another shallow furrow in the soil, place the seed in this furrow, cover the seed with another layer of potting soil, and water thoroughly with a fine mist. Consult the directions on seed packets for planting depth, spacing, and thinning recommendations.

Instant Color *vs.* a Longer Season

To add instant color with bedding plants, you can buy them in containers or flats already in flower. If you need a finished-looking garden immediately, buy the plants in flower, but for a longer blooming performance, look for smaller plants that have not yet formed flower buds. Since annuals grow fast, buying them small allows the plants to adapt to your garden conditions more easily before expending energy on flowers. You can also start fertilizing earlier, the plants are less likely to be rootbound (which stunts growth), and you can pinch back earlier to promote branching and compact growth.

Do a Little Exploring

To determine what annuals are doing well in your region and which are most attractive to you, visit public and private gardens in your area, consult your local nursery, or your University of California Cooperative Extension. There is also nothing wrong with the learn-by-doing method, especially with annuals, since they are relatively easy to grow, inexpensive, and can be replaced two or three times a year. As in life, there are no mistakes in gardening, only learning experiences.

With so many annual varieties, there is bound to be a suitable choice for any purpose— whether to brighten an area around the dark foliage of background shrubs, to fill in flower beds, to overplant bulb beds for color after spring-flowering bulbs are spent, or to bring the outdoors indoors with vases of cut-flower bouquets. With just a little effort and planning you can have a symphony of color from spring through fall, even all year-round in mild-winter regions, amidst your stalwart trees, shrubs, perennials, ground covers, and edible crops. The addition of annuals brings music to all your senses.

Ageratum

Ageratum houstonianum

Ageratum derives its name from Greek words meaning "not old," perhaps because it was an ancient remedy for ailments associated with old age. Another plausible explanation for the name may be that these plants are such prolific bloomers and are able to retain their color and fresh appearance for a long time, seeming never to age. So who are we to disagree with the wisdom of the ancients? The flowers appear at the ends of short stems and are dense clusters of puffy, button-shaped blossoms that emerge from heart-shaped mounds of crinkled, oval-shaped, dull-green leaves. Ageratums will die once temperatures dip below freezing or if drought and high temperatures prevail for an extended period without the availability of water. They tolerate soft breezes but desiccate when winds turn hot and dry. If you want to stay young at heart, be sure to include Ageratums in your mixed flower bed, or use as a border edge. Touring butterflies, industrious bees, and zooming hummingbirds will thank you. Ageratums make wonderful fillers for small, informal cut-flower arrangements if you pick them when their blossoms are just beginning to open. During the warmth of the summer and fall seasons, they can completely cover an area in a carpet of lavender-blue, lilac, white, mauve, or pink.

Family Name / Origin Compositae / Central America

Bloom Period and Color Blue, lavender, lilac, mauve, pink and white flowers bloom in summer.

Mature Height × Spread 6 to 8 in. × 8 to 10 in.

When and How to Plant Plant from seeds or from pony packs, color packs, or 4-in. containers in spring after the last frost, spacing them 8 in. apart. In mild-winter climates, plant seeds in late winter or early spring, after the garden soil has warmed. Plant the seeds by pressing *gently* into the soil, as they need light to germinate. Ageratums prefer a loam soil; if necessary, blend amendments such as humus mulch, compost, gypsum, and preplant fertilizer (2-10-6) to a depth of 12 in. Apply a root stimulator immediately after planting. See p. 398.

Climate & Culture

Preferred Zones
9–11

Sun Preference

Sun and Soil Preferences They do best in full sun but will also fare well in light shade. Plant in rich, moist, well-drained soil with a pH of 6.7 to 7.0.

Moisture Requirements Immediately after planting, soak deeply and thoroughly. For the first week, water daily; thereafter, adjust watering frequency and amounts according to climatic and growth conditions.

Fertilizing Once their roots are established, fertilize Ageratums once a month with a water-soluble food such as 12-55-6.

Pruning and Care Deadhead regularly to prolong the blooming season.

Pests and Diseases Because they grow so low to the ground, Ageratums are a haven for slugs and snails, but these pests are easily controlled with the application of a molluscicide such as iron phosphate. If it becomes necessary to control sow bugs and earwigs, use a granular pesticide such as Carbaryl™.

Companion Plantings and Design Phlox, Shasta Daisy, and Daylily are ideal companion plants.

Our Personal Favorites

NAME	SPECIAL CHARACTERISTICS
Ageratum houstonianum 'Blue Horizon'	A taller variety / blue flowers
A. houstonianum 'Blue Danube'	Very low growing / blue flowers

Alyssum
Lobularia maritima

*There is quite a lot of confusion about whether Alyssum is really the annual Lobularia. Most of us are content with referring to the mauve or white annual as Sweet Alyssum, except for the vigilant botanists. In the interest of botanical accuracy, Sweet Alyssum is really Lobularia maritima, one of the most popular annuals. In more temperate climates, it will reseed almost continually and appear in the garden just about all year-round. These are multibranched plants with spreading habits. Their leaves are erect and grayish-green in color. Atop the foliage, from spring to fall, they produce thick mounds of fragrant, one- to three-inch flower clusters. These petite four-petaled flowers come in hues of white, pink, rose-red, violet, and lilac. Their rich nectar provides satisfying nourishment for your garden gatherers such as bees, hummingbirds, and butterflies. Although they withstand short periods of drought, dry wind, heat, and temperatures slightly below freezing, they do best in mild weather with regular irrigation. Because of their tolerance to salt, they can be used in seaside gardens. **Note:** If you cannot find Lobularia maritima, look for Alyssum maritimum, another botanical name sometimes used for the same plant.*

Family Name / Origin Cruciferaea / Europe

Bloom Period and Color White, pink, rose-red, violet and lilac flowers bloom in spring and summer.

Mature Height × Spread 4 in. × 6 to 12 in.

When and How to Plant Plant in spring from seed or pony packs, color packs, or 4-in. pots, spacing them 6 to 8 in. apart. Alyssum prefers loam soil; if necessary, prepare the flower bed by blending soil amendments such as humus mulch, compost, gypsum, and preplant fertilizer (2-10-6) to a depth of 12 in. Since Alyssum seeds need light to germinate, tap the seeds very gently in the soil so they will not be buried too deeply. For additional information, consult Planting Techniques, p. 398.

Climate & Culture

Preferred Zones
9–11

Sun Preference

Sun and Soil Preferences Alyssum thrives in full sun, in well-drained, evenly moist soil with a pH of 6.8 to 7.0.

Moisture Requirements Immediately after planting, soak deeply and thoroughly. For the first week, water daily; thereafter, adjust watering frequency and amounts according to weather and growth conditions.

Fertilizing Fertilize once a month during the growing season with a water-soluble food such as 12-55-6.

Pruning and Care After the first flush of blossoms, clip back the plant by 50 percent to encourage a longer flowering cycle.

Pests and Diseases Alyssum is not susceptible to many diseases or pests, but as is true for many of our other favorite annual flowers, weekly inspection of the blossoms and foliage is prudent.

Companion Plantings and Design We use Alyssum in rock gardens, creating floral rivers of white or blue flowing down through the boulders; as ground cover in mixed flower beds; and as edging in containers. Sweet Alyssum grows well with Shore Juniper, Daylily, Lily of the Nile, and Wallflower.

Our Personal Favorite

NAME	SPECIAL CHARACTERISTICS
Lobularia maritima 'Royal Carpet'	Fragrant, very dark blue flowers

California Poppy
Eschscholzia californica

The Antelope Valley California Poppy Reserve, located on the high desert southwest of the bustling town of Mojave, is one of our favorite places to visit in spring. Near the end of the rainy season, a carpet of greenish-blue, finely dissected, fernlike foliage emerges from a seemingly barren desert floor. Within weeks these often-forgotten native plants grow, mature, and display a profusion of cup-shaped blooms that blanket the carpet of foliage with an overlay of brilliant orange. After the crepe-textured flowers have been pollinated, next season's seeds develop, the flower petals fall, and the seeds are dispersed. You can replicate this cycle in your own landscape and enjoy a field of brilliant orange or hybridized versions in shades of yellow, scarlet, creamy-white, copper, or pinkish-red each spring. Since the California Poppy is native to semidesert and prairie regions of the West, they thrive in somewhat dry conditions and cool, sunny temperatures, but they quickly die back during extended periods of drought; hot, dry winds; and high temperatures. During overcast or rainy days and in the evenings, their flowers remain tightly closed, but during bright, sunny days they will remain open until nighttime.

Family Name / Origin Papaveraceae / California

Bloom Period and Color Orange flowers bloom in spring.

Mature Height × Spread 8 to 12 in. × 8 to 12 in.

When and How to Plant Plant from pony packs or 4-in. pots, or broadcast seed before fall rains. California Poppies prefer sandy loam soil, but will tolerate denser textures. If needed, blend soil amendments such as humus mulch, compost, gypsum, and preplant fertilizer (2-10-6) to a depth of 8 in. See p. 398.

Sun and Soil Preferences They prefer full-sun areas of warm, dry, sandy, well-drained soil with a pH of 6.8 to 7.2.

Climate & Culture

Preferred Zones
7–11

Sun Preference

Moisture Requirements If planting from pony packs or 4-in. pots, soak deeply and thoroughly after planting. Water daily the first week; thereafter, adjust watering according to weather and growth conditions. If seed is sown, don't begin regular watering until seedlings are visible.

Fertilizing Fertilize monthly during the growing season with a water-soluble food such as 2-10-6. Do not overfertilize established plants.

Pruning and Care Leave the spent flowers alone for seed production and dispersal. Once you have successfully grown California Poppies in a particular area, they will continue to re-establish themselves. Thin out crowded seedlings and keep the area free of weeds for optimum growing conditions.

Pests and Diseases Unless damage is extensive, simply handpick and squash snails and slugs.

Companion Plantings and Design Grow *en masse* in expansive areas near edges of lawns, on sunny slopes, or naturalized in rock gardens. They make attractive but short-lived cut flowers if picked in the early morning while tightly budded. Plant with Bird of Paradise, Shore Juniper, and Silverberry.

Our Personal Favorites

NAME	SPECIAL CHARACTERISTICS
Eschscholzia californica 'Mission Bells'	Double and semidouble flowers
E. californica 'Milky White'	Single flowers / cream-colored with orange centers

Cosmos

Cosmos bipinnatus

*Although the Greek word Cosmos means "symmetrical beauty" or "perfection,"
beauty is indeed in the eye of the beholder: thinking it was a weed, Sharon yanked
a Cosmos out of a pot that a resident bird had thoughtfully "planted." While some
writers describe it as a scraggly, unattractive, large-flowered plant with pale-green,
thinly-divided leaves similar to wet feathers, others describe it as daisylike, with deeply
divided, feathery-textured leaves. I (Bruce) belong to the latter school and think these
crimson, maroon, pink, white, orange, violet, and red-hued flowers with bright-yellow
centers make delicate accents when planted randomly in front of hedges or walls, or
when used as fillers for the middle or background sections of flower beds. In addition to
attracting butterflies, they are also great as cut flowers. Pick them in the early morning
when the flower petals are just beginning to open but are not yet lying flat. Cosmos
plants are easy to cultivate as long as there is plenty of moisture and there are no
heavy summer rainstorms—their flowers tend to snap off from the stems during such
storms. They withstand heat as long as there is adequate moisture, but they do not
tolerate drought, blustery winds, or cold temperatures.*

Family Name / Origin Compositae / Mexico, Southern North America

Bloom Period and Color Pink, white, orange, violet, and red flowers bloom in spring and summer.

Mature Height × Spread 2 to 4 ft. × 12 to 18 in.

When and How to Plant Plant in spring from pony packs, color packs, or 4-in. pots, spacing 8 to 12 in. apart so they will support each other. Although Cosmos do self-sow (with help from the birds), you can plant from seed in spring after the last frost. They prefer loam soil, but will tolerate clayey textures; if necessary, blend soil amendments such as humus mulch, compost, gypsum, and preplant fertilizer (2-10-6) to a depth of 12 in. Also see p. 398.

Climate & Culture

Preferred Zones
9–11

Sun Preference

Sun and Soil Preferences Cosmos plants do best in full sun and prefer soil that is evenly moist and well drained, with a pH of 7.0.

Moisture Requirements Immediately after planting, soak deeply and thoroughly. During the first week, water daily; thereafter, adjust watering frequency and amounts according to climatic and growth conditions. During the hot summer months, these plants need lots of water.

Fertilizing Fertilize once a month with a water-soluble food, 12-55-6. Keep in mind that if the soil is too rich the stems will be weak and floppy, bearing few flowers.

Pruning and Care To prolong the bloom season, deadhead the spent flowers regularly.

Pests and Diseases The only problems these plants seem to have come from snails, slugs, or aphids. If damage is too extensive, try harvesting the pesky molluscs by hand and squishing them, or use a molluscicide such as iron phosphate. To control aphids, use Neem oil or insecticidal soap.

Companion Plantings and Design Ideal companion plants are Shasta Daisies, Blue Marguerites, and Foxgloves.

Icelandic Poppy

Papaver nudicaule

In ancient times, Poppy flowers, seeds, and sap were used for cooking and as a narcotic. Because of its toxic qualities, this plant was often associated with death. Even now, artificial Poppies are handed out as a remembrance of those who have died while serving their country. One of our memories of the Chelsea Flower Show in 1992 is of an elderly gentleman gently pinning such a Veteran's Day memorial on Bruce's lapel. Of all the Poppies, the Icelandic Poppy is our favorite for home gardeners: it has three-inch saucer-shaped flowers ranging in colors from bright red to hot pink to brilliant orange to soft salmon to sunny yellow and greenish-white. The ciliated, deeply indented, moss-green leaves form a thick circle of foliage from which thin, leafless stems emerge, bearing spectacular, delicately fragrant, crepe paper–textured flowers that bloom in spring. Strictly speaking, the Icelandic Poppy is a perennial, but you will have younger and stronger growth if you treat it as an annual or biennial. Icelandic Poppies grow best where the nights are cool and the days are warm. Although they tolerate extremely cold temperatures, they dislike drought; hot, dry winds; and intense heat. It is best, therefore, to use them during the cooler months.

Family Name / Origin Papaveraceae / Subarctic Regions

Bloom Period and Color White, yellow, orange, or red flowers bloom in spring.

Mature Height × Spread 8 to 12 in. × 10 in.

When and How to Plant Plant in fall from pony packs, color packs, or 4-in. pots, spacing 6 to 8 in. Icelandic Poppies prefer loam soil; blend amendments such as humus mulch, compost, gypsum, and preplant fertilizer (2-10-6) to a depth of 12 in. Also see p. 398.

Sun and Soil Preferences Where summers are hot and humid, select a spot with morning sun and afternoon shade; in cooler areas, full sun is preferable. An evenly moist, well-drained soil with a pH of 6.8 to 7.0 is best.

Moisture Requirements Soak deeply after planting. Water daily the first week; thereafter, water according to weather and growth conditions.

Fertilizing Fertilize monthly during the growing season with a water-soluble food such as 12-55-6.

Pruning and Care After the flower petals fall, remove the seed capsules to extend the blooming season. You can also extend the blooming season by planting at successive intervals of every three to six weeks. If planting from seed, tamp lightly and cover completely with soil, as darkness promotes better germination.

Pests and Diseases There are few disease or insect problems. Neem oil is an effective control if one is needed.

Companion Plantings and Design Poppies grow well with Pansies, Phlox, and Rock Rose. Use as an ornamental in mixed flower beds, as a border plant, and as an excellent cut flower. When using Poppies as cut flowers, cut when the flower petals are just beginning to open, then burn the ends with a flame or immerse in boiling water for a few seconds to prevent the loss of latex and avoid flower wilt. Before arranging, set in cold water for several hours. Re-sear the ends whenever you cut them again.

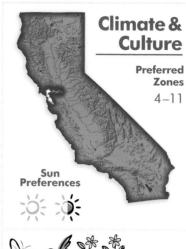

Climate & Culture

Preferred Zones
4–11

Sun Preferences

Our Personal Favorite

NAME	SPECIAL CHARACTERISTICS
Papaver nudicaule 'Garden Gnome Hybrids'	Dwarf / compact / yellow and pink flowers

Nasturtium

Tropaeolum majus

For many years Sharon wanted to plant Nasturtiums on a sloping bank below our raised vegetable beds, but I (Bruce) resisted because I always thought of them as rather common, weedlike plants. Now that they are flourishing on our slope, their cheerful red, orange, and golden-spurred flowers make a beautiful display of spring and summer color against a backdrop of lilypad-like, fresh, green leaves. In most areas of Southern California where climates are temperate, Nasturtiums may act like perennials, but in other areas they will die back after the first frost. Nasturtiums do not like excessive summer heat, frost, drought, or dry winds, preferring cool, even temperatures. They make lovely trailing or climbing accents in containers on patios or decks and look beautiful planted en masse on slopes, or tumbling over raised flower beds or rock gardens. Individual flower stems or lengths of blooming vines can be cut for fun, informal bouquets. Gather them in the early morning when the buds are still tight but showing color and they will last up to five days in water. Organically grown Nasturtium flowers and leaves add a peppery flavor to mixed salad greens and sandwiches, and their petite curving flower tips make natural straws from which children, hummingbirds, bees, and butterflies can sip their nectar.

Family Name / Origin Tropaeolaceae / Colombia, Bolivia

Bloom Period and Color Yellow and orange flowers bloom in spring and summer.

Mature Height × Spread 4 to 10 in. × 4 to 6 ft.

When and How to Plant Plant any time of year in frost-free zones, or after the last frost in colder areas. Nick the seeds with a file or knife and soak them overnight to speed germination; plant ½ in. deep, sowing them 4 to 6 in. apart for bush varieties, 8 to 10 in. apart for vine varieties. Make the soil a loam texture by adding amendments such as humus mulch, compost, gypsum, and preplant fertilizer (2-10-6) to a depth of 12 in. Also refer to Planting Techniques, p. 398.

Climate & Culture

Preferred Zones
9–11

Sun Preferences

Sun and Soil Preferences Nasturtiums do best in full sun except in areas where summers are hot and dry—then plant them in partial sun. They prefer well-drained, loose-textured soil with a pH of 7.0.

Moisture Requirements Soak deeply and thoroughly after planting. Water daily the first week; thereafter, water according to weather and growth conditions.

Fertilizing Using a water-soluble food such as 12-55-6, fertilize container plants twice a month during the leafy growth period, and after that only if the foliage begins to turn yellow. Fertilize only once a month if the plants are directly planted in the ground, and do not water too excessively or you may be rewarded with lush foliage but few flowers.

Pruning and Care Keep dried undergrowth cleared away to discourage families of rodents, such as mice, from setting up habitats.

Pests and Diseases Few pests and diseases affect Nasturtiums except snails, slugs, and sucking insects such as aphids. If damage is extensive, use Neem oil as a remedy against sucking, rasping, and chewing insects. If you are not using the plants as edibles, you can control snails and slugs with a molluscicide; otherwise, resort to the tried-and-true organic method of "pick and squish." Rabbits, gophers, groundhogs, and deer seem to dislike the peppery, spicy flavor.

Companion Plantings and Design Ideal companion plants are California Lilacs, Roses, Geraniums, Shasta Daisies, and Persimmon Trees.

Pansy
Viola × wittrockiana

You might think that Pansies are simple flowers, but on closer inspection you will find that they come in such a dazzling array of patterns, colors, and shapes that it is difficult to adequately describe them. When our family first began our nursery business, we were greatly impressed with these huge, intensely-colored faces that arrived as field-grown 'Majestic' hybrids packed in wooden strawberry trays. We could choose from single- to double-flowered hybrids in colors ranging from violet, lavender, wine-purple, lilac-blue, bronze, yellow, and orange. Some have dark, velvety faces that offer a contrasting color to their surrounding petals, and some come in single hues. Generally, the flowers are spurred with five petals, one forming a lower lip, two pointing sideways, and two pointing skyward. Their leaves are as varied as their colors, running the gamut from rounded, lobed, and toothed to heart-shaped. Depending on climate, they can bloom in the fall, winter, or spring, but because they are cool-weather annuals, they will die out in hot-summer areas. Pansies tolerate cold temperatures and wind but do not tolerate drought or high temperatures.

Family Name / Origin Violaceae / not found in the wild

Bloom Period and Color Violet, lavender, blue, purple, yellow, and orange flowers bloom fall, winter, or early spring.

Mature Height × Spread 8 to 10 in. × 6 to 10 in.

When and How to Plant Plant in early autumn from pony packs, color packs, or 4-in. pots, spacing 6 in. apart. Plant from seeds in midsummer in mild climates, but in hot-summer areas, wait until early to mid-fall. Pansies prefer a loam soil. If necessary, blend amendments such as humus mulch, compost, gypsum, and preplant fertilizer (2-10-6) to a depth of 12 in. Cover seeds with 1/8 in. of soil, then with a newspaper or piece of black plastic, for they need darkness to germinate. Be sure to remove the covers, not the soil, immediately after germination. See p. 398.

Climate & Culture

Preferred Zones 7–11

Sun Preferences

Sun and Soil Preferences They do best in full sun but will also grow in partial shade. Provide rich, moist, well-drained soil, pH 6.7 to 7.0.

Moisture Requirements Soak after planting. Water daily the first week; thereafter, water according to climatic and growth conditions.

Fertilizing Fertilize monthly during the growing and blooming seasons with a water-soluble food, 12-55-6.

Pruning and Care Deadhead regularly to extend the blooming cycle.

Pests and Diseases Damping off, a soil-borne fungus, is one of the few serious disease problems. It is quickly identified when the main stems deteriorate at ground level, eventually falling over. Remove the diseased plants, and solarize the soil by covering the area with 4 or 6 mil clear plastic, weighing down the edges with 2×4s or bricks. Leave in place for four to six weeks; the heat that builds up underneath the plastic should suppress the fungus. Although the problem will not be completely eradicated, solarization will keep it under control.

Companion Plantings and Design Pansies grow well with Wallflower, Candytuft, Ageratum, Alyssum, and Phlox.

Our Personal Favorite

NAME	SPECIAL CHARACTERISTICS
Viola × wittrockiana 'Majestic'	Very large, tricolored flowers

Phlox

Phlox drummondii

At Disneyland in Anaheim, Phlox are used en masse as border ornamentals within the park areas and throughout all Adventureland. Seeing them in full spring bloom, we realized the Greek translation of Phlox—"flame"—is one of the most appropriate descriptions for these brightly colored, multibranched annuals. Each branch has sharply pointed, long, ciliated leaves and rounded mounds of vivid purple, lavender, pink, salmon, and red-colored flowers. Just about the only color this plant does not come in is yellow. Its one-inch single or double flowers are somewhat flat with star-shaped petals and have a light fragrance. Since most Phlox come from northern temperate zones, they tolerate cold quite well and dislike drought, wind, and heat unless they are watered often. You can use them in vibrant summer arrangements if you harvest when the majority of the flowers have opened, cauterize the ends of the stems with a flame or immerse in boiling water for just a few seconds, then put them in cold water. Florists call this the "fire and ice" method for preventing the latex from oozing out of their stems, thus avoiding the problem of flower wilt.

Family Name / Origin Polemoniaceae / North America

Bloom Period and Color Red, pink, white, or purple flowers bloom in spring.

Mature Height × Spread 8 to 10 in. × 8 to 10 in.

When and How to Plant Plant in fall to early spring from pony packs, color packs, or 4-in. pots, spacing 8 in. In areas with mild winters, sow seeds in fall for early spring bloom. Otherwise, wait until spring, after the last frost. To lengthen the flowering season in cool-summer areas, plant seeds every four to six weeks. Phlox tend to die out in hot, humid weather. Also see p. 398.

Climate & Culture

Preferred Zones
7–11

Sun Preferences

Sun and Soil Preferences In warm climates, they like semishade, but in cooler regions, plant in full sun. They need moist, well-drained soil with a pH of 6.7 to 7.0. Phlox prefer loam soils. If necessary, blend soil amendments such as humus mulch, compost, gypsum, and preplant fertilizer (2-10-6) to a depth of 12 in.

Moisture Requirements Soak deeply after planting. Water daily the first week; thereafter, adjust watering according to weather and growth conditions.

Fertilizing Fertilize monthly during the bloom season with a water-soluble food such as 12-55-6.

Pruning and Care Cut back overgrown, scraggly plants to about 4 in. To prolong the bloom cycle, deadhead regularly.

Pests and Diseases Neem oil is an effective control for mites and mildew. For caterpillars, use *Bacillus thuringiensis* (*B.t.*). Handpick snails and slugs in the early morning or use a molluscicide.

Companion Plantings and Design Phlox is an excellent cool-weather plant for containers and mixed bedding areas. We particularly like to see them cascading over the edges of planters or pots, and so do hummingbirds. Ideal companion plants are Lily of the Nile, California Poppy, and Candytuft.

Our Personal Favorites

NAME	SPECIAL CHARACTERISTICS
Phlox drummondii 'Carnival'	Large flowers with contrasting centers
P. drummondii 'Palona Hybrids'	Dwarf / compact / multicolored flowers

Sweet Peas

Lathyrus odoratus

We always associate Sweet Peas with small children who delight in picking the fragrant, butterfly-shaped flowers. With their bush or vining habit, these plants are an ideal height for little ones to sniff, and they love to harvest their delicate blossoms on wiry stems. There are usually three winglike petals per flower with five to seven flowers on a single stem in warm hues of blue, lavender, rose-pink, white, salmon, and orange. Their leaves divide into feathery leaflets with curly tendrils that wrap around supports of string, wires, trellises, and tree branches. Since they were originally found in cool wooded areas, along riverbanks, in mountainous regions as high as 6000 feet, and even along seashores, it is easy to see why they do best in temperate to cool weather and bloom less in hot, dry climates. If left alone, the spent flowers will rapidly go to seed, signaling to the plant that its life cycle is about to end. When hot-weather conditions prevail, you should allow them to seed so you can gather the seeds and save to sow next year or to give away to friends and family. Be sure to store your seeds in airtight containers such as mason jars or cans, and place them in a cool, dry place.

Family Name / Origin Leguminosae / Italy

Bloom Period and Color Blue, pink, white, and red flowers bloom in summer.

Mature Height × Spread 4 to 6 in. (vining)

When and How to Plant Nick seeds with a file or knife and soak overnight to speed germination. Sow 1 in. deep in rows in early spring, spacing about 2 in. apart. In mild-winter areas, sow directly in the ground in late summer so you will have late-winter or early-spring blooms; otherwise, plant in late winter and early spring for late-spring and early-summer blooms. In colder zones, plant seeds as soon as you can work the soil. Anchor the trellis or the weight of the vines will topple them. Give the soil a loam texture by adding amendments such as humus mulch, compost, gypsum, and preplant fertilizer (2-10-6) to a depth of 12 in. We have been successful using a planting trench 18 to 20 in. long with a 4- to 5-in. cover of organic material. Do not plant Sweet Peas in the same place two years in a row. See p. 398.

Climate & Culture

Preferred Zones 6–11

Sun Preference

Sun and Soil Preferences They need full sun and well-drained soil with a pH of 6.0 to 7.2.

Moisture Requirements Soak thoroughly after planting. During the first week until the seeds germinate, water so the ground stays evenly moist. Thereafter, water according to climatic and growth conditions.

Fertilizing Fertilize with a complete food once seedlings sprout six to eight leaves. After that, fertilize monthly with a water-soluble fertilizer, such as a 12-55-6.

Pruning and Care To keep Sweet Peas flowering, deadhead spent flowers.

Pests and Diseases Unfortunately, these seeds are delectable appetizers for birds and mice, and the birds, snails, and slugs enjoy dining on the tender seedlings. Keep a vigilant eye out for pests.

Companion Plantings and Design As climbing annuals, Sweet Peas are among the best choices for cutting. They will last about one week in arrangements if you pick them in early morning and select stems whose top blossoms are still budded. Use a powdered floral preservative and keep your perfumed bouquets away from sources of ethylene gas such as fresh fruits, vegetables, and cigarette smoke.

Wood Violets
Viola odorata

According to Greek mythology, Io, daughter of the river god Inachus, was transformed from a lovely maiden into a large cow. This strange metamorphosis was the work of Zeus, who was protecting her from his jealous wife. Zeus wanted Io to graze on something less mundane than grass, so he created the dainty Viola for her meals. In addition to the fact that with a friend like Zeus one does not need enemies, would you believe the ancient classicists spent their time debating whether Io the heifer grazed upon Wood Violets or Pansies? Since the genus Viola includes both the Pansy and the Violet, I would rather spend my time planting and enjoying both. Wood Violets are the royalty of aromatic violets, with beautiful, heart-shaped, hunter-green leaves bearing March blooms of purple perfumed flowers. They add color and delicate flavor to salads and cakes and, of course, are one of the most romantic of cut flowers. Romantic as they may be, make sure your violets have not been sprayed with any pesticides or herbicides if you are using them as edibles. Wood Violets love cool climates and wither during drought, wind, and heat.

Family Name / Origin Violaceae / S Europe

Bloom Period and Color Violet flowers bloom in spring.

Mature Height × Spread 4 to 6 in. × 8 to 24 in.

When and How to Plant Plant in spring or fall from 4-in. pots or 1-gallon containers, spacing 6 to 10 in. apart. Wood Violets prefer loam soil; if necessary, blend amendments such as humus mulch, compost, gypsum, and preplant fertilizer (2-10-6) to a depth of 12 in. For more information, refer to Planting Techniques, p. 398.

Sun and Soil Preferences Pick a partial-shade location where there is cool, rich, well-drained soil with a pH of 6.8 to 7.2.

Moisture Requirements Soak deeply and thoroughly after planting. During the first week, water daily; thereafter, adjust watering frequency and amounts according to weather and growth conditions.

Fertilizing Fertilize monthly during the growing season with a water-soluble food such as 12-55-6.

Pruning and Care Although Wood Violets are technically perennials, you will have better results if you treat them as annuals, as they decline in winter. Propagate by division in spring or fall. To lengthen the bloom season, remove all spent flowers.

Pests and Diseases Because they grow close to the ground and their foliage is so tasty, Wood Violets may exhibit signs of pest damage. Neem oil is a good, biodegradable, combination fungicide and insecticide. Protect the plants from hoards of ravenous snails and slugs with early-morning hand-picking or with a molluscicide.

Companion Plantings and Design Our Wood Violets are nestled under the dappled light of Oak and Mulberry trees. In addition to their beauty in woodland areas, they make showy accents when peeking out of shady rock gardens and border edges. If using as cut flowers, pick just as they are beginning to open up, and avoid heat or direct sunlight in the house. Cyclamen, European Olive, and Southern Magnolia make ideal companion plants.

Climate & Culture

Preferred Zones
8–11

Sun Preference

Berries *for California*

Every summer when our children were youngsters, they would go on fishing and camping trips with their grandparents. When we could get away from our nursery business, we would join them near the Klamath and Trinity Rivers, close to the Oregon border. After our early-morning catches of steelhead, deep-water chinook, and King salmon, we would spend sun-soaked afternoons picking fresh-off-the-vine blackberries. Although we popped more of them in our mouths than in our buckets, there were enough for us to later stuff into butter-flaked pies. The aroma of those pies filled to their brims with the sweet goodness of glistening blackberries, simmering and bubbling in their rich maroon nectar, would tease and activate our salivary glands. When they were finally baked to golden perfection, we would all stampede to the oven, select one pie as our taste test, plop scoops of vanilla ice cream over each steaming, savory slice, and gulp down the fruits of our labor.

A Summer Parade of Berries

Plump, fresh berries picked at just the ripe moment punctuate sunny summer memories and motivate us to mulch, fertilize, water, weed, trellis, train, and prune our berry plants. We endure these chores because once our tangled mass of bare-rooted Strawberries, spindly Raspberry canes, and Blueberry sprigs are properly tended, a parade of berries rewards us during California's warm seasons. First to come are the sweet, juicy strawberries, the one backyard fruit that bears a sizable crop the same year it is planted, followed by deep-red raspberries in May, then a later appearance by jewel-like boysenberries, plump blueberries, and, as summer's glorious finale, succulent blackberries.

Grow the Berries That Are Right for Your Area

In California we can grow all kinds of berries, but it is important to select the right ones, as some are more suitable for specific regions. Depending on the

variety, Strawberries can be grown in nearly every part of California, while Boysenberries are commercially grown primarily around the Los Angeles area and pockets of Modesto and Watsonville (it was Walter Knott, of Knott's Berry Farm fame in Anaheim, who introduced this reddish-black jewel to the public).

Since Blueberries are native to bogs, they prefer high-acid soils and do best in mounded beds of amended soil or in containers. There are also variations in chill, pollination, and pruning requirements for all berries. Whether you live on the coast, inland, north, or south, your local nursery or University of California Cooperative Extension office can suggest the most area-appropriate and disease-resistant cultivars.

Wherever you plant them, allow plenty of room for aggressive brambles like Blackberries, Boysenberries, and Raspberries, and trellis or train them on wires. If you are working with thorned berries, wear thick, protective gloves, such as tough pigskin, to protect your skin from scratches.

Enjoy Spring and Summer Berries All Year

To enjoy spring and summer berries all year long, wash them, dry them with paper towels, place them one layer thick on baking sheets, and freeze uncovered until solid. Then package in air-tight containers or freezer bags.

There are certain rules in life that must be obeyed, and one is to use only the freshest, richest, and creamiest ingredients if you are making ice cream, otherwise do not bother. This is why our favorite way to freeze fresh-from-the-garden berries is to add them to homemade ice creams and sorbets. Extending the sweetness of summer into autumn and winter doesn't get much better than this.

Blackberry
Rubus fruticosus

As local bears have always known, eating Blackberries is one of the purest joys of summer. Blackberries grow best in the mild Pacific coastal and inland valley regions from Southern to Northern California. They are similar in appearance and growth habits to Raspberries, except they bear later in the summer and tolerate more heat but are less cold hardy. Once their prickly canes are covered with stems of deep-green leaves, pale pink or white flowers resembling miniature single roses emerge from their foliar nests. There are basically two types of Blackberries, the erect and semi-erect Eastern and the trailing Western types. Since the Western type grows primarily in California and the Pacific Northwest, we will highlight their characteristics. They are vigorous deciduous plants whose trailing, mostly thorny varieties are easier to cultivate on sturdy trellises. In addition to eating these mildly sweet, purplish-black jewels fresh, you can use them in jams, sauces, pies, and cobblers. If you plant them in the ground or in containers, provide their prickly, arching stems with plenty of support and give them lots of room. Extreme heat shortens the life span and reduces the yield and quality of the fruit, but if adequate moisture is provided, they will tolerate short periods of high heat, dry winds, drought, and subfreezing temperatures.

Family Name / Origin Rosaceae / North America

Fruit Berries mature in early summer.

Mature Size 6 to 15 ft. long

When and How to Plant Plant in late winter or early spring from bare-root stock, spacing 6 to 8 ft. apart. Build a watering basin 4 ft. in diameter or, if planting in a row, build a watering trench 2 ft. wide. Cover with 2 in. of organic material such as humus mulch or compost. See Planting Techniques, p. 398.

Sun and Soil Preferences They do best in full sun in well-drained, sandy loam soil with a pH of 6.0 to 7.0.

Climate & Culture

Preferred Zones 5–11

Sun Preference

Moisture Requirements Water deeply after planting. Water three times the first week; thereafter, adjust frequency and amount to climatic and growth conditions.

Fertilizing Fertilize in early spring with a complete granular food, 6-10-4.

Pruning and Care Blackberries bear on second-year canes, so allow first-year laterals to grow on a sturdy support system such as a trellis, pruning only diseased or weak canes. Train the canes by tying each one to the trellis. If you are not sure your Blackberry canes can survive winter, train them at an angle on the trellis; in winter, untie and drop them to the ground. Cover them with straw to protect from cold damage; when dormancy ends, re-tie to the trellis.

Pests and Diseases Few serious disease or insect problems affect Blackberries, except for occasional infestations of the fungus rust or attacks by chewing insects. If the problem persists, apply Neem oil.

Our Personal Favorites

NAME	SPECIAL CHARACTERISTICS
R. f. 'Marion'	Medium to large, bright-red, flavorful berries for fresh, freezing, or canning uses
R. f. 'Olallie'	Large, black, shiny 1½-in.-long berries / firm / sweeter than others
R. f. 'Navajo' (Plant patent #6679)	Thornless / the first fully erect, self-supporting Blackberry

Blueberry, Rabbiteye
Vaccinium ashei

Blueberries are tall, handsome deciduous shrubs that make attractive landscape plants, suitable for hedge or shrub borders or in containers. Their three-inch leaves start out reddish-bronze in spring, then gradually transform into dark-green hues. Fragrant white bell-shaped blossoms add a refreshing touch; when they flutter to the ground, clusters of green berries form and turn into plump, deep-blue mouth-poppers. The foliage later dons autumnal colors of scarlet reds and sunset yellows before dropping and signaling the start of winter dormancy. Sharon and I have spent many summer mornings gathering up these bluish-black morsels to eat fresh with our cereal or ice cream or in fruit salads. Any excess bounty is frozen, canned, or dried for later use in pies, muffins, breads, pancakes, sauces, and syrups. The Rabbiteye Blueberries are a popular choice for California home gardeners because they grow and taste like the high-bush and low-bush varieties that thrive in cold-winter areas but they do not need winter chill to set fruit. Like other types of Blueberries, they are not self-fruitful, so plant at least two compatible varieties that flower about the same time, for cross-pollination. If well mulched, they withstand temperatures as low as 10 degrees Fahrenheit.

Family Name / Origin Ericaceae /
SE United States

Fruit Berries mature in summer.

Mature Size 3 to 6 ft. × 3 ft.

When and How to Plant In mild-climate areas,
plant from early fall to early winter from 5-gallon
containers, spacing at 6 to 10 ft. Do not expose
the fibrous roots to sunlight because the ultraviolet
rays will harm them. Set plants at the depth of
their original containers. Build a 4- to 6-ft. watering
basin; cover with 1 to 2 in. of organic material
such as humus mulch or compost. See Planting
Techniques, p. 398.

**Climate &
Culture**

**Preferred
Zones**
7–11

**Sun
Preference**

Sun and Soil Preferences Blueberries do best in full sun, in mounded
beds of amended soil or in containers with a pH of 6.5 to 7.0. Amend the
preferred sandy loam soil with equal parts peat moss and humus mulch.

Moisture Requirements Water deeply after planting. Water three times
the first week; thereafter, adjust frequency and amount to climatic and growth
conditions. During prolonged periods of high temperatures, dry winds, or
drought, provide moisture, and partially shade young plants.

Fertilizing Fertilize twice a year, spring and late summer, with a complete
granular food like 9-12-9.

Pruning and Care Little pruning is required until about the third year.
During winter, remove about 1/3 of the oldest branches and any damaged or
dead wood. Unless you want to control the height to about 6 ft., avoid cutting
back shoots and terminals because most of the fruit buds emerge near the
ends. Remove all fruit buds to prevent fruiting during the first growing season
so that all the plants' energies will go into plant development.

Pests and Diseases No insects or diseases seriously affect the Rabbiteye
Blueberry other than your usual invasion of snails and slugs. Their worst
enemies are birds and squirrels—and if you have deer or bears in your
neighborhood, they too will help themselves to the blueberry feast. Rabbits
cause damage by foraging for tender leaves and twigs. Although it would
not hinder hungry bears or deer, plastic bird-netting might discourage the
smaller critters. As for snails and slugs, hand-squish or foot-stomp these
pests, or use a molluscicide.

Boysenberry

Rubus × *loganobaccus* 'Boysen'

Most Boysenberry crops are grown within a 150-mile radius of Los Angeles, with smaller crops from Modesto and Watsonville. These deciduous plants grow up to fifteen feet high on erect stems covered with bright-green oval leaves dusted with white underneath. From flat-topped clusters of white flowers come berries that taste and smell similar to Raspberries but are much larger, usually purplish-red in color, and have edible cores (Raspberries are hollow). Like Blackberries and Raspberries, their fruits are actually clusters of drupelets—individual bumpy, fleshy, seed-containing units that make up the whole berry. Since they grow so easily in mild climates in a variety of soils, they are popular berry plants for California home gardeners. With their big deep-maroon fruits and aromatic sweet-tart taste, they make excellent pies, cobblers, or shortcakes, and are just as delicious served with yogurt, ice cream, or cereal. They withstand drought, wind, cold, and high heat, but thrive when adequate moisture is provided. Since perennial weeds such as Bermuda Grass compete with Boysenberries for water and nutrients and are sources of disease and insect infestations, weed by hand regularly. Arrange the vines on a trellis in a fan shape to spread the fruiting wood over a greater area.

Family Name / Origin Rosaceae / California, not found in the wild

Fruit Berries mature in spring and summer.

Mature Size 8 to 15 ft. long

When and How to Plant Plant in late December or early January from bare-root stock or later in the year from 5-gallon containers. Space them 8 to 12 ft. apart and set at the same depth they were growing before transplanting. Build a watering basin 4 to 6 ft. in diameter and cover with 2 in. of organic material such as humus mulch or compost. Refer to the Planting Techniques section, p. 398, for additional information.

Climate & Culture

Preferred Zones
6–11

Sun Preference

Sun and Soil Preferences They do best in full sun in well-drained loam soil with a pH of 6.5 to 7.2.

Moisture Requirements Water deeply after planting. Water three times the first week; thereafter, adjust frequency and amount to climatic and growth conditions. Just before harvest, water lightly every three to four days.

Fertilizing Fertilize in early spring with a complete granular food such as 16-3-8.

Pruning and Care Start trellising as soon as the largest canes are long enough to reach the support's midpoint. Prune after the harvest season, removing all the wood that produced the current crop and tipping the ends of canes to force out laterals that will bear next season's fruit. To promote larger fruit, around Thanksgiving head back the long laterals at the top of the trellis to 12 to 15 in.

Pests and Diseases Most disease and insect infestations can be controlled by not watering overhead, pruning out damaged canes or foliage, not allowing the roots to stand in water, weeding regularly, and never planting near potential carriers of fungus such as nightshade, tomatoes, and potatoes.

Our Personal Favorite

NAME	SPECIAL CHARACTERISTICS
R. × l. 'Logan'	Hybrid of a Raspberry and a Blackberry / medium to large lavender-red berries with thornless canes / excellent for canning, juicing, wine-making, pies

Raspberry

Rubus idaeus

In Bruce's childhood backyard in Yellow Springs, Ohio, behind rows of corn and
a huge pear tree, stood a spreading bramble of Raspberries that became an emerald-
green mass of fresh six-inch leaflets with serrated edges. White five-petaled blossoms
would appear on the previous summer's sideshoots; when the flowers dropped in a
blizzard of snowy petals, clusters of green berries took their turn to ripen into ruby
drupelets. By June they would easily surrender from their stems as we harvested these
hollow-cored but tasty gems. From the frigid Arctic to the semitropics, Raspberries
adapt to an astonishing range of climatic conditions as well as a dazzling array of
colors. Don't just think red; think black, yellow, off-white, gold, pale orange, purple,
and reddish-black. Depending on the variety, there are also variations in taste, texture,
seediness, and thorniness. In California, the summer-bearing types do very well,
particularly in the Santa Cruz and Sonoma counties where the spring and summer
months are mild. They are self-fertile and are so vigorous and invasive they should be
supported on sturdy trellises and pruned regularly. These deciduous plants prefer slowly
warming, lingering spring weather. Once in bloom, they need to be protected from high
heat, drought conditions, dry or frigid winds, and late frosts.

Family Name / Origin Rosaceae / Northern Hemisphere

Fruit Berries mature in summer.

Mature Size 8 to 15 ft. long

When and How to Plant Plant in spring or fall in mild areas, or after the last spring frost in cold climates, from bare-root stock or from 1- or 5-gallon containers. Space 4 to 6 ft. apart and plant at the depth they were growing in their original containers. Build a 4-ft. watering basin and cover with 1 to 2 in. of organic material. See Planting Techniques, p. 398.

Climate & Culture

Preferred Zones
5–11

Sun Preference

Sun and Soil Preferences Raspberries do best in full sun. In hot climates, plant where there is some shade during peak temperatures or they will burn in the intense sunlight. They prefer a rich, well-drained but moisture-retentive soil with a pH of 6.0 to 6.7.

Moisture Requirements Using compost and amendments helps promote good drainage and aeration. Raspberries do not like their roots standing in water. Water deeply after planting. Water three times the first week; thereafter, adjust frequency and amount to climatic and growth conditions. Avoid wetting the canes when watering because the moisture can lead to fungal disease.

Fertilizing Fertilize twice a year, early spring and early summer, with a complete granular food such as 6-10-4.

Pruning and Care Immediately after planting, cut the canes down to 6 in. so all the energy goes into the plant's development and not into bearing fruit. Once established, remove second-year canes at ground level in winter after they bear a crop, and cut out dead, damaged, weak, or interfering canes. Remove the tops of canes in the late winter or early spring by 6 in. to force the lower buds into growth. Supporting the canes on a sturdy trellis or wires strung between two poles makes the training and harvesting of fruit easier.

Pests and Diseases Pruning regularly for good air circulation, using compost and soil amendments for good drainage, weeding, and watering sufficiently promote healthier plants and discourage the spread of disease or insects. Apply Neem oil if damage persists.

Strawberry

Fragaria × ananassa

Strawberries can be grown by the private gardener in nearly every part of our state, but they are region-specific, so selection of the right variety is important. For the best cultivars in your locale, consult your local nursery or cooperative extension. F. ananassa, a hybrid (F. chiloensis × F. virginiana), is the Modern Garden Strawberry. The plants consist of a crown and stems, from which some roots grow downward; some stems push upward, bearing leaflets. The "mother" plant spreads by sending out runners that bear "daughter" plants. The "fruit" we eat is actually the fleshy portion of the flower, and the hard yellow or black dots are the true fruits that contain the seeds. With their mint-green, serrated leaflets, five-petaled white flowers, and fragrant vivid-red berries, Strawberries are good to look at and even better to eat. They do not tolerate extended periods of drought but withstand heat, cold temperatures, and prevailing winds, provided there is adequate moisture. A fully ripe Strawberry should have a bright-red color, natural shine, and fresh-looking green caps. Once picked they do not continue to ripen, so pick one or two days after the entire berry turns red to eat fresh. For cooking, pick when slightly underripe. To prevent rot, do not wash the berries until ready to use.

Family Name / Origin Rosaceae / California, Eastern United States

Fruit Berries mature in spring and summer and decline in fall and winter.

Mature Size 4 in. tall (spreading)

When and How to Plant Plant in fall in warm-winter climates, in spring in cold-winter climates, from bare-root or pony pack containers. Space them 8 to 12 in. apart. Soak bare-root stock in water for one to two hours before planting. The plant crowns should be level with or slightly above the soil surface. Dig the holes deep enough for the roots to extend straight down; the roots can be trimmed to 4 in. before planting. Plant in rows with 4- to 6-in. irrigation furrows in between. Refer to Planting Techniques, p. 398.

Climate & Culture

Preferred Zones
9–11

Sun Preference

Sun and Soil Preferences They do best in full sun in deep, fertile, well-drained but moisture-retentive soil, pH 6.2 to 7.0.

Moisture Requirements Water deeply after planting. Water three times the first week; thereafter, water according to climatic and growth conditions. Try to avoid watering in the late evening. Use soaker hoses or drip irrigation.

Fertilizing Fertilize in spring with a complete granular food such as 6-10-4.

Pruning and Care Once plants begin to bear fruit, snip off the runners with scissors about once a week to encourage the growth of larger berries (if you handpinch or pull the runners, it may damage the parent plant). Replant Strawberries every two to three years, but to avoid disease, buy new plants rather than dividing the existing ones. Cut off any overripe or rotting fruits to discourage the development of disease or pests.

Pests and Diseases To reduce the risk of fungal and soilborne diseases, rotate the location of your Strawberry plants every two to three years and only use clean gardening tools. To avoid mold problems, cut off the affected berries and mulch to keep fruit off the ground and reduce weed growth. Planting Strawberries in elevated containers keeps them out of the reach of snails, slugs, and sowbugs. Spider mites and aphids are usually controlled by a forceful spray of water or insecticidal soap. Covering with plastic netting serves as a benign method for keeping hungry birds from pecking at your crop.

Bulbs, Corms, Rhizomes

When we kneel down in the cool autumn soil, scoop out holes, and plant our brown parchment–wrapped bulbs, we are acting on an optimistic gardening belief that from such plain, often ugly vessels will emerge breathtaking blossoms of every shape, size, form, color, and fragrance, transforming our garden into a shimmering tapestry of springtime magic. And with just a little effort, we truly can have bulbs that put on a radiant color show celebrating spring's beginning and winter's end.

Plan Your Bulb Showcase

Plan your design on paper and keep it simple, especially if you are a novice. Use two or three colors, or select just a few varieties of bulbs, picking out at least twelve of each kind, and group them in clusters or scatter in drifts.

One of the most important considerations when developing a bulb showcase is knowledge of heights and bloom times of the plants. Place the taller plants at the back or middle of the bed and plant the shorter ones in front. For maximum visual impact, select bulbs that bloom at the same time. If early-, mid-, and late-flowering varieties are mixed together, the look will be less dramatic, but the succession of blooms will make the season last longer. Daffodils come in a range of early- to mid- to late-season varieties; Persian Buttercups flower later than Daffodils and extend the bloom time after the others fade. Once the spring buds peak out, begin planting clusters of Lilies, Dahlias, Gladioli, and Tuberoses in anticipation of the warm summer months.

Don't forget that the adage about nice things coming in small packages applies to bulbs like Grape Hyacinth and miniature forms of Cyclamen and Daffodils.

& Tubers *for California*

Not All Bulbous Plants Are True Bulbs

The term "bulb" is often used loosely, as many bulbous plants are technically not true bulbs. True bulbs have pointed tops, short underground stems on basal plates, and new growths, called bulblets, that form from offshoots of the parent bulbs. Amaryllis, Grape Hyacinth, and Daffodils are considered true bulbs because they grow from enlarged buds with modified leaves called scales.

Included in the family of "bulbous plants that are not true bulbs" are those produced from corms, rhizomes, and tubers. Corms are similar to bulbs, except that each summer a new corm grows on top of the original one. As the parent corm disappears, the roots of the new corm grow downward into the hole left by the decayed corm. Gladioli and Freesias grow from corms that divide by growing small corms, called cormels, around the base of the parent bulb.

Unlike corms, which grow upwards, rhizomes are specialized stems that spread horizontally, underground, or on the surface with adventitious roots, and they sprout stems, leaves, and flowers from the rhizomes' upper sections. Peruvian Lilies and Tuberoses grow from rhizomes and are propagated by cutting out a section of their spreading layers.

Dahlias and Persian Buttercups grow from tubers, which are swollen rhizomes that produce pulpy, instead of scaly, stems. Tubers normally grow just below the surface of the soil and, like bulbs, store food for the plants. The buds on tubers become stems, leaves, and flowers, and clusters of roots form at the base. They multiply by division, and as they divide, the parent tuber deteriorates.

Whether bulbous plants derive from a true bulb, corm, rhizome, or tuber, there is a flowering bulb to suit every taste and to serve every garden purpose. And when it comes time to do the actual planting, choose the biggest, plumpest bulbs that are clean, solid, and free from scars. With faith in the magic of nature, bulbs bring forth spring and summer jewel-like colors in perennial borders, rock gardens, and random drifts in lawns or along slopes.

Amaryllis
Hippeastrum × hybrid

Every autumn Sharon and I put our potted Amaryllis to bed under our deck where their yellowed foliage will dry up and die back. They remain asleep until we return them to our deck in late winter and they awaken with the arrival of winter and spring rains. Soon thick, hollow, leafless stems emerge bearing enormous funnel-shaped flowers surrounded by deep-green, straplike leaves in the spring. They reward our seasonal routine when clusters of two to four buds open and stretch their petals until they each measure five or six inches across in colors of greenish-white with a lime-green throat, orange with green stripes, bright-red with a white star for its center, velvety-red with a deeper red throat, and soft pink tinted with streaks of white and pale yellow-green. If you do not recognize this plant, it is probably because you know it by another name. While both Hippeastrum and Amaryllis are commonly called Amaryllis, the genus Amaryllis comes from South Africa, is extremely poisonous, and consists of a single species, A. belladonna. Confusion reigns because the winter or early spring–flowering South American Hippeastrum bulbs, widely cultivated and sold during the winter holiday season, are marketed as Amaryllis and are also toxic. Just remember that what most gardeners think of as Amaryllis plants really belong to the genus Hippeastrum.

Family Name / Origin Amaryllidaceae / Americas

Bloom Period and Color Red, orange, yellow, pink, and white flowers bloom in spring.

Mature Height × Spread 1 to 2 ft. (clumping)

When and How to Plant Plant in fall from bulbs, spacing them 18 in. apart. Prepare a flower bed by adding a preplant fertilizer (2-10-6) and, if needed, a soil amendment such as compost or humus mulch. Plant so the top third of the bulb is above soil level. If planting in a pot, use potting soil, add a preplant fertilizer, and allow a 1- to 2-in. space between the bulb and the pot perimeter (they prefer cramped quarters). Refer to Planting Techniques, p. 398.

Climate & Culture

Preferred Zones
10–11

Sun Preference

Sun and Soil Preferences Plant in full sun in well-drained soil, pH 6.7 to 7.0.

Moisture Requirements Water sparingly at first. Adjust frequency and amount according to weather and growth conditions. In the late summer or early fall, stop watering until the foliage withers, then forget them until spring.

Fertilizing Fertilize once a week during the growth cycle with a water-soluble food such as 12-55-6, and continue to fertilize until no new leaves emerge and the mature leaves discontinue their growth.

Pruning and Care Remove spent flowers; the foliage needs the energy to return to the bulb rather than to be expended on the production of seeds.

Pests and Diseases Few diseases or insects affect these plants, but watch out for spotted wilt, a fungus that causes yellow or white spots on leaves. Remove damaged foliage and any mealybugs or aphids by hand, because many remedies such as Neem oil can also damage the flower buds.

Companion Plantings and Design Cut for flower arrangements when at least two buds are showing color and beginning to open. They will last up to two weeks if you also change the vase water regularly, add a powdered flower preservative, and keep them away from cold drafts. Prostrate Natal Plum, Dwarf Jade Plant, and Transvaal Daisy grow well with Amaryllis.

Our Personal Favorites

NAME	SPECIAL CHARACTERISTICS
H. × hybrid 'Apple Blossom'	Pinkish-white flowers
H. × hybrid 'Kalahari'	Large solid-red flowers

Cyclamen
Cyclamen persicum

We can never have enough Cyclamen nestled in the shady spots of our garden. When few plants are blooming in our winter garden, purple-tinged magenta flowers on six-inch stems burst forth from nests of deep-green, heart-shaped leaves marbled with silvery streaks. C. persicum is the florist's Cyclamen, with large, sweetly fragrant flowers composed of five upright, twisted petals in colors of white, pink, magenta, and red. They flower from spring to summer or in winter if weather conditions are mild. When their blooms are spent, stalks of straight seed capsules emerge, signaling the beginning of a rest period, usually during midsummer. Plant in the ground as long as the climate is temperate and frost-free, but in cooler regions, cultivate in containers and provide winter protection. Cyclamen are poisonous, but roasting diminishes their toxicity so that in many countries they are used to feed pigs. Pigs actually hunt for the buried tubers! This is probably the reason for Cyclamen's common name, "Sowbread." During dormancy they tolerate drought, wind, and heat, but they cannot withstand such conditions during growth. Although often sold as houseplants, they do not survive for very long indoors because they dislike heat. You will have much better results if you place them in a partially shaded, cool, frost-free location.

Family Name / Origin Primulaceae / Greece, Lebanon, North Africa

Bloom Period and Color Red, white, pink, or purple flowers bloom in winter.

Mature Height × Spread 8 to 12 in. × 10 in.

When and How to Plant Plant in early fall in mild-winter areas or spring in cooler regions, after the last frost, from corms or from 4- or 6-in. pots, spacing 4 to 6 in. apart. Make sure the tuber tops are just above the soil surface. If the soil does not drain freely, amend with compost, peat moss, or humus mulch. Consult Planting Techniques, p. 398.

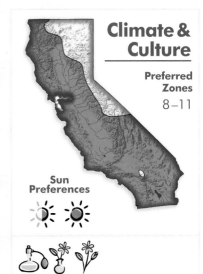

Climate & Culture

Preferred Zones
8–11

Sun Preferences

Sun and Soil Preferences They require shade or dappled light in well-drained, slightly alkaline soils, pH 6.8 to 7.2.

Moisture Requirements Soak deeply after planting. Water daily the first week; thereafter, adjust frequency and amount to weather and growth conditions. During the growth period, water around the edges of the tuber to avoid water settling in the tight mass of leaves and buds. Reduce frequency when the growth cycle ends, and gradually extend the dry period for about two to three months. Afterwards, repot or restart the growth cycle by watering regularly.

Fertilizing Fertilize during the growing and blooming season about twice a month with a water-soluble food low in nitrogen, like 6-10-4.

Pruning and Care Remove spent flowers from tubers to prevent root rot.

Pests and Diseases Be on the lookout for snails, slugs, sowbugs, and Cyclamen mites. If damage is severe, use snail bait or the pick-and-squash method of control. For mites, use Neem oil.

Companion Plantings and Design Colorful companion plants are Camellias, Azaleas, Clivias, and Impatiens.

Our Personal Favorite

NAME	SPECIAL CHARACTERISTICS
C. neapolitanum	A miniature Cyclamen / fragrant pink, white, or rose flowers from July through autumn / flowers followed by angular leaves marbled with silver that remain until May, then die back

Dahlia

Dahlia × hybrid

Whenever someone who claims to be "green-thumb impaired" pleads for a flowering plant that is easy to grow, we suggest Dahlias, named for Swedish botanist Andreas Dahl. Once their tubers are correctly planted, they do well in almost any garden throughout the world. With a minimum of effort they reward you with spectacular, almost limitless, shapes, sizes, and colors. From two-inch balls of pompons to twelve-inch plates of cactus or peony-shaped flowers, from anemone-like double-petaled blossoms to single-petaled ones surrounding a shorter collar-like form, they show off atop stems from two to six feet in height. Hot reds, oranges, yellows, pastel pinks, salmons, lavenders, rich magentas, bronzes, purples, and apricots are just a few of the colors available in single, double, or multicolored Dahlia varieties. The foliage is almost as variable, ranging from gray-green and bright-green to bronze. About the only color you cannot find is blue. If you need an extra 50,000 francs, the Caledonian Horticultural Society established this still unclaimed prize money in 1864 as an award for whoever successfully develops a blue Dahlia. Depending on the variety, they bloom from late spring and die back when the weather cools. Their only real enemies are drought, frost, and blustery winds. Adequate moisture resolves some of the damage caused by dry winds and high temperatures.

Family Name / Origin Compositae / Mexico, South America

Bloom Period and Color Red, orange, yellow, pink, and white flowers bloom in summer.

Mature Height × Spread 2 to 7 ft. × 2 to 4 ft.

When and How to Plant Plant in spring from tubers, 6- to 8-in. pots, or 1-gallon containers, spacing 2½ ft. for larger varieties, 2 ft. for pompons, and 12 to 18 in. for dwarf hybrids. Before planting, prepare a flower bed 8 to 12 in. deep and blend in a preplant fertilizer, 2-10-6. In frost-free areas you can leave the tubers in the ground, but in colder regions, dig them up, clean and dry, store in a cool, dry place in the fall, and replant in the spring. See Planting Techniques, p. 398.

Climate & Culture

Preferred Zones 10–11

Sun Preference

Sun and Soil Preferences Dahlias need full sun and rich, well-drained loam soil with a pH of 6.7 to 7.0.

Moisture Requirements Soak deeply after planting. Water three times the first week; thereafter, adjust frequency and amount to weather and growth conditions.

Fertilizing Do not fertilize during the growth cycle.

Pruning and Care When new growth is about 4 in. tall, thin out, leaving only the three strongest stems; cut any other shoots back to ground level. Repeat throughout the growth cycle, allowing only the three stems to flourish. Although disbudding is not necessary for dwarf or shorter varieties, for taller forms it encourages larger blooms and thicker stems. In July, when the first flower buds emerge, keep only the central bud. Just below the first group of buds are smaller flower buds which should also be removed, as well as any foliage. Deadhead spent flowers to keep Dahlias from seeding and shortening the bloom cycle. Where winters are mild, prune stems back to 4 to 6 in.

Pests and Diseases Dahlias are rarely diseased, with the exception of mildew, rust, slugs, snails, aphids, and spider mites. Air circulation is important. Insecticidal soap, squashing, and molluscicides are good controls.

Companion Plantings and Design English Ivy, Foxglove, Delphinium, and Lavender are ideal companion plants. For more Design Tips, see p. 407.

Freesia

Freesia × hybrid

This is Sharon's favorite late-winter to early-spring flower for bouquets. We also like
Freesias, named for Friedrich Heinrich Theodore Freese, because they cultivate easily,
naturalize in mild climates, and bear prolifically. The flower's elegant form, myriad
array of bright shades, and delicate perfume are the first signs of more scents and
colors to come into our warm-season garden. Fans of erect, narrow, irislike leaves bear
spiked stems. Along one side of each stem, five to seven trumpet-shaped flowers gather
single-file and politely wait to open one at a time. In single or double forms, these
spikes of sweetly scented flowers are painted in solid colors or two-toned combinations
of pale white, cream, yellow, pink, mauve, lilac, and lavender-blue, or in brilliant
orange, crimson, and dark blue. Where winters are mild, plant Freesias in the early
fall for winter and spring blooms; where freezing temperatures prevail, plant in the late
spring for summer flowering. As is true of most South African Cape bulbs, Freesias
dislike excessive heat, freezing temperatures, persistent winds, and drought. Do not
move Freesias while they are in their growth cycle, because they do not like their
roots disturbed.

Family Name / Origin Iridaceae / South Africa

Bloom Period and Color Red, orange, yellow, pink, and white flowers bloom in spring.

Mature Height × **Spread** 1 to 1½ ft. (clumping)

When and How to Plant Plant in fall in frost-free regions and in spring after last frost in colder climates, from corms, 4- or 6-in. pots, or 1-gallon containers, spacing 3 in. apart. Prepare a flower bed, sprinkle the bottom with a preplant fertilizer, place the corms pointed ends up, and plant 2 to 3 in. deep. If in a temperate climate, allow the corms to remain in place—otherwise, lift the corms out after the foliage is dead, store in a cool, dry place during winter, and replant in spring after the last frost. See Planting Techniques, p. 398.

Climate & Culture

Preferred Zones 9–11

Sun Preference

Sun and Soil Preferences They need full sun and average, well-drained soil, pH 6.7 to 7.0.

Moisture Requirements Soak deeply after planting. Water three times the first week; thereafter, adjust frequency and amount to weather and growth conditions. Water regularly during the growth cycle. Decrease watering when foliage yellows, and stop when the leaves dry. In late winter or spring (depending on the climate zone), resume watering as new growth appears.

Fertilizing Fertilize once a month beginning in spring or earlier, when new growth appears, with a water-soluble food like 12-55-6.

Pruning and Care It is not necessary to prune or deadhead.

Pests and Diseases With good air circulation, and if you respond immediately to the first signs of insect infestation, fungal and insect problems will be minimal. Try Neem oil, insecticidal soap, and washing off by hand.

Companion Plantings and Design Freesias make good companion plants for Candytuft, Transvaal Daisy, and Wallflower. See p. 407 for Design Tips and cut-flower ideas.

Our Personal Favorites

NAME	SPECIAL CHARACTERISTICS
F. × hybrid 'Aphrodite'	Double, soft pink to red flowers
F. × hybrid 'Uchida'	Semi-double flowers with yellow throats

Gladiolus

Gladiolus × hybrid

At Cape Town's world-famous garden Kirstenbosch, we saw massive plantings of so many different Gladiolus species and hybrids that it is understandable that these plants are classified into groups by height, flower size, and shape. With so many variables, the following must be a brief descriptive brushstroke. Gladiolus comes from the Latin word gladius, meaning "sword", referring to the plants' sword-shaped foliage. Stiff spikes with funnel-like florets arise, facing one way, from erect, coarse-textured, distinctively ribbed leaves. Their sun-loving faces are splashed with hues of white, green, yellow, orange, red, maroon, salmon, pink, mauve, or purple, but not blue— some are striped, streaked, or splattered with contrasting tints. Some flowers have ruffled or hooded petal segments; others have a flatter habit. Some stems are dainty at eighteen inches tall; others can reach just under five feet. Several have fragrances similar to honey, plums, or spicy carnations. In zones 8 to 10, the corms can remain in the ground, but in colder regions it is best to dig them up, clean them, and store in a cool, dry, dark place with good air circulation for the winter. With adequate moisture, most hybrids grow well where there is winter rainfall and summer heat. Except for some of the smaller hybrids, they need protection from wind and freezing temperatures.

Family Name / Origin Iridiaceae / South Africa

Bloom Period and Color Flowers in red, orange, yellow, pink, white, and other colors bloom in late spring and summer.

Mature Height × Spread 1 to 4 ft. (multiplying)

When and How to Plant Plant from corms in spring after the last frost, or in fall if winters are mild. Prepare a flower bed, blending in a preplant fertilizer (2-10-6). Plant the corms 2 to 4 in. deep and space 6 to 8 in. apart, depending on their size. If you plant bulbs at intervals every two to three weeks, from the first planting until July, you will have flowers until early fall, providing the weather remains mild. In temperate zones, you can plant from January to July, but in colder regions you may have to wait as late as May, after the last frost. For more planting information, see Planting Techniques, p. 398.

Climate & Culture

Preferred Zones
9–11

Sun Preference

Sun and Soil Preferences They need full sun and evenly moist, well-drained soil with a neutral to slightly alkaline pH, 6.5–7.0.

Moisture Requirements Soak deeply after planting. Water three times the first week; thereafter, adjust frequency and amount to weather and growth conditions. In hot, dry summer months, water roots and leaves generously.

Fertilizing Fertilize monthly with a water-soluble food such as 12-55-6.

Pruning and Care Cut off spent flowers, but leave as much foliage as possible while it is still green.

Pests and Diseases Some fungal diseases and insect infestations may be a problem in warm, humid conditions, but if you rotate your plant locations, remove debris (a breeding ground for disease and pests), and keep a watchful eye out for symptoms before they have a chance to proliferate, you will be rewarded with vigorous plants and spectacular blooms. If damage from aphids, red spider mites, thrips, snails, or slugs is extensive, use insecticidal soap, Neem oil, or a molluscicide.

Companion Plantings and Design Ivy Geraniums, Lilies of the Nile, and Canna Lilies are ideal companion plants. See p. 407 for Design Tips.

Grape Hyacinth

Muscari neglectum

Every summer I begrudgingly lug several of Sharon's heavy terracotta bowls that are home to her Grape Hyacinths to a place where the plants can dry out and rest during the heat of the long days and mild evenings. I try to tactfully persuade her to plant more perennials, but she just smiles and reminds me how much I enjoy Grape Hyacinth's abundant blooms at a time when the rest of our garden is pretty quiet. The effort of carrying those clay barbells is well worth it when the six-inch spikes of tiny, bell-like, intensely blue flowers peek out from their bed of tufted, grasslike leaves as a welcome prelude to spring. Flourishing in drifts amid grasslands, along meandering pathways, at the edge of woodlands, or underneath towering trees or flowering shrubs, nestling in rock gardens or borders, or accenting containers, their bright, fragrant, decorative blooms more than compensate for their diminutive size. Muscari comes from the Greek word moschos, meaning "musk", which no doubt refers to the delicate fragrance. Once planted, they can be left in place for several years and will cover the ground with a carpet of blue. Since Grape Hyacinth do not tolerate dry, hot, or arid conditions, it is best to plant them in cool, moist areas.

Family Name / Origin Liliaceae / Mediterranean, SW Asia

Bloom Period and Color Blue or dark-blue flowers bloom late winter and early spring.

Mature Height × Spread 4 to 6 in. (multiplying)

When and How to Plant Plant in early autumn from bulbs, spacing 2 in. apart. Prepare a flower bed, add a preplant fertilizer such as 2-10-6, and amend the soil with humus mulch, peat moss, or compost if needed. Plant the bulbs 2 in. deep. See Planting Techniques, p. 398.

Sun and Soil Preferences They need full sun or partial shade and cool, moist, well-drained soil with a slightly acidic pH of 6.0–6.5.

Moisture Requirements Soak deeply after planting. Water three times the first week; thereafter, adjust frequency and amount to weather and growth conditions.

Fertilizing Fertilize once a month after growth appears with a water-soluble food such as 12-55-6.

Pruning and Care Since one of the easiest methods of propagation is by division, dig them up when they are dormant, in the summer. Thin out the bulbs if they form growth that is too dense.

Pests and Diseases Grape Hyacinth are relatively impervious to most diseases, but since they grow so close to the ground, foraging snails and slugs can be a problem. If handpicking and squishing is ineffective, use a molluscicide.

Companion Plantings and Design They can be cut for miniature arrangements and will last for four to six days as long as you use a powdered floral preservative and keep them away from direct sources of heat, cool drafts, and sunlight. Azaleas, Magnolias, and White Birch are ideal companion plants in the landscape. Grape Hyacinths also grow well in low bowls with other bulbs such as Daffodils, Freesias, and Cyclamen.

Climate & Culture

Preferred Zones
7–11

Sun Preferences

Our Personal Favorite

NAME	SPECIAL CHARACTERISTICS
M. *armeniacum* 'Heavenly Blue'	Very fragrant / blue or white spiked flowers

Narcissus

Narcissus × hybrid

We are ashamed to admit it, but there is a narrow strip of ground in front of our Star Jasmine that rarely receives any care. Yet just before Valentine's Day, like clock-work, stems of fragrant, golden-yellow Narcissi lift their heads to wave hello. These are perfect bulbs that can grow under the most neglected conditions and not only survive, but flourish beautifully. Whether they are Jonquils, Daffodils, or Narcissi, all belong to the genus Narcissus. Generally speaking, the flowers have cups or trumpets known as coronas, most are surrounded by six petals or corollas, and they have a base of erect light-green leaves. Narcissus comes from the Greek word narkan, meaning "to stupefy"—the alkaloids in these bulbs are toxic and can affect the nervous system and stomach. Despite their poisonous property, their fragrance, colorful blooms, and easy maintenance make them one of the most popular spring bulbs for home gardeners. Keep bulbs in a cool (at most 45 degrees Fahrenheit), dark, dry place until ready to plant. Once in-ground, they can remain undisturbed for about five years, and can be dug up for division when dormant in the summer. Provided there is adequate moisture during the growth and bloom cycles, Narcissi tolerate wind, heat, and cold. While dormant, they will survive drought and freezing temperatures.

Family Name / Origin Amaryllidaceae / S Europe, Mediterranean, N Africa, W Asia, China, Japan

Bloom Period and Color Orange, yellow, or white flowers bloom in late winter and spring.

Mature Height × Spread 1 to 2 ft. (multiplying)

When and How to Plant In warmer climates, plant in fall from bulbs, spacing 4 to 8 in. apart in the ground or crowding them even closer in a pot (18 to 24 bulbs may be grown in a 14- to 16-in. pot). Prepare a flower bed 2 to 12 in. deep, depending on the size of the bulb, and blend with bonemeal (0-13-0) or preplant fertilizer (2-10-6) in the trench. See Planting Techniques, p. 398.

Climate & Culture

Preferred Zones
7–11

Sun Preferences

Sun and Soil Preferences They need full sun or partial shade and moist, well-drained, sandy, loam soil and a pH of 6.7 to 7.0.

Moisture Requirements Immediately after planting, soak deeply and thoroughly to collapse any air pockets in the soil. Water daily the first week; thereafter, adjust frequency and amount to weather and growth conditions. Water more lightly during fall and winter and more heavily during the spring growing season, and discontinue in the summer.

Fertilizing Fertilize monthly during the growing and blooming seasons with a water-soluble food such as 12-55-6.

Pruning and Care Remove only diseased or damaged foliage while in the growth cycle—the leaves are needed to manufacture food for current and future seasons.

Pests and Diseases The poisonous characteristic is a plus for the gardener because the alkaloids repel most insects and deer. In dense, moist soils with poor air circulation, aphids and fungal maladies can be problems.

Companion Plantings and Design To make any kind of display, plant at least three to six bulbs in a cluster. If you want your bulbs to naturalize in grassy or woodland areas, throw out the bulbs and plant them where they fall, in a freeform or random pattern. For a long bloom cycle, plant a mixture of early-, mid-, and late-blooming types. Ideal companions are Grape Hyacinth, Freesia, Pansy, Alyssum, Pink Indian Hawthorn, and Magnolia. See p. 408 for Design Tips.

Persian Buttercup

Ranunculus asiaticus

One April we visited the famous Flower Fields in Carlsbad, California, where acres of Persian Buttercup blossoms waved colorful greetings to appreciative tourists. It struck us that they were living examples of the truism "You can't judge a book by its cover," because their tubers look like pint-sized bunches of brown bananas with fuzzy berets. From such a homely embryo Mother Nature hatches another of her miracles. Deeply cut, feathery foliage, pale green in color, emerges on long stalks. Soon saucer-shaped blossoms, up to five inches in diameter with tight bundles of stamens in their centers, unfurl in the warmth of the spring sun. New hybrids have double or semi-double buttercup-like flowers painted in hues of green, yellow, orange, red, rose, pink, cream, and white; some are edged with a darker color while others are bi- and tricolored. Ranunculus is of Latin derivation from the word rana, meaning "frog," and they naturally share the same habitats as frogs in tranquil ponds, along banks overlooking bubbling brooks, and beside reedy marshes. Persian Buttercups do not tolerate frost, high temperatures, cold winds, or drought; they do best where winters are mild and autumns are warm during the days and cool during the evenings. The plants die back during the heat of the summer and awaken from their long sleep in fall.

Family Name / Origin Ranunculaceae / Mediterranean

Bloom Period and Color Flowers in red, orange, yellow, pink, white, and other colors bloom in late spring and summer.

Mature Height × **Spread** 12 to 18 in. (multiplying)

When and How to Plant Plant in fall where winters are mild, in spring after the last frost where winters are cold, from tubers, 4- or 6-in. pots, or 1-gallon containers. Prepare a flower bed, add a preplant fertilizer such as 2-10-6, and amend the soil with humus mulch, peat moss, or compost if needed. Before planting, soak the tubers in water for 30 to 45 minutes, but not too much longer or they may rot. Bury the tubers "toes down," spacing them 4 to 6 in. apart; if from 4-in. or larger containers, plant 6 to 10 in. on center in the ground. See Planting Techniques, p. 398.

Climate & Culture

Preferred Zones
8–11

Sun Preference

Sun and Soil Preferences They need full sun and rich, fast-draining soil with a pH of 6.5 to 7.0.

Moisture Requirements Soak deeply after planting. It should not be necessary to water again until the leaves appear, as long as the soil remains moist but not soggy. Once the root systems are established, adjust watering frequency and amount to weather and growth conditions.

Fertilizing Fertilize monthly with a water-soluble food such as 12-55-6.

Pruning and Care Deadhead the spent flowers. Although in mild climates you can leave the bulbs in the ground and in colder areas you can dig them up to put away for winter storage if foraging critters are a problem, eventually it will be preferable to buy new ones and discard the old for more prolific high-quality blooms.

Pests and Diseases Other than mildew resulting from airborne fungi spores and the ubiquitous snails and slugs, few diseases or insects pose a problem. You might protect the immature, tender leaves with netting or chicken wire because birds love to feed on them. For humans, however, all parts of *Ranunculus* are poisonous.

Companion Plantings and Design Ideal companions are Icelandic Poppies, Alyssum, Pansies, Shasta Daisies, Rock Cotoneaster, and Narcissus. See p. 408 for Design Tips and Recommended Varieties.

Peruvian Lily
Alstroemeria aurantiaca

The elegant spring- to summer-flowering Peruvian Lilies look so graceful in the rectangular terracotta pots placed as highlights in our backyard. Once their handsome flowers are spent, their seeds are dispersed by the wind and by our visiting birds. Come spring, we find more new Alstroemeria plants growing in serendipitous places: among our rosebushes, in other mixed-flower pots, standing tall in a mass of ivy, and peeking out in the middle of our raised vegetable plot. From fleshy tubers emerge long leafy stems that are gray-green in color and lance-shaped. At the end of their flower stalks are several trumpet-like blossoms that have been hybridized in hues of bronze, orange, yellow, purple, pink, red, and cream, and may be bicolored, multicolored, streaked, striped, spotted, or marbled. It is easy to see why they are so popular as cut flowers as well as dramatic garden accents in mixed-flower beds, as container plants, or along a warm, sheltered wall. They dislike hot, dry conditions such as drought and blustery winds and do not tolerate freezing temperatures, but they thrive in temperate regions with adequate moisture. **Note:** *If you cannot find Alstroemeria aurantiaca, look for Alstroemeria aurea, another botanical name sometimes used for the same plant.*

Family Name / Origin Alstroemeriaceae / Chile, Peru

Bloom Period and Color Pink and lavender flowers bloom in spring and summer.

Mature Height × **Spread** 2 to 3 ft. (clumping)

When and How to Plant Plant in spring after the last frost from seed, from rhizomes, or from 4- to 8-in. pots or 1-gallon containers. Space them 4 to 12 in. apart depending on the size of the rhizome or container. Amend the flower bed with compost or humus mulch if the soil does not drain freely. See Planting Techniques, p. 398.

Sun and Soil Preferences They need full sun and rich, well-drained, sandy soil with a neutral pH, 7.0. If the area has high temperatures, plant in partial shade to avoid the fading of flower color.

Moisture Requirements Soak deeply after planting. Water three times the first week; thereafter, adjust frequency and amount to weather and growth conditions.

Fertilizing Fertilize monthly during the growing and blooming seasons with a water-soluble food such as 12-55-6.

Pruning and Care Clip off the spent flowers if you do not want any seed production.

Pests and Diseases If you notice premature yellowing of leaves, this may be the nefarious work of thrips; if you see chewed-off leaves, you know they have been "slimed" by snails or slugs. If damage is extensive, use a mollusci-cide or squish the slimy pests by hand, and apply Neem oil for thrips.

Companion Plantings and Design Coreopsis, Candytuft, and Shasta Daisy make ideal planting companions. See p. 409 for Cut-flower Tips and Propagation information.

Climate & Culture

Preferred Zones 9–11

Sun Preferences

Our Personal Favorites

NAME	SPECIAL CHARACTERISTICS
A. a. 'Dover Orange'	Tall flowering stems / deep-orange flowers
A. a. 'Lutea'	Yellow flowers marked with red

Tuberose
Polianthes tuberosa

We can recall the heady fragrance of the Tuberose in the florist department at our nursery whenever our florists were designing corsages, boutonnieres, and arrangements for weddings and other festive occasions. We have long since retired from our retail operation, but to this day we associate the Tuberose with happy occasions. When we suggest Tuberose as an excellent summer plant, some people are underwhelmed because they think its scent is overwhelming, cloying, and sweet. While it can be pretty oppressive in a small room, when carried on a passing breeze in the garden, its perfume is rich and musky, similar to that of a Gardenia but much more complex. Rising from a gray-green mass of clumping, grasslike leaves are two- to three-foot-tall spikes of creamy-white flowers packed closely together. As buds, they are tinged with pink; once they open, each waxy flower reveals six petals that come from a funnel-shaped tube. If you want erect spikes rather than curved, remove the top bud. Like many other bulb plants, if they are overwatered in dense, clay soils, they may rot. Tuberose plants are easy to grow, but the real skill is to develop a high-quality bloom, which requires an extended period of warm weather and protection from cold wind, overcast skies, freezing temperatures, and drought.

Family Name / Origin Agavaceae / Mexico

Bloom Period and Color Creamy-white flowers bloom in summer.

Mature Height × Spread 2 to 3 ft. (multiplying)

When and How to Plant Plant in April after the last frost from rhizomes, planting one to three rhizomes per 6-in. pot—or plant directly in the ground, spacing 8 to 12 in. apart. Prepare a flower bed, add a preplant fertilizer such as 2-10-6, and amend the soil with humus mulch, peat moss, or compost if needed. Once a rhizome has flowered, it will not bloom again. Although you can use the "baby" rhizomes that develop around the "mother," it takes four years for them to reach maturity. If you have the patience in cold-winter climates, dig and store the young rhizomes in a warm, dry place after the leaves have yellowed and died back. Where winters are mild, allow them to remain in place for several years before you dig them up to divide. If expediency is more important, throw away the rhizomes that have bloomed and buy new ones each year. See Planting Techniques, p. 398.

Sun and Soil Preferences Tuberose needs light shade or full shade in desert climates, full sun in milder climates. The plants thrive in fertile, well-drained, slightly acidic soil, pH 6.7.

Moisture Requirements Soak deeply after planting. Water three times the first week; thereafter, adjust frequency and amount to weather and growth conditions. Watering needs are increased during growth and bloom periods.

Fertilizing Fertilize monthly during the growth and bloom seasons with a water-soluble food like 12-55-6.

Pruning and Care Deadhead spent flowers.

Pests and Diseases Since they are toxic, there are few insect infestations.

Companion Plantings and Design Gladiolus, Delphinium, Foxglove, Daylily, and Roses are ideal companions for the Tuberose. See p. 409 for more Design Tips.

Climate & Culture

Preferred Zones

10–11

Sun Preferences

Our Personal Favorite

NAME	SPECIAL CHARACTERISTICS
P. t. 'Excelsior Double Pearl'	An improved, highly fragrant variety / pearl-white clusters of flowers

Citrus *for California*

Originating in Southern China and Southeast Asia, citrus has been cultivated for over four thousand years. Today there are hundreds of varieties and subspecies, including the popular Grapefruit, Lemon, Lime, Mandarin, Sweet Orange, and, to a lesser extent, Calamondin, Citron, Kumquat, Pummelo, and Tangelo that are propagated in California's sun-drenched mild-winter regions.

The Virtues of Citrus

Citrus trees are handsome throughout the year and are ideal additions to orchards and mild-climate gardens. They are quite ornamental with their lustrous-green foliage, large clusters of intensely perfumed, creamy or purplish blossoms, immature green fruits, and mature bright nuggets of sunshine. The crops of tasty fruits are a bonus, particularly in winter when other trees are dormant. Our idea of a perfect day is to sit on the deck and listen to the chitchat of our resident jays, mockingbirds, robins, and mourning doves while savoring a homemade biscotti dipped in a glass of freshly-squeezed orange juice, lemonade, or limeade. Like the Chinese, we believe citrus fruits represent the sweetness in life.

Although citrus plants belong to either the Citrus or Fortunella genus and have been hybridized to create one of the most complex fruits on earth, they share many common characteristics. They are evergreen with fragrant flowers that are mostly creamy white, often tinged with pink or purple. The fruits have leathery rinds and fleshy interiors that are divided into sections and separated by parchment-like membranes. Many varieties are available both as

standard twenty-foot and dwarf six- to ten-foot trees. Standard trees provide a shaded respite from the sun, and dwarf varieties make wonderful hedges, espaliers, or container plants.

Most citrus trees sold at nurseries are *composite trees*, meaning their rootstocks differ from their tops, which are called *scions*. The rootstocks have been genetically developed to resist pests, diseases, or less-than-optimum soil conditions and are grafted on to compatible scions that have superior fruit quality.

Select a Healthy Tree

Select well-grown one- or two-year-old trees that are between one-half to one inch in diameter when measured one inch above the graft union. Older trees tend to be rootbound and do not establish as quickly when they are planted. A healthy, vigorous tree should have large leaves all along the length of its trunk with a uniform green color, free from pest damage. The branching should be symmetrical and the bark should be bright and clean with a healed graft union that is six inches above the ground.

Grow a Variety for Your Climate

Growing tasty fruit begins with selecting a variety that suits your climate. Some citrus do not produce sweet fruit near the coast where temperatures are cool. Lemons and Limes require less heat, and they do produce good fruit near the coast. The Valencia Orange needs higher temperatures, and produces good fruit from the coast to the desert. Navel Oranges, Mandarins, and Tangelos require more heat and do best in inland valleys. Grapefruit need prolonged periods of high heat to develop peak flavor, and they grow best in the desert, although recent hybrids such as the 'Oroblanco' have a lower heat requirement.

Resistance to cold weather is variable, with the Satsuma Mandarin being the most tolerant, Sweet Oranges, Grapefruits, Tangelos, and other Mandarins intermediate, Lemons less tolerant, and Limes the least tolerant. Unlike other fruits, citrus do not contain much starch, so they do not sweeten once plucked from the tree; thus, they should be picked only when fully ripe.

Provide Proper Care

In addition to a suitable climate, successful citrus cultivation depends on year-round care. Proper irrigation is very important. All citrus need well-drained soils—if allowed to

stand in water, the roots will be damaged and leaf drop will result. To resolve drainage problems, plant citrus in raised beds filled with potting soil and mulch. Do not plant shallow-rooted plants that need frequent watering (like lawns, ground covers, annuals) beneath citrus trees, or the soil will be too moist for the trees. Keep water at least six inches away from the trunk to prevent *brown rot gummosis*. When left untreated, gummosis causes the bark to scale, fall off, and ooze from the infected site, eventually leading to the tree's demise. If infected, scrape and paint with a paste made of Bordeaux

powder mixed with water. Reapply until there is
no more scaling or oozing.

Add two inches of mulch under the
tree to conserve water, prevent weeds, and absorb
damaging salts from the water. Fertilize with a complete
citrus food in late winter after the fruit has set and grown
one-half inch in diameter, and again in early summer. Follow
the directions on package labels because different manufacturers
formulate different ingredients and percentages. If new leaves are
turning yellow, iron deficiency may be the problem. Iron chelate is
an appropriate remedy for iron chlorosis. Zinc deficiency causes
yellow mottling or blotching of the green leaves and can be remedied
with chelated zinc as a foliar spray or as a soil application.

Keep Pruning to a Minimum

Prune citrus any time since there is rarely a time when a tree does not have
fruit or flowers on it—but keep pruning to a minimum, just for shape and to
remove dead wood, broken or damaged limbs, water sprouts, and suckers. Protect the inner
branches from exposure to the sun by painting with whitewash or latex paint.

"June drop" and insect infestations are some common citrus maladies. "June drop" is the
sudden shedding of immature fruit, which is nature's way of adjusting the crop size to the tree's
capability to produce good fruit. If the weather is unusually hot or dry, the drop may be sizable.
The fruit may also split and drop off if there is too much water. If it becomes necessary to control
aphids, scale, mealybugs, thrips, mites, and leafrollers, select methods that are appropriate for
the particular pest and locality.

More Than Fruit Factories

Whether displayed as an ornamental or grown in an orchard, citrus trees are more than
fruit factories: they are handsome shade, hedge, container, and specimen trees. But to be
perfectly candid, they are probably one of our favorite plants because of their fruits that
feed us and sweeten our days.

Calamondin

Citrofortunella microcarpa

In China, Calamondin is known as Sechi Chief, meaning "four seasons," an appropriate appellation since it bears fruit practically all year-round. It is a natural hybrid cross between a Sour Mandarin and a Kumquat (Citrus reticulata × Fortunella marginata). On a mature tree there may be hundreds of fruits bearing at the same time, making it a spectacular sight to behold. This shapely evergreen tree grows upright with a columnar habit. Covering the delicately textured, almost thornless branchlets are small, glossy-green, oval-shaped leaves. The petite, one-and-one-half-inch, spherical fruits have reddish-orange rinds and bright-orange pulp. Because it has few seeds, tender pulp, and acid-tasting juice, the Calamondin makes excellent marmalade, refreshing drinks when sweetened with sugar, and flavorful additions to foods—as long as you have grown them organically, or if you have not used any pesticides, herbicides, or fungicides that have long-term residual affects. When I (Bruce) served in the Navy, aboard the carrier USS Kitty Hawk, one of our ports of call was at Subic Bay in the Philippines. This was my first introduction to "Calamondins," as they are commonly called there, and they are used there as culinary substitutes for lemons and limes. They tolerate heat if there is sufficient humidity and water, but do not like drought or wind.

Family Name /Origin Rutaceae / Philippines

Mature Height × Spread 6 to 10 ft. × 6 to 8 ft.

When and How to Plant Plant in spring after the last frost from 5- or 15-gallon containers, spacing them 12 to 15 ft. apart. Construct a watering basin 6 to 10 ft. in diameter and cover with 2 in. of organic material such as humus mulch or compost. For more information, refer to Planting Techniques, p. 398.

Climate & Culture

Preferred Zones 10–11

Sun Preference

Sun and Soil Preferences Calamondins prefer full sun in porous, well-drained soil that has a pH of 6.7 to 7.0.

Moisture Requirements Immediately after planting, soak deeply and thoroughly. During the first week, water twice; thereafter, adjust watering frequency and the amount according to weather and growth conditions.

Fertilizing Fertilize in late winter or early spring and early summer with a granular citrus and avocado food.

Pruning, Care, and Harvest Prune for shape and remove dead wood between two of the harvest cycles. In the coastal areas of Southern California and the coastal valleys of Northern California, Calamondins are harvested from winter through fall. In Southern California's inland regions, they are picked from winter through midsummer. The harvest season lasts from early winter to late summer along California's central valleys, but only lasts from early winter to early spring in the desert areas.

Pests and Diseases Snails can happily spend the majority of their lives in the dense canopy of the Calamondin. Remove them by hand and feed them to your ducks, or use the foot-stomp method of eradication. Watch out for aphids, particularly when tender growth emerges in the spring; as the weather warms, inspect for mites. An effective biodegradable control is Neem oil.

Companion Plantings and Design Calamondin is a wonderful ornamental background or shade tree in the landscape and a perfect indoor or outdoor container plant as long as there is sufficient light, humidity, and moisture. Because it is cold hardy, it grows where other citrus are either unavailable or cannot be grown.

Citron
Citrus medica

The Citron has a long history of cultivation. Originally known as the Persian Apple, it was the first citrus known to Europeans and was grown by the Hebrews, Greeks, and Romans hundreds of years before Christ. In the fifteenth century, Columbus brought the Citron to America. This evergreen tree is referred to in the Bible as the "hadar" or "goodly fruit," but is now grown primarily as a novelty and for religious ceremonies such as the Jewish Feast of the Tabernacles. We first saw this strange, deformed citrus growing at Casa Pacifica, President Nixon's former home in San Clemente. Its new growth and flowers are tinged with purple, and it grows fruit practically year-round. Like lemons and limes, it bears sour fruit, but unlike its more popular relatives, its flesh and pulp is skimpy with very little juice. Citron fruits look like large, bumpy lemons with thick but highly aromatic rinds. These fragrant fruits are great room and closet deodorizers and moth repellents. High in vitamin B as well as vitamin C, the rind can be grated for a healthy and tangy addition to salads and vinegars, and the peel can be candied. The plants are sensitive to frost and cool temperatures, drought, and wind, but tolerate heat if there is sufficient humidity and moisture available.

Family Name / Origin Rutaceae / E Indies, Mediterranean

Mature Height × Spread 10 to 15 ft. × 6 to 8 ft.

When and How to Plant Plant in spring after the last frost from 5- or 15-gallon containers and space them 10 to 15 ft. apart. Construct a watering basin 6 to 8 ft. in diameter and cover with 2 in. of organic material such as humus mulch or compost. *Avoid persistent and systemic pesticides, fungicides, and herbicides if you want to use the Citron as an edible.* For more information, refer to Planting Techniques, p. 398.

Climate & Culture

Preferred Zones
10–11

Sun Preference

Sun and Soil Preferences Citron prefers full sun in sandy loam soil with a pH of 6.7 to 7.0.

Moisture Requirements Immediately after planting, soak deeply and thoroughly. During the first week, water twice; thereafter, adjust watering frequency and the amount according to weather and growth conditions.

Fertilizing Fertilize in late winter or early spring and early summer with a granular citrus and avocado food.

Pruning, Care, and Harvest Prune for shape and to remove dead wood.

Pests and Diseases Snails and citrus woolly whitefly are common enemies, but are easily controlled by a granular snail bait, hand-harvesting, and Neem oil.

Companion Plantings and Design The tree can hardly be thought of as decorative since it is a small, scraggly, thorny plant with large, leathery, oval-shaped leaves. If you place a single fruit in a room, its delicate and penetrating perfume will waft throughout the house for several days.

Our Personal Favorite

NAME	SPECIAL CHARACTERISTICS
C. *medica* 'Buddha's Hand'	Elongated, lemon-sized, fragrant fruit / popular in Asia for its finger-like fruit / in China, a symbol of happiness

Grapefruit

Citrus paradisi

Even without their large yellow or pink-blushed fruits that grow so extravagantly in clusters near the outside of trees, these would be handsome evergreen ornamentals. Their large, shiny, dark-green leaves provide a lush background for their equally impressive fruits. There are two types of Grapefruit: white-fleshed and pigmented. The latter need long periods of heat to color, but there is no flavor difference between the two. There is a difference, however, between seeded and seedless varieties—the former tends to be more flavorful and separates into segments easily. If you have grown your Grapefruits organically or if you have not used any pesticides, herbicides, or fungicides that have long-term residual affects, use them as you would oranges in freshly-squeezed juice; in salads, especially paired with avocado; and as marmalade, candied peel, and sorbet. Where winters are warm and summers are long and hot, such as in the California low desert, the fruits ripen in twelve to fourteen months; in cooler, coastal regions they may need eighteen months, but their rinds will be thicker and their juice tarter in flavor. This is why we are considering taking out the two Grapefruit trees growing in our orchard. There is not enough heat for proper sugar development and the fruits are almost as sour as lemons.

Family Name /Origin Rutaceae / China

Mature Height × Spread 10 to 15 ft. × 15 ft.

When and How to Plant Plant in spring from 5- or 15-gallon containers, spacing at least 15 to 20 ft. apart for large varieties and closer for smaller ones. Build a watering basin 10 to 12 ft. in diameter and cover with 2 in. of organic material such as humus mulch or compost. Grapefruit have the highest heat requirement of all citrus and need a long, hot growing season. For additional information, see Planting Techniques, p. 398.

Sun and Soil Preferences They require full sun in rich, well-drained soil with a pH of 6.7 to 7.0. They tolerate strong sunlight and gusty winds, but there will be some sun and wind damage.

Climate & Culture

Preferred Zones
10–11

Sun Preference

Moisture Requirements Immediately after planting, soak deeply and thoroughly. During the first week, water three times and thereafter adjust the frequency and the amount according to weather and growth conditions. They are sensitive to drought.

Fertilizing Fertilize in late winter or early spring and early summer with a granular citrus and avocado food.

Pruning, Care, and Harvest Prune only for shape and to remove dead wood. You can allow the fruits to hang on the tree for up to eighteen months, but do not leave them on too much beyond that time because it diminishes the flavor. For the juiciest fruits at their peak prime, pick those that are heavy, smooth, and thin-skinned, and avoid those that have sandpaper-like, puffy rinds.

Pests and Diseases Giant whitefly and mites are common problems that are controlled by Neem oil.

Companion Plantings and Design They make ideal background, ornamental, or shade trees in the landscape, and are great outdoor container plants.

Our Personal Favorite

NAME	SPECIAL CHARACTERISTICS
C. p. 'Oroblanco'	A white grapefruit / thrives in the cool, coastal areas of California

Kumquat

Fortunella japonica

Often called the "little gems of citrus," Kumquats are unique in that they do not belong to the genus Citrus and their fruit is eaten whole. We like to pick the small orange fruits, gently press and roll them between our fingers, pop them in our mouths, and savor the combination of the peel's sweet flavor with the pulp's tart taste. They are attractive, symmetrical, compact evergreen trees that during the growing season are covered with tiny, lustrous, dark-green leaves. In China it is a common custom to place a fruiting bonsai Kumquat plant in front of dinner guests so they can pick and eat the "golden oranges" between the many courses of a Chinese feast. Chefs also like them in sauces for rich meats, as marmalade, as garnishes, and as piquant preserves. Just avoid harmful pesticides, fungicides, and herbicides if you want to use the Kumquat as an edible. Kumquat trees do not begin their growth cycle until the onset of warm weather, and they do not bloom until midsummer. They produce the sweetest and juiciest fruit where summers are hot and humid, but they can adapt to other zones. In the California desert, the fruits are large but a bit more acid in flavor, and in the coastal regions, the fruits are smaller but juicier.

Family Name / Origin Rutaceae / Japan

Mature Height × Spread 10 to 15 ft. × 15 ft.

When and How to Plant Plant in spring after the last frost from 5- or 15-gallon containers, spacing them 12 to 15 ft. on center. Construct a watering basin 6 to 10 ft. in diameter and cover with 2 in. of organic material such as humus mulch or compost. See Planting Techniques, p. 398.

Sun and Soil Preferences They require full sun in rich, well-drained soil with a pH of 6.7 to 7.0.

Moisture Requirements Immediately after planting, soak deeply and thoroughly. Water three times during the first week; thereafter, adjust watering frequency and amounts according to weather and growth conditions.

Fertilizing Fertilize in late winter or early spring and early summer with a granular citrus and avocado food.

Pruning, Care, and Harvest Prune as needed for shape and to remove dead wood. Because they stay dormant in the cooler fall and winter months, Kumquats withstand temperatures below 20 degrees Fahrenheit with little damage to their foliage. They need protection from drought and wind.

Pests and Diseases Few diseases affect Kumquats, but citrus red scales and brown soft scales can be a problem. A horticultural oil is an effective treatment for these sucking insects if you follow the manufacturer's directions.

Companion Plantings and Design With their brightly colored fruit, they are prized as ornamentals and make excellent foundation shrubs and plants for terrace and patio containers. They are used as decorative centerpieces with dainty foliage clipped and jeweled fruits attached.

Climate & Culture

Preferred Zones
9–11

Sun Preference

Our Personal Favorites

NAME	SPECIAL CHARACTERISTICS
C. f. 'Nagami'	An oval-shaped Kumquat / the variety most commonly sold in American supermarkets
C. f. 'Meiwa'	A round fruit with a spicy flavor

Lemon
Citrus limon

Lemons were cultivated in the ancient gardens of Media (an ancient country of southwest Asia in present-day Iran). They were brought to America by Christopher Columbus in 1492. Where temperate conditions prevail, we think every garden should have a Lemon tree because there is nothing more satisfying than being able to pick fresh fruits anytime you need them. It is a necessary luxury. We have always believed that "when life hands you lemons, make lemonade," as well as marinade, Hollandaise sauce, pie filling, sorbet, pudding, and preserves—provided, of course, you have grown your lemons organically or have not used any pesticides, herbicides, or fungicides that have long-term residual effects. These are attractive, vigorous, upright trees with light-green leaves that are tinged with purplish-red when immature, highlighting their bright-yellow fruit. Although they do not need too much heat to ripen, they are frost-sensitive and may damage when temperatures dip below 30 degrees Fahrenheit for prolonged periods. In regions where winters and summers are mild, such as coastal areas, they bear all year-round, but in interior regions they bear primarily in winter and late summer. Like most citrus, a Lemon tree (probably a hybrid of C. medica × C. aurantifolia) does not tolerate drought or wind.

Family Name /Origin Rutaceae / Asia

Mature Height × Spread 10 to 15 ft. × 12 to 15 ft.

When and How to Plant Plant in spring after the
last frost from 5- or 15-gallon containers, spacing
15 to 20 ft. on center. Build a watering basin 6 to
10 ft. in diameter and cover with 2 in. of organic
material such as humus mulch or compost. Consult
Planting Techniques, p. 398.

Sun and Soil Preferences Lemon trees require full
sun in loam-textured, well-drained soil, pH 6.7 to 7.0.

Moisture Requirements Soak deeply after planting. Water twice the first week; thereafter, adjust
watering frequency and the amounts according to
weather and growth conditions.

Fertilizing Fertilize in late winter or early spring with a citrus and
avocado food.

Pruning, Care, and Harvest If left alone, Lemon trees become too tall,
rangy and unsightly. Regularly pruned trees are more productive and the
fruits are easier to harvest. For best flavor, pick Lemons that are completely
yellow—those with a greenish cast are more acid and less flavorful. If you
leave them on the trees too long, they become pithy.

Pests and Diseases Lemon trees are prone to mite infestations that result
in a condition called russeting or silvering, a blemishing of the rind. Since
russeting or silvering does not destroy the quality of the lemons, do not inter-
vene unless the infestation becomes severe. If necessary, you can introduce
predacious mites from agricultural insectaries, or apply Neem oil.

Companion Plantings and Design Lemon trees can be pruned into
espaliers. They are desirable as ornamentals and background trees, and
in containers for terraces and patios.

**Climate &
Culture**

Preferred
Zones
9–11

Sun
Preference

Our Personal Favorite

NAME	SPECIAL CHARACTERISTICS
C. meyeri	Commonly known as Meyer Lemon / very hardy / thin, smooth rind / excellent container plant

Lime
Citrus aurantiifolia

There are two main types of Limes produced in California, the small-fruited Mexican Lime and the large-fruited Persian or Tahiti Lime. Limes are evergreen hybrids, probably C. medica × another species. Mexican Lime is often referred to as Key Lime or Bartender's Lime because it was once grown commercially in the Florida Keys and is also used in drinks. It is a round, thorny, shrublike tree with a wiry, open habit. Small pale-green leaves cover its canopy of twiggy growth and it bears dark-green fruits that are seeded, aromatic, and juicy. The fruit's flavor develops best in areas where summers are hot and humid. Although it bears fruit year-round, the main harvest occurs in winter. Persian or Tahiti Limes do well in Southern California and are a few degrees hardier than Mexican Limes. They have a more compact and attractive growth habit with limes that are lighter colored, less seeded, and less fragrant, but they are larger and just as juicy and flavorful. The trees have darker-green leaves, their branches have fewer thorns, and they do not require as much heat to ripen. Avoid harmful pesticides, fungicides, and herbicides if you want to use the lime as an edible. Lime trees are very sensitive to frost, drought, and strong winds, but thrive in heat as long as there is adequate moisture.

Family Name / Origin Rutaceae / Asia

Mature Height × Spread 8 to 12 ft. × 10 ft.

When and How to Plant Plant in spring from
5- or 15-gallon containers, spacing 10 to 15 ft. apart.
Build a watering basin 8 to 10 ft. in diameter and
cover with 2 in. of organic material such as humus
mulch or compost. See Planting Techniques, p. 398.

Sun and Soil Preferences Limes prefer full sun
and well-drained loam soil, pH 6.7 to 7.0.

Moisture Requirements Immediately after
planting, soak deeply and thoroughly. During the
first week, water three times; thereafter, adjust
frequency and the amount according to weather
and growth conditions.

Fertilizing Fertilize in late winter or early spring and early summer with a
granular citrus and avocado food.

Pruning, Care, and Harvest Prune for shape and to remove dead wood
during late winter or early spring. Limes can be picked when they are green
to yellow, but they do not hold well on the tree once they have turned yellow.

Pests and Diseases Few disease or insect problems affect these trees, but
keep a watchful eye out for spider mites, citrus woolly whitefly, and snails. If
damage is extensive, apply Neem oil for mites and a molluscicide for snails.

Companion Plantings and Design A Lime tree is a great container plant
as well as a foundation plant. If you want to plant only one type of Lime tree,
we would choose the Tahiti or Persian Lime because it is a much more attractive ornamental, and it bears larger fruits that are about as juicy and flavorful
as the Mexican Lime.

**Climate &
Culture**

**Preferred
Zones**
10–11

**Sun
Preference**

Our Personal Favorite

NAME	SPECIAL CHARACTERISTICS
C. a. 'Bearss Lime'	Thought to be a seedling of Tahiti Lime / the most popular lime for home gardeners / our Bearss Lime is a prolific producer and has had minimal disease or insect problems

Mandarin
Citrus reticulata

Historically, the Mandarin is named after a group of high-ranking Chinese officials who traditionally wore bright orange robes and button-shaped hats, similar to the fruit. An important "do you know?" fact is that some Mandarins are called Tangerines, but the name has no botanical significance and was merely used by distributors to help sell the bright, reddish-orange varieties. Mandarins are alternate bearing, which means they yield a large crop of small fruit one year, followed by a less prolific crop of large fruit the next year. The foliage is dark green, and the fruit is usually borne on the outside of the canopy. One of our favorite pleasures is to walk down to our orchard, pluck off a couple of perfectly ripe Mandarins, "zip" off their rinds, and eat them out-of-hand, section by juicy section. The trees are very frost-hardy, tolerating short dips in temperatures as low as 28 degrees Fahrenheit, but their fruit is much more cold-sensitive and cannot survive such frost (although early-maturing varieties do better in cold climates). Some adapt to desert and hot inland areas, but most do best in subtropical regions where high heat in the late stage of ripening produces the sweetest and juiciest fruit as long as there is adequate moisture. They do not tolerate hot, dry winds.

Family Name / Origin Rutaceae / SE Asia

Mature Height × Spread 10 to 15 ft. × 12 to 15 ft.

When and How to Plant Plant in spring from
5- or 15-gallon containers, spacing 10 to 15 ft. apart.
Construct a watering basin 10 ft. in diameter and
cover with 2 in. of organic material such as humus
mulch or compost. For additional information, see
Planting Techniques, p. 398.

Sun and Soil Preferences These evergreens prefer
full sun in well-drained loam soil with a pH of 6.7
to 7.0.

Moisture Requirements Immediately after planting, soak deeply and thoroughly. Water three times
during the first week; thereafter, adjust frequency and amount according to
weather and growth conditions.

Fertilizing Fertilize in late winter or early spring and early summer with a
granular citrus and avocado food .

Pruning, Care, and Harvest Prune just after the fruits set to even out
alternate-bearing fruit production, to remove any dead wood, and to provide
good air circulation by thinning out the interior of the tree. Pick Mandarins
when they are heavy with juice, and avoid puffy, lightweight fruits that have
soft spots. If left too long on a tree, the fruits will become dry and bland. To
avoid tearing off the rinds around the stems when harvesting, use clippers to
snip off the fruits.

Pests and Diseases If you thin the trees' interiors, it will help prevent
pest and disease infestations by promoting good air circulation. Washing
the foliage weekly with a strong stream of water will help keep the insect
population down.

Companion Plantings and Design Most Mandarins are pollinated by
bees, but a few varieties need cross-pollinators that bloom during the same
time, normally a different type of Mandarin or Tangelo.

Climate & Culture

Preferred Zones
10–11

Sun Preference

Our Personal Favorite

NAME	SPECIAL CHARACTERISTICS
C. r. 'Owari-Satsuma'	Exceptionally sweet fruit that ripens early / a good choice for colder climates such as the California foothills

Pummelo
Citrus grandis

What is the largest citrus fruit in the world? The trivia answer is the Pummelo, reaching up to eight inches in diameter and weighing in at several pounds. Its botanical name, Citrus grandis, accurately describes this giant among citrus. Closely related to the Grapefruit but sweeter, less acidic, and larger, use it as you would a Grapefruit (provided, of course, you have grown your Pummelos organically or you have not used any pesticides, herbicides, or fungicides that have long-term residual effects). *We like the evergreen Pummelo for a prosaic but practical reason— because its shelled segments taste so good. Some Pummelo trees are small with mound-like canopies, others are about the same size as Grapefruit plants. Some have a drooping habit while others are large, open, and wide-spreading. There are also differences in the color and flavor of the fruits, and there are seeded and seedless, thorny and thornless varieties. Most have thick branches covered with distinctively wide, winged leaf stems that bear large, thick-textured blossoms. Because the rind of the fruit is so thick, they are a bit hardier in cool weather than Grapefruit trees. They grow best in warm tropical regions close to the sea in sheltered areas; they even tolerate brackish water but dislike extended periods of drought, wind, or freezing temperatures.*

Family Name / Origin Rutaceae / Polynesia

Mature Height × **Spread** 10 to 15 ft. × 12 ft.

When and How to Plant Plant in spring from 5- or 15-gallon containers, spacing 15 to 20 ft. Construct a watering basin 10 ft. in diameter and cover with 2 in. of organic material like humus mulch or compost. See Planting Techniques, p. 398.

Sun and Soil Preferences Plant in full sun in rich, well-drained soil, pH 6.7 to 7.0.

Moisture Requirements Soak deeply after planting. Water three times the first week; thereafter, adjust frequency and amount to weather and growth conditions.

Climate & Culture

Preferred Zones
10–11

Sun Preference

Fertilizing Fertilize in late winter or early spring and early summer with a granular citrus and avocado food.

Pruning, Care, and Harvest Prune for shape and to remove dead wood before spring growth. For maximum sweetness, ripen a freshly picked Pummelo at room temperature for ten to fifteen days or until its skin is a deep yellow with a heavy fragrance.

Pests and Diseases Few diseases affect Pummelos, but citrus red scale, brown soft scale, and citrus woolly whitefly can cause problems, particularly during the warm, growing seasons. Horticultural oil or Neem oil are effective controls.

Companion Plantings and Design In Asia, it is believed that this fruit is a symbol of prosperity and that good fortune will happen to those who eat it. They are in great demand during Chinese New Year celebrations; if you want to create a stir at your next dinner, set out a few of these giants as table decorations.

Our Personal Favorites

NAME	SPECIAL CHARACTERISTICS
C. g. 'Chandler'	Pink-fleshed / a sweet, acidic flavor / does best in warm inland regions
C. g. 'Reinking'	White-fleshed / slightly larger than the 'Chandler' / thrives in warm inland areas

Sweet Orange
Citrus sinensis

There are three major types of Sweet Oranges: Navel, Common, and Blood Oranges. The Navel Orange has a sweet, rich flavor and develops a secondary fruit at the blossom end of the primary fruit. When the secondary fruit enlarges, it creates a small protrusion that resembles a navel. Navels are the best for eating fresh because they are seedless, easy to peel, and have just the perfect blend of sweetness and acidity. Optimum growing conditions in California are in the subtropical interior regions where the summers are warm and the nights are cool. Common Oranges do not have navels and are seedier, harder to peel, and juicier. They are perfect juicing oranges and can be fresh or frozen. Most of the oranges grown in the world are Common Oranges because they adapt to most citrus-growing regions, except frost areas. Blood Oranges have reddish pulp and juice. The taste is rich and tangy, with just a hint of raspberries and strawberries. As a general rule, ideal conditions for the best internal coloration and taste are hot, dry summers paired with cold winters. When sliced or wedged, they are wonderful as dramatic garnishes on fish, soups, salads, and tarts, and make delicious sauces and sorbets. Sweet Oranges do not tolerate windy locations or extended periods of drought.

Family Name / Origin Rutaceae / China, Vietnam

Mature Height × Spread 10 to 15 ft. × 12 ft.

When and How to Plant Plant in spring from 5- or 15-gallon containers, spacing them 10 to 15 ft. apart. Build a watering basin 10 ft. in diameter and cover with 2 in. of organic material such as humus mulch or compost. See Planting Techniques, p. 398.

Sun and Soil Preferences These evergreens prefer full sun in rich, well-drained soil with a pH of 6.7 to 7.0. The bark and fruit of citrus are sensitive to sunburn, especially in arid areas of California. As a preventative, plant your trees in an easterly exposure, paint the trunk with a reflective surface, or use a tree wrap, available at your local garden center.

Climate & Culture

Preferred Zones
10–11

Sun Preference

Moisture Requirements Immediately after planting, soak deeply and thoroughly. Water three times the first week; thereafter, adjust frequency and amount according to weather and growth conditions.

Fertilizing Fertilize in late winter or early spring and early summer with a granular citrus and avocado food.

Pruning, Care, and Harvest Prune for shape or to remove dead wood as needed.

Pests and Diseases Be vigilant regarding infestations of aphids, mealybugs, and citrus red scale. Control with applications of Neem oil or horticultural oil when necessary.

Companion Plantings and Design If you have the space and live in a frost-free area, plant a 'Washington Navel' and a 'Valencia' orange and you will have fresh oranges for about ten months out of the year.

Our Personal Favorites

NAME	SPECIAL CHARACTERISTICS
C. s. 'Valencia'	Tall trees with vigorous growth / the best common orange for the California gardener / produces excellent fruit for making juice
C. s. 'Washington Navel'	The most widely grown navel / large, thick-skinned fruits with few seeds and sweet taste

Tangelo

Citrus × tangelo

Tangelos are hybrids of Mandarins crossed with Grapefruits or Pummelos. Fruit colors range from pale yellow to deep orange, fruit size from small to medium large. As do the fruits, the form of the tree will resemble one parent or the other, but the taste will combine the best qualities of both parents. At the edge of our orchard, we are growing a fifteen-year-old, twelve-foot-tall 'Minneola' Tangelo that continues to bear generous crops, particularly on the southwest side of the tree where the warmth of the late-winter and early-spring sun ripens the fruits. An 'Owari-Satsuma' Mandarin is nearby. Because the trees are relatively sheltered from prevailing winds, the honeybees industriously cross-pollinate the two citrus trees. From late winter to mid-spring we harvest these flavorful and aromatic jewels when they are heavy and full of juice. Other varieties adapt to hot climates if there is sufficient humidity and moisture available. Some also adapt to cooler weather, but their flavor will be more tart. A Tangelo's cold hardiness generally falls between that of a Grapefruit and an Orange, or intermediate between its parents' tolerance to cold. Like our 'Minneola', most Tangelos are sensitive to wind, freezing temperatures, and drought.

Family Name / Origin Rutaceae / China

Mature Height × Spread 10 to 15 ft. × 12 ft.

When and How to Plant Plant in spring from 5- or 15-gallon containers, spacing 15 ft. apart. Build a watering basin 10 ft. in diameter and cover with 2 in. of organic material such as humus mulch or compost. For more information, see Planting Techniques, p. 398.

Sun and Soil Preferences These evergreens prefer full sun in well-drained soil with a pH of 6.7 to 7.0.

Moisture Requirements Soak deeply after planting. Water three times the first week; thereafter, adjust frequency and amount according to weather and growth conditions.

Climate & Culture

Preferred Zones
10–11

Sun Preference

Fertilizing Fertilize in late winter or early spring and early summer with a granular citrus and avocado food.

Pruning, Care, and Harvest Prune anytime for shape and to remove dead wood.

Pests and Diseases Despite infestations from the exotic giant whitefly and citrus woolly whitefly, the tree will continue to thrive with an occasional application of horticultural oil alternating with Neem oil during the cool season.

Companion Plantings and Design Because Tangelos do not cross-pollinate with each other, cross-pollination with a Mandarin will usually produce a more prolific crop.

Our Personal Favorites

NAME	SPECIAL CHARACTERISTICS
C. × t. 'Minneola'	Cross between a Duncan Grapefruit and a Dancy Mandarin / bears fruit from mid-December through April / slightly elongated, deep-orange fruit with knob-like formations at the stems / fruit peels and segments easily and has a sweet, tart flavor
C. × t. 'Orlando'	Available from November through January / light-orange fruit is slightly flat, medium-large, pebble-textured, with a taste that is tangy yet mildly sweet

Fruit Trees *for California*

There is something magical about trees that bear flowers and edible fruit. With their fresh spring blossoms, summer and fall bounty, and blaze of autumn color, they transform a bland landscape into a Garden of Eden. Exquisite pink and white clouds of perfumed Apricot, Nectarine, and Plum blossoms fall in a blizzard of floral snowflakes to make way for their sun-warmed fruits. Plucking a crisp, crunchy red Apple or a golden-orange Persimmon from your own tree is a particular delight.

Even in Winter

Even in their winter guise, these trees continue to have an allure. The winter-slanting sun's rays highlight the sweeping branches of a Fig tree and gild the bark of the Sweet Cherry with the rich color of chestnut brown. Winter also brings unexpected color in the form of

Pomegranates, dangling red baubles that add a festive holiday flair to bare limbs.

Orchard or Edible Landscape

Many people think fruit trees should be grown in an orchard setting, planted in militarily-precise rows apart from everything else. The advantage of this agricultural style is convenience, especially if you grow several standard fruit trees over a large area; the disadvantage is that it is not aesthetically pleasing and tends to interfere with the harmony of the landscape.

If space is limited or your preference is towards a blended design, without fruit trees set apart, then an edible landscape is a wonderful alternative. You double your pleasure by growing fruit trees not only for their crops, but for their ornamental value. If your yard is small, plant dwarf varieties or espalier to make a decorative screen, or to camouflage a sterile wall.

Three Steps to a Thriving Fruit Tree

Whether your intent is to create an orchard or an edible landscape, the first step to having a thriving fruit tree is to select a suitable site. Most fruit trees need a sunny location where fragile blossoms and pollinating bees, butterflies, and birds are sheltered from blustery, prevailing winds. All fruit trees do best in well-drained soils, but if the soil is not well-drained, it is still possible to grow dwarf fruit trees in raised beds. Consider dwarf rather than standard varieties for small spaces—not only do they take up less room, but they bear normal-sized fruit, and most produce about twenty percent as much fruit as a standard tree. The second step is to select plants adapted to your climate. You should consider the *chilling requirement*, which is defined as the number of cool-temperature hours below 45 degrees Fahrenheit that a particular plant needs during winter before it breaks out of dormancy and starts growing again. Some trees need a larger number of winter-chill hours than others. Another important consideration is a plant's cold hardiness, which reflects the lowest temperature it can tolerate and survive during winter dormancy. For fruit trees to flourish, there needs to be a balance between winter-chill hours and cold hardiness. In cold regions, you can select high-chill cultivars, which remain dormant until dangers of frost have passed—in mild-winter areas, their long dormancy would probably produce weak shoots, and they might not bloom at all. Further complicating proper selection is the fact that temperatures vary in specific regions depending on elevation, and they may vary even in your own garden. We have several different microclimates in our yard. Our low-elevation areas are frost pockets, and the middle and top of our slopes are much warmer. If you keep all of these variables in mind, you can select the right tree for the right spot.

The third step is to determine how your tree of choice is pollinated, and whether or not it is self-fruitful. Many Apples, Sweet Cherries, Pears, and Plums are not self-fruitful and need at least one or two compatible cultivars planted within one-hundred feet of each other in order to bear fruit.

Consult your local nursery, University of California Extension fruit specialist, or talk to your neighbors about the kinds of fruits and specific cultivars that thrive where you live, as well as pest and disease problems you may encounter and how to manage them.

An Ode to Nature

There is nothing quite like eating Figs, Nectarines, or Cherries picked fresh from your own trees and preserving them in jams, stuffing them in pies, baking them in breads, or freezing them for summer reminders in winter. While harvesting the edible bounty is the most obvious reward, there are other lessons to be learned. Whenever we look at our fruit trees, Vivaldi's symphonic ode to nature, "The Four Seasons," comes to mind. Each tree's leaves, flowers, fruits, and branching silhouette are magical metaphors for the circle of life.

Apple
Malus sylvestris

Our Apple trees once again trumpet their presence when their delicate pastel-pink blossoms appear and scent the warming breezes with their fragrance. These are our orchard harbingers of spring, and the honeybees, butterflies, hummingbirds, orioles, and robins fly, flutter, and flock to their welcoming buds. The dainty flowers fall in a blizzard of petaled snowflakes to reveal newly leafed branches of bright-green elliptical leaves that are smooth on top and downy underneath. Come the end of summer to early fall, there are apples for making pies, strudels, bread, applesauce, and jam, and for munching fresh off the trees and sharing with the birds. Though not found in tropical and arctic regions, there are more than two thousand varieties of Apples throughout the world. The rounded, ornamental trees are available as standard, semi-dwarf, and dwarf varieties, from forty-foot giants to six-foot miniatures. Most Apple tree roots are less tolerant of frost than their branch tips, so although their dormant period requires temperatures ranging from 32 to 55 degrees Fahrenheit, they do not withstand extended periods of below-freezing temperatures. They need adequate amounts of moisture to protect them from the damaging effects of high temperatures, drought, and cold or dry winds.

Family Name / Origin Rosaceae / Europe, Asia, North America

Mature Height × Spread 20 to 40 ft. × 20 to 30 ft.

When and How to Plant Plant in spring from bare-root stock or 5- or 15-gallon containers. Space 20 ft. apart if dwarf or semi-dwarf, 35 to 40 ft. if standard. Build a 10-ft. watering basin and cover with 2 in. of organic material. See p. 398.

Sun and Soil Preferences Plant in full sun in rich, well-drained, medium-textured soil, pH 5.5 to 6.5.

Moisture Requirements After planting, soak deeply and thoroughly. Water three times the first week; thereafter, adjust frequency and amount to climatic and growth conditions.

Fertilizing After planting, apply a root stimulator such as IBU, idole-3 butyric acid. Once established, fertilize with 16-4-8 in late winter or early spring.

Pruning, Care, and Harvest Since fruits develop on wood that is at least one year old, selective pruning is very important. For detailed Pruning information, see p. 409.

Pests and Diseases If you select disease-resistant varieties, plant in the right place, handpick bugs, remove diseased wood, and are satisfied with less-than-picture-perfect fruits, pesticides are usually not necessary.

Companion Plantings and Design Yellow drifts of Daffodils or a blue blanket of Grape Hyacinth make beautiful underplantings for blossoming Apple trees. For other Design Tips, see p. 410.

Climate & Culture

Preferred Zones
4–10

Sun Preference

Our Personal Favorite

NAME	SPECIAL CHARACTERISTICS
'Anna'	Self-fruitful / large / light greenish-yellow with a slight red blush, creamy white flesh / sweet, slightly tart / stores well / requires only 200 to 300 hrs. of winter chill / ripens in late June / for better production, plant a pollinizer such as Dorsett Golden

See p. 410 for other excellent Apple selections.

Apricot

Prunus armeniaca

In winter our Apricot tree looks rather forlorn and ungainly with its untidy bare branches and stout grayish-brown trunk, but come spring a miraculous transformation takes place. Clouds of pink and white flowers settle on the branches and a bevy of honeybees hover to gather the sweet nectar. In late spring, a rounded crown of deep-green, oval, leathery leaves provides a proper background-in-waiting for the summer-blushed jewels of yellow and reddish-orange fruit. We look forward to picking the first perfectly ripe Apricot with its velvety-soft, rouge-kissed, golden skin, and biting into its plump meat. Savoring its sweetness is the beginning of summer for us. If only to provide this experience, every garden should have an Apricot tree. This common orchard variety bears freestone fruit, which means the flesh separates easily from the stony pit, and it is self-fruitful, making it unnecessary to plant more than one tree. The ancient Persians called Apricots "the seeds of the sun." If you live in cold regions, plant Apricots as ornamentals—if they bear fruit, consider it a serendipitous bonus. Provided there is adequate moisture, Apricots love summer heat and frost-free spring weather. They need protection from drought, cold winds, and sharp variations in weather. If your soil is heavy, consider planting a dwarf variety in a container.

Family Name / Origin Rosaceae / China, Mongolia

Mature Height × Spread 10 to 15 ft. × 15 to 20 ft.

When and How to Plant Plant in late winter from bare-root stock or 5- to 15-gallon containers. Space dwarf or semi-dwarf plants 10 to 15 ft. apart and construct a 5- to 8-ft. watering basin (space at 20 ft. if standard, and construct a 12-ft. watering basin). Cover with 2 in. of organic material. See Planting Techniques, p. 398.

Sun and Soil Preferences Plant in full sun in rich, well-drained, loam soil, pH 5.5 to 6.5.

Climate & Culture

Preferred Zones 5–10

Sun Preference

Moisture Requirements Immediately after plant-ing, soak deeply and thoroughly to collapse the air pockets. Water three times the first week; thereafter, adjust frequency and amount to climatic and growth conditions. As a general rule, water weekly during warm weather from spring to harvest time; supplement water in winter only if there is a winter drought.

Fertilizing Fertilize in late winter or early spring with a complete food, 16-4-8.

Pruning, Care, and Harvest To beat other garden critters to your harvest, pick Apricots when all traces of green have disappeared but they are still firm. For important Pruning and Winter-Chill information, see p. 410.

Pests and Diseases Aside from the usual warm-weather infestations of aphids, mites, scale, and caterpillars, there are few serious disease or insect problems. If insect damage is severe, apply an appropriate dormant spray in fall when the leaves drop, at the end of December, and just before the buds swell and show color.

Companion Plantings and Design Apricots do very well in California as espaliers against an otherwise stark wall, as cooling shade trees, and even in cut-flower arrangements.

Our Personal Favorite

NAME	SPECIAL CHARACTERISTICS
'Goldkist'	Self-fruitful / medium size, orange blush / sweet, good for eating, canning, and drying / a predictable producer / ripens midseason / winter chill: 300 hrs.

See p. 410 for other excellent selections.

Fig

Ficus carica

Relaxing under the cool shadow cast from the wide crown of a Fig tree at Sydney's Royal Botanic Gardens, we happened to look up and saw dozens of "flying foxes," as the Australians affectionately call their fruit bats, suspended upside down, wings wrapped tightly around themselves in deep slumber. What a wonderful life they have, sheltered from the summer heat among low sweeping branches covered with luxuriant, deeply-lobed, dark-green leaves. Growing like pear-shaped offshoots from the branches were succulent groupings of purplish-black Figs, ready and waiting for their nocturnal guests' moonlit feast. Imagine a fully ripe Fig, so plump its skin has stretch marks, and so sweet a drop of honey hangs at its tip. As you take your first bite, the soft, sweet, juicy red pulp melts in your mouth and you must remind yourself to savor its goodness slowly instead of gobbling it down. Figs are not really fruits in the botanical sense— rather, they are hundreds of minuscule flowers encased in fleshy balloonlike receptacles. New varieties vary in skin color from black, purple, lavender, brown, and green to white and in pulp shades from red, purple, pink, and yellow to white. These trees are sun- and heat-lovers. Once established, they are somewhat drought tolerant, but severe cold temperatures and blustery winds may cause branch dieback.

Family Name / Origin Moraceae / Asia Minor

Mature Height × Spread 15 to 25 ft. × 15 to 20 ft.

When and How to Plant Plant in December or January when bare-root trees are available, or from 5- or 15-gallon containers any time of the year, spacing 35 ft. apart. They need to be planted where fruit drop and aggressive root systems are not problems, such as alongside houses, driveways, patios, and walkways. Build a watering basin 12 to 15 ft. in diameter and cover with 2 in. of organic material such as compost or humus mulch. See Planting Techniques, p. 398.

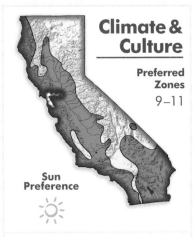

Climate & Culture

Preferred Zones 9–11

Sun Preference

Sun and Soil Preferences Plant in full sun in average, well-drained soil, pH 6.5 to 7.0.

Moisture Requirements Soak deeply after planting. Water twice the first week; thereafter, adjust frequency and amount to climatic and growth conditions. As a general rule, water deeply and slowly every ten to fourteen days in dry regions.

Fertilizing Fertilize in late winter or early spring with a food like 16-4-8.

Pruning, Care, and Harvest Pick Figs when they are full-size, soft to the touch, and come off easily. For important Pruning and Harvesting information, see p. 411.

Pests and Diseases While Fig trees do not have serious disease or insect problems, their tender spring leaves are targets for sucking and chewing insects, and their fruits are delectable treats for birds. Cover the trees with netting or helium-filled mylar balloons before harvest, surround them with chicken wire before planting, and pick off any infested leaves or fruit.

Companion Plantings and Design A Fig tree is a source of cool shade and can be pruned into a spreading shrub or trained as an espalier.

Our Personal Favorite

NAME	SPECIAL CHARACTERISTICS
F. c. 'Black Mission'	Medium to large fruit / pear-shaped, purplish-black skin / strawberry-colored flesh with a good flavor / a large, long-lived tree

See p. 411 for other good selections.

Japanese Plum

Prunus salicina

Although commonly known as Japanese Plums, these trees are native to China. They can grow up to twenty feet tall, and in spring bear delicate white, sweet-scented flowers that turn into round yellow, gold, red, or purplish-black plums. The juicy red or yellow-fleshed fruits taste pleasantly sugary close to their soft skin but are surprisingly tart around the pits. Smooth green leaves with sharply pointed tips cover the rough-textured branches; they turn into yellows, oranges, and reds in fall. Although some varieties are partly self-fruitful, most are not, and even the partly self-fruitful will be more productive when planted among compatible cross-pollinizing varieties. Consult your local retail nursery for the appropriate varieties. Like most fruit trees with showy flowers, Japanese Plums rely on insects such as honeybees to carry the pollen. Their fruits are wonderful eaten fresh, but as clingstone fruits they are less suitable for canning, drying, or preserving. If you do use them in cooking, drying, or preserving, remove the pits because they contain cyanic acid. Japanese Plum trees are vulnerable to frost during their fruiting and growth cycles, and are better suited for warmer climates. They need protection from prevailing winds and extended periods of drought, but thrive in heat as long as it is not tropical and adequate moisture is provided.

Family Name / Origin Rosaceae / China

Mature Height × Spread Maintain at 5 to 25 ft. × 10 to 15 ft.

When and How to Plant Plant in December or January from bare-root stock or in spring from 5- or 15-gallon containers. Space dwarf or semi-dwarf varieties 6 to 10 ft. apart; space standards 15 to 20 ft. apart. Construct a watering basin 6 to 8 ft. in diameter for dwarf or semi-dwarf varieties, 10 to 15 ft. in diameter for standards; cover with 2 in. of organic material such as humus mulch or compost. See Planting Techniques, p. 398.

Sun and Soil Preferences They need full sun and well-drained, medium-textured soil with a pH of 5.5 to 6.5.

Moisture Requirements Soak deeply after planting. Water twice the first week; then, adjust frequency and amount to climatic and growth conditions. As a general rule, periodic deep watering during the summer is important.

Fertilizing Once established, fertilize with a complete food such as 16-4-8 in late winter or early spring.

Pruning, Care, and Harvest Japanese Plum trees fruit on year-old shoots and older spurs, so prune selectively each year during dormancy. See p. 411 for detailed Pruning and Harvesting information.

Pests and Diseases Few diseases or insects pose a serious problem.

Climate & Culture

Preferred Zones
7–10

Sun Preference

Our Personal Favorites

NAME	SPECIAL CHARACTERISTICS
P. s. 'Santa Rosa'	Large oval fruit with purplish-red skin, firm yellow to dark-red flesh, and rich, pleasing, tart flavor / self-fruitful / the most important commercial and home variety / requires 400 hours of winter chill / ripens in mid-June
P. s. 'Satsuma'	Large, nearly round fruit with dark solid-red skin and firm, rather juicy, dark-red flesh / requires 300 hours of winter chill / ripens late July to August / an excellent pollinizer for 'Satsuma' is 'Santa Rosa'

Nectarine

Prunus persica 'Nectarina'

Whenever clients tell us they do not care for fuzzy fruit, we recommend Nectarine trees. They have growing requirements identical to those of Peach trees, and fruit that has a similar taste but not the fuzz. Peaches and Nectarines belong to the same species and are identical except for one gene. Nectarines are the gene- and fuzz-deprived fruit. Although Nectarine trees are less productive, bear smaller fruit, and ripen later, from the end of August to mid-September, they are just as beautiful in a landscape. In March when the spring weather turns mild, delicate pink flowers and long, pointed, shiny leaves emerge on trees ranging from four to twenty feet tall. There are clingstone, freestone, and intermediate types of fruit, yellow- or white-skinned with a ruby-red blush and a rich golden-yellow or creamy-white flesh. Their edible qualities are the same as Peaches, so enjoy them fresh, canned, dried, and baked. During their dormancy, they need a winter chill of 650 to 950 hours of 45 degrees Fahrenheit or below, unless you select a low-chill variety. Once in the bloom or fruit cycles, they need a dry, warm spring and a long, hot summer. They are sensitive to extreme winter cold, blustery winds, and late-season frosts, and grow best in the San Joaquin Valley and Fresno, Tulare, and Kern counties.

Family Name / Origin Rosaceae / China

Mature Height × Spread 12 to 20 ft. × 10 to 15 ft.

When and How to Plant Plant in late winter from bare-root stock, or any time from 5- or 15-gallon containers. Space dwarfs or semi-dwarfs 6 to 10 ft. apart; space standard trees 8 to 20 ft. apart. Construct a watering basin 12 ft. in diameter and cover with 2 in. of organic material such as compost or humus mulch. Refer to Planting Techniques, p. 398, for additional information.

Sun and Soil Preferences They need full sun and light, loose, well-drained topsoil with heavier soil underneath, pH 5.5 to 6.5.

Moisture Requirements Soak deeply after planting. Water twice the first week; thereafter, adjust frequency and amount to climatic and growth conditions.

Fertilizing Once established, fertilize in January or February with a complete food like 16-4-8.

Pruning, Care, and Harvest For detailed Pruning information, see p. 411. Ripe fruits will give easily when you gently twist them.

Pests and Diseases Few pests and diseases pose serious problems, but consult your local agricultural expert for the best disease-resistant and weather-appropriate variety for your specific area. To control brown rot, use dormant spray only when the tree is dormant, according to the label.

Companion Plantings and Design Since they are self-fruiting, you need only one in your orchard, or use it as a patio container tree or espalier, or in a mixed border.

Climate & Culture

Preferred Zones
5–10

Sun Preference

Our Personal Favorites

NAME	SPECIAL CHARACTERISTICS
P. p. 'N. Goldmine'	Large, freestone, white-skinned fruit with a red blush / juicy, sweet, white-fleshed, excellent flavor / good for home use / ripens in early August
P. p. 'N. Panamint'	Medium-sized freestone fruit / rich, red skin / golden flesh / heavy bearer in mild-winter areas / ripens early to mid-July

Peach

Prunus persica

Few pleasures can compare with the taste of a freshly picked, perfectly ripe peach. It is impossible to pass a Peach tree without plucking the fruit, sinking your teeth into its sweet-scented meat, and slurping its sun-warmed juice before the excess trickles down your chin. Next to Apples, Peaches are the most popular fruit trees. In early spring, before their glossy lance-shaped leaves emerge, a snowy haze of rose-colored blossoms blankets their bare branches. Soon the fragrant flowers give way to velvet-covered fruits in shades of reddish-yellow, orange, or white. Their yellow or white meat surrounds furrowed flat seeds called stones, either freestone or clingstone, depending on the variety. Standard trees grow from eight to fifteen feet and dwarf varieties stand on their tip-toes at three to five feet. Whether you eat them fresh or preserve, bake, freeze, or dry them, Peaches are among the most versatile and delectable fruits. The trees normally need several hundred hours of temperatures below 45 degrees Fahrenheit for normal flower and leaf production, but fortunately there are varieties that adapt to warmer winter climates. They dislike extreme freezing conditions and their buds need protection from late-spring frosts and dry, cold prevailing winds. During periods of drought, provide moisture when the trees are in their bloom and fruit cycles.

Family Name / Origin Rosaceae / China

Mature Height × Spread 8 to 15 ft. × 10 to 12 ft.

When and How to Plant Once topsoil has settled after watering or winter rains, plant in January or February from bare-root stock, or later in the year from 5- or 15-gallon containers. Space dwarf or semi-dwarf trees 6 to 10 ft. apart, standard 12 to 20 ft. Plant at the depth the tree grew in the nursery and only deep enough to cover the roots well. Construct a 6-ft. watering basin for a dwarf or semi-dwarf, a 12-ft. basin for a standard, and cover with 2 in. of organic material. See Planting Techniques, p. 398.

Climate & Culture

Preferred Zones
5–10

Sun Preference

Sun and Soil Preferences They need full sun and light, loose topsoil with a pH of 5.5 to 6.5. Make sure you have 4 ft. or more of loam soil, as well-drained soil is essential. If you have only 12 to 18 in. of topsoil, add 6 to 12 in. from the yard by mounding or terracing before planting your tree. Do not dig deep holes in the hardpan and backfill with soil or compost—this will create a pit of soggy soil that will kill the tree.

Moisture Requirements Soak deeply after planting. Water twice the first week; thereafter, adjust frequency and amount to climatic and growth conditions.

Fertilizing Once established, fertilize in January or February with a complete food such as 16-4-8.

Pruning, Care, and Harvest Prune annually in December or January because fruit is produced on the shoots of the previous season's growth. For important Pruning and Harvesting information, see p. 412.

Pests and Diseases A number of diseases and pests attack Peaches. Consult your local farm advisor or nursery for information about the most disease-resistant and weather-appropriate varieties as well as the latest facts about annual sprays. See p. 412 for more Pest and Disease information.

Companion Plantings and Design Dwarf trees are ideal deck or patio container plants. Their branches are among the most beautiful of all flowering trees for cut arrangements.

See p. 412 for recommended varieties.

Pear

Pyrus communis

There are many different varieties of dwarf and standard Pear trees, with fruits that vary in flavor, shape, size, and texture. When I (Bruce) was a youngster growing up in Yellow Springs, Ohio, my family had a forty-foot-tall Pear in our backyard. It looked so beautiful during the bleak days of winter, when drifts of glittering snow fell on its chestnut-colored bark and glistening icicles hung from its branches. Around late March or April it would awake from its winter slumber and burst forth with umbels of alabaster flowers painted with violet-red anthers. Shiny-green, deeply-pointed, serrated leaves would begin to form a shaded canopy for emerging fruits. Bumblebees buzzed and pollinated the floral cups and by summer, dark-yellow pears with brown freckles hung in all their glory. Their white meat was buttery sweet with a touch of spiciness. My mother served them fresh, canned, dried, juiced, and preserved, but no matter how many ways we ate them and no matter how many we gave away, there would still be a large mass of fallen fruit that would squish and slide underfoot. In the fall, its leaves would turn a fire-engine red before the tree shed its autumn coat and awaited its winter slumber. My childhood Pear tree was my first lesson about the circle of life.

Family Name / Origin Rosaceae / Europe

Mature Height × Spread 20 to 30 ft. × 20 ft.

When and How to Plant Check on compatibility
before purchasing because some varieties need a
pollinizer. Plant in January from bare-root stock or in
spring or summer from 5- or 15-gallon containers.
Space dwarf varieties 6 to 8 ft., semi-dwarf 10 to
15 ft., and standard 20 ft. Construct a watering basin
4 to 6 ft. in diameter for dwarf and semi-dwarf varieties and 12 to 15 ft. for standards; cover with 2 in.
of organic material such as humus mulch or compost.
See Planting Techniques, p. 398.

**Climate &
Culture**

**Preferred
Zones**
6–9

**Sun
Preference**

Sun and Soil Preferences Plant in full sun in deep,
fertile, well-drained soil, pH 6.5 to 7.0.

Moisture Requirements Soak deeply after planting. Water twice the
first week; thereafter, adjust frequency and amount to climatic and growth
conditions.

Fertilizing Once established, fertilize with a food such as 16-4-8 in winter.

Pruning, Care, and Harvest At planting, prune to about 30 in. and cut
away any broken or injured roots. See p. 412 for important information on
Pruning and Harvesting.

Pests and Diseases With the exception of fireblight (a sudden wilting
and browning of new growth), few disease or insect problems affect Pears.
Control fireblight by pruning the diseased areas 6 in. beyond the infection—
or select one of the new varieties that are resistant to this bacterial disease.

Companion Plantings and Design Dwarf varieties make perfect espaliers
on trellises. Standards can be grouped in the middle of yards and make ideal
hedgerow plants when spaced 8 to 14 ft. apart.

Our Personal Favorite

NAME	SPECIAL CHARACTERISTICS
P. c. 'Sensation Red Bartlett'	Large, dark-red fruit with bluish over-ones / white flesh is juicy and tender / medium-sized tree / self-fruitful / requires 900 hours of winter chill / ripens in late August

See p. 413 for other excellent selections.

Persimmon

Diospyros kaki

The Persimmons that grew at our nursery were lovely fifteen- to twenty-foot-tall trees with full, spreading branches that provided perfect shade. Their large four- to six-inch glossy-green leaves turned into hues of rich gold and orange-red in fall, matching the brilliant orange fruits that hung like glowing lanterns from their gray branches. In winter they dropped their leaves and awaited the warmth of spring to blossom in the shelter of their new foliage. After their waxy, white flower petals floated away, tiny fruits emerged, eventually growing to the size of apples, ready to be harvested in early or late fall. There are two popular varieties in California. The astringent 'Hachiya' is deep orange and heart-shaped, and must be completely ripe before eating because its tannins pack more pucker-power than the most sour lemon. When the fruits are smushy soft, their flavor is like a ripe peach with a hint of clove and vanilla. The non-astringent 'Fuyu' is the same color, but flatter, more tomato-shaped, and its apple-crisp flesh can be eaten before peak ripening without suffering the dire consequences of a green 'Hachiya'. Both types adapt well to subtropical and warm, temperate regions and tolerate cold, frosty conditions during winter dormancy. For high-quality fruit, the non-astringent varieties need warmer climates than the astringent types, and both need protection from drought and cold, strong winds.

Family Name / Origin Ebenaceae / Japan

Mature Height × Spread 15 to 20 ft. × 15 to 20 ft.

When and How to Plant Plant in January from bare-root stock, or in spring or summer from 5- or 15-gallon containers. Space 6 to 10 ft. apart if dwarf or semi-dwarf, 15 to 20 ft. if standard. Build a watering basin 4 to 8 ft. in diameter for dwarf and semi-dwarf varieties, 10 to 15 ft. for standards; cover with 2 in. of organic material. See Planting Techniques, p. 398.

Sun and Soil Preferences Persimmons need full sun and soil with a pH of 6.5 to 7.0. The soil should be well drained and sandy so that water percolates down and through the root zones. If the soil is heavy and clayey, amend with organic matter and gypsum.

Moisture Requirements Soak deeply after planting. Water twice the first week; thereafter, adjust frequency and amount to climatic and growth conditions. As a general rule, water regularly from fruit set to harvest, making sure root systems do not dry out.

Fertilizing Fertilize in late winter with a complete food such as 16-4-8.

Pruning, Care, and Harvest At planting, prune sparingly and cut away any broken or injured roots. See p. 413 for detailed Pruning and Harvesting information.

Pests and Diseases If damage from the usual warm-weather pests such as mealybugs is extensive, insecticidal soap is an appropriate remedy.

Companion Plantings and Design Use the trees as attractive background plants or in front of evergreens. Train them as shade umbrellas above lawns or as espaliers in patio containers, or plant a row along a fence for a visual screen.

Climate & Culture

Preferred Zones
8–10

Sun Preference

Our Personal Favorite

NAME	SPECIAL CHARACTERISTICS
D. k. 'Fuyu'	Large, round, flattened fruit with reddish-orange skin / non-astringent / excellent, apple-like flavor / heavy producer / ripens in November / bears as a young tree

Pomegranate

Punica granatum

Two Pomegranate trees grow at the ends of our road, as if to punctuate its ingress and egress, and we always notice their seasonal presence as we pass by. In early spring, small clusters of glossy green foliage bush out the shrublike trees; in spring and summer, bell-shaped red-orange flowers wave greetings in the gentle breezes. By autumn the leaves take on a reddish or bright-yellow tint, and soon decorative balls of crimson fruit appear. As the fruits grow heavy, the slender new branches are pulled down, creating a weeping effect. These red ornaments can provide a festive holiday touch to the bare limbs from late fall through winter. We live in an area with a year-round mild climate, but the Pomegranates remind us that seasonal changes occur even without sharp fluctuations in weather. An ancient symbol of prosperity and fertility, Pomegranates were grown in the Hanging Gardens of Babylon, depicted in Egyptian hieroglyphics, and mentioned throughout the Bible. Thick leathery rinds with membranous compartments of pink, white, or scarlet seeds have a tart-sweet, nutty flavor. They thrive in areas where summers are hot and dry and tolerate freezing temperatures when dormant. If in a growth, bloom, or fruiting cycle, they are sensitive to frost, but once established, they withstand periods of drought and dry winds.

Family Name / Origin Punicaceae / Mediterranean, Asia

Mature Height × Spread 10 to 20 ft. × 8 to 15 ft.

When and How to Plant Plant in December or January from bare-root stock or in spring or summer from 5- or 15-gallon containers. Space dwarf varieties 4 to 6 ft. apart, standards 20 ft. apart. Build a watering basin 4 ft. in diameter for dwarf varieties, 10 ft. for standards, and cover with 2 in. of organic material. See Planting Techniques, p. 398.

Sun and Soil Preferences Pomegranates need full sun. They do best in deep loam, well-drained soil, pH 6.5 to 7.0, but also grow in sandy or adobe-clay soils.

Climate & Culture

Preferred Zones
9–11

Sun Preference

Moisture Requirements Soak deeply after planting. Water twice the first week; thereafter, adjust frequency and amount to climatic and growth conditions. Although they withstand extended periods of drought, they will grow vigorously and produce more abundant crops if watered regularly, particularly throughout the growing season until autumn.

Fertilizing Once established, fertilize with a complete food such as 16-4-8 in late winter or early spring.

Pruning, Care, and Harvest See p. 413 for detailed Pruning information. Pick Pomegranates when they are plump and heavy for their size. Their crowns should give when pressed slightly and their rind should be shiny rather than dull.

Pests and Diseases Few diseases or insects seriously affect Pomegranates, but as a preventative, remove old fruit from the trees during pruning, and keep a watchful eye out for mites and leafrollers. If damage is extensive, pick off the damaged foliage and fruit or apply a Neem oil.

Companion Plantings and Design These trees are beautiful ornamentals for backyard gardens and canyon lots, and make decorative accents in arrangements.

Our Personal Favorite

NAME	SPECIAL CHARACTERISTICS
P. g. 'Wonderful'	Extra-large fruit with blush-red skin and crimson seeds / juicy and sharp in flavor / most commonly grown of all the Pomegranates / ripens in September

Sweet Cherry
Prunus avium

Sweet Cherry trees are the largest of fruit trees and are just as lovely as their cousins, the Flowering Cherries. In Europe, some grow as tall as a hundred feet, but whatever their size, they are a wondrous sight to behold in spring. With reddish-brown bark, their stout, rising branches form graceful pyramidal crowns and are draped each April in fragrant white blossoms and lance-shaped, rough-textured leaves. When the blossoms flutter to the ground, plump heart-shaped cherries festoon the trees. Their sweet flesh ranges in color from purple-black, cerise, and yellow to white, and some taste as powerful as a superb red wine without the fermentation. From November to February, most Sweet Cherry trees require 900 hours of winter chill. When the bloom cycle begins, they do not tolerate frost or frigid winds. High temperatures may result in double or spur fruits, but this is merely a cosmetic situation. If there are prolonged periods of high heat, the trees stress and their limbs suffer sunburn damage. Early-summer rainfall during harvest time is harmful because their fruit skins absorb the moisture, swell, and crack. They do well in the northern and central coastal regions, Sacramento–San Joaquin Valley areas, and the foothills of the Sierra Nevada Mountains. In Southern California, unless the trees are grown above 2000-foot elevation, fruit production is minimal.

Family Name / Origin Rosaceae / Europe, W Asia

Mature Height × Spread Maintain at 15 to 20 ft. × 12 to 15 ft.

When and How to Plant Plant while still dormant, from January to March, from bare-root stock or 5- to 15-gallon containers, spacing 25 to 30 ft. apart. To avoid crown root rot and fungal disease, plant no deeper and preferably 1 to 2 in. higher than they were in the nursery. Construct a watering basin 12 ft. in diameter and cover with 2 in. of organic material such as compost or humus mulch. See Planting Techniques, p. 398.

Sun and Soil Preferences Sweet Cherries need full sun and well-drained loam soil with a pH of 5.5 to 6.5.

Moisture Requirements Soak deeply after planting. Water three times the first week; thereafter, adjust frequency and amount to climatic and growth conditions. During the growth and bloom cycles, water more often. Supplement during the winter and spring months if rainfall is insufficient.

Fertilizing Once established, fertilize in late winter or early spring with a complete food such as 16-4-8 .

Pruning, Care, and Harvest At planting, prune to about 24 to 30 in., cut away any broken or injured roots, and protect the trunk with a commercial tree wrap down to the soil surface to prevent sunburn. See p. 414 for detailed Pruning and Harvesting information.

Pests and Diseases The trees are relatively free from disease and insects, but net them before harvesting if they need protection from birds. Set traps if you notice gophers.

Climate & Culture

Preferred Zones
4–9

Sun Preference
☼

Our Personal Favorite

NAME	SPECIAL CHARACTERISTICS
'Black Tartarian'	Medium, round fruit / purplish-black skin / dark-red flesh / semisweet, juicy, delicious flavor / tree is vigorous and erect / needs 900 hours of winter chill / ripens in early June / pollinizers are 'Bing', 'Royal Ann', 'Stella'

Ground Covers *for California*

Ground cover is a carpet for the earth beneath your feet. A less poetic definition of ground cover is this: any dense, low-growing plant that covers an area when planted *en masse*. To be worthy of the name it must grow quickly, and it is often fiercely aggressive by nature.

A Living Mulch

Ground covers play both practical and aesthetic roles in the garden. Often referred to as "living mulch," once they are established their dense growth chokes out unwanted weeds, retains moisture, prevents erosion, and serves as a fire retardant. They require less maintenance and expense than lawns. They decorate a garden by creating a carpet of foliage and flowers, adding an important landscape dimension by drawing the eye down to themselves and other low-lying neighbors. Without them, landscape grounds can be forlornly barren.

How to Grow

For successful cultivation, prepare the planting area by turning over the soil, raking it free of weeds, and adding organic amendments. Whether bare-root, in pint-, quart-, or gallon-size containers, or in flats, the spacing of the plants is determined by variety and mature size. A ground cover normally requires one to two years to cover an area,

unless the plants are spaced farther apart than recommended—then an additional twelve to twenty-four months may be needed. Cuttings are usually spaced eight to ten inches apart on center (measuring from the center of one plant to the center of the next).

After planting, water well, and add two inches of organic mulch. Pull out any weeds or use a pre-emergent product until the ground cover has filled in sufficiently.

Maintaining a Ground Cover

Maintenance of an established ground cover is much less demanding than that of a lawn. Some ground covers—like Minor Periwinkle and Algerian Ivy—actually tolerate partial shade, and most others consume less water, fertilizer, and pesticides than do

lawns to keep them looking their best. Fertilize once a year during the growth cycle, water during extended periods of drought or high heat, and rake off leaves and debris from the top of a planting.

Woody plants such as Dwarf Coyote Bush, Kinnikinnick, and Shore Junipers need only selective pruning to remove dead wood or to reduce their size if they are beginning to cover a walkway. For vining or trailing ground covers, carefully use an edger in areas around the base of a tree—the smallest nick can open up a tree to fungal and insect infestations. Set the lawn mower six inches high and mow Dwarf Coyote Bush once a year to improve its appearance and keep it low. Any ground cover that has been scorched brown from a combination of full sun and severely cold winter will also be rejuvenated by a lawn-mower trim, which stimulates fresh growth and removes damaged foliage.

Keeping a Ground Cover Under Control

The yin and the yang of ground cover is that many of them can cover a large area so quickly and thickly that they become pests, invaders of garden areas where they are not welcome. To effectively tame their wild nature, first observe how they grow. Plants like Algerian Ivy that have holdfasts or suckers have a reputation for swallowing anything immobile, including entire buildings, but they can be controlled if their new growth is cut back several times a year. Ground covers that spread by rhizomes can be stopped with metal or vinyl edging or other physical barriers placed directly in the ground. Others that spread by runners or stolons, like Red Apple, Beach Strawberry, Rosea Iceplant, Trailing African Daisy, and Minor Periwinkle, can run over edging and settle on the other side—they can be curtailed by trimming their young runners several times a year.

Ground-Level Dimensions

Whether in a sunny spotlight or shadowy shelter, ground covers soften a landscape, hide bare soil in all seasons, stabilize soil, and provide fire-retardant buffers. Red Apple, Beach Strawberry, Rosea Ice Plant, Trailing African Daisy, and Minor Periwinkle provide a broad expanse of vibrant color. The berries produced by Dwarf Coyote Bush, Kinnikinnick, Red Apple, and Shore Juniper are not only attractive but are also food sources for wildlife. Kinnikinnick, Dwarf Coyote Bush, Rosea Ice Plant, and Shore Juniper are handsome ground covers suitable for many different garden designs, including xeriphytic, Mediterranean, and woodland. Beach Strawberry and Shore Juniper are excellent choices for seashore plantings or rock gardens. While trees allow us to touch the sky and shrubs capture the "middle" world, floral and foliar carpets encourage us to enjoy the ground-level dimensions of our gardens.

Algerian Ivy

Hedera canariensis

Pepper trees, Peach trees, and Victorian Box shade a long slope that parallels a meandering brick path in our backyard. The trees provide a perfect shelter for migrating birds, but covering such a long expanse of slope is a challenge. We finally decided to plant a ground cover commonly used in California because of its ability to carpet an area quickly and its tolerance for shade: the Algerian Ivy. Despite its reputation for swallowing anything motionless, when properly tended it is a beautiful ground cover for shady slopes, underneath trees, and around bushes, as well as an effective climber for silhouetting pillars and walls. Whether stabilizing steep banks, tumbling over ledges, hiding unsightly foundations, or providing a fresh green scent after a spring rain, Algerian Ivy is an excellent choice, particularly in frost-free regions. It is dimorphic, which means it has two forms. The smaller, more vinelike, non-flowering form with light-green three- or five-lobed leaves is the two- to six-inch-tall juvenile form, while the unlobed, darker green adult form produces flowers and fruits and grows twelve to fifteen inches high. Algerian Ivy does not tolerate extended periods of frost or drought, but it can withstand high temperatures and dry winds if there is sufficient moisture. **Note:** If you don't find Algerian Ivy by the botanical name Hedera canariensis, *look for* Hedera algeriensis.

Family Name / Origin Araliaceae / North Africa, Algeria, Tunisia

Bloom Period and Color White blossoms appear in late spring or early summer, on adult growth only.

Mature Height × Width 8 to 12 in. (spreading)

When and How to Plant Plant any time from flats, spacing 10 to 14 in. See Planting Techniques, p. 398.

Sun and Soil Preferences These plants prefer semi-shade or shade, but will tolerate full sun in well-drained soil with a pH of 6.5 to 7.2.

Moisture Requirements Soak deeply after planting. During the first week, water daily; thereafter, adjust frequency and amount according to weather and growth conditions.

Climate & Culture

Preferred Zones 10–11

Sun Preferences

Fertilizing Fertilize in fall and early spring with a complete granular food such as 16-4-8.

Pruning and Care Prune after the bloom cycle but just before the fruits ripen in December. Control growth by regularly cutting away from walls, trees, or other climbing surfaces, and edging the ivy's borders. Since its leaves are toxic and its sap can irritate skin, wear gloves and be careful when handling Algerian Ivy. The best way to remove ivy from its tight grip of "holdfasts" on trees, houses, and walls is to snip it off at the base, wait a few weeks for remaining material to die, then remove it.

Pests and Diseases Algerian Ivy's white blossoms attract bees, and birds can build nests in the protected safety of its espaliered dense branches, but it is also a haven for slugs and snails. Control the slimy marauders with a molluscicide or by handpicking and squishing. If you live in a county that allows Decollate snails, colonize these beneficials in your ground cover— they will prey on small and medium-sized brown garden snails without harming your mature plants.

Companion Plantings and Design Camellias, Clivias, Lilies of the Nile, and Golden Mirror Plants are ideal companions.

Our Personal Favorite

NAME	SPECIAL CHARACTERISTICS
Hedera helix	Commonly known as English Ivy / has smaller leaves and is less aggressive than Algerian Ivy

Beach Strawberry
Fragaria chiloensis

"*Tucked away in a mental time capsule are many fond memories of camping trips we took with our daughter and son when they were youngsters. They liked to splash in the waves, build fanciful castles, hunt for sand crabs, and collect seashells. Those trips were great opportunities to spend time with the family, to get away from the cares of work, and to enjoy all that nature had to offer along the seashore. Our introduction to the Beach Strawberry was on one of these summer sojourns, just beyond Santa Barbara. While walking towards the beach, we noticed a ground cover that seemed to be flourishing between some otherwise desolate sand dunes. It was a low-growing, evergreen mat of glossy-green strawberry leaves that supported a white frosting of blossoms. We discovered that once the flowers fell to the ground, deep-red fruits resembling elfin strawberries took their place. Although not as sugary as hybrid strawberries, these fruits smell just as sweet, and deserve their Latin name* fraga, *which means "sweet-smelling." The name* chiloensis *refers to Chile, one of this plant's native habitats (California is another). Whenever we include Beach Strawberry in one of our landscape designs, it conjures up the sights and smells of that family seashore vacation as if it were yesterday.*"

Family Name / Origin Rosaceae / Chile, California

Bloom Period and Color White flowers appear in spring.

Mature Height × Width 4 to 6 in. (spreading)

When and How to Plant Plant in fall or spring from flats, spacing 8 to 14 in. apart. It does best in cool, temperate areas. It tolerates some foot traffic, but try to plant it where there are no regular pathways. See Planting Techniques, p. 398, for more information.

Sun and Soil Preferences The plants require full sun in coastal regions, partial shade in inland areas. Plant in well-drained, porous soil, pH 6.7 to 7.2.

Climate & Culture

Preferred Zones
10–11

Sun Preferences

Moisture Requirements Soak deeply after planting. Water daily during the first week; thereafter, adjust frequency and amount according to weather and growth conditions. This 4- to 6-in.-tall, silky-leafed ground cover needs regular watering. It tolerates some heat and dry wind if there is adequate moisture but cannot withstand extremely high temperatures or extended periods of drought.

Fertilizing Fertilize in early spring and early summer with a complete granular food such as 6-10-4. To treat yellow leaves, use chelated iron.

Pruning and Care If mowed in early spring, this rapidly spreading plant forms a more compact and dense mat.

Pests and Diseases Few serious disease or insect problems affect Beach Strawberry, with the exception of rust and other fungal infestations. Consult your local garden center or county agricultural department for correct identification and appropriate remedies. If planted in your landscape in dappled shade, slugs and snails may also cause problems. Control the slimy marauders with a molluscicide or by handpicking and squishing. If you live in a county that allows Decollate snails, colonize these beneficials in your ground cover—they will prey on small and medium-sized brown garden snails without harming your mature plants.

Companion Plantings and Design Because Beach Strawberry spreads by means of offsets, it is excellent for rock gardens, as a substitute for lawns, as attractive ground covers in woodsy or beachfront areas, and in front of shrubs and around trees. California Lilac, Japanese Mock Orange, and New Zealand Christmas Tree make ideal companion plants.

Dwarf Coyote Bush

Baccharis pilularis 'Twin Peaks'

One of our friends lives on a hillside that offers privacy and a spectacular view. The good news and the bad news is that her priceless view and solitude come with a cost of steep terrain and tinder-dry brush. To make matters worse, whatever ground cover she planted as erosion controls and fire-retardant measures was quickly devoured by salad-aficionado rabbits, rodents, and other wildlife. We suggested she try the Dwarf Coyote Bush. It is a low, prostrate, and woody shrub that grows one to two feet tall and quickly spreads to ten feet wide. If they are planted too close to each other, they grow into each other as they compete for light. If this happens, they will become woody underneath. So plant them farther apart for denser foliage. Because its evergreen leaves have sharp, serrated edges and a sticky surface, it is not a very palatable entree for most herbivores, but it is one of the best plants to retard fires and to stabilize banks with its deep roots that go down four to six feet. Adaptive to a variety of conditions, Dwarf Coyote Bush is found from high deserts to coastal areas. It tolerates heat, drought, dry winds, and salt spray but does not withstand foot traffic.

Family Name / Origin Compositae / California, Oregon

Bloom Period and Color In summer, the pale creamy-yellow flowers that bloom and the nutlike fruits that follow are of little ornamental value.

Mature Height × **Width** 12 to 24 in. × 6 to 10 ft.

When and How to Plant Plant in early fall or winter where climates are mild, or in spring after the last frost, from flats or 1-gallon containers, individually spacing them 3 to 6 ft. apart. See Planting Techniques, p. 398, for additional information.

Sun and Soil Preferences Plant in full sun in sandy, well-drained soil with a pH of 6.0 to 7.0.

Climate & Culture

Preferred Zones
8–11

Sun Preference

Moisture Requirements Soak deeply after planting. Water twice during the first week; thereafter, adjust frequency and amount according to weather and growth conditions. After the first year, Dwarf Coyote Bush should be established enough that it can survive on moisture from average rainfall, with occasional supplemental watering during summer. It will appreciate an occasional misting to clean its foliage.

Fertilizing Fertilize in fall and early spring with a complete granular food such as 16-4-8.

Pruning and Care As it matures, the Dwarf Coyote Bush tends to get woody and lumpy; prune for shape and appearance before new growth emerges, in late winter or early spring. If it is clipped back once a year, light and air can reach the lower leaves, encouraging lush growth. Regular pruning prevents any buildup of dead or damaged wood. When pruning, look toward the base of the stems and leave in a few buds that are beginning to green. Propagate from male cuttings because female plants produce a messy, cottony substance.

Pests and Diseases Few disease or insect problems affect Dwarf Coyote Bush except for black sooty mold and aphids. Promote good air circulation by thinning out the plant's woody canopy. If the conditions persist, apply Neem oil or consult your local nursery for another appropriate fungicide.

Companion Plantings and Design Ideal companion plants are Butterfly Bush, California Sycamore, White Birch, and Crimson Bottlebrush. Plant Dwarf Coyote Bush around entryways, as borders, and along sidewalks.

Kinnikinnick

Arctostaphylos uva-ursi 'Point Reyes'

Native Americans call it Kinnikinnick, but its botanical name is of Greek derivation, from arctos, meaning "bear," and staphyle, meaning "a cluster of grapes." Uva-ursi translates as "the bear's grapes." This cumbersome and almost unpronounceable name simply means that bears enjoy noshing on this species' berries and that the berries resemble grapelike clusters. Also known as Barberry or Manzanita, it is native to the coastal regions of California. It's a prostrate, low-growing plant with wide-spreading, woody branches covered with inch-long, leather-textured, deep-green, teardrop-shaped leaves. In the fall and winter months, its leaves turn a brilliant red-dish-bronze color, coordinating perfectly with its red berries. By spring, its leaves regain their green luster and provide a lush background for minuscule, urn-shaped white flowers tinged with a blush of pink. After the flowers are spent, grapelike clusters of glossy-green berries emerge. The Kinnikinnick leaves were used by Native Americans to brew a tea for kidney disorders, while others used them to stop bleeding or to facilitate birth contractions. In Russia and Scandinavia, they took advantage of its high tannin content to tan hides. Today, this ground cover is appreciated for its drought-tolerant, erosion-resistant, and ornamental qualities when planted on steep slopes, in rock gardens, along seashores, and in natural or informal landscapes.

Family Name / Origin Ericaceae / California

Bloom Period and Color Small white flowers appear in spring.

Mature Height × Width 1 ft. × 3 to 6 ft.

When and How to Plant Plant in fall from 4-in. pots to 1-gallon containers, spacing 36 in. to 48 in. apart. It not only withstands some foot traffic, but tolerates prevailing winds, salt spray, high temperatures, drought, and below-freezing temperatures. For more information, consult Planting Techniques, p. 398.

Sun and Soil Preferences Plant in full sun in well-drained soil with a pH of 7.0. Sandy loam soil is a suitable medium for this amazingly adaptive ground cover.

Climate & Culture

Preferred Zones 8–11

Sun Preference

Moisture Requirements Soak deeply after planting. Water three times during the first week; thereafter, adjust frequency and amount according to weather and growth conditions.

Fertilizing Fertilize in fall and early spring with a complete granular food such as 6-10-4.

Pruning and Care Prune for errant growth and dead wood.

Pests and Diseases Few serious disease or insect problems affect Kinnikinnick if it is planted in full sun. Even the ubiquitous slug and snail dislike its woody habitat. The woody growth and low-creeping habit can be a shelter of choice for rats; if they become a serious problem, a good hunting cat is an excellent solution. If there are no accommodating felines in the neighborhood, a trap or bait is the next-best remedy.

Companion Plantings and Design When we are asked to design a native or xeriphytic garden, *A. uva-ursi* is our ground cover of choice. Trees such as Magnolias, Bronze Loquats, and European Olives are ideal companions.

Our Personal Favorite

NAME	SPECIAL CHARACTERISTICS
A. *u-u.* 'Vulcan's Peak'	Same growing characteristics as those of 'Point Reyes', but pink flowers

Minor Periwinkle
Vinca minor

“ *On our long strolls through the neighborhood we pass many gentle slopes that are blanketed with the vinelike ground cover* Vinca minor, *commonly known as Minor Periwinkle. Its trailing tendrils are covered with small, dark-green, oval-shaped leaves that glisten in the sun. In the spring, miniature five-petaled flowers in shades of lilac-blue, blue, or white stretch their faces out of the low, green undergrowth; they put on a less profuse show in the fall. As its botanical name indicates, the plant's size and leaves are smaller than those of V. major, growing to about four to six inches high with long, slender foliar fingers that spread and root at every knuckled node. It is a plant rich in history. In Medieval times, the heads of convicted criminals were adorned with stems of Minor Periwinkle just before their execution—perhaps this is why the Italians called it Fiore di Morte, "flower of death." The Celts believed witches used it during their sabbaths. Our current uses are less sanguine, but equally magical. These flowers make such a lovely display that they are easily forgiven for their lack of fragrance. Because their tough runners bind the soil, they also prevent soil erosion. Surprisingly, the plants survive cold temperatures as low as -10 degrees Fahrenheit. They prefer little or no foot traffic.* ”

Family Name / Origin Apocynaceae / Europe

Bloom Period and Color Lilac, blue, or white flowers bloom in spring and summer.

Mature Height × Width 6 in. (spreading)

When and How to Plant Plant from flats in spring after the last frost, spacing 10 to 15 in. apart. See Planting Techniques, p. 398.

Sun and Soil Preferences Plant in partial sun in rich, well-drained soil, pH 6.5 to 7.0.

Moisture Requirements Soak deeply after planting. Water daily during the first week; thereafter, adjust frequency and amount according to weather and growth conditions. The plants tolerate short periods of drought, high temperatures, and dry winds, but produce more flowers and develop more vigorously if adequate moisture is provided.

Fertilizing Fertilize in late winter or early spring with a complete granular food such as 16-4-8.

Pruning and Care To revitalize and thicken Minor Periwinkle, cut with a rotary mower in the fall. This encourages dense growth and discourages the development of weeds.

Pests and Diseases Except for aphids, slugs, and snails, few serious disease or insect problems affect this dense ground cover if it is planted in dappled shade. Aphids and other sucking insects are easily controlled by washing them off the foliage with a strong stream of water or applying Neem oil. Control slugs and snails by handpicking and squishing, or by applying a molluscicide. If you live in a county that allows Decollate snails, colonize these beneficials in your ground cover.

Companion Plantings and Design Minor Periwinkle makes lovely green carpets sprinkled with splashes of lilac, blue, or white winking flowers alongside meandering paths, in woodlands, underneath the shade of trees, cascading over rocks, at the base of hedges, or around shrubs.

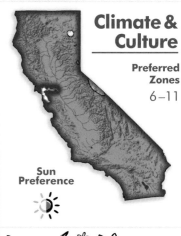

Climate & Culture

Preferred Zones
6–11

Sun Preference

Our Personal Favorite

NAME	SPECIAL CHARACTERISTICS
V. m. 'Alba'	Growth habit similar to that of the species / white blossoms

Red Apple

Aptenia cordifolia

The name A. cordifolia is of Greek derivation, from apten, *meaning "wingless," referring to its wing-deprived seed capsules, and* cordifolia, *meaning the foliage is heart-shaped. A blanket of Red Apple covers our north slope next to a grizzled, weeping California Pepper Tree. Only a few inches tall, but spreading to four feet, this green-lacquered ground cover bears a profusion of reddish-pink flowers. At the bidding of their queen, regiments of industrious bees teem over all the blossoms, intent on harvesting every last drop of precious nectar. Our Apricot, Carambola, Pomegranate, Orange, Lime, Tangerine, and Grapefruit trees are nearby, and they benefit from these buzzing pollinators. Whenever we cut back the succulent creeping stems of glossy leaves, we share our cuttings with friends and neighbors—because Red Apple grows so easily, our original patch has spread throughout the neighborhood. Instead of Johnny Appleseed, perhaps Bruce will become known as the Red Apple man. In addition to covering small to medium areas, Red Apple looks wonderful cascading over planters or nestling in rock gardens. Once established, Red Apple requires little maintenance. It tolerates dry winds and heat if there is adequate moisture, as well as short periods of drought, but it does not hold up well in temperatures below 40 degrees Fahrenheit.*

Family Name / Origin Aizoaceae / South Africa

Bloom Period and Color Pink flowers bloom in spring, summer, and fall.

Mature Height × **Width** 8 in. (spreading)

When and How to Plant Plant any time of the year from cuttings or flats and space them 10 in. to 12 in. on center. For additional information, refer to Planting Techniques, p. 398.

Sun and Soil Preferences Plant in full or partial sun in well-drained soil with a pH of 6.0-7.0.

Moisture Requirements Soak deeply after planting. Water daily during the first week; thereafter, adjust frequency and amount according to weather and growth conditions. During extended periods of drought or high temperatures, water more frequently.

Fertilizing Fertilize twice, in late winter or early spring and fall, with a complete granular food such as 15-15-15.

Pruning and Care Since Red Apple spreads via creeping stems, give them plenty of room to run, or thin them out once every two or three years. Propagate by stem cuttings any time of the year.

Pests and Diseases Except for slugs and snails, few serious disease or insect problems affect Red Apple if it is planted in full sun or dappled shade. Control the slimy marauders by handpicking and squishing them, or by applying a molluscicide. If you live in a county that allows Decollate snails, colonize these beneficials in your ground cover—they will prey on small and medium-sized brown garden snails without harming your mature plants.

Companion Plantings and Design Because Red Apple is such a bee-magnet, plant it with fruit trees like Peaches, Plums, Nectarines, and Apricots that benefit from pollination.

Climate & Culture

Preferred Zone

11

Sun Preferences

Our Personal Favorite

NAME	SPECIAL CHARACTERISTICS
A. c. 'Variegata'	Smaller, variegated leaves edged in creamy white

Rosea Ice Plant

Mesembryanthemum roseum

Traveling along the famed Garden Route from Port Elizabeth to Cape Town, South Africa, we saw the native Rosea Ice Plant spilling over sheer cliffs overlooking the Indian Ocean. From April to June, hot-pink daisylike flowers with sun-yellow faces emerge from fleshy needlelike leaves. These long-blooming evergreen plants reach six to twelve inches high, with one-and-one-half-inch blossoms resting on semi-succulent foliar pillows. They are a popular ground cover for the steep slopes along the French Riviera. Wherever the climate is sunny, hot, and dry, the Rosea Ice Plant will show off its dense mat of gray-green leaves and glistening blossoms. As California's most spectacular carpet-maker, it thrives with a minimum of water and very little attention. We planted Rosea Ice Plant along our barren southern-exposure slope and within a year, not only did it cover the bank, it also provided a vista of intense pink outside our dining-room window. It blankets an unsightly slope, improves our spring-season view, and serves as an erosion control and fire retardant. It is one of the most beautiful ground covers when in bloom, and it tolerates short periods of frost, drought, prevailing winds, and high temperatures. **Note:** *If you cannot find* Mesembryanthemum roseum, *look for* Drosanthemum floribundum, *another botanical name sometimes used for the same plant.*

Family Name / Origin Aizoaceae / South Africa, Namibia

Bloom Period and Color Pink flowers bloom in summer.

Mature Height × Width 6 to 10 in. (spreading)

When and How to Plant Plant in spring or fall from flats, spacing 12 to 18 in. apart. Refer to Planting Techniques, p. 398, for additional information.

Sun and Soil Preferences Plant in full sun in a sandy, well-drained soil with a pH of 6.5 to 7.0. Try cultivating Rosea Ice Plant if you have sandy soil and difficulty establishing a ground cover. It will grow where few other plants survive.

Moisture Requirements Soak deeply after planting. Water daily during the first week; thereafter, adjust frequency and amount according to weather and growth conditions

Fertilizing Fertilize in early spring and fall with a complete granular food such as 16-4-8.

Pruning and Care After Rosea Ice Plant matures, thin out its woody undergrowth. Propagate by cuttings any time of the year, except winter, and keep fairly dry until roots develop.

Pests and Diseases Except for slugs and snails, few serious disease or insect problems affect Rosea Ice Plant if it is planted in full sun. Control the slimy marauders by handpicking and squishing them, or by applying a molluscicide. If you live in a county that allows Decollate snails, colonize these beneficials in your ground cover—they will prey on small and medium-sized brown garden snails without harming your mature plants.

Companion Plantings and Design Because Rosea Ice Plant attracts bees, plant it near fruit trees that benefit from pollination, like Sweet Oranges, Mandarins, and Avocados. Other suitable companion plants are California Lilac, Dwarf Coyote Bush, and Silverberry.

Climate & Culture

Preferred Zones
10–11

Sun Preference

Our Personal Favorite

NAME	SPECIAL CHARACTERISTICS
M. barklyi	Grows to 18 in. high / white flowers

Shore Juniper

Juniperus conferta

Overlooking Monterey Bay where otters frolic, seals sunbathe, pelicans dive-bomb, and seagulls soar is one of the most graceful and low-upkeep ground covers in California: the Shore Juniper. Its botanical name, J. conferta, is of Latin origin and means "crowded juniper," which adequately refers to its thick leaf structure but does not do justice to its stunning architectural form. It is a dense horizontal plant that stands about six to twelve inches tall and spreads six feet wide. Its needlelike leaves are green and prickly to the touch; when wet, they release a pleasing resinous scent. Native to the misty coastal areas of Japan, it has adapted very well to the diverse temperature zones of California. Hardy to -10 degrees Fahrenheit, it is drought- and wind-resistant, and survives high temperatures if there is adequate moisture. Few plants can challenge its ability to survive in the face of adversity, even growing near seaside bluffs, exposed to the ocean wind, misty mornings, and an occasional sea gull roosting on its branches. Shore Juniper is a perfect choice for sunny slopes because it is strong-rooted and thrives on dry conditions caused by water runoff. The plant's only significant weaknesses are that it cannot tolerate foot traffic and it is slow growing.

Family Name / Origin Cupressaceae / Japan

Bloom Period and Color Shore Junipers are confiers that produce cones that provide a summer and fall buffet for birds, squirrels, rabbits, deer, and other wildlife.

Mature Height × Width 6 to 12 in. × 3 to 6 ft.

When and How to Plant Plant in spring or fall from 1- or 5-gallon containers, spacing 3 to 4 ft. apart. For more planting information, see Planting Techniques, p. 398.

Sun and Soil Preferences Shore Juniper prefers full sun but tolerates partial shade. Plant in well-drained soil that has a pH of 6.5 to 7.0.

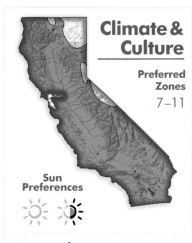

Climate & Culture

Preferred Zones
7–11

Sun Preferences

Moisture Requirements Soak deeply after planting. Water twice during the first week; thereafter, adjust watering frequency and amount according to weather and growth conditions.

Fertilizing Fertilize in spring and fall with a complete granular food such as 16-4-8.

Pruning and Care Because it is a slow-growing ground cover, prune selectively for shape or to remove dead or damaged wood.

Pests and Diseases Except for slugs and snails, few serious disease or insect problems affect this hardy ground cover when it is planted in full sun or dappled shade. Control the slimy marauders by handpicking and squishing, or by applying a molluscicide. If you live in a county that allows Decollate snails, colonize these beneficials—they will prey on small and medium-sized brown garden snails without harming your mature plants. Shore Juniper is subject to occasional attacks from juniper tip moths and twig girdlers, but they are easily controlled with a systemic insecticide.

Companion Plantings and Design Ideal companion plants are Hollywood Twisted Juniper, Rock Rose, and Dwarf Jade Plant. We recommend the Shore Juniper as a substitute for lawns, as an erosion control on moderately steep slopes, as plantings in front of trees and shrubs, and in rock and seashore gardens. It is a popular choice for bonsai.

Trailing African Daisy

Osteospermum fruticosum

Osteospermum fruticosum *is a Greek tongue-twister from the words* osteon, *meaning "bone";* sperma, *"seed"; and* fruticosum, *"shrubby"—meaning the seeds are hard and the growth is shrubby. This is another plant species from South Africa that has adapted easily to diverse regions throughout the world. It was introduced to California by the Los Angeles State and County Arboretum, and we now see the plants spreading their oval-shaped light-green leaves all along freeway embankments from coastal to inland areas, and along northern to southern byways. Although they are sometimes taken for granted as "those freeway daisies," we use them as soil stabilizers for steep slopes, as ground covers for difficult-to-reach berms and terraces, as salt-tolerant seashore plantings, and as a low-maintenance alternative to a flower garden. From early spring to fall they show off a glistening blanket of white or lilac daisylike flowers that poke through a twelve-inch-thick evergreen mattress. They are somewhat fire retardant and can withstand short periods of cold as low as 30 to 40 degrees Fahrenheit, but they cannot withstand foot traffic.*

Family Name / Origin Compositae / Southern South Africa

Bloom Period and Color White or lilac flowers bloom in winter and spring.

Mature Height × Width 1 ft. (spreading)

When and How to Plant Plant in spring or fall from flats, spacing 12 to 20 in. apart. See Planting Techniques, p. 398.

Sun and Soil Preferences Trailing African Daisies prefer full sun in moderately rich loam soil, but they tolerate other soils as long as they are well drained, with a pH of 6.5 to 7.0.

Climate & Culture

Preferred Zones
10–11

Sun Preference

Moisture Requirements Once established, Trailing African Daisy is drought-, wind-, and heat-tolerant, but supplemental watering in the summer months is best for optimum growth and appearance. Soak deeply after planting. Water daily the first week; thereafter, adjust frequency and amount according to weather and growth conditions.

Fertilizing Fertilize in fall and late winter or early spring with a complete granular food, 6-10-4.

Pruning and Care Prune back trailing stems as they overgrow their borders. If you thin old growth, light penetration and air circulation will be increased, initiating new growth and improving the plant's appearance. Propagate by cuttings in spring, fall, or winter.

Pests and Diseases Except for fungal diseases such as damping-off, and slugs and snails, few serious disease or insect problems affect Trailing African Daisy planted in full sun or afternoon shade. Fungal diseases result from too much moisture and poor soil drainage; do not overwater. Control slugs and snails with a molluscicide or by handpicking and squishing. If you live in a county that allows Decollate snails, colonize these beneficials—they will prey on small and medium-sized brown garden snails.

Companion Plantings and Design Canna Lilies, Angel's Trumpet, and Pride of Madeira are ideal companions.

Our Personal Favorite

NAME	SPECIAL CHARACTERISTICS
O. f. 'African Queen'	Deeper-green foliage / rich, purple flowers

Houseplants *for California*

Houseplants are gifts of Mother Nature brought indoors. They decorate our homes, produce oxygen, cleanse the air, and serve as effective dustmops. Corn Plants and Umbrella Trees soften vaulted rooms and bring an architectural flair to sterile spaces. Chinese Evergreen, Cast-Iron Plants, and Peace Lilies provide touches of fresh greenery in low-light corners, and the Butterfly Orchids, African Violets, and Zebra Plants paint the indoors with splashes of purples, lavenders, pinks, reds, and yellows. Houseplants

such as Peace Lilies, Chinese Evergreens, and Orchids help to clean the air of tobacco smoke and fumes from paints, construction materials, and household cleaners.

The Stresses of Indoor Life

While interior plants brighten our spirits and senses, indoor life can be stressful for them. Low light stunts growth and interferes with photosynthesis, dust particles coat leaves and clog pores, and warm air and cold drafts reduce humidity. With the pleasures of interior plantscaping come the responsibilities of finding proper locations for sufficient light and providing adequate moisture, fertilizer, and pest control.

The Importance of Light

Just as "in the beginning there was light," so is light one of the most important considerations for successfully growing houseplants. Without sufficient illumination, photosynthesis cannot occur, which eventually leads to a plant's demise. Illumination is measured in foot candles (fc): 1 fc is equivalent to the light produced by a candle at a distance of 1 foot.

Although most plants do well in diffused light (light that comes through a thin curtain, for example), specific light requirements are

Light Intensity Chart

Foot Candle to Photographic Light Meter Conversion Table

Foot Candles	Photo "F" Stop
150 foot candles	F 4.0
300 foot candles	F 5.6
600 foot candles	F 8.0
1200 foot candles	F 11.0

*Set photographic light meter at ASA 25. Set shutter speed at 1/60. Hold a white card in the same location as your plant. Take a reading of the reflected light at a distance of 18 inches away from the card. Take readings at 9 a.m., noon, and 4 p.m. Add readings together and divide by 3. The result should then be rounded to the nearest F stop or interpolate.

dependent on species and variety. North-facing windows generally receive less light than south-facing ones, and plants with flowers, bracts, or brightly colored foliage need more light than others. Unless the plant has very low light needs, do not place a plant where you cannot read a newspaper without turning on a light.

Once a new plant has been put in a location, observe how it adjusts to its new environment; if it does not do well within the next couple of weeks, find a more suitable spot. Sudden changes can lead to foliar sunburn or yellowing, sagging leaves or bud drop, as well as increasing vulnerability to disease and pests. Since plants naturally lean towards light, a half-turn of the pot every few days will maintain even growth.

If you are considering artificial lights, use either special plant-growing fluorescent lights that concentrate more on the red and blue spectrums, or use a combination of cool (emits more blue) and warm white (emits more red) fluorescent tubes.

Watering, Fertilizing, and Cleaning Houseplants

How often to water a container plant is probably the most frequently asked question on our program. Our replies usually begin with "it depends," because the answer is contingent on a variety of factors: the kind of plant and its size in a container; growth cycle; room temperature; type of container; and soil mix. When you stick your finger in the soil about one-half or one inch below the surface and it feels dry to the touch, this is a good cue to water. While most house-plants do well when they are allowed to go a little dry, some such as Butterfly Orchids prefer to be kept evenly moist but not soggy, while others like to go very dry. A resting plant needs less water than a growing one, and a small plant in a large container needs less water than a large plant in a small container. And the warmer the room temperature, the more porous the container (clay pots are more porous than plastic or glazed), and the lighter and sandier the planting mix, the more frequent the watering should be. Because most houseplants originally come from tropical or subtropical habitats, the ideal temperature range for most of them is between 68 to 72 degrees Fahrenheit.

Water according to each plant's need for water and not by a rigid time schedule. Let your "fingers do the talking" and your eyes do the diagnosing when answering the mystifying question, "How often should I water?"

Fertilize during the growth and bloom cycles with a liquid or controlled-release type of food, closely following package directions.

Avoid wax or shine products to clean the plants, because they tend to clog the pores. Simply wipe the leaves with a wet cloth or sponge. Periodically wash them off with tepid water in the sink or shower to clean them thoroughly and to leach out any accumulated salts.

Some Problems of Indoor Plants

As is true of outdoor plants, indoor plants can have problems that need to be remedied. Brown leaf tips may be the result of too much fertilizer, dry air, or accumulated salts; these problems can be corrected by reducing the dosage of fertilizer, increasing humidity by regular misting or the use of humidity trays, flushing out salts with deep soakings, or switching to de-ionized water found at local grocery stores. Cut off the brown parts, but leave a slight edge and do not cut into healthy tissue.

If a plant has mottled or yellow leaves, look for sucking insects such as aphids, mealy-bugs, or mites. If there are no signs of insects, reduce the amount of water or move the plant to an area with more light. When insect damage is apparent, syringe with a spray of water or houseplant insecticide-miticide, or apply a systemic houseplant insecticide. Use only products specifically labeled for houseplants, and follow the directions—because the label is the law.

Pay Attention

Before buying a houseplant, make sure you know what its needs are and what its mature size will be. If you want to buy a cute palm in a six-inch pot, know that with proper care it can grow up to ten to fifteen feet. Regularly inspect the stems and leaves of any houseplant, topside and underneath, for signs of insect damage. Look under the pots to see if any roots growing out of drainage holes need to be pruned, or if the plant needs to be repotted. As in all gardening, there are no hard and fast rules to successfully maintain houseplants, but trial and error and keen observation are important keys to helping Mother Nature with our interiors.

African Violet

Saintpaulia ionantha

Whenever callers to our garden radio program ask about their African Violets, we jokingly tell them that people have to be at least thirty years old before these plants will bloom. Since African Violets are the most popular blooming houseplants in the world, we have many opportunities to talk about them. If given proper care, once they are mature they can bloom almost continuously, bearing clusters of fragrant flowers in shades of pink, red, purple, blue, or white with single or double blooms that are bicolored, wavy, or ruffled. Their rosettes of ciliated foliage come in solid or variegated tints of deep to light greens, edged or streaked in cream, white, or pink, and are available as standard two- to four-inch leaves or Lilliputian one-half- to one-inch leaves. Display them single file in decorative pots on your windowsill, or mass them in a shallow basket for a table arrangement, or simply place one wherever you want a miniature touch of color. The ideal temperature range is 65 to 75 degrees Fahrenheit, provided there is adequate moisture, humidity (40 to 60 percent), and air circulation. Keep them away from sources of heat, air conditioning, cold drafts, and direct sunlight. Specialized African Violet pots permit watering from the bottom, but make sure you use de-ionized, distilled, or reverse-osmosis water.

Family Name / Origin Gesneriaceae / East Africa, Tanzania

Bloom Period and Color Pink, white, red, purple, and variegated flowers bloom in spring, summer, and fall.

Mature Height × **Spread** 3 to 6 in. × 8 to 12 in. (clumping)

When and How to Plant Transplant any time of year from 2-, 4-, or 6-in. pots, spacing 6 to 10 in. apart if in a grouping or mixed planter. Since they like their roots crowded, repot only when necessary, in the spring—which is also a good time to propagate by division or by leaf-cutting. Dip the leaves in a rooting hormone, place in a suitable growing medium such as coarse vermiculite, and pot up when sufficient root systems develop.

Soil and Light Preferences Use a well-drained, all-purpose African Violet potting soil that is high in organic matter and has a pH of 6.0 to 6.5. The plants grow and flower best in filtered light of 600 to 1000 foot candles.

Moisture Requirements Immediately after planting, soak deeply and thoroughly; thereafter, adjust watering frequency and amount to temperature, humidity, and growth conditions. Once established, water when dry to the touch—do not overwater, but keep the soil barely moist. Stand the pots in a shallow dish filled with room-temperature water that is distilled or de-ionized, allowing the plants to wick up their water needs without getting any moisture on their sensitive foliage. Ugly splotches on the leaves appear when cold water drips on them. After they have wicked up a sufficient amount of moisture, remove them from the tray and return them to their original location.

Fertilizing Fertilize twice a month during their growth cycle, from spring to fall, with a complete African Violet liquid food such as 2-10-6, at half-strength.

Pruning and Care When growth becomes too dense or additional crowns form, thin out with a sharp, clean knife any time of year. To control disease, remove spent flowers and any dead or damaged leaves.

Pests and Diseases Setting African Violets on trays filled with moist pebbles is an effective way to meet their high humidity needs as well as to offset the dry air conditions that attract mealybugs and aphids. Root rot and mildew are common maladies of African Violets when the soil is too cold and soggy.

Our Personal Favorite

NAME	SPECIAL CHARACTERISTICS
S. magungensis	Clusters of deep-purple flowers are grouped closely against the foliage

Corn Plant

Dracaena fragrans 'Massangeana'

"*On a windy road towards the Arenal Volcano in Costa Rica, we passed numerous pastures with grazing cattle and frolicking goats. The pastoral scenery was quite beautiful, and the "living fences" were even more impressive. These were stumps of leafed-out Corn Plants bound with wire, effectively defining property boundary lines and confining their herding residents. Their rough-textured trunks grow up to six feet tall, with broad, arching, greenish-yellow- or greenish-white-striped leaves similar to those of corn stalks. Corn Plants normally do not have any conspicuous flowers, but when mature, their foliage has a slight perfumed fragrance. They have distinctively smooth roots that are yellow-orange in color. Not only are these bold-looking plants ideal fenceposts, they are effective standing on their own on staircase landings, under skylights, or as focal plants in indoor atrium gardens where there is some height to display their scale and broad, cascading foliage. Since they are salt-sensitive, the leaves may turn brown at the tips. If this happens, switch from tap water to de-ionized or the distilled water available at your grocery store. The ideal temperature range is 65 to 75 degrees Fahrenheit, provided there is adequate moisture, humidity, and air circulation. Keep the plant away from sources of heat, air conditioning, cold drafts, and direct sunlight.*"

Family Name / Origin Agavaceae / Tropical Africa

Mature Height × **Spread** 6 to 8 ft. (clumping)

When and How to Plant Plant any time of year from 6- to 8-in. pots or 1- or 5-gallon containers, spacing 6 to 12 in. apart if in a grouping. Once established, repot about every two years, as needed.

Soil and Light Preferences Use a well-drained, all-purpose potting soil that is high in organic matter and has a pH of 6.5 to 7.0. Corn Plants require filtered light of 400 to 800 foot candles. Keep them out of full sun. If your plants are exposed to too much light, the leaves fade and eventually burn; too little light will result in droopy, dull foliage.

Moisture Requirements Immediately after planting, soak deeply and thoroughly; thereafter, adjust frequency and amount to temperature, humidity, and growth conditions. Once established, do not overwater, but keep the soil evenly moist. Corn Plants require high humidity (50 percent).

Fertilizing Fertilize twice a month during their growth cycle, from early spring to late fall, with a complete liquid food such as 6-10-4, at half-dosage strength.

Pruning and Care Prune for shape or to remove any damaged, diseased, or dead foliage. If leaf tips or edges turn brown, snip them off following the natural leaf shape but leaving a small edge of brown, because cutting into healthy tissue leads to more dieback. Do not use a commercial leaf shine or the oil might clog the plant pores.

Pests and Diseases Excessive sogginess or dryness may cause leaf drop. Infestations of scale and spider mites or leaf edges turning brown might indicate the air is too dry from central heating or air conditioning. Setting them on trays filled with moist pebbles without allowing the plants to stand in water, misting regularly with room-temperature water, and moving them away from heat sources or air-conditioner vents will help increase humidity around the plants. After washing off with soapy water and rinsing with tepid water, keep an eye out for subsequent infestations. Should damage continue, use an insecticidal soap, systemic houseplant granules, or an appropriate spray for houseplant pests.

Our Personal Favorite

NAME	SPECIAL CHARACTERISTICS
D. marginata	Twisted trunk / long, narrow leaves with red margins

Moth or Butterfly Orchid

Phalaenopsis amabilis

The loveliest of all spray orchids, Butterfly Orchids, whose name comes from Greek words meaning "mothlike," has rounded petals that resemble floral Lepidoptera in full flight. As epiphytes, they are found in their native habitats high in the upper canopies of trees where forest growth is too dense for them to establish in the ground. They come in a dazzling palette of magentas, lavenders, pinks, whites, pale greens, yellows, browns, and reds, as well as contrasting patterns of spots, splashes, streaks, and stripes. From deep-green, tongue-shaped, leathery leaves come flowering spikes laden with four to ten blooms that last from two to three months. A mature Butterfly Orchid can remain in bloom for up to eight to ten months of the year and form two or three budding offshoots. Despite their fragile, exotic appearance, they are great for beginners because they are one of the most forgiving orchids. The ideal temperature range is from 65 degrees Fahrenheit in the evening to 75 or higher during the day, provided there is adequate moisture, 50 to 70 percent relative humidity, and good air circulation. If flower buds drop, it may mean insufficient light. Keep them away from sources of heat, air conditioning, cold drafts, and direct sunlight.

Family Name / Origin Orchidaceae / Australasia

Mature Height × **Spread** 8 to 12 in. × 12 to 18 in.

When and How to Plant Repot about every two years when the plants are in an active stage of growth. Remove dead and decaying roots and place a layer of styrofoam "peanuts" at the bottom of a pot for drainage. I prefer the lighter-weight plastic over clay containers because the former retains moisture longer and there is not as much salt buildup.

Soil and Light Preferences Use a fir bark mixture, fine-grade 1/4-in. for seedlings, 1/2- to 5/8-in. medium-grade for larger sizes. Filtered light of 600 to 800 foot candles is best during most of the year; in winter, the plants require 1000 foot candles.

Moisture Requirements To allow the injured roots time to heal, do not water for a couple of days after planting. Then soak deeply; thereafter, adjust frequency and amount to temperature, humidity, and growth conditions. Once established, do not overwater, but keep the soil evenly moist.

Fertilizing Fertilize every time you water during the growth cycle, fall to winter, with a complete liquid food like 30-10-10, at half-dosage strength. During spring and summer, switch to a half-strength 10-30-20 or 10-20-10 liquid.

Pruning and Care When flowers wilt, leave spikes so additional buds can form. If a spike tip dies back, cut off at the nearest bump or node on the stem and a lateral shoot should emerge in about four weeks. Water before noon to let the plants dry by night. In fall, keep temperatures around 61 degrees Fahrenheit for four to six weeks to stimulate flower spike development. When Butterfly Orchids grow a new leaf, they will probably drop an older, bottom leaf.

Pests and Diseases Thrips, scales, aphids, mealybugs, and spider mites can be problems when the air is too warm and dry. Setting these tropical orchids on trays filled with moist pebbles without allowing the plants to stand in water, misting periodically with room-temperature water, and moving them away from heat sources help increase humidity. After washing off with soapy water and rinsing with tepid water, keep an eye out for subsequent infestations. Should damage continue, use an insecticidal soap, systemic houseplant granules, or an appropriate spray for houseplant pests.

Our Personal Favorites

NAME	SPECIAL CHARACTERISTICS
P. amboinensis	Star-shaped flowers with brown markings
P. equestris	A compact plant / small deep-rose flowers / prolific bloomer

Peace Lily
Spathiphyllum floribundum 'Mauna Loa'

About seven miles north of Hilo is a nature preserve known as the Hawaii Tropical Botanical Garden where trails wind through groves of Coconut, Mango, and Monkeypod trees. Overlooking the rugged ocean coast amidst waterfalls, meandering streams, and forests of giant tree ferns, this tropical paradise shelters a vast array of flowers, fruits, and plants. Few are as spectacular as the giant 'Mauna Loa', a variety of S. floribundum. Standing three feet high, its giant, glossy, arching, forest-green leaves are similar in scale to palm fronds, except the leaves grow in dense tufts on stems that hug the mulch-rich ground. From spring to early fall, four-foot-tall white flowers or spathes beckon butterflies and birds to pollinate their spiked inflorescence. Most of us do not have the year-round warmth, humidity, and shade of a tropical rain forest, but because Peace Lilies are so adaptive, they can be successfully grown indoors. Their elegant foliage and fragrant snow-white flowers make perfect accents in modern or minimalist interiors. Combined with other flowering houseplants, 'Mauna Loa's' pale spathes provide a welcome cooling contrast to the more hotly colored species. The ideal temperature range is 64 to 77 degrees Fahrenheit, provided there is adequate moisture, humidity (50 percent), and air circulation. Keep them away from sources of heat, air conditioning, cold drafts, and direct sunlight.

Family Name / Origin Araceae / South America

Mature Height × **Spread** 2 to 3 ft. (clumping)

When and How to Plant Plant any time of the year from 4-in., 6-in., 8-in., or larger containers, spacing 12 to 18 in. apart if in a grouping or mixed planter. Once established, repot in February or March—only if needed, because they prefer to be crowded. Repotting time is also a good time to propagate by division.

Soil and Light Preferences Use a well-drained, all-purpose potting soil, high in organic matter, pH 6.0 to 6.5. The plants do best in filtered light with 400 to 600 foot candles.

Moisture Requirements Immediately after planting, soak deeply and thoroughly; thereafter, adjust frequency and amount to temperature, humidity, and growth conditions. Water moderately most of the year, except during winter, when you should water sparingly. Never allow the plants to dry out completely and keep the soil evenly moist, never overwatering.

Fertilizing Fertilize twice a month during their growth cycle, from spring to fall, with a complete liquid food such as 8-8-8, at half-dosage strength.

Pruning and Care Cut back damaged, diseased, or dead leaves, particularly during the less-active cycle in winter. Remove spent spathes for appearance's sake. Use room-temperature water when irrigating your plants, and avoid wetting the spathes because moisture causes them to rot. Wear gloves when handling Peace Lily as the flowers may irritate your skin.

Pests and Diseases Few insects bother Peace Lilies unless the air is warm and dry. Then they may become havens for spider mites, scale, mealybugs, and aphids. Setting them on trays filled with moist pebbles without allowing the plants to stand in water, misting regularly during warm weather with room-temperature water, and moving them away from heat sources help increase humidity around the plants. After washing off with soapy water and rinsing with tepid water, keep an eye out for subsequent infestations. Should damage continue, use an insecticidal soap or cover with a plastic bag for a couple of days to increase humidity and kill those bothersome pests. Salt accumulation in the soil is the most common cause of foliar tip burn, and changing from tap to de-ionized water (the kind you find at a store that sells steam irons) is an effective remedy.

Our Personal Favorite

NAME	SPECIAL CHARACTERISTICS
S. × 'Petite'	Compact, upright form / glossy green leaves

Umbrella Tree
Schefflera actinophylla

Commonly known as Umbrella Trees because they resemble foliar umbrellas, these plants have compound lacquered leaves that are palmate, meaning their six to nine leaflets are arranged in the shape of a hand at the ends of twelve-inch-long petioles. When we see them sold in dainty four- to six-inch pots, we think about our friend who planted one under the shade of his front porch believing it would develop into a nice four-foot bush. After only a few years, it is now thirty feet tall with a fifteen-foot canopy and still growing and reaching for the sun. Had he asked, we could have told him Umbrella Trees are among the tallest of all houseplants, develop multiple trunks, and reach heights of forty feet when grown outdoors. They give a tropical look to dish gardens and planters when pruned back to control their size and make excellent specimens in large containers in residential entryways. Ideal temperature range is 65 to 80 degrees Fahrenheit, provided there is adequate moisture, humidity, and air circulation. If placed a distance from vents they withstand air-conditioned rooms, but keep them from sources of heat, frost, wind, and direct sunlight. **Note:** *If you cannot find* Schefflera actinophylla, *look for* Brassaia actinophylla, *another botanical name sometimes used for the same plant.*

Family Name / Origin Araliaceae / Northern Australia, New Guinea

Mature Height × Spread 8 to 15 in. × 4 to 6 ft.

When and How to Plant Plant any time of the year from 4- to 8-in. or 1- or 5-gallon containers. It may be necessary to repot younger plants every year, but once established, repot only as needed. Since they are rather difficult to propagate from seed, air layering or tip cuttings are the preferred methods of propagation.

Soil and Light Preferences Use a well-drained, all-purpose potting soil that is high in organic matter and has a pH of 6.5 to 7.0. Although the plants tolerate lower light conditions, bright indirect light in excess of 600 to 1000 foot candles is best—but never place them in full sun.

Moisture Requirements Immediately after planting, soak deeply and thoroughly; thereafter, adjust frequency and amount to temperature, humidity, and growth conditions. Once established, do not overwater, but keep the soil on the dry side—otherwise, the leaves may turn yellow and drop.

Fertilizing Fertilize twice a month during their growth cycle, from spring to fall, with a complete liquid food like 8-8-8, at half-dosage strength.

Pruning and Care To encourage a fuller growth habit, prune back the stems in spring. If you do not want a large plant, pinch or cut back regularly. Use gloves whenever you handle Umbrella Trees, for they may be a skin irritant. Just as we do, they appreciate an outdoor summer vacation if there is a shady, protected area.

Pests and Diseases There are few disease or insect problems, but scale and spider mites may appear when the air is too warm and dry. Setting the plants on trays filled with moist pebbles without allowing them to stand in water, misting periodically with room-temperature water, or moving them away from heat sources helps increase humidity around the plants and discourages insect infestations. After washing off with soapy water and rinsing with tepid water, if insects are still damaging your Umbrella Trees, use an insecticidal soap, systemic granules, or an appropriate spray for houseplant pests. Their leaves tend to drop when temperatures fall below 55 degrees Fahrenheit.

Our Personal Favorite

NAME	SPECIAL CHARACTERISTICS
S. arboricola	Commonly known as Dwarf Schefflera / smaller version of the Umbrella Tree / maximum height 4 to 8 ft.

Variegated Cast-Iron Plant
Aspidistra elatior 'Variegata'

" *Cast-Iron Plant was once found in every Victorian's parlor room because it was one of the few houseplants that could survive gas lighting. It is still our choice for people who tell us all their houseplants wither, shrivel, and die. Our Variegated Cast-Iron Plants are almost indestructible and are great choices for low-light, low-humidity, low-maintenance areas indoors as well as outdoors. Originally from the briskly cool, shadowy mountains of China and Japan, they grow to over three feet tall and expand horizontally with the help of spreading rhizomes. Evergreen foliage emerges upright as tightly rolled, tubular shapes, before unfurling into twenty-five- to thirty-inch-long leaves. They maintain their deep-green, dense form in surprisingly dark stairways, hallways, and offices, in forgotten corners, in temperate and shady xeriscape land-scapes, or simply displayed in an old-fashioned pot on a pedestal, just as in Victorian times. This long-lived plant can become quite large. Since the gray-violet flowers are insignificant, it is not necessary to deadhead spent flowers. As long as temperatures do not dip below 50 degrees Fahrenheit, they endure poor soil; low light; high heat; humid, stagnant, dry air; and even smoke—but keep them away from direct sunlight.* "

Family Name / Origin Liliaceae / China, Japan

Mature Height × Spread 2 to 3 ft. (clumping)

When and How to Plant Plant any time from 6- or 8-in. pots, or 1-gallon containers, spacing 12 in. apart if in a grouping. When a plant outgrows its container, divide into individual plants or clumps of two to three plants.

Soil and Light Preferences Although they tolerate low light levels of 300 foot candles, they grow more compactly in bright, filtered light of 300 to 600 foot candles. Use a well-drained, all-purpose potting soil, high in organic matter, pH 6.5 to 7.0.

Moisture Requirements Soak deeply after planting; thereafter, adjust frequency and amount to temperature, humidity, and growth conditions.

Fertilizing Fertilize twice a month during the growth cycle, spring to fall, with a complete liquid food such as 8-8-8, half-strength.

Pruning and Care Prune only to remove any damaged, diseased, or dead leaves. The day before dividing, water thoroughly. After removing the plant from its old pot, trim off any tangled, dried, or dead roots and spread the sides of the root mass. You can divide by selecting one plant per stem and potting it up singly or grouped with others, or cut the rootball into two or three sections. Once divisions are potted, press the soil around the rootball with your fingertips, and water thoroughly and deeply to eliminate air pockets.

Pests and Diseases There are few serious problems with the exception of root rot or leaf burn, and these are easily remedied by removing the plants from standing water or from the damaging rays of sunlight. If your plants harbor spider mites, scale, mealybugs, or aphids, the air is probably too warm and dry. Setting them on trays filled with moist pebbles without allowing the plants to stand in water, misting periodically with room-temperature water, and moving them away from heat sources help increase humidity around the plants. After washing off with soapy water and rinsing with tepid water, keep an eye out for subsequent infestations. Should damage continue, use an insecticidal soap, systemic houseplant granules, or an appropriate spray for houseplant pests.

Our Personal Favorites

NAME	SPECIAL CHARACTERISTICS
A. e. 'Green Leaf'	Large leaves that are shiny and solid green in color
A. e. 'Milky Way'	Speckled-white variegations

Variegated Chinese Evergreen

Aglaonema commutatum

With the Variegated Chinese Evergreen's pleasing dome-shaped growth habit, low light requirements, and minimal care needs, it was one of our mainstay selections for commercial interior plant design at our family's nursery. It is high on our list of recommended houseplants for people who ask what they can grow indoors without too much light and care. Growing in clumps of broad, twelve-inch, spear-shaped leaves that camouflage a twenty-inch stalk from top to bottom, they are also very attractive. Depending on the variety, the foliage is deep green with boldly marked spots, dots, or stripes in pale green, white, or silvery gray. Some hybrids have leaves that are so pale they almost appear to lack chlorophyll. From spring through fall, tiny flowers form on short spikes surrounded by three-inch, greenish-white spathes that resemble flags. In the fruiting stage, these tiny flowers transform into reddish-orange seedpods. Although they add a touch of welcome fall and winter color, keep the seedpods away from children and pets because they are toxic. The ideal temperature range is 60 to 80 degrees Fahrenheit, provided there is adequate moisture, humidity (50 percent), and air circulation. Keep them away from sources of heat, air conditioning, cold drafts, and direct sunlight.

Family Name / Origin Araceae / Phillipines, E Indonesia

Mature Height × Spread 10 to 12 in. (clumping)

When and How to Plant Plant any time from 4- to 8-in. pots, spacing 12 in. apart if in a grouping or mixed planter. It may be necessary to repot younger plants every year, but once established, repot only as needed. Repotting time is also a good time to propagate by division.

Soil and Light Preferences Use a well-drained, all-purpose potting soil, high in organic matter, pH 6.0 to 6.5. Low light levels of 400 foot candles are tolerated, but the plants grow more compactly in 600 to 800 foot candles.

Moisture Requirements Soak deeply after planting; thereafter, adjust frequency and amount to temperature, humidity, and growth conditions. Once established, do not overwater, but keep the soil evenly moist.

Fertilizing Fertilize twice a month during the growth cycle, spring to fall, with a complete liquid food such as 8-8-8, half-dosage strength.

Pruning and Care Remove the spent spathes or allow them to remain on the stems to develop seedpods. If an older plant becomes overgrown, divide it or prune back to encourage a more compact growth from the base. If leaves turn yellow, it may be the result of overwatering, lack of nutrients, or insufficient light. The greener the variety, the less light needed. Handle Variegated Chinese Evergreen with gloves because the sap may irritate your skin.

Pests and Diseases If your plants harbor spider mites, scale, mealybugs, or aphids, the air is probably too warm and dry. Setting them on trays filled with moist pebbles without allowing the plants to stand in water, misting periodically with room-temperature water, and moving them away from heat sources help increase humidity around the plants. After washing off with soapy water and rinsing with tepid water, keep an eye out for subsequent infestations. Should damage continue, use an insecticidal soap, systemic houseplant granules, or an appropriate spray for houseplant pests. If their foliage margins turn brown, either they need de-ionized water (the kind you find at a store that carries steam irons) or the temperature is too cold.

Our Personal Favorite

NAME	SPECIAL CHARACTERISTICS
A. modestum	Commonly known as Chinese Evergreen / same growth and bloom habits as A. commutatum, but lacks the distinctive variegation and tolerates slightly dimmer light conditions / dark-green foliage

Zebra Plant

Aphelandra squarrosa

A customer came into our nursery asking for a blooming houseplant with bright-yellow flowers and we told her such a plant was not available. She was persistent enough to walk around our store and within a few minutes triumphantly plunked down the plant she was looking for: a Zebra Plant, known for its dramatic, dark-green leaves with distinctive creamy-white veins. These were popular in Victorian conservatories because of their bold foliage and brilliant yellow spikes that bloom as long as six weeks in the autumn months. Actually, as Bruce explained to our customer, the flowering spikes are not flowers but are overlapping bracts that form a tiled-roof pattern. She shook her head, convinced that her selection was a "flowering" houseplant, and left happily with her purchase. We knew she had stumped us with her description, but by her persistence, she got exactly what she wanted. If kept to a compact height of twelve to eighteen inches, Zebra Plants are ideal in small decorative pots or as focal accent plants in a mixed houseplant basket or planter. They like 50-percent humidity; keep them away from sources of forced air heating, air conditioning, cold drafts, direct sunlight, smoke, and stagnant air.

Family Name / Origin Acanthaceae / Brazil

Bloom Period and Color Yellow bracts appear in summer.

Mature Height × Spread 2 to 3 ft. × 1 ft.

When and How to Plant Plant any time from 4- to 8-in. pots, spacing 12 in. apart if in a grouping or mixed planter. Repot in spring, if needed; its also a good time to propagate from cuttings.

Soil and Light Preferences Use a well-drained, all-purpose potting soil, high in organic matter, pH 6.0 to 6.5. Although they tolerate low light levels of 600 foot candles, they grow more compactly at 800 to 1000 foot candles.

Moisture Requirements Immediately after planting, soak deeply and thoroughly; thereafter, adjust frequency and amount to temperature, humidity, and growth conditions. Do not overwater, but keep the soil evenly moist.

Fertilizing Fertilize twice a month during the growth cycle, from March to August, with a complete flowering liquid food like 6-10-4 at half-dosage.

Pruning and Care Remove spent flowering bracts. In March, prune back about 50 percent of the previous season's growth, and repot in a suitable potting soil to encourage compact, more attractive development. Unless the Zebra Plant is maintained at 50 degrees Fahrenheit for eight weeks during the winter under a plant light, it will probably not "flower" more than once. After the bracts fade, it may be simpler to enjoy its beauty as a vegetative houseplant. As long as it is cut back regularly, it will remain a bushy plant with vigorous, dramatic leaves.

Pests and Diseases If your plants harbor spider mites, scale, mealybugs, or aphids, the air is probably too warm and dry. Setting them on trays filled with moist pebbles without allowing the plants to stand directly in water, misting periodically with room-temperature water, and moving them away from heat sources help increase humidity around the plants. After washing off with soapy water and rinsing with tepid water, keep an eye out for subsequent infestations. Use an insecticidal soap, systemic houseplant granules, or an appropriate spray for houseplant pests. If foliage curls and drops, the probable cause is cold drafts, dry air, or a drop in temperature.

Our Personal Favorites

NAME	SPECIAL CHARACTERISTICS
A. s. 'Snow Queen'	Pale, lemon-yellow bracts
A. tetragona	Same foliage characteristics as Zebra Plant, but bracts are scarlet-red

Lawns *for California*

Like our freeways, fast-food chains, shopping malls, and multiplex movie theaters, the lawn is an icon of American culture. In spaces as diverse as suburban yards, sport fields, fairways, parks, and corporate headquarters, a lawn may be the object of obsessive care and attention. A common image of a perfect landscape is an impeccably manicured velvety lawn, flecked with sunlight amidst the shadows of a couple of trees. Unfortunately, this image of perfection too often comes at the cost of high maintenance: mowing, watering, aerating, fertilizing, weeding, broadcasting, and spraying for insects and diseases, which raises some valid economic and environmental concerns.

Go for "Healthy and Attractive," Not "Perfect"

For a lower maintenance and more environmentally friendly lawn, consider reducing its size by incorporating more trees, shrubs, flowers, vines, and ground covers into your landscape. It is helpful to realize that a perfect lawn is an ideal difficult to attain. But even if your lawn has some weeds it can be healthy and attractive. When you mow at the correct height, water properly, fertilize correctly, and choose the best-adapted type of grass for your growing conditions, you are providing the optimum components for a healthy lawn that is less susceptible to weeds, pests, and diseases.

What Kind of Grass Should I Plant?

To determine the kind of grass you should plant, ask yourself (1) What is the best match between the grass type and my location? and (2) What do I want from my lawn? Stolons are specialized stems that grow along the ground; at the point where leaf nodes touch the ground, new roots develop, creating a dense, thick lawn. If you want rough-and-tumble areas for children, pets, or heavy foot traffic, then a stoloniferous grass is a good choice. Bermuda, Seashore Paspalum, and 'El Toro' Zoysia are stoloniferous warm-season grasses that grow actively

during the summer months, but go dormant when temperatures dip below 55 degrees Fahrenheit. Depending on the species and the climate, dormancy will begin in the fall and last until mid-spring.

On the other hand, cool-season clumping grasses like Perennial Rye and Fescue grow most actively during spring and fall, remain green in the winter, and may turn brown during hot, dry summer weather. Unlike warm-weather species, cool-season grasses grow in bunches that tend to clump rather than form a tightly interlaced sod, and they are a much finer-textured turf. Unless they are sown thickly, some bare ground may be exposed. Perennial Rye does well in coastal fog belts and performs adequately elsewhere, but Bermuda and Zoysia grasses do better in the warm regions of California. Fescue is appropriate for shaded areas, but Bermuda, Seashore Paspalum, and Zoysia are better selections for drought tolerance.

When trying to decide, don't forget to talk to neighbors whose lawns you admire and consult your local nursery and University of California Cooperative Extension advisor. Every year there are new and improved grass varieties that better tolerate shade, sun, and drought; slower-growing cultivars that do not require frequent mowing; and still others that are more disease- or insect-resistant.

Installation and Care

Whether planting from seed, stolon, or sod, soil preparation is exactly the same. Once the soil has been raked and cleared of debris and a rough grading has been completed, test the soil's pH. If it is alkaline, refer to p. 402 for the appropriate application of sulfur. If you have clay soil, improve its texture to allow easy air and moisture movement by blending in gypsum, and mixing about 20 to 30 percent organic material to a depth of eight to twelve inches.

Once planted, firm the soil by pushing a roller over the surface—this enables seeds to germinate or ensures that stolons or sod make close contact with the soil. Before rolling seeds, mulch the surface with one-fourth inch of topdressing such as humus or topsoil; mulch with one-half inch before rolling stolons.

Keep the surface well watered until the seeds, stolons, or sod are established. Do not fertilize until the lawn has been mowed twice. Feed with a granular or liquid lawn fertilizer according to the manufacturer's instructions.

The Rewards of a Well-Kept Lawn

Although lawns pose a number of challenges, with proper forethought and care the rewards will be well worth the effort. A well-kept lawn sustains the summer rites of barbecues, water fights, and lawn parties and remains the best possible surface for bare feet, frolicking children, and pets. Grass is the background beat to the grand rhythm of a complete landscape.

Bermuda Grass

Cynodon dactylon

Bermuda Grass has a reputation for being a troublesome invader of gardens, and to a certain extent it deserves its nickname "devilgrass." Sharon complains its wiry stems can spread like weeds from our neighbor's yard into her flower and vegetable beds. The shoots appear where they are not welcome unless you border your bedding plant areas . . . but when properly tended, Bermuda is an excellent turfgrass. Think about the sea of grass you admire during a Super Bowl game—it's more than likely the sod is a mixture of hybrid Bermuda Grass for toughness, overseeded with Rye for color. For home landscapes, playing fields, even animal fodder, Bermuda is ideal as a low-maintenance warm-season turf. The grass by itself is gray-green, coarse-textured, and spreads by stolons (specialized above-the-ground stems), rhizomes (specialized underground stems), or seed, forming relatively dense turf. Its blades are smooth, short, flat, and pointed, with papery sheaths covering prostrate stems at each node. Upright flowering seedheads have three to seven spike-like branches resembling crow's feet. It grows best under extended periods of high summer temperatures and mild winters such as the low-elevation (below 3000 feet) areas from Mexico's border to the Southern California coast, the north end of Sacramento Valley, and in certain temperate zones surrounding San Francisco Bay.

Family Name / Origin Gramineae / South Africa

Maintenance Height ¾ to 1½ in.

Climate & Culture

Preferred Zones
8–11

Sun Preference

Installation Plant common Bermuda Grass from seed in late spring or summer, hybrid Bermuda from sod or stolons from March to November. To prepare the soil, create a sandy loam down 8 to 12 in. by amending with organic material such as humus mulch or compost. When seeding common Bermuda Grass, sow the seeds, topdress with ⅛ in. of loam soil or humus, and use a water roller to press seeds into the ground. One pound of seed covers approximately 1000 sq. ft. Water immediately after installation and keep moist until the seeds germinate. When stolonizing, distribute evenly across the prepared soil, press into the earth with a water roller, topdress with ¼ in. of loam soil, and keep moist until the stolons take root. For sod installation, lay the sections on the prepared soil, press with a water roller, and thoroughly water. If the seams between the sections separate, fill the gaps with sand and press again with a water roller. Refer to Planting Techniques, p. 398.

Sun and Soil Preferences Bermuda Grass grows best in full sun and loam soil with a pH of 7.0.

Moisture Requirements Once established, adjust watering frequency and amount according to climatic and growth conditions. This turf needs the least amount of water because of its deep roots; it withstands sustained, summer-long droughts and adapts to hot, sunny, windy conditions.

Fertilizing Fertilize every other month during the growth season after Bermuda Grass comes out of dormancy and is uniformly green, with a complete lawn fertilizer such as 16-6-8. Do not fertilize in fall or winter months.

Mowing and Care Bermuda lawns need frequent mowing to maintain a neat, restrained, attractive appearance. Mow with a rotary lawn mower set ¾ to 1½ in. high. Although drought-resistant and low-maintenance, Bermuda lawns look best when well watered, closely mowed, and fertilized in summer.

Pests and Diseases Few serious disease or pest infestations affect Bermuda Grass with the exception of sod webworm, which can be controlled by periodic applications of Diazinon™ or *B.t.*

See p. 414 for information on improved hybrid Bermudas.

Fescue

Festuca arundinacea × hybrid

Many of our clients are from the East Coast or Midwest, and when they visualize a lawn they think of blade-grass lawns like Kentucky Bluegrass. But most California regions do better with stoloniferous grasses such as Bermuda, which unfortunately goes dormant in winter, turning an unsightly brown unless overseeded with an annual like Rye. For those who insist on a landscape with an evergreen blade-grass lawn, Fescue fits the bill. It has the good looks of springtime Bluegrass, but stays green year-round. A bunch-type cool-season grass, Fescue traces its heritage to pasture grasses. It has the widest leaves of most turf species and a rough, somewhat clumping appearance. The surface of each leaf is coarse-textured and ribbed, but underneath it is shiny and smooth. It is a popular grass in Southern and Northern California, but is not recommended for low-desert or high-altitude mountain regions. In addition to home use, Fescue is excellent for playgrounds, parks, race tracks, erosion control on banks, and farm fodder. It is drought-tolerant and adapts moderately well to heat if there is adequate moisture, but it does not withstand temperature extremes. Consult your local garden center for cultivar blends appropriate for your area. **Note:** *Fescue Grass is sometimes given the botanical name* Festuca elatior.

Family Name / Origin Gramineae / Europe

Maintenance Height 1½ to 4 in.

Installation To prepare the soil for seeding or sodding, create a sandy loam down to a depth of 8 to
12 in. by amending with organic material such as
humus mulch or compost. Plant from sod any time
of the year during mild weather, or from seed in the
spring. If seeding, sow 8 to 12 lbs. per 1000 sq. ft.—
it needs to be densely sown because Fescue does not
have runners. Sow the seeds, topdress with ⅛ in. of
loam soil or humus, and use a water roller to press
the seeds into the ground. Water immediately after
installation and keep moist until the seeds germinate.
For sod installation, lay the sections on the prepared
soil, press with a water roller, and thoroughly water. If
the seams separate between the sections, fill the gaps with sand and press
with a water roller again. For more information, see Planting Techniques,
p. 398.

Climate & Culture

Preferred Zones
9–11

Sun Preferences

Sun and Soil Preferences Fescue grass grows best in full sun or partial
shade and well-drained, medium-textured soil with a pH of 5 to 7.2.

Moisture Requirements Once established, whether from seed or sod,
adjust watering frequency and amount according to climatic and growth
conditions. Fescue needs more water than Bermuda or Zoysia.

Fertilizing Fertilize every other month during the cool season, fall through
spring, with a complete lawn fertilizer such as 16-8-4.

Mowing and Care Mow with a rotary mower set 1½ to 2½ in. high
during the cool season and 3 to 4 in. high during the warm season. Since
Fescue is a bunch-type grass, its open areas need to be reseeded. Once
established, its vigorous growth discourages weeds. Do not mix other lawn
seeds with Fescue or the latter will look like coarse weeds rather than grass.

Pests and Diseases Brown patch can be controlled with a fungicide
such as Daconil, and sod webworm can be controlled with a pesticide
such as Diazinon™.

Perennial Ryegrass
Lolium perenne

" *When our family owned a nursery, many new homeowners came to us for advice about an appropriate grass that would be inexpensive, easy to install, quick to germinate from seed, and green all year-round. We would usually recommend the handsome Perennial Ryegrass because of its bright-green coloration and its ability to quickly cover a bare expanse with a moderate amount of maintenance. Ryegrass grows in bunches with medium to coarse leaves that are pointed at the tips, forming a soft, open sod, often a clumping habit. Like Bluegrass it is a perennial, but its blades are heavily veined on the upper surfaces and glossy underneath. Because of the veination and coarse texture it is difficult to mow, but improved varieties are finer textured, darker green, and more resistant to certain diseases. This cool-season grass is excellent in inexpensive seed mixtures and in Bluegrass mixtures. Lacking rhizomes or stolons, it spreads by tillering and does best in coastal fog belts, but grows adequately in other areas. It grows best during periods of cool temperatures and adapts well to sunny or partially shady conditions, but does not tolerate extended periods of heat. Consult your local garden center for a cultivar blend, such as a Bluegrass/Ryegrass mix, that is appropriate for your area.* "

Family Name / Origin Gramineae / Europe

Maintenance Height 1½ to 4 in.

Installation Plant from seed any time of the year, as long as the weather is mild. To prepare the soil for seeding or sodding, create a sandy loam down 8 to 12 in. by amending with organic material such as humus mulch or compost. When seeding Perennial Ryegrass, sow the seeds, topdress with ⅛ in. of loam soil or humus, and use a water roller to press the seeds into the ground. For sod installation, lay the sections on the prepared soil, press with a water roller, and water thoroughly. If the seams separate between the sections, fill the gaps with sand and press with a water roller again. See Planting Techniques, p. 398.

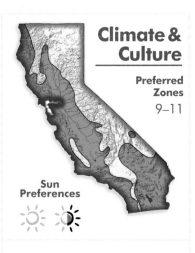

Climate & Culture

Preferred Zones

9–11

Sun Preferences

Sun and Soil Preferences Perennial Ryegrass grows best in full sun (although it withstands partial shade) and loam soil with a pH of 6.5 to 7.0.

Moisture Requirements Water immediately after installation and keep moist until the seeds germinate. Once established, whether from seed or sod, adjust watering frequency and amount according to climatic and growth conditions.

Fertilizing Fertilize every other month during the cool season, from fall to spring, with a complete lawn food such as 16-6-8.

Mowing and Care While the common Perennial Rye is most often used in new lawns, the improved but costlier varieties might be well worth the extra money for ease of mowing and their ability to persist under a wider range of conditions. Frequent mowing to maintain a neat, restrained, and attractive appearance is necessary. Mow with a rotary mower set 1½ to 2½ in. high during the cool season and 3 to 4 in. high during the warm season. Since Perennial Rye seldom forms a tightly knit turf, any open or worn areas should be reseeded.

Pests and Diseases With its ability to sprout quickly and its vigorous growth, weeds are kept to a minimum. The most common diseases and insects are rust, which can be controlled with a fungicide such as Daconil, and sod webworm, which can be controlled with Diazinon™.

Seashore Paspalum

Paspalum vaginatum 'Adalayd'

"*One of the luxuries of country living is having the space for farm animals, from common ducks, chickens, geese, pigs, goats, and horses to the more exotic ostrich, peacock, llama, and buffalo. Our community is criss-crossed with many fine horse trails, and the sight of our equestrian friends sashaying by provides a tranquil respite from the hustle and bustle of appointments, commitments, and never-ending things-to-do lists. Several nearby stables are situated on dusty, highly alkaline river-bottom soils that require a turf rugged enough to retain its density after the wear and tear of galloping horses. The turf of choice for our local stables is Seashore Paspalum, commonly known as Adalayd. This perennial warm-season grass is a loose, medium-low, spreading turf with a somewhat coarse appearance. It has a color similar to that of Bluegrass and is exceptionally tolerant of heavy foot, paw, and hoof traffic, as well as saline water and soil. Since it roots deeply, it is a good grass for sandy areas and is relatively pest-free. Use this turf on problem sites such as seashore landscapes, equestrian areas, high soil salinity locations, rugged coastal sites, dog runs, and pockets of light shade.*"

Family Name / Origin Gramineae / subtropical and tropical Americas, New Zealand, Australia

Maintenance Height 1 to 3 in.

Installation Plant from stolons or sod in spring or summer. To prepare the soil for stolonizing or sodding, create a sandy loam down 8 to 12 in. by amending with organic material such as humus mulch or compost. When stolonizing, distribute evenly across the prepared soil, press into the earth with a water roller, topdress with ¼ in. of loam soil, and keep moist until the stolons take root. For sod installation, lay the sections on the prepared soil, press with a water roller, and thoroughly water. If the seams separate between the sections, fill the gaps with sand and press with a water roller again. Consult Planting Techniques, p. 398, for additional information.

Climate & Culture

Preferred Zones
9–11

Sun Preferences

Sun and Soil Preferences Seashore Paspalum grass grows best in full sun, although it tolerates partial shade, and requires loam soil with a pH of 6.5 to 7.2.

Moisture Requirements Once established, whether from stolon or sod, adjust watering frequency and amount to climatic and growth conditions. Although drought-resistant, 'Adalayd' looks best when watered about twice a week during the growth cycle.

Fertilizing Fertilize lightly every other month, between May and October with a complete lawn food such as 16-6-8.

Mowing and Care Mow with a front-throw reel mower set to about 1 to 2 in. In interior areas in late summer, 'Adalayd' produces tough stems that brown after scalping. To avoid this problem and to conserve water, mow the lawn at a height of 2 to 3 in.

Pests and Diseases Seashore Paspalum has a few drawbacks, because just like humans, lawns are not perfect. It is occasionally susceptible to brown patch, which can be controlled by a fungicide such as Daconil, and sod webworm, which can be controlled with Diazinon™. It does not tolerate extended periods of sub-freezing temperatures; it goes dormant if temperatures dip below 55 degrees Fahrenheit and remains dormant for a longer time than Bermuda Grass. Its tolerance of drought, high temperatures, soil and water salinity, and resistance to foot traffic more than compensate for its small failings.

Zoysia Grass

Zoysia japonica 'El Toro'

For gardeners who love to entertain in the summer on a picture-perfect lawn and do not mind patiently waiting for a few seasons to get what they want, the 'El Toro' Zoysia Grass is the answer to their dream. It is an attractive, uniformly dense, erect, high-quality turf that forms a verdant carpet. 'El Toro' spreads through rhizomes and stolons. As young blades of grass each leaf is rolled, but the seedheads emerge as single spikes. It does well in much of Southern California and San Joaquin Valley, where the days are warm and the nights remain mild. It needs less fertilizer, water, and mowing than cool-season turf. With stiff stems and fine, tight texture, this grass provides a rebounding resiliency to heavy foot traffic, has a low thatch, displays its spring greenup earlier, offers better color, and discourages weed invasions. In addition to home land-scapes, Zoysia is ideal for golf courses, playgrounds, and parks. During winter or whenever temperatures dip below 55 degrees Fahrenheit, Zoysia goes dormant and turns a golden brown color until spring. Another Zoysia, Z. tenuifolia, commonly known as Korean Grass or Bump Grass, has a fibrous, shallow root system and is very slow growing—use it in a small planting area such as a rock garden combined with ornamental shrubs, succulents, and palms.

Family Name / Origin Gramineae / a cultivar
not found in the wild

Maintenance Height ½ to 1 in.

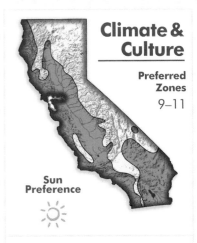

**Climate &
Culture**

Preferred
Zones
9–11

Sun
Preference

Installation Plant from stolon, sod, or plugs in
spring or summer. To prepare the soil for stolonizing,
sodding, or plugging, create a sandy loam down 8 to
12 in. by amending with organic material such as
humus mulch or compost. When stolonizing, distribute
the stolons evenly across the prepared soil, press
them into the earth with a water roller, topdress with
¼ in. of loam soil, and keep moist until the stolons
take root. For sod installation, lay the sections on
the prepared soil, press with a water roller, and
water thoroughly. If the seams separate between
the sections, fill the gaps with sand and press with a
water roller again. Depending on how fast you want plugs to fill in, space
them 4 to 6 in. on center, press in with a water roller, and water thoroughly.
For additional information, see Planting Techniques, p. 398.

Sun and Soil Preferences Zoysia grows best in full sun and loam soil
with a pH of 6.5 to 7.0.

Moisture Requirements Once established, whether from stolon, sod,
or plugs, adjust watering frequency and amount to climatic and growth
conditions. Water only when blades begin to lose their bright green shine
and start to turn a dull blue-gray. If water runs off, stop until the soil absorbs
the excess moisture, then turn on the water again.

Fertilizing Fertilize during the growing season with a complete lawn food
such as 16-6-8.

Mowing and Care Zoysia lawns need frequent mowing to maintain a
neat, attractive appearance and to control weeds until establishment. Mow
with a rotary mower set ½ in. to 1 in. high. If you broadcast stolons at
¾ bushel per 50 sq. ft. in May, you can establish a Zoysia lawn in three
to six months.

Pests and Diseases Rust can be controlled with a fungicide such as
Daconil. Billbugs, white grubs, sod webworms, and mole crickets can
become pests, but an application of Diazinon™ should remedy an infestation
before it causes extensive damage.

Nut Trees *for California*

Although no poet has immortalized the spreading Pecan or Walnut tree, and no songwriter has "tied a yellow ribbon 'round" the old Pistachio, Almond, or Macadamia tree, they are among the most romantic reminders of seasonal changes. In late winter or early spring, magnificent pink Almond blossoms hurriedly flower ahead of their more reticent leaves. In late spring, clusters of green, hard-shelled Macadamia nuts hang from their branches like oversized grapes. By late autumn or early winter, the fiery golden hues of Pecan leaves and the brilliant reds and oranges of Pistachio leaves decorate our gardens.

Nut Trees and the Home Gardener

Impatient nuts ripen and fall to the ground. By winter, the autumn leaves have long gone, allowing us to appreciate the trees' roughly textured bark and outstretched branches, still regal in their barren simplicity. With the exception of Almonds, nut trees can grow into very large specimens and create wonderful shade wherever they plant their feet. Unfortunately, most are ill-suited for small yards, but if there is plenty of elbow room

they bring beauty, stature, and crops to the landscape. As long as the climate is suitable, even exotic Macadamias and Pistachios can be yours for the picking, almost as easily as from the grocery store.

A nut is technically a single-seeded dry fruit with a tough exterior shell that does not split when ripe.

It is a mistaken belief that a plentiful nut crop requires the expertise of a knowledgeable orchardist. Unless you are a stickler for maximum fruit production, the home gardener can harvest a decent-sized crop without interminable spraying, feeding, and pruning schedules. Like any fruit tree, nut trees are susceptible to bouts of disease and insect infestations, but their size limits the average homeowner's ability to effectively spray with the usual assortment of fungicides and insecticides. Think of nut trees as beautiful shade habitats for people and for wildlife that often, but not always, reward you with a large harvest.

Select the Right Tree for the Right Site

All nut trees prefer deep, fertile soil with good drainage and an even supply of water. When planted in full sun, some trees, such as the Pecan, can become arboreal ninety-foot skyscrapers, while the comparatively diminutive Almond can mature on its tip-toes to twenty feet. It is therefore very important that you choose the right tree for the right site. Many nut trees, including Pecans and most Walnuts, are not self-fruitful and need one or two compatible cultivars planted within a hundred feet of each other for successful cross-pollination. Pistachio trees are dioecious, and they need one male tree for up to ten female trees in order to bear properly. Where there is adequate summer rainfall, little irrigation is required, but where the climates are hot and dry, they need occasional and deep irrigation.

The deep taproots of Almond and Walnut trees make them difficult to transplant. Plant them in permanent spots in holes deep enough to accommodate their entire taproots without bending them.

One of the best trees for cold climates is the Walnut or Almond, but for milder climates consider Pistachios, Pecans, and Macadamias. Keep in mind that nut crops drop, so do not plant them where falling fruits would be a problem.

Nut Trees and Wildlife

We are continually amazed at the protective systems plants have developed to stave off competition from other plants. The English Walnut, for example, manufactures a chemical compound called juglone. This compound deters many species of plants, including Tomatoes, from growing too close to it. Interestingly enough, it has no effect on brambles, such as Blackberries. Perhaps allowing thorny brambles on the tree's trunk is a way to discourage foraging squirrels, rats, and raccoons.

With the exception of Walnuts, most nut trees are viewed as tasty buffets for wildlife. A friend of ours who manages thousands of acres of Almond trees in the Sacramento and San Joaquin Valleys developed an ingenious, benign deer repellent. He suspends small hotel-size soap bars in the trees' canopies and the scent keeps the deer away. As for ravenous birds and other wildlife, either be prepared to battle them away, or plant enough trees so there will be plenty for all to share.

The Odds Are Getting Better

Improved varieties with better fruiting, disease resistance, and tolerance of special soil and climate conditions are increasing the odds in your favor for successful cultivation of nut trees. As long as you learn about your site, choose suitable varieties, and give them proper care and attention, your nut-bearing trees will provide edible fruits, natural beauty, shade, and wildlife shelter for years to come.

Almond
Prunus dulcis

Flying into Fresno one spring morning, we saw a panoramic patchwork quilt of pastel pinks in varying hues. Grove after grove of Almonds provided this captivating view and dispelled our former notion that Fresno's main claim to fame was the California Raisin. The Almond is one of the earliest blooming and most beautiful of all flowering trees. Even in dormancy, it has a lovely spreading form with grayish-black bark and an airy, open center and sky-reaching branches. In late winter or early spring, magnificent pairs of pink blossoms hurriedly bloom ahead of the more reticent leaves. When the clusters of two-inch flowers are just about spent, fresh green foliage emerges and clothes the bare limbs with six-inch, oval-shaped, somewhat serrated leaves. In summer, flattened velvety fruits resembling small peaches dangle from the spreading branches. The fruits shrivel and split in the late-summer heat, revealing pitted husks that contain hidden treasures of sweet, crunchy almond kernels ready for fall harvest. For optimum growth and fruit production, Almond trees prefer hot, dry summers and cool winters, but they do not tolerate extended periods of drought. When the trees are budded, they do not withstand blustery winds. Young trees are frost-tender and need protection, but once mature, they tolerate temperatures down to 10 degrees Fahrenheit.

Family Name / Origin Rosaceae / E Mediterranean, N Africa

Bloom Period and Color Pink and white flowers bloom in early spring.

Average Height / Average On-Center Spacing 15 to 20 ft. / 20 ft.

When and How to Plant Plant in December or January from bare-root stock, or from 5- or 15-gallon containers in spring or summer, spacing 20 ft. apart. Build a watering basin 12 ft. in diameter and mulch with 2 in. of organic material such as humus or compost. See Planting Techniques, p. 398.

Climate & Culture

Preferred Zones 7–10

Sun Preference

Sun and Soil Preferences For optimum growth and production, plant in full sun in sandy loam, well-drained, salt-free soil with a pH of 5.5 to 6.5.

Moisture Requirements Soak deeply after planting. Water three times the first week; thereafter, adjust frequency and amount to climatic and growth conditions.

Fertilizing Fertilize in late winter with a food such as 16-4-8.

Pruning, Care, and Harvest Prune during dormancy for an open vase shape with three or four main branches. Remove any dead, damaged, or interfering wood.

Pests and Diseases Watch for peach leaf curl, almond leaf scorch, and shot hole fungus. Apply dormant spray, usually three times—in autumn when the leaves fall, in December, and just before the buds swell and show color. Few insects cause serious damage with the exception of ants, which penetrate the almond skins and hollow out the nuts. They can be controlled by applying to the tree trunks a sticky barrier paste that is available at your local nursery.

Our Personal Favorite

NAME	SPECIAL CHARACTERISTICS
P. d. 'All-in-one' (Patent #4304)	Number-one Almond tree for the home orchard / self-fruitful / requires 500 hrs of winter chill / soft-shelled / ripens in late September to early October

See p. 414 for other excellent varieties and for more information about Almond trees.

English Walnut

Juglans regia

*While driving in the Sacramento Valley, from Chico to Redding, we passed groves of Walnut trees with distinctively colored trunks. Up to two to three feet off the ground, they were a light buff color, but above three feet they were a charcoal color, almost as if each tree had stood in a shallow tub of bleach. Their two-toned trunks were really the grafting points of English Walnuts on top of California Black Walnut rootstock. For the home gardener, a well-tended Walnut tree is a handsome sight to behold with its sturdy trunk, elegant broad-leaf canopy, and spicy, aromatic foliage. In spring, chartreuse male catkins develop on previous-season's growth and inconspicuous flowers appear on the tips of new shoots, both on the same tree. Gentle spring breezes help pollinate the flowers and large purplish-bronze pinnate leaves emerge. As the foliage matures, it provides a rich reddish-green background for ripening oval-shaped nuts encased in green husks. Walnut trees do not tolerate prolonged periods of drought, and high temperatures sunburn the nuts. During dormancy, Walnuts withstand prevailing winds and sub-zero temperatures, but once the buds show color, freezing temperatures will destroy the set. **Note:** Please refer to p. 415 for more words of caution about Walnut trees.*

Family Name / Origin Juglandaceae / SE Europe, China

Bloom Period and Color Catkins appear in early spring.

Average Height / Average On-Center Spacing
30 to 50 ft. / 30 ft.

When and How to Plant Plant in December or January from bare-root stock, or plant in spring after the last frost from 15-gallon containers, spacing 40 to 50 ft. apart. Dig a planting pit deep enough to accommodate the long taproot, but shallow enough that the tree is higher than it was in its original container. Construct a watering basin 12 to 15 ft. in diameter and mulch with 2 in. of organic material such as humus or compost. See Planting Techniques, p. 398.

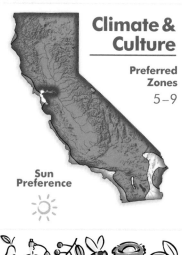

Climate & Culture

Preferred Zones
5–9

Sun Preference

Sun and Soil Preferences For optimum growth and production, plant in full sun in deep, well-drained loam soil, pH 6.5 to 7.0.

Moisture Requirements Soak deeply after planting. Water three times the first week; thereafter, adjust frequency and amount to climatic and growth conditions. Water slowly and more frequently during summer. Since its roots spread out over $1\frac{1}{2}$ times the canopy area, make sure that area is watered, but do not water within 4 ft. of the trunk. Give the trees a long soak (four to six hours) two weeks before harvest.

Fertilizing Fertilize twice a year, once in spring when the buds form and again in fall just before harvest, with a complete granular food such as 16-4-8. Broadcast over the root area, but do not make contact with the trunk.

Pruning, Care, and Harvest Prune young trees in early spring, right after the buds swell. See p. 415 for detailed Pruning and Harvesting information.

Pests and Diseases Their spread averages 40 to 50 ft., so do not plant English Walnuts too close to structures, curbs, foundations, and paved walkways. If you plant lawns or flower beds too close to their trunks, the excess moisture may lead to water mold fungi and crown rot. They are also susceptible to aphids and walnut husk fly. If the tree is mature and the infestation is extensive, contact a licensed pest control advisor for appropriate insecticidal remedies.

See p. 415 for excellent varieties.

Macadamia Nut
Macadamia tetraphylla

While visiting the island of Hawaii, we oohed and aahed over the tropical wonders, from cascading Phalaenopsis Orchids to giant Jak fruit. One of the highlights of our tour was an off-the-beaten-track Macadamia plantation in Honokaa. The magnificent thirty- to forty-foot trees were handsome enough to be ornamentals. Their immature pinkish-red branchlets contrasted beautifully with older, darker, thicker limbs. The glossy, leathery leaves were dark green, prickly, and serrated, forming a dense canopy of shade. In late winter or early spring, pendulous spikes of pink-blushed flowers precede clusters of green hard-shelled nuts that hang like oversized grapes. By late autumn or early winter, the nuts ripen and fall to the ground. It must have taken patience, time, and brute strength for that first person to discover the crisp, rich, creamy-white treasure inside the hard shell. And Macadamias do bear delicious, meaty nuts . . . but just consider that a bonus. With proper pruning, they can fit into almost any landscape plan as a round bush, tall upright tree, and even hedging. Ideal growing locations are one to ten miles inland from coastal areas, away from damaging salt spray and frost. Protect young trees from hot, dry winds, drought, and sun damage; once established, with adequate moisture and humidity Macadamias survive high heat. See p. 415 for instructions on how to prepare Macadamia nuts for eating.

Family Name / Origin Proteaceae / Australia

Bloom Period and Color Pinkish-white flowers bloom in early spring.

Average Height / Average On-Center Spacing
15 to 30 ft. / 20 ft.

When and How to Plant Plant in spring from 5- or 15-gallon containers, spacing 20 ft. apart. Construct a watering basin 10 ft. in diameter and mulch with 2 in. of organic material such as humus or compost. See Planting Techniques, p. 398.

Sun and Soil Preferences For optimum growth and production, plant in full sun in deep, fertile, well-drained soil with a pH of 6.5 to 7.0.

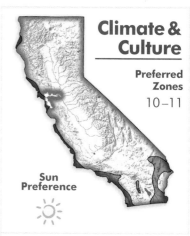

Climate & Culture

Preferred Zones
10–11

Sun Preference

Moisture Requirements Soak deeply after planting. Water three times the first week; thereafter, adjust frequency and amount to climatic and growth conditions. Although mature trees tolerate some drought, they produce best with regular irrigation.

Fertilizing Fertilize in late winter or early spring with a complete granular food such as 6-10-4. Fertilize newly planted trees lightly for six months with a granular food such as 16-4-8.

Pruning, Care, and Harvest Early pruning is necessary to develop a central leader with strong lateral branches that begin 3 to 4 ft. above the ground. Macadamia trees begin producing in three to five years, and many live over 100 years. In fact, the two earliest trees introduced to California in 1879, at the University of California Berkeley, are still bearing fruit. A reasonably healthy tree will produce about 30 to 50 pounds at ten years of age. Do not shake the tree to harvest its nuts because that causes immature nuts to fall. When they are ripe, they will naturally drop. To find implements developed especially for cracking the cement-hard Macadamia shells, contact the California Macadamia Society.

Pests and Diseases Macadamias are resistant to avocado root rot fungus and have few serious insect problems with the exception of mealybugs, aphids, ants, thrips, and scale, all of which can be controlled with Neem oil.

See p. 416 for excellent Macadamia selections.

Pecans

Carya illinoinensis

Our next-door neighbor has a garden that is large enough to sustain five graceful sixty-foot Pecan trees. In the spring and summer months, their branches are dappled with light- to deep-green compound leaves composed of eight to ten pairs of narrow lance-shaped leaflets. Their billowy canopies shade his entire yard, creating a cool oasis in the middle of a sizzling summer day. By early fall, elongated nuts hang in clusters, providing food for our resident chattering squirrels and squawking jays. Since jays lack the gnawing powers of their furry neighbors, they cleverly soar high above our road and drop their precious cargo so that the force of the fall cracks the hard outer shells. After a successful drop, life becomes a pecan buffet for our jays. By winter, the autumn leaves have long gone, and we appreciate the roughly fissured charcoal-gray bark of the multiple trunks, still regal in their barren simplicity. While Pecan trees do well in mild-summer climates, their yield is not as fruitful as in areas where the summers are long and hot with warm nights, such as parts of the Sacramento and San Joaquin Valleys. Even in desert areas, Pecan trees are very resistant to high temperatures (but do not withstand drought). When dormant, they withstand cold temperatures as low as -10 degrees Fahrenheit and blustery winds.

Family Name / Origin Juglandaceae / Iowa, Indiana, south to Texas and Mexico

Bloom Period and Color Greenish-white flowers bloom in early spring.

Average Height / Average On-Center Spacing 30 to 60 ft. / 50 ft.

When and How to Plant Plant in December or January from bare-root stock, or in spring or summer from 5- or 15-gallon containers, spacing 50 ft. apart. After planting, head back to 30 in. above the ground. Build watering basin 10 ft. in diameter and mulch with 2 in. of organic material such as humus or compost. See Planting Techniques, p. 398.

Climate & Culture

Preferred Zones 5–9

Sun Preference

Sun and Soil Preferences For optimum growth and production, plant in full sun in well-drained loam soil, pH 6.5 to 7.0.

Moisture Requirements Soak deeply after planting. Water three times the first week; thereafter, adjust to climatic and growth conditions.

Fertilizing After the first year, fertilize in late winter with a complete granular food such as 16-4-8.

Pruning, Care, and Harvest Prune lightly for shape, to remove crossing or damaged branches, and to retain strong limbs and fruiting wood. Many varieties produce better with a cross-pollinator. Plant two or more varieties that have similar pollen release and receptivity periods. When the hulls lose color and start to split, knock or shake the nuts to the ground. Hull them, dry them, remove the nutmeats, and store in air-tight containers in the freezer.

Pests and Diseases Few serious diseases affect Pecan trees, except that sucking insects such as aphids may appear in spring. If aphid infestation persists, release lady beetles as a beneficial control.

Our Personal Favorite

NAME	SPECIAL CHARACTERISTICS
C. i. 'Mahan'	Nuts are very large with a rich flavor / bears heavily as a young tree / good for home shade / prefers arid climates / ripens in November / does well in mild-winter areas

See p. 416 for another excellent Pecan variety.

Pistachio

Pistacia vera 'Kerman'

These wide-spreading twenty- to thirty-foot trees are covered with pale- to moss-green pairs of leaflets on compound leaves that turn red and gold in fall. After waking from winter dormancy, male trees bear red flowers and female trees bear white blossoms. Around April, spring winds carry pollen from male to female flowers, and soon suspended clusters of rose-colored husks ripen in the summer sun. By mid-September to October, the nuts are ready to be shaken from their sheltering branches, their hulls removed within twenty-four hours of harvest to prevent stained shells, then dried in the sun until their chartreuse or yellow kernels are crisp. If you do not live in an area where the summers are hot and dry and the winters are moderately cold with at least 1000 hours of chill below 45 degrees Fahrenheit, plant a Pistachio tree as an ornamental instead of a nut-bearing specimen. Desiccating winds, late spring frosts, and heavy spring rains interfere with pollination and reduce crop set. Prolonged summer rain and high humidity near harvest time may damage the quality of the nuts. For optimum production, Pistachios need arid conditions and extended periods of heat, but when dormant they can withstand cold winds and chilling temperatures down to 15 degrees Fahrenheit. See p. 416 for a bit of California agricultural history and a description of another Pistachio variety.

Family Name / Origin Anacardiaceae / W Asia, Middle East

Bloom Period and Color Red or white flowers appear in early spring.

Average Height / Average On-Center Spacing 15 to 30 ft. / 15 to 20 ft.

When and How to Plant Plant in December or January from bare-root stock, or in spring after the last frost from 5- or 15-gallon containers, spacing 15 to 20 ft. apart. Build a watering basin 10 to 15 ft. in diameter and mulch with 2 in. of organic material such as humus or compost. At least one male pollinator tree is needed for every ten female trees since Pistachios are dioecious (male and female flowers are borne on separate trees); if space is limited, graft a male branch onto a female tree. See Planting Techniques, p. 398.

Climate & Culture

Preferred Zones
10–11

Sun Preference

Sun and Soil Preferences Although they can grow in alkaline, saline, or high-lime soils, for optimum growth and production plant in full sun in deep, fertile, well-drained soil with a pH of 6.5 to 7.0.

Moisture Requirements Soak deeply after planting. Water three times the first week; thereafter, adjust frequency and amount to climatic and growth conditions. Water more frequently during development of the nuts from June to August, stop in mid-August to promote ripening, and resume watering after the harvest.

Fertilizing Fertilize in late winter with a complete granular food such as 16-4-8.

Pruning, Care, and Harvest Prune according to a modified leader system with well-spaced lateral branches. See p. 416 for more information on this system. Pistachio trees are alternate bearing, meaning they produce heavily one year and little or none the next. Once fully mature, at about eight years, they can bear for 600 years or more if given proper care!

Pests and Diseases Most serious disease and insect problems are best resolved with preventative measures—avoid root rot by making sure the trees are not in standing water; do not plant near carriers of Verticillium wilt like Strawberries or Melons; and wash off sucking insects like aphids with a strong stream of water.

See p. 416 for excellent Macadamia selections.

Palms *for California*

The lure of lush tropical landscapes in Hawaii, Bali, and other exotic locales is the stuff dreams are made of, and universally appealing for those of us who do not live in such places. Most people associate the flamboyant and contrasting silhouettes of Palms with the tropics. Langorous landscapes of swaying Palms are synonymous with that South Seas island atmosphere. This is because the majority of the world's 2800 Palm species are found in tropical and subtropical regions, although their natural range is from as far north as Southern Europe to as far south as the North Island of New Zealand.

Princes in the Landscape

Palms are regarded as the "princes" of plants. In fact, the noted Swedish botanist and founder of the modern binominal system of nomenclature, Carl von Linnaeus, labeled them "Principes." Following his lead, the members of the Palm Society have named their quarterly journal *Principes.*

California has many areas that are ideal for the culture of Palms. Rather than describe all Palm species, we have chosen those that behave themselves in average home landscapes with temperate climates—not the 150-foot "Paul Bunyan" varieties or the vining or twelve-inch miniature types.

Distinctive Features of Palms

Palms are fibrous monocotyledons, members of the Palmae family of plants, which makes their appearance easily recognizable. We have also included the unrelated Sago Palm, a Cycad, because of its similar appearance.

Superficially these plants may all seem to look alike because many have clustering or clumping trunks with stalks of long evergreen fronds. On closer inspection you can see there are differences. Palms can be categorized according to frond shape: the fan-frond, also called palmate, like the Lady Palm, and the feather-frond or pinnate, like the Pygmy Date. Palmate fronds are round or semicircular in outline, while pinnate fronds are linear or oblong with segments arranged like the pattern of a feather. Although Sagos are a unique group of plants that form seed-bearing cones rather than flowers, they have evergreen pinnate fronds.

Although Palms are usually used in garden designs for their form rather than color, there are many Palms with bright fruits such

as the stranded clusters of ruby-red jewels on the Fishtail Palm, the brownish-orange fruits of the Mediterranean Fan Palm, and the bright-red, egg-shaped seeds of the Sago Palm.

Palms are monocots, which means they lack a main taproot. Instead, Palms grow fibrous, adventitious roots from the trunk bases. They do not produce successive layers of growth in their trunks or stem; their trunks enlarge over time because their tissues expand, not because of the new wood development. This is why injuries to the trunk should be avoided—such damage is permanent and cannot be repaired.

Care for Your Palms

Since Palms are primarily surface feeders, they need regular supplies of moisture and soil nutrients. They do well on 3-1-3 or 3-1-2 food. Most Palms prefer frequent deep irrigation, although some, like the Mediterranean Fan Palm, are drought-resistant.

Since Palms lack a deep root system, they can be moved relatively easily and transplanted successfully as long as a planting hole has been prepared in advance and the trunks are buried a little deeper than before. They may be transplanted any time of the year, but the warm spring or summer months are best since root growth is highest during those months.

Once a Palm is established, use a pruning saw to cut off dead or damaged leaf stalks and make sure the cuts are flush with the trunk. Mulching is beneficial since it conserves water, stabilizes root zone temperatures, adds nutrients, and improves the soil's porosity and water infiltration. Lawns, ground covers, and weeds should be kept away from Palm trunks because they compete for water and nutrients and increase the danger of damage from mowers and weed-whackers.

Tropical Magic for the Landscape

Smaller Palms such as the Fishtail, the Mediterranean Fan, and Pygmy Date Palms normally grow only ten to twenty-five feet tall and are ideally suited for average-size yards. Others, like the Lady Palm and Sago Palm, are also excellent on the patio in containers or near the house. Palms have great value for use near swimming pools or other bodies of water because they rarely drop fronds or other litter. Their graceful foliage is beautiful when silhouetted by back lighting. Palms play a variety of roles in the landscape that few other plants can duplicate. Whether indoors or out, sun or shade, coastal to interior areas, there are species to fill many landscape situations. All Palms cast a spell of tropical magic.

Fishtail Palm

Caryota mitis

While on a leisurely stroll through Australia's magnificent Royal Botanic Gardens in Sydney, we came upon an impressive stand of very different-looking fifteen-foot palm trees. Against the heart-stopping panoramic view of Sydney Harbor and Opera House stood multitrunked Fishtail Palms with a thicket of sucker growths at their bases, giving a lush, full appearance. Their eight-foot-long bipinnate fronds were further divided into distinctive wedge-shaped and feathered leaflets. The glossy, dark-green fronds provided a verdant canvas against which long, necklace-like strands of silvery-green seeds hung in clusters of fifty or more beaded strings. The seeds ripen into stunning ruby-red marbles throughout the year. Once mature, the trees die, but this takes quite a long time, about thirty years. Although they are monocarpic palms, meaning they die after fruiting, it is more accurate to describe each stem as mono-carpic. Flowering panicles first appear near the top of the palm and open successively downward. When the last set of fruit matures, the entire stem dies, but not before it is replaced by a new basal sucker. Fishtail Palms need sheltered, humid environments and dislike drought, dust, or dry winds. They prefer warm weather with adequate moisture, but are surprisingly tolerant of cold temperatures down to 30 degrees Fahrenheit for short periods of time.

Family Name / Origin Palmae / S China

Mature Size 10 to 20 ft. tall (clumping)

When and How to Plant Plant in spring from 5- or 15-gallon or specimen-size containers; plant singly or group in clusters of three to five. Construct a watering basin twice the diameter of the original container and mulch with 2 in. of humus or compost. For additional information, see Planting Techniques, p. 398.

Sun and Soil Preferences Fishtail Palms require partial shade outdoors and medium to high light levels indoors. Plant in rich, well-drained soil with a pH of 6.0 to 6.5.

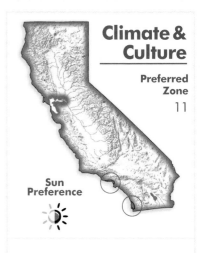

Climate & Culture

Preferred Zone

11

Sun Preference

Moisture Requirements Immediately after planting, soak deeply and thoroughly. Water three times the first week; thereafter, adjust watering frequency and amount according to weather and growth conditions.

Fertilizing Fertilize every other month during the growth cycle, spring through summer, with a complete granular palm food such as 6-3-6.

Pruning and Care Unless the fronds are thinned, the continual growth of suckers will cause the development of dense foliage from the tops to the bottoms of the clumps. Either form—thinned or left natural—is stunning, but the leaf outlines do not stand out unless some fronds are removed. Propagate by division of suckers or from seed, which takes about four to six months to germinate. Wear protective gloves and clothing when handling the fruit; the fibrous flesh contains caustic crystals of calcium oxalate that will irritate skin and mucous membranes. And never, ever eat the fruit unless you have the cast-iron stomach of a Cassowary bird, one of the few feathered creatures whose digestive systems are uniquely adapted to the caustic fruit.

Pests and Diseases Few diseases or insects seriously affect Fishtail Palms, with the exception of leaf spots caused by fungus and infestations of spider mites and scale. Consult your local University of California Cooperative Extension for recommendations of fungicides appropriate for your area. For insect control, use Neem oil or systemic insecticidal granules.

Companion Plantings and Design Ideal companion plants are Victorian Box, Gold Dust Plant, Azalea, Camellia, and Heavenly Bamboo.

Lady Palm

Rhapis excelsa

Beneath the protective shade of our Cork Oak and Mulberry Trees are two R. excelsa plants, commonly called Lady Palms. The common name was probably given to them because of their small stature and graceful appearance. These are multistemmed fan palms that form dense thickets of light- to rich-green fronds from the base of each plant. With age, tan fibers weaving around the five- to eight-foot trunks become a dark charcoal color. The stiff, glossy leaves are deeply divided and have five to eight wide-spread segments that resemble fingers on a hand. In summer, tiny spikes of creamy flowers and greenish-yellow blossoms appear on separate male and female plants near the tops of their canes and among their lower leaves; when pollinated, they form clusters of small berries, each berry containing a single seed. With their beautifully textured trunks and shimmering palmate leaves, they are among the most popular of dwarf palms. Their elegant silhouettes can create a soothing rainforest atmosphere in a garden on hot summer days. They can be grown indoors if placed in an area of medium to bright light. Although tolerant of short bouts of freezing temperatures and full sun, they prefer partial shade and temperate areas protected from prevailing winds and intense heat.

Family Name / Origin Palmae / S China

Mature Size 5 to 8 ft. tall (clumping)

When and How to Plant Plant in spring or summer from 1-, 5-, or 15-gallon or specimen-size containers; plant individually or in clusters of three, spaced 2 to 3 ft. apart. Construct a watering basin twice the diameter of the combined rootballs (three times the diameter of the rootball if planted individually), and mulch with 2 in. of humus or compost. For additional information, see Planting Techniques, p. 398.

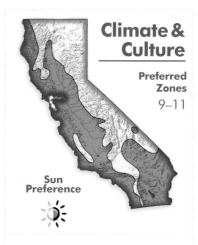

Climate & Culture

Preferred Zones
9–11

Sun Preference

Sun and Soil Preferences Although Lady Palms tolerate full sun, their foliage coloration will fade or burn. For beautiful deep-green hues, plant in partial shade protected from the harsh midday sun, in well-drained loam soil with a pH of 6.5 to 7.0.

Moisture Requirements Soak thoroughly after planting. Water three times the first week; thereafter, adjust frequency and amount according to weather and growth conditions. Since Lady Palms are not drought tolerant, they require regular watering.

Fertilizing Every other month during the growth cycle, fertilize with a complete granular palm food such as 6-3-6.

Pruning and Care Prune for shape and appearance by thinning out some of the crowded trunks to create a more artistic silhouette. Remove dead or damaged fronds. Since seedling plants grow very slowly, division by clumps is the more popular method of propagation. Lady Palm's slow growth is an advantage when container grown, because they can remain in the same pots for years without replanting.

Pests and Diseases Few outdoor diseases or insects seriously affect Lady Palms, but indoors they are susceptible to occasional infestations of mealybugs and spider mites. Treat with Neem oil or systemic insecticidal granules.

Companion Plantings and Design Clivia Lilies, English Ivy, and Variegated Cast-Iron Plant are good companion plants. The compact size and dense habit of Lady Palms make them ideal for foundation planting, as hedges, as focal points for small gardens, and in container plantings for patios or decks. For formal or exotic cut-flower arrangements, use some of their stems as dramatic greenery accents.

Mediterranean Fan Palm

Chamaerops humilis

Few springtime experiences are as pleasant as strolling along La Promenade des Anglais overlooking Nice's sparkling Cote D'Azur. With the warmth of the sun cooled by gentle sea breezes, outdoor cafes filling the air with delicious aromas, bright red-tiled roofs splashing the hillsides, and elegant hotels landscaped with exotics befitting a tropical paradise, it is easy to understand why we never wanted to leave the south of France. Whenever we see a Mediterranean Fan Palm, it carries us back to Nice, where they flourished along the promenade. These are low-growing clustering palms with dark, shaggy fibers covering graceful, curved trunks. Their stiff olive-green or blue-gray fronds are deeply divided like the ribs of a fan, eighteen inches long, segmented, and split at the top. They are dioecious, meaning there are male and female plants and both are needed to pollinate. The lightly perfumed male flowers are yellow and form in thick, small panicles, while the female flowers are green, sparse, and stubby, and when pollinated produce shiny, brownish-orange fruits similar to dates that make treats for wildlife. Although best suited to temperate regions, they are one of the hardiest of all palms, enduring temperatures down to 15 degrees Fahrenheit, as well as drought, hot sun if adequate moisture is provided, and wind and salt spray from the seacoast.

Family Name / Origin Palmae / S Europe

Mature Size 8 to 15 ft. (clumping)

When and How to Plant Plant from spring to fall from 5- or 15-gallon or specimen-size containers, spacing them 15 to 20 ft. apart. Build a watering basin three times the diameter of the rootball and mulch with 2 in. of humus or compost. For more information, see Planting Techniques, p. 398.

Sun and Soil Preferences Mediterranean Fan Palms require full sun or partial shade and rich, well-drained soil with a pH of 6.5 to 7.0.

Moisture Requirements Immediately after planting, soak deeply and thoroughly. Water three times the first week; thereafter, adjust the frequency and amount according to weather and growth conditions. Keep in mind that they need plenty of water.

Fertilizing Fertilize every other month, March through October, with a complete granular palm food such as 6-3-6.

Pruning and Care Remove the oldest fronds to expose the trunk structure and maintain a tidy appearance. Be cautious when handling Mediterranean Fan Palms because they are armed with very sharp, straight or hooked spines along their frond stalks. Propagate by seed or division. These slow-growing palms take many years to reach a respectable size.

Pests and Diseases Few diseases or insects seriously affect Mediterranean Fan Palms, with the exceptions of leaf spots caused by fungus and infestations of spider mites and scale. Consult your local University of California Cooperative Extension for recommendations of fungicides appropriate for your area. For insect control, use Neem oil.

Companion Plantings and Design Ideal companion plants are Pink Indian Hawthorn, Golden Mirror Plant, and Bougainvilleas.

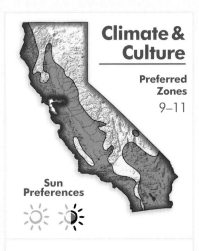

Climate & Culture

Preferred Zones
9–11

Sun Preferences

Our Personal Favorite

NAME	SPECIAL CHARACTERISTICS
C. excelsa (syn. *Trachycarpus fortunei*)	Commonly known as Hemp Palm / has a solitary, straight trunk

Pygmy Date Palm

Phoenix roebelenii

On our way to Australia's Great Barrier Reef, we stopped off at Port Douglas and visited the Tropical Rainforest Habitat, a wildlife park with eighty-five species of endemic birds and animals such as Kookaburras, Cassowaries, King Parrots, Rainbow Lorikeets, Koalas, Kangaroos, and Platypus. Even if these fabulous creatures of nature were not present, you would want to stroll around to see all the stunning tropical plants. Along one of the bird sanctuary pools was a diminutive stand of P. roebelenii, graceful solitary-trunked palms ranging in height from six to ten feet. These are the smallest of the Phoenix palms, but we think they are the most elegant. With slender trunks and compactly mounded crowns of arching gossamer leaves, we wonder why this palm was burdened with the mundane name Pygmy Date Palm. The four-foot pastel-green leaves are lightweight and soft textured and accompanied by evenly spaced darker-green leaflets that glisten in the sunshine. Small yellow flowers grow in clusters; the spent flowers are followed by fruits. Despite their delicate appearance, established Pygmy Date Palms withstand short periods of drought, wind, and cold temperatures down to freezing, and tolerate heat as long as there is adequate moisture. If you have a bright spot with sufficient humidity, they will also grow indoors.

Family Name / Origin Palmae / Laos

Mature Size 4 to 10 ft. tall (single trunk)

When and How to Plant Plant in spring or summer from 5- or 15-gallon or specimen-size containers; plant individually or in groups of three, spaced 2 ft. apart. Build a watering basin twice the diameter of the combined rootballs if planting in a group, or three times the diameter of the rootball if planted individually. Mulch with 2 in. of humus or compost. See Planting Techniques, p. 398.

Sun and Soil Preferences Pygmy Date Palms look their best when in full sun or partial shade along coastal areas, and complete shade for inland regions. They prefer rich, well-drained soil with a pH of 6.0 to 7.0.

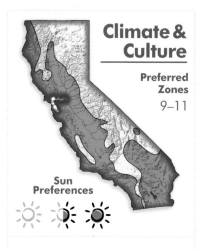

Climate & Culture

Preferred Zones
9–11

Sun Preferences

Moisture Requirements Immediately after planting, soak deeply and thoroughly. Water three times the first week; thereafter, adjust the frequency and amount according to weather and growth conditions. Since they are native to tropical rain forests, they are water lovers.

Fertilizing Fertilize every other month from March to October with a complete granular palm food such as 6-3-6.

Pruning and Care Prune only to remove dead fronds. Pygmy Date Palms are dioecious and need both male and female plants for pollination and seed production. After sowing, seeds need three months to germinate. The fruits, small black egg-shaped drupes, are edible, but they are not very palatable since they only have very thin layers of flesh.

Pests and Diseases Few diseases seriously affect Pygmy Date Palms, but they are susceptible to occasional infestations of spider mites and mealybugs. For insect control, use Neem oil or horticultural oil, following label instructions.

Companion Plantings and Design Ideal companion plants are Sago Palms, Japanese Mock Orange, and Shore Junipers. In our landscape designs, we use them in groupings of two or three as a focal silhouette in smaller gardens, as foundation plantings, or beside a swimming pool or pond. Since they mind their manners in small spaces, they make ideal container plants on a patio or deck, or along a walkway, where their lacy form and elegant detail can be fully appreciated.

Sago Palm
Cycas revoluta

After almost forty years of marriage, two children, and eight moves, we have collected
a lot of baggage and what I (Bruce) call "stuff." I do not regret the marriage and
children—as for the excess "stuff," if I include all the plant material that we have dug
up and transplanted during our nomadic life, well, I am glad we collected and kept
that too. Whenever I tend to these "heritage" plants, they remind me of their former
owners, close friends and family. Decades ago our Sago Palms were tiny pups, growing
from the bases of two stately Sagos in the atrium garden of my parents' home. Now
that the pups have matured into four-foot adults, I am anxiously awaiting to see
which ones will become the male pollen-bearing "cone-heads" and which will become
the female seed-bearing "dome-heads." Since they live for a hundred years or more,
perhaps our children and grandchildren will want to inherit some of them, as a living
tie to us and to my parents. Young Sago Palms are single-trunked, but with age they
can branch out into multiple trunks. Their feathery pinnate fronds are bluish green
when immature; once mature, they crown the fibrous brown trunk with four-foot
fronds that become a rich dark-green color. Under ideal conditions, a single plant
may have over a hundred stiff, decorative leaves.

Family Name / Origin Cycadaceae / S Japan

Mature Size 4 to 6 ft. tall (clumping)

When and How to Plant Plant any time of the
year in mild climate areas or in spring after the
last frost, from 1-, 5-, or 15-gallon or specimen
size containers and use them singly or in groups of
three. Construct a watering basin three times the
diameter of the original container and mulch with
2 in. of humus or compost. Sago Palms tolerate high
temperatures, drought, wind, and cold weather down
to freezing. Refer to Planting Techniques on p. 398 for
more information.

**Climate &
Culture**

Preferred
Zones
9–11

Sun
Preferences

Sun and Soil Preferences Sago Palms require full
sun or partial shade in deep, well-drained soil with a
pH of 6.5 to 7.0.

Moisture Requirements Immediately after planting, soak deeply and
thoroughly. Water three times the first week; thereafter, adjust the frequency
and amount according to weather and growth conditions.

Fertilizing Fertilize every other month during the growth cycle, with a
complete, granular palm food such as 6-3-6.

Pruning and Care Remove dead or damaged fronds as needed. Propagate from seed or detached offsets. When the female plant is pollinated,
red egg-shaped seeds will mature in a nest of furry, brown, twisted fronds.
When handling the seeds, use protective gloves because the seeds may
irritate the skin.

Pests and Diseases Few diseases or insects seriously affect Sago Palms,
with the exceptions of iron chlorosis and infestations of mealybugs and brown
soft scale. Apply chelated iron twice a year to correct iron deficiency. For
insect control, use Neem or horticultural oil, adhering to label directions.

Companion Plantings and Design Ideal companion plants are Rock
Cotoneaster, Dwarf Jade Plant, and Heavenly Bamboo. Sago Palms are
a geologically ancient genus, dating back to the times of dinosaurs—the
Jurassic Period. Prized by collectors and landscape contractors, Sago Palms'
handsome but slow-growing habit makes them a valuable addition to
Japanese-style landscapes, tropical gardens, courtyards, plazas, and
containers for porch or patio.

Perennials *for California*

Perennials are flowering or foliage plants with lifespans of more than two years; they are technically *herbaceous,* since they lack the woody stems and branches characteristic of shrubs and trees. Although some perennials will last only a few years, others survive for decades. Some have topgrowth that dies back every winter, but their roots live from year to year and send up new shoots each spring. Perennials give color and texture to gardens in shady spots, slopes, and meadows, and take center stage in casual cottage landscapes. Their abundant foliage and flowers bursting forth from intimate or expansive spaces produce a glorious potpourri of scents, textures, and colors.

Good Marriages Between Plants

Before planting, determine if your perennial selections are compatible with each other and with the site, considering light, soil, and water needs. Study the bloom times of perennials in your neighborhood and select plants that flower together, as well as those that flower when nothing else is in bloom. Shasta Daisies, Coreopsis, Delphiniums, and Yarrow bloom from late spring through the end of summer, while Daylilies blossom early, midseason, or late depending on the variety, and Candytuft bloom throughout the year in warm-winter regions. While some, like Coreopsis, bloom for up to twelve weeks, others, like Delphiniums, rebloom after their first flush of flowers are cut back and before they set seed. Clivia Lilies and Impatiens are perfect for shaded nooks and crannies under trees or shrubs, but if you need heat lovers and drought-tolerant types, Transvaal Daisies and Wallflowers are better choices.

Think about foliage as well as flowers, and mix bold-leaved Ivy Geraniums with finely-textured Marguerite Daisies. When designing a perennial border, start with tall, long-lived specimens such as Delphinium, Foxglove, and Daylilies, and stand them in the back. To support their taller neighbors and peek over their tinier friends, Lily of the Nile, Coreopsis, and Shasta Daisies are great fillers for the middle. Towards the front, plant groundhuggers like Candytuft, Ivy Geraniums, or Impatiens. Near ponds, a tropical stand of thirsty Canna Lilies can effectively show off

their lush, bold foliage and burgeoning flowers of eye-popping reds, oranges, yellows, and pinks.

In most mild-winter western regions, October is the best time to plant perennials or to divide or take cuttings from established ones. Planting or propagating in autumn gives perennials a head-start over those that are planted in the spring.

Heirlooms and Cut Flowers

Part of the joy of gardening is being able to share your plants with others and, in turn, to receive plants from family and friends. Our Asakawa parents grow an Ivy Geranium variety called 'Rouletta' with magnificent semi-double white-and-magenta- striped clusters of blooms. They gave us some cuttings, and we think of them every time we pass the hanging basket brimming with its trailing foliage and blossoms. Gifts of plants from people who mean so much give a whole new meaning to the word "heirloom."

A drift of Daisies, Lilies, or Woolly Yarrow is not only a feast for our eyes, but the petals are perfect cushions for fluttering butterflies, whirring hummingbirds, and buzzing bees. Nectar- and berry-rich perennials are important food sources for your garden wildlife. Whether they are flowering or fruiting, we enjoy cutting them to use in colorful mixed bunches of flowers arranged loosely in a favorite vase or in formal, more elegant designs. From the ornate to the minimal, from hot, intense splashes of yellows, reds, oranges, magentas, and rusts to cool whites, delicate lavenders, pinks, salmons, and creams, perennials make excellent cut-flower arrangements suitable for any decor.

The Spice of Life

Perennials prove that "variety is the spice of life." They add color and texture for mass planting displays in meadow and woodland gardens, provide punctuation points for beds and borders, brighten pond and rock landscapes, nourish neighborhood wildlife, and beckon the outdoors in with fresh-flower arrangements. Whether you find them while treasure hunting at local nurseries or propagate them from seed, division, or cuttings, perennials serve as precious threads in your garden tapestry.

Blue Marguerite Daisy

Felicia amelloides

While on a winding bus trip toward the Cape of Good Hope in South Africa, we saw Blue Marguerite Daisies the color of the sky peeking over wind-eroded boulders perched precariously on steep cliffs overlooking the converging Indian and Atlantic Oceans. This was the famous Fynbos, one of the most biologically diverse regions on the face of this earth, where majestic Black Eagles, cuddly guinea pig–like Hyraxes, and fluttering butterflies share the magical land with the sprawling bushes of Blue Marguerite Daisies (named for Herr Felix, mayor of Regensburg on the Danube). These fast-growing perennials have elliptical-shaped, matte-green foliage and single blue-petaled, yellow-centered flowers balancing on extended wiry stems. Flowering is almost continuous, depending on the climate, but it occurs most definitely during early summer through fall. These plants require warm weather and frost-free areas; once established, they are drought and wind tolerant. To enhance appearance and floral display, however, make sure an even amount of soil moisture is available. In mass plantings they are spectacular, and they also make subtle container plants for patios and decks. You can cut them just before their petals unfurl for use in loose bouquets.

Family Name / Origin Compositae / Africa

Bloom Period and Color Blue flowers bloom in spring, summer, and fall.

Mature Height × Spread 3 ft. × 4 ft.

When and How to Plant Plant in spring after the threat of frost has passed, from 4-in. pots or 1-gallon containers, spacing 3 ft. apart. Construct a watering basin 3 ft. in diameter and mulch with 1 in. of organic material. See Planting Techniques, p. 398.

Sun and Soil Preferences *F. amelloides* prefers full sun and well-drained soil with a pH of 6.7 to 7.0.

Climate & Culture

Preferred Zones
9–11

Sun Preference

Moisture Requirements Soak deeply after planting. Water three times the first week; thereafter, adjust frequency and amount to climatic and growth conditions. Keep in mind that Felicias prefer occasional deep watering to frequent shallow watering.

Fertilizing Fertilize in early spring with a complete food, 6-10-4 or 12-55-6.

Pruning and Care Following their bloom cycle, prune to shape the plants, to lace out the dense growth, and to maximize the next flowering cycle. Pinch the plant back when it is only a few inches high by nipping off the tip of the main stem. Thereafter, pinch back the lateral growths a couple of times to develop a bushier, multibranched plant. Remember, the bushier the plant and the more numerous the lateral growth, the more profuse the production of flower buds. You also need to deadhead the flowers, because they do not fall off naturally.

Pests and Diseases Control snail and slugs with iron phosphate or "pick-and-squish." Aphids can be controlled with Neem oil or insecticidal soap.

Companion Plantings and Design They are best used in informal gardens such as in mixed borders, at edges of lawns, or in rock gardens. Ideal planting companions are Pink Indian Hawthorn, English Ivy, and Prostrate Natal Plum.

Our Personal Favorites

NAME	SPECIAL CHARACTERISTICS
Felicia amelloides 'Santa Anita'	Flowers much larger than those of the species
F. amelloides 'Alba'	White flowers

Candytuft

Iberis sempervirens

We like to use Candytuft as a rock garden accent. The shiny, verdant, linear foliage creates cushioned pockets of vegetation between the weathered stones. Candytuft is also effective when planted en masse as a foreground plant. During the warmth of spring and summer, these compact evergreens are completely masked by large, abundant, four-petaled, snow-white flowers arranged in multiple clusters of delicately scented blooms. In fact, that is how they came to be known as Candytuft, for their mounds of sweetly fragrant blossoms. Iberis is of Greek derivation, from Iberia, the ancient name for Spain, where several species grow wild. The pure-white flowers contrast beautifully with the dark-green foliage of most other plants. Keep in mind that these plants do not appreciate too much moisture. Although disease, insects, heat, and long periods of drought are not bothersome problems to Candytuft, they do not like too much shade, severe cold, or frigid winds. When used as cut flowers, they will last for five to six days as long as they are in a cool room.

Family Name / Origin Cruciferae / Iberia

Bloom Period and Color White flowers bloom in spring and summer.

Mature Height × Spread 6 to 10 in. × 10 in.

When and How to Plant Since growth is so slow, plant in the spring or summer from pony packs, color packs, or 4-in. or 1-gallon containers, spacing 8 to 12 in. apart. Construct a watering basin 1 ft. in diameter and mulch with ½ in. of organic material such as compost or humus. Also see p. 398.

Sun and Soil Preferences Plant in hot, sunny locations, preferably facing south. They prefer well-drained soil with a pH of 6.6 to 7.1.

Moisture Requirements Soak deeply after planting. During the first week, water every day; thereafter, adjust watering frequency and amount according to weather and growth conditions.

Fertilizing During the growing season, feed Candytufts monthly with a water-soluble fertilizer such as 12-55-6.

Pruning and Care To promote a tidy, compact appearance, prune back the foliage by a third immediately after the flowers are spent. Be diligent about removing the dead flower heads and you will be rewarded with a continuous and abundant supply of blooms.

Pests and Diseases There are no serious pest problems.

Companion Plantings and Design These low, semi-woody, densely-spreading mounds are terrific as edgings for raised beds, borders, pathways, and terrace margins, and as ground cover atop retaining walls, where they can meander shyly over the sides. We cut the flowers just as they are opening in the early morning and arrange them with bulb flowers such as Grape Hyacinth and Tulips.

Climate & Culture

Preferred Zones
9–11

Sun Preference

Our Personal Favorites

NAME	SPECIAL CHARACTERISTICS
Iberis amara	Annual / also known as Hyacinth-flowered Candytuft / fragrant white flowers develop into Hyacinth-like spikes
I. gibraltarica	Perennial / purplish flowers

Canna Lily

Canna × generalis

If you want a tropical garden, you must include an area where expansive beds of Cannas can display their lush, bold foliage and burgeoning flowers of eye-popping reds, oranges, yellows, and pinks. As long as there is no frost and water is abundant, these exotics add snap to an otherwise bland foliage border. In summer, their attractive foliage runs the color gamut from plain green, red, purple, and bronze to a rainbow of variegation. Spectacular four- to six-inch flowers spread their fiery hues from sturdy clumps of two- to eight-foot stalks. Canna × generalis, a hybrid not found in the wild, resembles ginger and banana plants in that it has what appear to be thick stalks but are actually tightly rolled leaves that emerge from surface rhizomes. Although the plants tolerate heat if sufficient humidity and moisture are present, they do not withstand drought; hot, dry winds; or severe cold. Cannas can be reproduced by severing the rhizomes from the parent plant, making sure each cut section has an eye that will produce new vegetation, and allowing the exposed sections to callous. Dust with sulfur as a preventative against fungus and insect damage, and then replant.

Family Name / Origin Cannaceae / South America

Bloom Period and Color Red, white, pink, yellow, or orange flowers bloom in spring and summer.

Mature Height × **Spread** 3 to 6 ft. (rhizotomaceous, clumping)

When and How to Plant Plant rhizomes in spring after the last frost from 1- or 5-gallon containers, spacing 1 to 2 ft. apart. Build a watering basin twice the diameter of the original container and mulch with 1 in. of organic material such as humus or compost. See Planting Techniques, p. 398.

Climate & Culture

Preferred Zones 9–11

Sun Preference

Sun and Soil Preferences Plant in full sun, in rich moisture-retaining soil that has a pH of 6.5 to 7.0.

Moisture Requirements With good drainage, it is almost impossible to overwater Canna Lilies.

Fertilizing Fertilize in early spring after the last frost with a complete food such as 6-10-4.

Pruning and Care To prevent seed formation and to encourage a longer flowering season, remove spent blooms. If you have freezing winter temperatures, prune to 6 to 8 in. in the fall and dig up the rhizomes; wipe them off, apply a dusting sulfur, and place them in dry peat. Maintain at a temperature of 45 to 50 F. in a dry, dark place with good air circulation, letting them rest for the winter. In temperate zones, allow Cannas to naturalize in your garden.

Pests and Diseases Few disease or insect problems affect these perennials, except for giant whitefly or snails during spring and summer. Control is easily managed by an application of insecticidal soap, Neem oil, or molluscicide.

Companion Plantings and Design Cannas show off best when massed as all-season accents beside a water garden. Their exotic looks are best set apart, so try not to squeeze them in tiny beds with more mundane Salvias, Ageratums, or Marigolds. Daylilies, Bearded Irises, and Birds of Paradise are suitable companions in a tropical setting.

Our Personal Favorite

NAME	SPECIAL CHARACTERISTICS
Canna × generalis 'Race Track Red'	A spectacular cultivar with a bright red-orange color

Clivia Lily
Clivia miniata

Along the side of our home leading to the backyard is a meandering brick pathway where the bent overhead branches of a California Pepper Tree, Fruiting Mulberry, and Victorian Box provide protection from the intense brightness of the sun. Their cool shadows are a haven for our thirty-four Clivia Lilies planted on a slope among trailing tendrils of English Ivy. In the springtime, umbels of apricot-orange, creamy yellow, and fiery carmine funnel-shaped flowers shoot up from thick, straplike, dark-green leaves. On stocky stems, these brilliant yellow-throated flower clusters emerge out of rhizomes with heavy, tangled surface roots. Blooming occurs over several weeks, after which clusters of large berrylike fruits form, ripen, and turn red or yellow. Clivias grow well in frost-free, temperate climates. They tolerate heat if planted in the shade and if there is sufficient humidity and soil moisture. Because their leaves are so thick and waxy, persistent breezes and short periods of drought are not too troublesome. Because they have surface roots, they dislike being disturbed. Propagate them by division after the bloom cycle.

Family Name / Origin Amaryllidaceae / South Africa

Bloom Period and Color Red, orange, or yellow flowers bloom in spring.

Mature Height × Spread 2 ft. (clumping)

When and How to Plant Plant anytime during the year, in shaded or dappled-sun locations, from 1- or 5-gallon containers, spacing 2 to 3 ft. apart. Although you can plant by seed, it will be slow to flower, about three to five years. Create a watering basin 2 ft. in diameter and mulch with 1 in. of organic material such as humus mulch or compost. See p. 398.

Climate & Culture

Preferred Zones
10–11

Sun Preferences

Sun and Soil Preferences Clivias prefer shade and well-drained soil with a slightly acidic pH of 6.6 to 7.0.

Moisture Requirements Immediately after planting, soak deeply and thoroughly. During the first week, water two to three times to settle the soil against the roots, and then adjust the frequency and amount according to weather and growth conditions. As a general rule, decrease watering in winter and increase in spring and summer.

Fertilizing Fertilize in late winter or early spring with a complete food such as 6-10-4.

Pruning and Care Remove the outer, older, yellowing leaves periodically.

Pests and Diseases Few diseases or insects affect these plants, with the exception of the shade- and moisture-loving snails and slugs. They can be easily controlled with molluscicide applications, or just handpick them in the early-morning hours.

Companion Plantings and Design Sharon enjoys cutting a single flowering or fruiting stem to use in a simple arrangement, adding just a few leaves as dramatic contrast. You can also tie several together just beneath the flower or berry heads and place them firmly in a water-soaked oasis to create a topiary-tree arrangement with a domed pompon shape.

Our Personal Favorite

NAME	SPECIAL CHARACTERISTICS
Clivia miniata 'Flame'	Commonly known as Flame Clivia Lily / one of the most brilliant red-orange varieties

Coreopsis
Coreopsis grandiflora

Whenever a novice gardener calls my (Bruce's) radio program and asks for an easy-to-grow, colorful perennial in an informal setting, I usually recommend Coreopsis. Linnaeus unfortunately named this genus Coreopsis from the Greek words koris, *meaning "lice or tick," and* opsis, *meaning "similarity," because of the seeds' resemblance to those obnoxious bugs—but the name is certainly an inaccurate description of these plants' cheerful beauty. Their smooth, lance-like, light-green leaves spring from rosette-shaped mounds, creating a vision of dense, feathery vegetation. Solitary, puffy, daisylike buds open into two-inch golden-yellow flowers with bright-orange centers, standing at attention on erect stems from early summer to mid-fall. Just be sure you harvest them when they are nearly open in the early morning—if you allow them to go to seed, mourning doves, scrub jays, robins, and other seed-eating birds will have a late-summer feast and help propagate your plants all over your yard and neighborhood. Since their flower stalks become long and thin, they are easily damaged and broken during strong winds and heavy rains. Once established, they are very drought tolerant and can even survive freezing temperatures—but if their roots stand in water, they will develop root rot. They are sun worshipers and love heat as long as there is adequate soil moisture.*

Family Name / Origin Compositae / Central and Southeastern North America

Bloom Period and Color Orange flowers bloom in spring and summer.

Mature Height × Spread 1 to 2 ft. × 1 ft.

When and How to Plant Plant in the spring from pony packs, color packs, 4-in. pots, or 1-gallon containers, spacing about 15 to 18 in. apart. Build a watering basin 1 ft. in diameter and mulch with ½ in. of organic material such as humus or compost. If planting in a pot, make sure the container has a diameter of at least 24 in. See p. 398.

Climate & Culture

Preferred Zones
7–11

Sun Preference

Sun and Soil Preferences Plant in full sun. If the soil is too rich, you will get more leaves but fewer flowers, so it is best to plant in loamy soil without too much organic material. They thrive in well-drained soil with a slightly acidic pH, 6.7 to 7.0.

Moisture Requirements Soak thoroughly after planting. Water in-ground plantings twice the first week; thereafter, adjust watering according to climatic and growth conditions. Water container plants every day during the first week; then decrease watering according to the plant's growth rate and the weather conditions.

Fertilizing Fertilize in early spring after the last frost when the tender leaves begin to sprout, with a 6-10-4 granular food.

Pruning and Care If you remove all the dead blooms regularly, you will be rewarded with a multitude of fresh blooms in the summer months. To slow the bloom cycle, prune back every few weeks beginning in mid-September.

Pests and Diseases Coreopsis is susceptible to several diseases and insects, but these pests are usually not life-threatening. The worst affliction is powdery mildew—Neem oil is a good remedy for mildew as well as insect infestations.

Companion Plantings and Design There are few colorful perennials as effective when planted in large masses at the edges of lawn areas, in country meadow gardens, as background for borders, and in patio containers. They also make excellent fillers in mixed bouquets. Ideal companion plants to surround Coreopsis are Shasta Daisies, Daylilies, and Nasturtiums.

Daylily

Hemerocallis × hybrids

The genus name Hemerocallis *comes from the Greek words* hemera, *meaning "day," and* kalo, *meaning "beautiful." Both the Greek and common names tell you these lovely blooms are short-lived, but there are always more buds eagerly waiting to open in your garden. The hybrids tend to have a longer bloom life. When we shop for hybrids, we look for those that have won awards from the American Daylily Society. The premier awards are the Stout Silver Medal, usually listed in catalogs as "ST"; Award of Merit, "AM"; and Lenington All-American Award, "LEN." From mounds of arching, narrow grasslike leaves emerge tall, flowering stalks whose color selections include astounding shades of cream, yellow, orange, red, pink, a deep maroon that is almost black, and many bicolored varieties. Daylilies are among the easiest evergreens to grow, requiring very little attention, and they offer gorgeous splashes of color throughout the spring and summer months. They make stunning floral arrangements. They are hardy in cold zones that dip down to 10 degrees Fahrenheit, and once established, their thick roots store water, making them drought tolerant for short periods of time. Their foliage will yellow and wither during extended times of drought, but they should rebound once moisture is restored. Providing there is adequate moisture, they do quite well in hot and windy locations.*

Family Name / Origin Liliaceae / E Asia

Bloom Period and Color Yellow, red, orange, pink or white flowers bloom in spring and summer.

Mature Height × **Spread** 2 to 3 ft. (clumping)

When and How to Plant Plant in late winter or early spring from 1-gallon containers, spacing 2 to 3 ft. apart. Construct a watering basin 1 to 2 ft. in diameter and mulch with 1 in. of organic material. Also see p. 398.

Sun and Soil Preferences Although Daylilies grow in full or partial sun or full shade, they prefer full sun in temperate areas. They appreciate deep, cool, fertile, moderately moist, loose-textured soil, pH 6.5 to 7.0.

Climate & Culture

Preferred Zones
8–11

Sun Preferences

Moisture Requirements Soak deeply after planting. Water three times the first week; thereafter, adjust frequency and amount according to weather and growth conditions.

Fertilizing Fertilize in early summer with a complete food such as 15-15-15.

Pruning and Care Harvest the flowers while they are still tightly budded but just beginning to show some color, and they will last as cut flowers for a week. Remove the stamens to avoid unsightly stains on your furniture or clothes.

Pests and Diseases Slugs and snails sometimes graze on the tender shoots. If damage is extensive, go on a snail- and slug-stomping expedition, or use a molluscicide.

Companion Plantings and Design As a landscape architect I (Bruce) use Daylilies in planting beds or borders, along meandering paths, at the edges of lawns or woodlands, among shrubs, as mass plantings on steep slopes, or reflected in nearby water gardens. Some companion suggestions for Daylilies are spring bulbs like Persian Buttercups and Freesias and annuals such as Ageratums and Phlox. Woolly Yarrow and Coreopsis are a wonderful combination to make an all-yellow area.

Our Personal Favorite

NAME	SPECIAL CHARACTERISTICS
Hemerocallis × hybrids 'Allegretto'	Extra-large, 6-in. flowers / orchid-colored, deepening to a rich wine hue in the flowers' throats

Delphinium

Delphinium elatum

When we hear the words "cottage garden," a vision comes to mind: a rustic wood-frame house surrounded by a white picket fence, front yard carpeted with sun-drenched color dominated by towering true-blue Delphiniums reaching for the sky. While you still have this vision of loveliness in your mind's eye, let us warn you that Delphiniums are not for people who want plants to thrive on benign neglect. Nor do they belong in regions where the summers are hot and dry and the winters are cold. If you live where the climate is cool and moist, such as the coastal areas of northwest California, and you equate landscape maintenance chores with pleasure, then Delphiniums are meant to be part of your garden. These hybrids have pale-green, eight-inch, handlike leaves with flower spikes occupying the top halves of straight, stiff stems. Each bloom can be four inches across and is packed together, forming tall, stately spires of dense florets. Delphiniums generally develop one main flower stem with small auxiliary stems that fill in the blank spaces, creating a massive summer show. After two or three years, Delphiniums need to be replaced with new plants. Be aware that all parts of Delphiniums are toxic, even seeds, so keep them away from young children.

Family Name / Origin Ranunculaceae / North America, Europe

Bloom Period and Color Although the flowers are most commonly dressed in blues and purples, they are also available in pink, lavender, magenta, red, and white; they bloom in summer and fall.

Mature Height × Spread 2 to 8 ft. × 2 to 4 ft.

When and How to Plant Plant in spring from color packs or 1-gallon containers, spacing 2 to 3 ft. apart. Build a watering basin 3 to 4 ft. in diameter and cover with 1 to 2 in. of organic material. See p. 398.

Sun and Soil Preferences They prefer full sun and well-drained fertile soil, pH 6.6 to 7.0.

Moisture Requirements Soak deeply after planting. Water three times the first week; thereafter, adjust watering according to weather and growth conditions.

Fertilizing Fertilize with water-soluble food, such as a 12-55-6, every two to three weeks during spring and summer months.

Pruning and Care To promote better air circulation and to strengthen the plant, thin out all but three or four stalks. Deadhead spent flowers just above the foliage to promote continuous blooms. When stems die back, prune them off, allowing new foliage to grow from the base.

Pests and Diseases Leaf miners, caterpillars, slugs, snails, and powdery mildew may attack. If damage is extensive, remove the infested leaves or stems and squish those obnoxious slugs and their hard-shell relatives.

Companion Plantings and Design Even though they require patient tending, Delphiniums are one of our favorites for background ornamentals in flower beds, mass plantings in a large setting such as a meadow garden, or cottage gardens. They combine well with Lilies of the Nile, Roses, Ivy Geraniums, Canna Lilies, and Dahlias.

Climate & Culture

Preferred Zones
5–11

Sun Preference

Our Personal Favorites

NAME	SPECIAL CHARACTERISTICS
Delphinium elatum 'Blue Jay'	Beautiful medium- to dark-blue flowers
D. elatum 'Percival'	White flowers with black centers

Foxglove
Digitalis purpurea

The genus name Digitalis *refers to the fingerlike shape of these biennial or perennial flowers; the common name does not mean a glove for a fox but a glove with the fingers cut off for little "folks"—or fairy gloves. Unfortunately, the handsome Digitalis is stuck with its all-too-precious common name, but at least its genus name is now known the world over as an effective heart medication—pardon the pun, but when planted on slopes in dappled shade, the attractive five-foot flowering spikes in pastels of pink, peach, yellow, and cream will steal your heart. They also come in shades of purple and red, and we use them as medium-height perennials in our terraced garden. They grow on alpine slopes and meadows in their natural habitats, so they are perfect for partial-shade or full-sun gardens. Their wrinkled leaves are rough-textured, covered with creamy hairs, and more numerous towards the base of the plants. Each trumpet-shaped flower faces downward, clustered together on one side on stout, erect spikes. They are perfect food sources for active hummingbirds and bees. They withstand cold and some wind, but they are thirsty plants and do not like drought, nor are they at their best in hot, dry weather. Since all parts of Foxglove are toxic, do not use if you have children or pets who like to chew on plants.*

Family Name / Origin Scrophulariaceae / Europe, W Asia

Bloom Period and Color Once in bloom, early spring to midsummer, there are six weeks of flowering enjoyment in purple, pink, white, rose, or yellow.

Mature Height × Spread 2 to 4 ft. × 2 ft.

When and How to Plant Plant in early spring from 4-in. pots or 1-gallon containers, spacing 18 in. apart. Build a watering basin 1 to 2 ft. in diameter and mulch with 1 in. of organic material. See p. 398.

Sun and Soil Preferences Plant in full sun or dappled shade in a well-drained acidic soil, rich in organic material, pH 6.5 to 6.8.

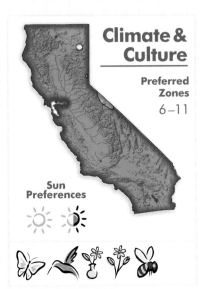

Climate & Culture

Preferred Zones
6–11

Sun Preferences

Moisture Requirements Soak deeply after planting. Water three times during the first week; thereafter, adjust frequency and amount according to climatic and growth conditions.

Fertilizing Fertilize in early spring with a complete flower food such as 6-10-4.

Pruning and Care If you snip off spent flowers, the energy will go into the plants, which will become more vigorous, increasing their rosettes of foliage; there will be a second bloom, but the spikes will be shorter with fewer flowers.

Pests and Diseases If you cut back any leaves damaged by snails and slugs, a flush of new, vital foliage will usually emerge. If you need more control than early-morning foot-stomping slime hunts, use a molluscicide.

Companion Plantings and Design Use as cut flowers, mass planting displays in meadow and woodland gardens, and colorful punctuation points for beds and borders. Mix with Phlox, Roses, Impatiens, Pink Indian Hawthorn, and Lily of the Nile.

Our Personal Favorites

NAME	SPECIAL CHARACTERISTICS
Digitalis purpurea 'Excelsior'	An annual Foxglove / many mixed colors / grows slightly shorter than the species
D. purpurea 'Campanulata'	Upper flowers unite to form large, cupped blooms with many segments

Impatiens

Impatiens walleriana

On the deck outside our dining room window are two hanging pots filled with
Impatiens. Even though there is a hummingbird feeder with homemade nectar nearby,
our "hummers" first dip their beaks into the throats of the Impatiens. In addition to
enjoying the sight of our resident hummers, we also appreciate the simple beauty of
the Impatiens' flowers tumbling over the pots. Their Violet-shaped single and double
flowers contrast nicely with their lance-shaped, fresh green leaves. Although the
flowers are slightly fragrant, they are more popular for their vibrant colors. The name
Impatiens truly refers to their impatience to germinate and grow: when their seed
capsules are barely touched, they explode, dispersing their seeds over a wide area. In
India, the juices are extracted from Impatiens balsamina and they are used to dye
fabrics in reds and yellows. Since they come from tropical habitats, Impatiens are not
frost hardy, nor do they tolerate drought or dry, blustery winds—but they withstand
heat if adequate moisture is provided. Cuttings from the mother plant establish so
easily that you can just stick them in the ground and most will root and grow.

Family Name / Origin Balsaminaceae / SE Africa

Bloom Period and Color Vibrant flowers of deep crimson, violet, pink, or speckled white bloom from spring to fall.

Mature Height × Spread 2 ft. × 3 ft.

When and How to Plant Plant in spring from pony packs, color packs, 4-in. pots, or 1-gallon containers, spacing 18 in. on center; or place single plants in 8-in. pots. Build a watering basin encompassing the planting area and mulch with 1 in. of organic material. Also see p. 398.

Climate & Culture

Preferred Zone
11

Sun Preferences

Sun and Soil Preferences Along coastal areas, they thrive in full sun, but as you move inland where it is hotter and drier, partial shade is best. Provide highly organic, well-drained soil, pH 6.5 to 7.0.

Moisture Requirements Immediately after planting, soak deeply and thoroughly. Water three times the first week; thereafter, water according to climatic and growth conditions.

Fertilizing Fertilize lightly once a month during the spring and summer seasons with a water-soluble food such as fish emulsion.

Pruning and Care For a more compact growth and abundant flower production, pinch back tip growth. Because established Impatiens have large root systems, they can be dug up and moved without too much trouble. If transplanting, provide plenty of water until their roots have a chance to re-establish.

Pests and Diseases They are relatively free from disease and insect infestations except for spider mites, snails, and slugs. These are not life-threatening problems, but if damage is extensive, snip off the affected foliage and fertilize to encourage new growth.

Companion Plantings and Design We recommend using Impatiens in sunny or shaded color beds, borders, window boxes, or containers on patios or decks. Camellias, Azaleas, and English Ivy are wonderful companions.

Our Personal Favorite

NAME	SPECIAL CHARACTERISTICS
Impatiens balsamina	Grows quickly to 12 to 18 in. tall/ produces clusters of colorful, 1/2 in., full flowers

Ivy Geranium

Pelargonium peltatum

Here's a perennial with an identity crisis. Is it a Geranium or is it a Pelargonium? Let's add to the confusion with the thought that although it is commonly known as Ivy Geranium, it belongs to the genus Pelargonium. The fact is, not all Pelargoniums are Ivy Geraniums, but all Ivy Geraniums are Pelargoniums. There are other geraniums that belong to the genus Geranium—the main difference between Geranium and Pelargonium is in their flowers. Pelargonium flowers have two irregular-shaped upper petals that are different in size and shape, and often in color, from the three lower ones. They also have nectar tubes at the base of each petal. Geranium flowers, on the other hand, have symmetrical petals. We selected the Ivy Geranium not to befuddle you, but because it adds such vibrant colors to summer gardens, and in frost-free areas it flowers from March to November. The flowers range in hue from lavender, pink, white, and red to veined purple and have star-shaped, bright-green leaves similar to Ivy foliage but with dark circular zones. If sufficient humidity and moisture are available, these perennials do well in most areas of California, withstanding heat, gentle breezes, and even short periods of drought—but they are not frost tolerant.

Family Name / Origin Geraniaceae / South Africa's Fynbos

Bloom Period and Color Red, pink, lavender, or white flowers bloom in summer.

Mature Height × Spread 8 to 12 in. (spreading)

When and How to Plant Plant in spring after last frost from color packs, 4-in. pots, or 1-gallon containers, spacing 18 in. on center. Construct a 12-in. watering basin and mulch with 1/2 in. of organic material. See Planting Techniques, p. 398.

Sun and Soil Preferences Full sun is best, but they will grow in partial shade. The soil should be well drained and have a pH between 6.0 and 7.0.

Climate & Culture

Preferred Zones 10–11

Sun Preferences

Moisture Requirements Soak deeply after planting. Water three times the first week; thereafter, water according to weather and growth conditions.

Fertilizing Fertilize from spring to fall with a liquid food, 16-4-2, once a month.

Pruning and Care Regularly deadhead spent blooms, including stalks, during the flowering cycle. Remove dead or yellowing foliage. To propagate by cuttings, take 5-in. stem sections, each including three nodes, in late summer. Make a slightly angled cut just under the bottom node and dip the end into rooting hormone. Cut off all leaves except the top one, and root in presoaked, medium-textured vermiculite. Place in a sheltered, shaded area. Do not water too much and roots will form in about two weeks. Transplant into containers with potting soil when a sufficient root system has developed.

Pests and Diseases Snails and slugs can be easily controlled with a molluscicide or by squishing underfoot.

Companion Plantings and Design Use Ivy Geranium in color baskets, windowboxes, terraces, balconies, or on trellises. Shasta Daisies, Lilies of the Nile, and Pink Indian Hawthorn are ideal companion plants.

Our Personal Favorites

NAME	SPECIAL CHARACTERISTICS
Pelargonium peltatum 'Galilee'	Pretty, double, rose-pink flowers
P. peltatum 'La France'	Semidouble, mauve-veined, white or purple flowers

Lily of the Nile

Agapanthus africanus

When I (Bruce) design a landscape, Lily of the Nile is one of my favorites to use as a foreground plant, in front of larger shrubs. With their dense fountain-like clumps of foliage and showy blue umbrella-shaped clusters of flowers, Lilies of the Nile resemble a river of blue against a sea of green. Depending on climate and variety, they bloom in late spring through early summer, and their small funnel-shaped flowers shoot up on leafless stalks at least one to three feet high. In addition to blue, their flowers come in hues of violet-blue and white. Their beauty is accentuated by fleshy tubular roots that surround dark-green, ribbonlike, thick leaves. Agapanthus comes from the Greek words meaning "flower of love" and I do love to see them in mass plantings near water or woodlands; as edging along a wall, fence, or driveway; in cut-flower gardens; as ground cover blanketing hilly, rocky mounds; or in containers on decks and patios. Once established, they withstand strong winds, temperatures slightly below freezing, and even short periods of drought, although they prefer slightly moist soils on dry slopes near the coast.

Family Name / Origin Liliaceae / South Africa

Bloom Period and Color Blue or white flowers bloom in summer.

Mature Height × Spread 18 in. (strap leaves)

When and How to Plant Plant in spring from 1-gallon containers, spacing 18 in. Construct a watering basin 1 ft. in diameter; mulch with 1 in. of organic material such as compost or humus. See p. 398.

Sun and Soil Preferences They prefer full-sun areas and well-drained soil, pH 6.5 to 7.0.

Moisture Requirements Soak deeply after planting. Water three times the first week; thereafter, water according to weather and growth conditions. They require minimal water in winter; water much more frequently in early spring and summer. Remember, in their native habitat they grow near streams and ponds.

Fertilizing Fertilize in spring with a complete granular food like 6-10-4.

Pruning and Care Pruning is unnecessary, but remove spent flowers, including the dried stalks and dead leaves. Propagation by division is best after the flowering cycle is completed in late summer or early fall. Mature plants produce young side shoots that can be removed and repotted as long as there are sufficient root structures. In about six to eight months the roots will have established themselves enough to replant in the ground; they will bloom in about two or three years.

Pests and Diseases Lilies of the Nile are not susceptible to pests except for snails and slugs, and a molluscicide or handpicking and foot-smashing methods easily control these slimy creatures.

Companion Plantings and Design Because of their large simultaneous blooms, they give an exotic look to fresh flower arrangements. Cut when one-third of the flowers on the cluster are open in the early morning. If you frequently recut stem ends, regularly change the water, and add powdered flower preservative, they should last seven to fourteen days.

Climate & Culture

Preferred Zones
9–11

Sun Preference

Our Personal Favorite

NAME	SPECIAL CHARACTERISTICS
Agapanthus africanus 'Peter Pan'	Known as Dwarf Lily of the Nile / more compact than the species / blooms and foliage have finer texture

Shasta Daisy

Chrysanthemum × superbum

*Luther Burbank, one of America's premier horticulturists and plant breeders, developed the Shasta Daisy in 1890 after crossing two European daisies (L. maximum × L. lacustre). The result was a plant far stronger and larger than its parents. When we visited his historical home while passing through Santa Rosa, California, and saw Shastas growing in his garden, it struck us that no matter how many times they are used in landscapes, they never seem commonplace. The pure white, fringe-petaled flowers on sixteen-inch-long, naked stems add sparkle to any garden. A drift of Shasta Daisies is not only a feast for our eyes, but the flat petals are perfect cushions for resting swallowtails as they dip into the nectar, which is stored in hundreds of miniature yellow florets that are compacted into the golden centers of each flower head. From mid-June to September, three- to four-inch blooms dance in the warm summer breezes out of rosettes of coarsely toothed, dark-green, spoon-shaped, ten-inch leaves. During their blooming and growing season, they need warmth and adequate water but tolerate some drought for short periods of time. Since the species was also found naturalized on Mount Shasta in Washington state, it is apparent that these plants survive freezing temperatures and blustery winds. **Note:** If you cannot find* Chrysanthemum × superbum, *look for* Leucanthemum superbum, *another botanical name sometimes used for the same plant.*

Family Name / Origin Compositae / Iberia

Bloom Period and Color White flowers bloom in summer.

Mature Height × Spread 2 ft. (clumping)

When and How to Plant Plant in spring from 4-in. pots or 1-gallon containers, spacing 12 in. apart. Build a watering basin 1 ft. in diameter and mulch with 1 in. of organic material such as compost or humus mulch. Also refer to p. 398.

Sun and Soil Preferences Shastas thrive in full sun in rich, well-drained soil with a pH of 6.5 to 7.0.

Moisture Requirements Immediately after planting, soak deeply and thoroughly. During the first week, water three times; thereafter, adjust watering frequency and amount according to weather and growth conditions.

Fertilizing Fertilize lightly once a month with a water-soluble food suitable for bloom and foliage production.

Pruning and Care It is not necessary to prune, but deadhead regularly to encourage a longer flowering cycle. If you want to share your Shastas with your gardening friends, wait until the plants are about three years old and divide the clumps in the fall.

Pests and Diseases Shastas may have occasional insect and disease problems, but damage is usually minor.

Companion Plantings and Design Shastas are great additions to informal borders in front of hedges or in cottage-style perennial gardens. Sharon uses them in colorful mixed bunches of flowers arranged loosely in her favorite vase, or sometimes she arranges them in an elegant, all-white bouquet. Harvest when the flowers are only half open and they will last as cut flowers for seven to ten days. Ideal plant companions are Daylilies, Anemones, Phlox, and Woolly Yarrow.

Climate & Culture

Preferred Zones
8–11

Sun Preference

Our Personal Favorites

NAME	SPECIAL CHARACTERISTICS
Chrysanthemum × superbum 'Esther Read'	Used by the florist industry
C. × superbum 'Marconi'	Full-flowered, all-white variety

Transvaal Daisy

Gerbera jamesonii

A bare area with a southern exposure in our backyard needed a lot of work. After some "gentle" prodding from Sharon, I (Bruce) decided to terrace that space, using railroad ties as retaining structures. Once the terracing was completed and soil amendments added, my "honey-do" list included selecting plants appropriate for cut flowers that were heat and drought tolerant and required little care. I immediately thought of one of South Africa's plant gifts to the world: the Transvaal or Gerber Daisy, which was named for the German naturalist Traugott Gerber. It is one of the most decorative, symmetrically formed, daisylike flowers, known for varieties that offer hot, intense splashes of yellows, reds, oranges, magentas, or rusts, and some that have cool, delicate tints of pinks, salmons, creams, and greenish-whites. In fact, they come in just about all the colors of the rainbow except blue and purple. From May to September, dull-green crowns of large, jagged, coarse-textured leaves support their straight, bare, flowering stems. They need a warm, dry, frost-free climate, and once established, they withstand prevailing breezes.

Family Name / Origin Compositae / South Africa

Bloom Period and Color Yellow, pink, red, or white flowers bloom in summer.

Mature Height × **Spread** 8 to 12 in. × 12 to 16 in.

When and How to Plant Plant in spring from 4-in. pots or 1-gallon containers, spacing 12 in. apart. To help prevent crown rot, plant the crown slightly higher than finished soil level. Build a watering basin 12 in. in diameter and cover with 1 in. of organic material. Also see Planting Techniques, p. 398.

Sun and Soil Preferences These plants need full sun, or partial shade in hot areas, and loose, well-drained, loam soil, pH 6.7 to 7.1.

Moisture Requirements Soak deeply after planting. Water three times the first week; thereafter, adjust watering according to climatic and growth conditions.

Fertilizing Fertilize in early spring with a complete food like 6-10-4.

Pruning and Care The spent flowers look unsightly—if this bothers you, deadhead them, cutting them off at the base of their stalks.

Pests and Diseases Slugs, snails, earwigs, and aphids can be easily controlled with Neem oil, Diazinon™, and a molluscicide.

Companion Plantings and Design The large stiff-petaled flowers on long stems make excellent cut-flower arrangements suitable for any decor, from ornate to minimalist. They are also terrific in rock gardens or perennial gardens, or as border plants or ground covers. Wallflowers, Woolly Yarrow, and Blue Marguerite Daisy are ideal companion plants. As cut flowers, they can last up to three weeks if correctly treated. Recut their stems frequently because they are prone to blockage, and change the water daily, adding just a drop of bleach or some powdered flower preservative each time. Place them in a cool spot, away from direct sunlight.

Climate & Culture

Preferred Zones
10–11

Sun Preferences

Our Personal Favorites

NAME	SPECIAL CHARACTERISTICS
Gerbera jamesonii 'Double Parade'	Double flowers / many color variations
G. jamesonii 'Ebony Eyes'	Flowers with dark centers

Wallflower
Erysimum linifolium

While on a ship traveling from England to Belgium, we noticed the mauve blooms of the Wallflower growing nonchalantly on the steep, white, windswept cliffs of Dover. With their habit of decoratively clamoring over castle walls and stone houses, it is easy to see how they got their common name. While young, the flowers are rarely fragrant, but as they mature, their flowers become scented. Their four-petaled, sweetly perfumed flowers gather into compact spikes and bloom all year round in mild climates, and only in spring in cooler zones. In addition to mauve, E. linifolium is available in colors of orange, purple, violet, or white. Growing from rounded mounds are oblong, narrow, wavy-shaped leaves that are silvery-gray in color. Just be aware that they dislike wet winters and generally do much better in drier conditions such as rock gardens or on walls rather than in flower beds. They are tolerant of wind, drought, temperatures below freezing, and heat. These plants get woody as they age, and if you find that severe pruning or lacing is not encouraging new growth, it is time to replace them with younger, more vigorous plants.

Family Name / Origin Cruciferae / Spain, N Portugal

Bloom Period and Color Orange, purple, violet, or white flowers bloom in spring.

Mature Height × **Spread** 1 to 2 ft. × 2 to 3 ft.

When and How to Plant Plant in spring or fall from 1-gallon containers, spacing 2 to 3 ft. Build a watering basin 3 ft. in diameter and cover with 1 in. of organic material. Also see p. 398.

Sun and Soil Preferences They prefer full sun and well-drained soil, pH 7.0.

Moisture Requirements Soak deeply after planting. Water three times the first week, then adjust watering to climatic and growth conditions. Once established, they prefer to be on the dry side.

Fertilizing Feed Wallflowers once a month with a water-soluble food such as a 12-55-6.

Pruning and Care After a bloom cycle, prune back the plant 20 percent to encourage new growth and avoid the "crater-in-the-center" look. To propagate, take 6-in. semi-hardwood cuttings during late summer or early fall, dip in a rooting hormone, and plant in coarse vermiculite. By the following spring, the roots should be strong enough to plant in the garden.

Pests and Diseases Wallflower plants are free from disease and insect infestations as long as they have cool summers and full sun. They will also do fine in warmer areas if they are in partial shade.

Companion Plantings and Design At our home, Wallflowers are planted in a mixed perennial terrace with drifts of Lavender and Birds of Paradise. They also display well as a border or ground cover, in a rock garden, as a wall planting, or on slopes. Combine with Dwarf Lily of the Nile, Lavender, Woolly Yarrow, and Bird of Paradise.

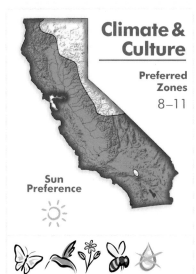

Climate & Culture

Preferred Zones
8–11

Sun Preference

Our Personal Favorites

NAME	SPECIAL CHARACTERISTICS
Erysimum linifolium 'Bicolor'	White and pink-violet colors appear in the same flower cluster
E. linifolium 'Bowles Mauve'	Deer-resistant / light violet flowers mature into deep violet

Woolly Yarrow

Achillea tomentosa

In the south of France near Aix-en-Provence, growing beside the remains of an ancient cobbled Roman road, can be seen outcroppings of Woolly Yarrow. While they are not as showy as some other perennials, they have a pretty silvery-gray, woolly sheen to their fernlike foliage. Their flat-topped flowers are tiny, canary yellow, and densely packed at the ends of stiff, erect stems. They have a vigorous spreading habit with leaves that are thin and lance-shaped. According to mythology, they were named after Achilles who used the plants to heal wounds. While other species of Yarrow have indeed been used for their medicinal properties, the Woolly Yarrow has more modest claims. It blooms all summer, and if you brush up against the plants or bruise them, they release a spicy fragrance. Once established, it is drought, heat, wind, and cold tolerant. Woolly Yarrow have even been found at altitudes as high as 12,000 feet. In addition to attracting butterflies, they look wonderful in cut-flower, herb, or meadow gardens, as ground cover, as border plants, or as mass plantings along walkways. Since they spread vigorously, select your planting sites carefully—a bit of thought beforehand will eliminate future gardening headaches. Do not provide too much fertilizer; they prefer poor soil, as they grow in rocky areas in their native habitats.

How and Where to Buy Roses

Our advice about how and where to buy roses is to first do your homework. Visit several public and private rose gardens in your area, and contact the local Rose Society chapter, the University Cooperative Extension, and your nearby nursery. Rose Hills in Whittier, Exposition Park in Los Angeles, Descanso Gardens in La Canada, Huntington Gardens in San Marino, Berkeley Municipal Garden in Berkeley, Quail Botanical Gardens in Encinitas, Golden Gate Park Rose Garden in San Francisco, Wasco Community Garden in Wasco, Capitol Park Rose Garden in San Francisco, and Filoli Center in Woodside are just a few of many wonderful gardens to visit for ideas.

When a rose has won your heart and nose, purchase only Grade #1 plants from a source which guarantees the success of the plant. To qualify as Grade #1, hybrid teas and grandifloras must have three or more vigorous canes, all at least eighteen inches long. Polyanthas must have four or more canes that are at least twelve inches long, and climbers must have three or more canes not less then twenty-four inches long. The cane lengths are actually the field lengths when the plants are lifted from the ground, but for more efficient shipping space the growers may trim them back before shipment.

A careful inspection of the canes will reveal even to the novice gardener the differences between a #1, #1½, and #2 grade. #1 canes are husky and vigorous, #1½ are thinner and less vigorous, and #2 are very small. With roses, you get what you pay for, and buying cheap is usually not economical in the long run.

Indoor Bouquets

If you planted the right rose in the right place, provided adequate moisture and fertilizer, applied fungicide and insecticide when necessary, and pruned correctly, you will be rewarded with a rich bounty of flowers not only for your garden display but for indoor bouquets as well. To insure the maximum longevity of cut roses, pick them in the early morning or late afternoon. Select a rose that is just beginning to open, not too tightly budded nor too open. Use sharp, sterilized shears to cut the stems just above a leaf that has five or more leaflets, because a new branch will not form if you cut above a three-leaflet leaf. Be sure to cut above a leaflet that is facing outward from the center of the bush, the direction where replacement roses are to grow.

Layer them in a wicker basket so they do not crush each other. Once indoors, immerse in hot water (not scalding, but comfortable for you to work in, similar to the temperature you use for dishwashing) mixed with a powdered floral preservative or one-half ounce of bleach per eight gallons of water; recut one-fourth inch off each stem while it is still underwater. Air bubbles form in the stems when cutting them dry from the mother bush—cutting them underwater seals the stems so that air bubbles cannot form, thereby doubling the life of your blooms. The preservative or bleach will keep bacteria from clogging the cut tips. Allow the water temperature to cool to room temperature before arranging. If you really want to extend the bloom life, recut the stems underwater every two days, and change the water and preservatives as well.

Classes of Roses

Although roses can be classified into numerous categories and we are mindful that it is impossible to cover everything, in this book we have included climbing roses, floribundas, grandifloras, hybrid teas, and miniatures as the major classes.

Climbing roses bring a garden indoors by framing a window or covering part of a house, and they are perfect for framing arches, poles, fences, pergolas, walls, and old trees. They provide beauty and texture as a background for border plants, including bush roses, and add spectacular color without taking up too much space. Most climbers bear blossoms in clusters with some blooming just once, while others flower on and off from late spring through summer. For any style landscape, from the more formal or tailored to the more casual or cottage types, from the expansive to the intimate, climbing roses give just the right touch of emphasis.

As their name implies, *floribundas* bloom abundantly and, in most cases, in clusters, which means that a bouquet of three to six flowers on one stem offers flowers at the same stage of development at the same time. There are some varieties that bloom in sprays, which means they have many flowers on a single stem in different stages of development, from tight buds to completely open inflorescences, often as many as two dozen blooms and buds.

Grandiflora roses, developed from a hybrid tea and a floribunda, are taller than either parent and have double flower forms of thirty-five to forty petals. They display

solid hues of white, red, pink, yellow, and orange as well as blends and bicolors.

With their long-lasting blooms on long stems that open from pointed buds to reveal velvety or satiny petals arranged in single or multiple rows, *hybrid teas* are often used as focal points in the garden. They are classic cut flowers, and they can be combined with other perennials in border plantings.

Although the word "miniature" refers to the bloom size, not the bush size, the leaves and stems of *miniature roses* also tend to be petite versions of full-sized plants, ranging in height from six inches to three feet. Since miniatures grow upright, long, short, or compact depending on the variety, they can be used in many different ways, and their small stature allows a gardener to have an extensive rose display in a tiny space. They grow indoors, provided there is sufficient indoor lighting. For outdoors, use miniatures in low borders, windowboxes, and hanging baskets, climbing on small trellises or nestling in rock gardens, wherever you can enjoy their delicate and winsome size up close.

The Roses in This Book

After dividing the roses into five major classes, we describe specific varieties that are particularly near and dear to our hearts and noses. Most of our favorites that we have selected for fragrance, looks, and manners are available at nurseries or through mail-order catalogues.

Climbing Rose

Rosa spp.

When we moved into our current home we were so busy unpacking, organizing, cleaning, and painting that we barely noticed spring's cycle of renewal in our garden—until one day as we were hurriedly eating our lunch, anxious to return to our chores, something quite beautiful caught our attention outside our dining-room window. It was a perfect "stop and smell the roses" moment, for scrambling, spilling, and stretching fifty feet over our fence down below were thousands of nosegay-sized clusters of pale-yellow flowers. On closer inspection we realized that this was an old but still very vigorous Banksia Climbing Rose, whose carefree looks and profuse blooms spread like butter over its dark-green foliage. We took a deep breath, inhaled the delicate floral fragrance, and realized we were home at last. Unlike vines, climbing roses do not spread and attach themselves via tendrils or other growths, but instead have long canes that must be tied to a support. Some climbers look best when grown horizontally along a fence because their canes are more pliable; others have stiffer canes and adapt well when trained upright on a pillar or trellis. Most withstand short periods of cold temperatures, blustery winds, and high temperatures if adequate moisture is provided, but they do not tolerate drought.

Bloom Period and Color Blends and white, lavender, pink, yellow, orange, red, striped, and bicolored flowers bloom in mid-spring.

Mature Height × Spread (Variable) × 10 to 20 ft.

When and How to Plant Plant in late winter or early spring from bare-root stock, or any time of year from 5-gallon containers, spacing 15 ft. to 20 ft. apart. Construct a watering basin 4 ft. in diameter and mulch with 2 in. of humus or compost. See Planting Techniques, p. 398.

Sun and Soil Preferences Some climbing roses tolerate partial shade, but most prefer full sun and sandy loam soil with a pH of 6.5 to 7.0.

Climate & Culture

Preferred Zones
8–11

Sun Preferences

Moisture Requirements Soak deeply after planting. Water three times the first week; thereafter, adjust to climatic and growth conditions.

Fertilizing Fertilize in late winter, early spring, and early summer with a complete granular rose food such as 10-12-10.

Pruning and Care Climbing roses usually bloom on second-year or older growth, so it is only necessary to prune out dead or diseased wood on newly planted climbers. Once established, in late winter or early spring, but still during dormancy, remove lingering leaves and prune any errant canes that stray from the horizontal, arching, or upright pattern, leaving four to eight structural canes, including some of last year's laterals. Clear the ground of all leaves and weeds, and apply dormant spray to the plants and the soil. When removing this year's foliage, do not harm the latent buds that are hidden under the petioles, because spring flowers will emerge from those buds.

Pests and Diseases Susceptibility to diseases and insects depends on a host of variables such as climate, soil conditions, care, location, and the specific variety of climbing rose. Generally speaking, climbing roses are less vulnerable to mildew than other types of roses, but blackspot, rust, and aphid infestations can occur during growth and bloom cycles; use Neem oil for these problems.

Companion Plantings and Design Ideal companion plants are Clematis, Carolina Jessamine, and California Lilac.

See p. 417 for more information on climbing roses, as well as specific varieties.

Floribunda Rose
Rosa spp.

Like most gardeners, we devoted the greater part of our rose garden to hybrid teas, until one day we planted a floribunda. Once we saw the blooms, we wished we had selected more floribundas instead of so many hybrid teas. While it is true that floribundas lack the size, symmetrical beauty, and fragrance of their more popular counterparts, they flower from summer to fall, provide more color coverage on bushes, and are generally hardier, easier to maintain, lower growing, and less susceptible to wet-weather conditions. As the name implies, floribundas bloom abundantly and, in most cases, in clusters. Whether single- or multipetaled, flattened, cup-shaped, or high-centered, floribundas come in a wide array of colors, some with stripes, from the softest whites, creams, yellows, peaches, pinks, and mauves to brilliant golds, oranges, and reds. With a light and fruity fragrance, they are the roses of choice for formal or informal settings, or for any place that calls out for a large number of flowers. The taller varieties make ideal hedges, while the dwarf varieties are perfect for the fronts of borders, as container plants, or in mass plantings. Most floribundas withstand short periods of cold temperatures, blustery winds, and high temperatures if adequate moisture is provided, but they do not tolerate drought.

Bloom Period and Color Blends and white, pink, lavender, yellow, orange, red, bicolored, and striped flowers bloom from summer to fall.

Mature Height × Spread 2 to 4 ft. × 3 ft.

When and How to Plant Plant in late winter or early spring from bare-root stock, or any time of year from 5-gallon containers, spacing 4 ft. to 6 ft. apart. Construct a watering basin 4 ft. in diameter and mulch with 1 in. of humus or compost. See Planting Techniques, p. 398.

Sun and Soil Preferences Floribundas prefer full sun and sandy loam soil with a pH of 6.5 to 7.0.

Climate & Culture

Preferred Zones
8–11

Sun Preference

Moisture Requirements Soak deeply after planting. Water three times the first week; thereafter, adjust frequency and amount to climatic and growth conditions.

Fertilizing Fertilize in late winter, early spring, and early summer with a complete granular rose food such as 10-12-10.

Pruning and Care Do not prune a newly planted floribunda, just remove any dead wood. Once established after twelve months, prune lightly for shape and remove 1/3 of its total height. For prolific blooms, *disbud* the plant, which means to take out the center flower bud shortly after the side buds emerge so that the plant's energy is directed toward the side buds. As the plant goes dormant, remove any remaining leaves, clear the ground of all leaves and weeds, and apply dormant spray to the plants and the soil. Once you have broken out the first center bud, it is possible that three or more clusters of side shoots will form, and if you pinch out each successive center bud you may have as many as nine or more buds and blooms on a single stem—an instant bouquet of roses.

Pests and Diseases Susceptibility to diseases and insects depends on a host of variables such as climate, soil conditions, care, location, and the specific variety of floribunda. Generally speaking, they are less vulnerable to mildew than other types of roses, but blackspot, rust, and aphid infestations can occur during growth and bloom cycles; use Neem oil for these problems.

Companion Plantings and Design Ideal companion plants are Japanese Mock Orange, hybrid tea roses, and Foxglove.

See p. 417 for more information on floribundas, as well as specific varieties.

Grandiflora Rose

Rosa spp.

Once upon a time, a young human princess was about to be crowned while at the same time, two rose parents, 'Charlotte Armstrong' from the hybrid tea family and 'Floradora' from the floribunda family, gave birth to a new class of rose. The All-America Rose Selections Committee in 1955 named the class grandiflora, and crowned the 'Charlotte Armstrong'-'Floradora' offspring 'Queen Elizabeth' in honor of the real Princess Elizabeth's accession to the throne. From our family-room window we see our most recent rose addition, standing seven feet tall on thornless stems, covered with deep-green leaves glimmering in the sunlight. Adorning it are massive clusters of fragrant four-inch clear-pink blossoms whose ruffled edges are tinged with a darker pink. Without a doubt, the 'Queen Elizabeth' deserves to be the reigning monarch of grandifloras. She produces bouquets of high-centered flowers at the identical point of development at the same time on one stem. The 'Queen Elizabeth' and her royal followers derive their form and long cutting stems from the hybrid teas, and inherit their hardiness and near continuous, abundant clustered blooms from the floribundas. Most grandifloras withstand short periods of cold temperatures, blustery winds, and high temperatures if adequate moisture is provided, but they do not tolerate drought.

Bloom Period and Color Blends and white, pink, lavender, yellow, orange, red, bicolored, and striped flowers bloom from summer to fall.

Mature Height × Spread 6 to 8 ft. × 4 to 6 ft.

When and How to Plant Plant in late winter or early spring from bare-root stock, or any time of year from 5-gallon containers, spacing 8 ft. to 12 ft. apart. Construct a watering basin 4 to 6 ft. in diameter and mulch with 2 in. of humus or compost. See Planting Techniques, p. 398.

Sun and Soil Preferences Grandifloras prefer full sun and sandy loam soil with a pH of 6.5 to 7.0.

Climate & Culture

Preferred Zones
8–11

Sun Preference

Moisture Requirements Soak deeply after planting. Water three times the first week; thereafter, adjust frequency and amount to climatic and growth conditions.

Fertilizing Fertilize in late winter, early spring, and early summer with a complete granular rose food such as 10-12-10.

Pruning and Care Do not prune a newly planted grandiflora, just remove any dead wood. Once established, prune in late winter or early spring before new growth. Remove dead or weak wood and prune back to an outward-facing bud, about 1/3 of its original height. Clear the ground of all leaves and weeds and apply dormant spray to the plants and the soil.

Pests and Diseases Susceptibility to diseases and insects depends on a host of variables such as climate, soil conditions, care, location, and the specific variety of grandiflora. Generally speaking, they are more disease resistant than other types of roses, but powdery mildew, blackspot, rust, and aphid infestations can occur during growth and bloom cycles. To control powdery mildew, wash off the foliage in the early morning. Use Neem oil for blackspot, rust, and aphids.

Companion Plantings and Design Ideal companion plants are hybrid teas, floribundas, and climbing roses. Grandifloras are the largest of the bush roses. Because of their size, it is best to use them as single specimen shrubs, grouped in a hedge, or as background roses behind lower-growing plants. They make ideal specimen plants in large containers.

See p. 418 for more information on grandifloras, as well as specific varieties.

Hybrid Tea Rose

Rosa spp.

We were in the florist business for so long that whenever the word "rose" is mentioned, the image that springs to our minds is that of a long, elegant stem bearing a single, symmetrical, high-centered ruby-red bloom glittering with dew. This is the aristocrat of all roses, the hybrid tea, the long-stemmed beauty of choice for Mother's Day, Valentine's Day, May Day, weddings, graduations, coronations, and ovations. With the exception of black and true blue, there are varieties in every color of the rainbow including white, pink, red, lavender, yellow, orange—even green—as well as bicolors and blends. Many are fragrant and, depending on the region, bloom from spring through fall. Plant size varies from two to six feet. Despite the fact that they are the most selected rose plant in gardens, there are a few caveats one should keep in mind: hybrid teas have an upright, rigid growth habit, bloom less frequently than floribundas, are less adaptable to wet weather, and are less tolerant of adverse climatic and soil conditions. Most hybrid teas withstand short periods of cold temperatures, blustery winds, and high temperatures if adequate moisture is provided, but they do not tolerate drought.

Bloom Period and Color Blends and white, pink, lavender, yellow, green, orange, red, bicolored, and striped flowers bloom from spring through fall.

Mature Height × Spread 4 to 6 ft. × 3 to 5 ft.

When and How to Plant Plant in late winter or early spring from bare-root stock, or any time of year from 5-gallon containers, spacing 4 ft. to 6 ft. apart. Construct a watering basin 4 ft. in diameter and mulch with 1 in. of humus or compost. See Planting Techniques, p. 398.

Sun and Soil Preferences Most hybrid teas prefer full sun and sandy loam soil with a pH of 6.5 to 7.0.

Climate & Culture

Preferred Zones
8–11

Sun Preference

Moisture Requirements Soak deeply after planting. Water three times the first week; thereafter, adjust frequency and amount to climatic and growth conditions.

Fertilizing Fertilize in late winter, early spring, and early summer with a complete granular rose food such as 10-12-10.

Pruning and Care Do not prune a newly planted hybrid tea, just remove any dead wood. Once established after twelve months, prune in January or February when the plants are dormant to remove old, woody canes that have "dog legs" (where one stem grows out of another); leave the vigorous newer canes that are green and growing straight out of the plant's base. See p. 418 for more detailed, important Pruning information.

Pests and Diseases Mildew, blackspot, rust, and chlorosis are the typical rose maladies, especially for hybrid teas. For mildew, blackspot, and rust, use Neem oil, or consult your local nursery for other appropriate remedies. Chelated iron is an effective corrective for iron deficiencies such as chlorosis. Insect infestations of aphids, thrips, scale, and caterpillars can occur during growth and bloom cycles from April to November. Handpick and squish caterpillars or use *B.t.*, wash off aphids with a stream of water in the early morning, and try introducing beneficial insects such as ladybugs and praying mantis to control sucking insects. If insect infestation persists, use Neem oil.

Companion Plantings and Design Ideal companion plants are other hybrid teas, 'Edward Goucher' Abelia, and Rock Rose.

See p. 418 for more information on hybrid teas, as well as specific varieties.

Miniature Rose

Rosa spp.

Given time, something old becomes new again, which is exactly what happened to the miniature rose. In Victorian times it was one of the most popular potted plants, but it fell out of favor when fashion whims changed, and it was thought to have completely disappeared by the end of the nineteenth century. Then in 1918, Major Roulet saw a tiny rose growing on a window ledge in Switzerland, and he named this tenacious survivor Rosa rouletii. Major Roulet's rediscovery earned him a place in horticultural history, and his double-flowered, deep-rose-pink elfin specimen became the founding member of the modern miniature rose class. These are the smallest of roses in flower size, some no bigger than the head of a hatpin, while others are thimble-sized or larger, and they come in an ever-widening range of colors from pure white to an almost black-red, with many blends and striped patterns. In form they are just as varied, from simple five-petal flowers to the full, high-centered types that resemble scaled-down versions of hybrid teas. They go dormant in winter, leaf out in March, bloom in mid-summer, and continue to flower until the first frost. While most miniatures are winter hardy and tolerate short periods of blustery winds and high temperatures if adequate moisture is provided, they do not like drought conditions.

Bloom Period and Color Blends and white, pink, lavender, yellow, orange, red, bicolored, and striped flowers bloom midsummer to first frost.

Mature Height × Spread 6 in. to 3 ft. × 6 in. to 1 ft.

When and How to Plant Plant in spring or early summer from 4- to 6-in. pots; grow as a container specimen or space 6 to 12 in. apart. If planted in the ground, construct a watering basin 1 ft. in diameter and mulch with 1 in. of humus or compost. See Planting Techniques, p. 398.

Sun and Soil Preferences Most miniatures prefer full sun for at least six hours a day and sandy loam soil with a pH of 6.5 to 7.0.

Climate & Culture

Preferred Zones
8–11

Sun Preference

Moisture Requirements Soak deeply after planting. Water daily during the first week; thereafter, adjust frequency and amount to climatic and growth conditions. Regular watering is most important, especially in dry weather, because miniatures do not have the root systems of larger varieties.

Fertilizing Fertilize every week from spring to late summer with a complete water-soluble rose food at half-strength, or use a slow-release food.

Pruning and Care Do not prune a newly planted miniature rose, just remove any dead wood. Once established after twelve months, prune in January to train and remove old leaves and dead wood, and trim for shape. Clear the ground of all leaves and weeds and apply dormant spray to the plants and the soil. As flowers fade, snip stems back to an outside bud.

Pests and Diseases Susceptibility to diseases and insects depends on a host of variables such as climate, soil conditions, care, location, and the specific variety of miniature rose. Generally speaking, they are susceptible during growth and bloom cycles to mildew, blackspot, rust, and insect infestations of aphids and thrips. For blackspot, mildew, and rust use Neem oil. To control aphids and thrips, use Neem oil or a systemic pesticide.

Companion Plantings and Design Ideal companion plants are Transvaal Daisies, Candytuft, and Alyssum.

See p. 419 for more information on caring for miniature roses, as well as specific varieties.

Shrubs *for California*

While at New Zealand's Taranaki Rhododendron Festival, we visited several private gardens, including one owned by a sprightly eighty-five-year-old. Her garden was like entering a painting, filled with a variety of textures and a rainbow of colors, all accomplished by massive plantings of Azaleas and Rhododendrons interspersed with areas of lush lawns, brilliant pink and red Camellias, lemon-scented Mock Oranges, and assorted Pine trees, as well as alabaster-white Gardenias and canary-yellow Hibiscus. With forethought, dedication, and a gifted painter's eye, she had used her shrubs as more than mere multitrunked woody plants plopped in a landscape between trees, flowers, and lawns. Instead they were grouped in borders and hedges, interplanted in flower beds, highlighted as specimens, and clustered in foundation plantings—proving that shrubs can be the base coat, top coat, or colorful trim for any garden.

First Do Your Homework

Before purchasing and planting a shrub, carefully consider local climatic conditions, site locations, and the shrub's particular needs and habits. A little homework beforehand will save time, money, and effort afterward as you try to maintain the plant's health or prune it to keep it within bounds. A cute little Yew Pine or Hollywood Twisted Juniper from a one-gallon-size container can grow much taller, just as a young child grows until reaching full adulthood. If such a shrub is planted as a foundation shrub in front of an average-sized home, in a few years it might be much too tall, obscuring the house or blocking window views. For foundation plantings and borders, it is wiser to plant low to medium-height evergreen or deciduous shrubs.

A Multitude of Choices

Whether the landscape calls for evergreen or deciduous, berry or flower-bearing, screening or showcasing, there are shrubs for every purpose. For showy spring flowers and deep-green foliage in shaded areas, few plants can compete with Azaleas, Camellias, and Hydrangeas. Others are known less for their flowers but have variegated foliage, including Gold Dust and Golden Mirror Plants that look as if a painter took a paintbrush and

stippled the leaves with gold dust. Some, like Heavenly Bamboo, Laurustinus, and Cotoneaster, provide blazing autumn color and bright berries. If fluttery visitations from ruby-tinged hummingbirds, plump bees, and boldly patterned monarch and swallowtail butterflies are important to you, find sunny areas for the Butterfly Bush, Pride of Madeira, and California Lilac—their delicate fragrant, spiked flowers and sweet nectar are perfect metaphors for the sweetness of life. For those who think good hedges make good neighbors, Hibiscus, Rose of Sharon, Yew Pines, and Laurustinus are ideal choices. Dwarf Jade Plants, Silverberry, Rock Rose, California Lilac, and Pride of Madeira make good companions for other drought-tolerant trees, shrubs, and ground covers. Hollywood Twisted Junipers are excellent accent plants in areas that allow for their mature dimensions, often grouped or planted in pairs on opposite sides of driveways and walkways in formal landscapes. On warm spring and summer days, the blossoms of Saucer Magnolias, Mystery Gardenias, and Japanese Mock Orange scent gentle breezes with their perfume.

A Multitude of Uses

Instead of planting in linear, single-file formations, add depth by planting taller shrubs towards the back and low-spreading or ground-covering varieties in the front. Cluster identical shrubs for focal points, or combine with trees to create a shade garden or wooded landscape. Evergreen shrubs that prefer pruning are great when planted for formal hedges or verdant walls. Use taller evergreen shrubs as a backdrop for the seasonal changes of shorter deciduous shrubs, annuals, and bulbs.

Avoid combining drought-tolerant shrubs with thirsty ones, or shade-lovers with sun-seekers. While upright and pyramidal shapes draw the eyes skyward and lend themselves to the more formal landscape, the weeping, mounding, or spreading shapes anchor our vision to ground level and reflect a more relaxed plan.

Leaf shapes, textures, sizes, and colors bring contrasts to gardens. Shrubs offer colors that cover the spectrum from gold to blue-gray to all shades of green as well as red, burgundy, purplish-bronze and variegated splashes, stipples, or stripes. In winter, many deciduous plants have colorful bark patterns or interesting branch structures that more than compensate for their leafless state.

To soften or camouflage, to brighten or shade, to flower or green, whatever the purpose, there are shrubs for every need. They make graceful bridges between tall trees and smaller perennials, lawns, ground covers, and annuals, and also shine as gregarious floral showpieces or hide in the muted shade of more forceful plants. Use them as a gifted artist would use a rainbow palette of texture and color.

Angel's Trumpet
Brugmansia suaveolens

A member of the Nightshade family of plants, Angel's Trumpet is a large bush that can be pruned into a small tree. Each leaf of its lovely blue-gray foliage measures six to ten inches in length and width and has a fuzzy surface. But even though Angel's Trumpet has spectacular pendulous, funnel-shaped flowers that range in color from pink to white to yellow, it is one of the most poisonous plants in the home landscape and should be used cautiously. Because its leaves and flowers are toxic and the entire plant is a narcotic, never use it in cut-flower arrangements or plant in your garden if you have small children or pets. When working with it, wear protective clothing and gloves. Despite these ominous warnings, the beauty of the flower and its light musk perfume are well worth the extra care as long as children and pets are not a consideration. Angel's Trumpets are easy to maintain if you have selected the correct growing environment. **Note:** *If you cannot find Brugmansia suaveolens, look for Datura suaveolens, another botanical name sometimes used for the same plant.*

Family Name / Origin   Solanaceae / South America

Bloom Period and Color   Pink, white, or yellow flowers

Mature Height × Spread   8 to 12 ft. × 8 ft.

When and How to Plant   The best time to plant is in spring, from 1- or 5-gallon containers, in a frost-free location protected from wind. If you want to plant several, space them 6 to 10 ft. apart. Use a preplant fertilizer, 2-10-6, following manufacturer's directions. For more information on soil preparation refer to Planting Techniques, p. 398.

Sun and Soil Preferences   Plant in full sun in loam soil with a neutral pH of 6.5 to 7.0.

Moisture Requirements   Deep-water infrequently, about once a week depending on weather conditions and maturity of the plant. Two inches of organic material such as humus mulch or compost will minimize moisture loss.

Fertilizing   Fertilize with a granular acid food, 6-10-4, just before the flush of spring growth, and water-in well after the application.

Pruning and Care   To develop this plant into a small tree form, remove the lateral branches up to 4 ft. with a pruning shear. Since this plant is toxic, use latex or other waterproof gloves when pruning and washing the shears; use warm water with liquid detergent; and don't forget to dry off the shears.

Pests and Diseases   Control aphids by washing them off with a stream of water or by applying Neem oil.

Companion Plantings and Design   Angel's Trumpet contrasts well with plants such as Rock Rose, California Lilac, and Pride of Madeira. It can also be used to great effect as an accent plant in a large container.

Climate & Culture

Preferred Zones 10–11

Sun Preference

Our Personal Favorites

NAME	SPECIAL CHARACTERISTICS
B. suaveolens 'Charles Grimaldi'	Pale orange-yellow flower / developed by crossing B. s. 'Dr. Seuss' with B. s. 'Frosty Pink'
B. s. 'Equador Pink'	A spectacular cultivar / pastel pink-and-white flower

Azalea
Azalea indica

People are often confused about whether a plant should be called a Rhododendron or an Azalea. All Azaleas are Rhododendrons, but not all Rhododendrons are Azaleas. In other words, Azaleas, whether evergreen or deciduous, are one of the three main categories of Rhododendrons (the others being Vireyas and true Rhododendrons). Azaleas are one of the most popular shade plants used in California landscapes. In spring, their single or double funnel-like flowers cluster on almost every branch tip and come in just about every color except bright blue. Once their flowers are spent, you can appreciate their elliptical-shaped, dense, hunter-green foliage that has delicate hair-like filaments covering its surface. Their profuse blooms and dome-like form lend themselves to formal and informal landscapes and can be effectively used as shrubs or topiaries. I (Bruce) include them in many of my landscape designs. One of my favorite Azaleas is A. indica 'Rosea'—its semi-double flowers open from rose-like buds and bloom rose-red in color. A midseason bloomer is 'California Snow', whose large pure-white blooms are true double flowers. Remember, Azaleas are Rhododendrons, so don't be surprised if you see them tagged as Rhodys—they take the same care.

Family Name / Origin Ericaceae / Asia

Bloom Period and Color Red, white, pink, orange, and variegated flowers bloom in spring.

Mature Height × Spread 4 to 6 ft. × 4 to 6 ft.

When and How to Plant Plant in the spring, from 1- or 5-gallon containers. See p. 398.

Sun and Soil Preferences There are sun-tolerant Azaleas, but all varieties do much better in partial shade, and all need porous-textured organically rich soil which permits air and moisture movement. If you have dense, clay soils, plant Azaleas in containers, raised beds, or mounded areas. A soil pH of 5.5 to 6.5 is a fundamental requirement for growth.

Climate & Culture

Preferred Zones
9–11

Sun Preference

Moisture Requirements Moisture should always be available in the root zone, but don't keep the soil saturated. Begin by watering thoroughly, then adjust amount and frequency to growth and climatic conditions.

Fertilizing Fertilize after blooms are spent with a Camellia/Azalea food, following manufacturer's instructions. Since Azalea foliage tend to become chlorotic because of a lack of iron, periodically apply chelated iron to the foliage or the soil in amounts specified by the manufacturer.

Pruning and Care If any flower petals remain after the bloom cycle, deadhead them—do not allow them to go to seed.

Pests and Diseases The fine-textured foliage hair traps dust that should be washed off periodically. Monitor Azaleas for spider mites and thrips.

Companion Plantings and Design Azaleas combine well with Camellias and Hydrangeas.

Our Personal Favorites

NAME	SPECIAL CHARACTERISTICS
A. *indica* 'Rosea'	A Southern Indian Azalea with semi-double rose-red flowers that open from rose-like buds / grows 4 to 6 ft. tall and 4 to 6 ft. wide
A. *indica* 'Chimes'	One of the most radiant, semi-double blossomed varieties of the Belgian Indian group / dark-red blooms occur midseason

Bird of Paradise

Strelitzia reginae

There are few flowers more dramatic in form and color than the Bird of Paradise flower, with its pointed, waxy beak, three erect orange petals, and blue spiked corolla resembling a crown of plumage. In California it blooms in the spring and the fall, as it does in its native South Africa. It makes a superb cut flower because of its longevity and its spectacular form, especially in highly stylized arrangements such as Ikebana displays. Do not throw a cut flower away when the initial bloom period is over; simply remove the old flower, reach in, and carefully lift the new flower out of the sheath. This is a clumping herbaceous plant with large, deep green, glossy leaves growing from the base. The leaves are three to four feet long with distinctive ribs. It makes a colorful addition and accent to any tropical garden. You can display these plants in large terracotta pots and use them as colorful architectural focal points in your patio or entryway, provided there is full sun. Although Bird of Paradise does not tolerate cold, it is still an easy plant to maintain since it withstands drought, heat, and wind. It's best to plant from a five-gallon container; if you choose a one-gallon container plant, it will take about two or three years to bloom. The best time to divide and transplant is in summer.

Family Name / Origin Strelitziaceae / South Africa

Bloom Period and Color Orange flowers bloom in spring and fall.

Mature Height × Spread 3 to 5 ft. (clumping)

When and How to Plant Plant from a 5-gallon container just about any time of year, but spring and fall months are best. Space 6 ft. on center. Build a watering basin 4 ft. in diameter with a berm 4 to 6 in. high. Mulch the basin's surface with 2 in. of compost or humus mulch. See Planting Techniques, p. 398.

Sun and Soil Preferences Plant in full sun to maximize flower production. It prefers porous, well-drained, loam soils but will survive in denser, clay soils. Soil pH needs to be a bit on the acidic side, 6.5 to 7.0.

Moisture Requirements As a general rule, these plants do best when watered deeply and thoroughly every seven to ten days in summer, less frequently in winter.

Fertilizing Fertilize twice a year, early spring and early fall, with a complete food, 6-10-4.

Pruning and Care Remove spent flowers and stems all the way down to the base, or it will look unsightly and stalks will not rebloom. Remove tattered and dried leaves.

Pests and Diseases Snails are common around Birds of Paradise; control them with the pick-and-squish method or use a molluscicide, such as iron phosphate.

Companion Plantings and Design Pink Powder Puff, Mystery Gardenias, and Hibiscus are tropical plants that go well with the Bird of Paradise.

Climate & Culture

Preferred Zones
10–11

Sun Preference

Our Personal Favorite

NAME	SPECIAL CHARACTERISTICS
Strelitzia nicolai	Known as the Giant Bird of Paradise / reaches a height of 10 to 20 ft., a diameter of 6 to 8 ft. / greenish-blue and white flowers appear in the summer / characteristic growth resembles the form of a banana tree

Butterfly Bush
Buddleja davidii

Imagine hundreds of brilliant orange-and-black-edged monarch and yellow-and-orange-dotted swallowtail butterflies gliding along their flyway to and from the central California coast. As the winds carry them towards their destination, they light upon our Butterfly Bush, decorating the flowers with their pulsing wings. They are not alone. Bumblebees and honeybees buzz industriously, red-crowned and ruby-throated hummingbirds whir their wings in a blur, and lucky us, we get to watch all this beauty while butterflies, birds, and bees hungrily extract nectar. If you enjoy such visitations, you need this shrub with its clusters of delicate, fragrant, spiked flowers. It is a wonderful choice for a summer-blooming plant because of its vibrant purple color, which is probably the reason for its other common name, the Summer Lilac. (Buddleja davidii was named for the English botanist Adam Buddle and the French missionary-naturalist Father Armand David.) The leaves are dark green, felted underneath, and grow six to ten inches in length. In full sun or in partial sun, the Butterfly Bush thrives in almost any growing condition, including seaside exposures. This is a hardy, cold-tolerant shrub; it is deciduous, but its upright structure provides a picturesque silhouette in winter.

Family Name / Origin Loganiaceae / China

Bloom Period and Color Dark violet, pink, white, and purple flowers bloom in summer.

Mature Height × **Spread** 6 to 10 ft. × 8 ft.

When and How to Plant You can plant Butterfly Bushes any time of year, but the best times are fall or early spring. Plant this vigorous-growing plant at least 10 to 15 ft. on center, especially if planting in groups. Mulch the surface of the ground with humus mulch or compost. As the plant continues to grow, increase the size of the watering basin so that its diameter is slightly beyond the drip line, just beyond the edge of the outermost branches. For more planting information, see Planting Techniques, p. 398.

Climate & Culture

Preferred Zones
6–11

Sun Preferences

Sun and Soil Preferences Plant in partial or full sun. Prepare the planting pit with 20 to 30 percent organic material mixed with the native soil to encourage rapid root development. Soil pH needs to be 6.5 to 7.0.

Moisture Requirements Irrigate thoroughly every seven to ten days depending on weather and soil conditions. Once established, Butterfly Bushes are drought tolerant and require little attention.

Fertilizing Fertilize in early spring and early summer.

Pruning and Care Remove spent flowers to promote and extend a profuse blooming season. Since flowers develop on the current season's growth, prune back the canes 80 to 90 percent in late winter. Once the flush of new growth occurs in spring, pinch back the tips of the growth to encourage new flowering branches to develop at a lower level for a fuller plant and more abundant blooms.

Pests and Diseases Aphid infestations can be controlled by washing the critters off with a strong stream of water or applying Neem oil.

Companion Plantings and Design Combine Butterfly Bush with other nectar-rich plants like Pride of Madeira, Crape Myrtle, and California Lilac.

Our Personal Favorites

NAME	SPECIAL CHARACTERISTICS
B. davidii 'Black Knight'	Deep-violet flowers
B. d. 'Charming'	Lavender-pink blooms

California Lilac

Ceanothus tomentosus

Just about the same time as the bees begin to swarm, the birds start to nest, and the butterflies slowly emerge from their cocoons, we start putting on our hiking boots so we can explore the spring beauty of the foothills. Covering these Southern California foothills is a California native species, C. tomentosus, commonly called California Lilac. Its thick, spiked, lilac-blue blossoms form a spectacular carpet when compared to its more camouflaged companions. Providing a showy contrast to these blue spikes is dark-green foliage, the texture of crepe paper, with serrated margins. When mature, these plants grow into large shrubs, reaching heights and widths of ten feet. Since they tolerate windy conditions and temperatures below freezing as well as the other extreme of high 90s and even, for short periods of time, temperatures in the 100s, California Lilacs are adaptable to many otherwise adverse environments. They have the added benefit of attracting nature's helpers, birds and bees. Be sure the soil is well drained. Lack of adequate percolation is probably the most common reason a California Lilac will perish.

Family Name / Origin Rhamnaceae / California

Bloom Period and Color Blue flowers bloom in spring.

Mature Height × **Spread** 6 to 12 ft. × 10 ft.

Climate & Culture

Preferred Zones
8–10

Sun Preferences

When and How to Plant Fall is the best season to plant because it is at the beginning of the rainy season and the flush of root growth occurs during this time. The second-best time to plant is in spring. Select a 1- or 5-gallon plant that is not rootbound. Space the plant 10 ft. on center in a triangular or rectangular pattern. Mulch the surface of the ground with compost or humus mulch immediately after planting California Lilac because this will conserve moisture, stabilize the temperature, and limit the growth of weeds. Refer to Planting Techniques, p. 398, for further planting information.

Sun and Soil Preferences Plant in an area of full sun or partial shade. Make sure the location has well-drained soil and is just beyond the limits of the sprinkler pattern. It grows best in soils that develop from decomposed granite with a slightly acidic pH, 6.5 to 7.0.

Moisture Requirements Once California Lilac is established, Mother Nature provides adequate moisture and nutrients, provided there is an average amount of rainfall during the months of November to March. Since infrequent, deep watering is the rule, make sure you isolate your California Lilac from plants that need more frequent watering, or root rot may result.

Fertilizing If there is a need to fertilize, do so once a year in December or January.

Pruning and Care There is no need to deadhead, and prune only to shape the plant or to avoid an unruly canopy.

Pests and Diseases Very few insects or diseases affect California Lilac.

Companion Plantings and Design When landscaping a drought-tolerant area with California Lilac, plant it behind medium-sized shrubs and ground covers because of its width and height. Combine with other natives that are drought tolerant and thrive in full sun, such as Red Clusterberry Cotoneaster, Silverberry, and Rock Rose.

Camellia
Camellia japonica

C. japonica *is the most popular of all the Camellias because of its wide variety of colors, including yellow, and because it is easy to grow in a shady environment. Since the roots are not invasive, this is an ideal shrub to grow in shaded plant groupings about three feet from the foundation of a home. Glossy bright-green leaves and symmetrical four-inch flowers, either single or double in form, decorate these multiple-branched evergreen shrubs. For short periods of time they can tolerate temperatures as low as 10 degrees Fahrenheit, but if it is hot and dry, their foliage will scorch. Be on the lookout for Camellia blight, a fungus with an interesting cycle. During winter and spring rains, moisture splashes the soil and moves the fungus from the soil to the branches and foliage and then to the buds and opening flower petals. When and if the buds open, the petals decay and are brown and mushy. If infected buds, flowers, and leaves are left on the ground, the cycle will continue and destroy your plant's flower production. If you prefer an approach more aggressive than clearing away spent flowers and fallen leaves, use a fungicide to control the blight, but be aware that this will not eliminate the fungus; it will only serve as a control.*

Family Name / Origin Theaceae / China, Japan, Korea

Bloom Period and Color Red, white, pink, or variegated flowers bloom late winter and early spring.

Mature Height × **Spread** 6 to 15 ft. × 4 to 8 ft.

When and How to Plant Plant 4 to 8 ft. apart from 1- or 5-gallon containers in late winter or early spring. For specific information, refer to Planting Techniques, p. 398.

Sun and Soil Preferences Choose a shaded area with sun exposure until ten in the morning. Camellias need acidic soil, pH 6.0 to 6.5.

Climate & Culture

Preferred Zones
8–11

Sun Preference

Moisture Requirements It is most important to avoid overwatering—once established, keep the soil a bit on the dry side. If planted in loam soil, water thoroughly about once a week or as weather and growing conditions dictate.

Fertilizing Fertilize as the bloom season ends and the new growth begins, with a specially formulated food designed for Camellias. If it is a granular fertilizer, make sure you distribute it evenly in the watering basin, and soak-in thoroughly.

Pruning and Care Unless the plants are overgrown, you do not normally need to hard-prune the canopies. It is a good idea to clear away and dispose of any spent flowers and fallen leaves to help control Camellia blight.

Pests and Diseases Bud drop is another malady, caused by unfavorable temperatures, moisture stress, malnutrition, frost, bud mite, or root rot. Monitor these conditions to minimize the bud drop symptom.

Companion Plantings and Design Plant with other shade lovers such as Azaleas, Japanese Maples, and Hydrangeas.

Our Personal Favorites

NAME	SPECIAL CHARACTERISTICS
C. *japonica* 'Kramer's Supreme'	Grows 6 to 10 ft. / very large Peony-form flowers in a deep red color / unlike most C. *japonicas*, has a slight fragrance / blooms midseason
C. *j.* 'Debutante'	Abundant, large, light-pink, Peony-form flowers / early bloomer

Carmel Ceanothus
Ceanothus griseus

Carmel Ceanothus plants are huge, bushy plants with bright, shiny, crinkled leaves. Like many other California native plants, they are drought and seaside tolerant, and once established, they require little maintenance. At the end of the rainy season, about the middle of March, large bright-blue flowering spikes appear that are two to three inches in length. Once they mature, they can survive several adverse conditions, including cold, wind, and heat, but they cannot tolerate clay soils or sites where soil aeration is poor. The ideal percolation rate for Carmel Ceanothus is one inch per hour. This is important because their roots systems rot if they remain in saturated soils for an extended period of time. It is best to use Carmel Ceanothus with other native or drought-tolerant plants. Try not to mix native plants with tropicals or subtropicals because of their different water requirements. Most root systems of native plants are very efficient at making use of small amounts of water. For this reason, do not use an automatic irrigation system unless your system has numerous zones keyed to specific plant grouping needs. There is no need to deadhead or prune Carmel Ceanothus, because the plant's natural form is open and graceful.

Family Name / Origin Rhamnaceae / California

Bloom Period and Color Blue flowers bloom in spring.

Mature Height × Spread 4 to 6 ft. × 6 to 10 ft.

When and How to Plant In fall, select 1- or 5-gallon plants that are not rootbound, and plant them 10 ft. apart. If the soil dug from the planting pit is soft and friable, there's no need to amend it for backfill. Just eliminate the large rocks and dirt clods. If the soil needs amendment, use one-third organic material, such as humus mulch, compost, or planting mix, and two-thirds loam soil. Mulch the ground's surface out to the outermost branches with 2 to 3 in. of compost or humus mulch to help keep the soil moist, soft, and friable. See Planting Techniques, p. 398.

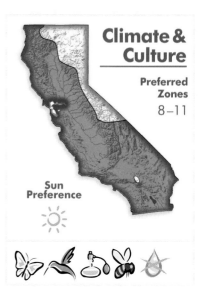

Climate & Culture

Preferred Zones 8–11

Sun Preference

Sun and Soil Preferences Plant in full sun. Soil pH should be neutral, 7.0.

Moisture Requirements Although a mature plant will survive on natural rainfall, infrequent deep watering is essential for a young plant. Water about every seven to ten days, unless there is a drought or period of heavy rainfall—then adjust your irrigation schedule accordingly.

Fertilizing Fertilize in late summer and early winter, just before the plant's two growth cycles, with a complete fertilizer, 6-10-4.

Pruning and Care There is no need to deadhead or prune.

Pests and Diseases Aphid infestations can be controlled by washing the critters off with a strong stream of water or applying Neem oil.

Companion Plantings and Design Rock Cotoneaster, Rock Rose, and Dwarf Coyote Bush are good companions.

Our Personal Favorites

NAME	SPECIAL CHARACTERISTICS
C. *griseus* 'Horizontalis'	Grows up to 2 to 3 ft. in height / known as Carmel Creeper / clusters of blue flowers in spring / excellent ground cover
C. *griseus* 'Frosty Blue'	Large blue flowers on 2- to 3-ft.-long spikes / rapid growth / spectacular spring bloom

Crimson Bottlebrush
Callistemon lanceolatus

Crimson Bottlebrushes are large plants that are particularly useful as visual screens. They have feathery red flowers that bloom from late spring to summer, and the masses of flowers give the plants their common name. When you crush the leaves, they release a wonderful lemon scent, and cut-up leaves can be used as a potpourri mixed with dried citrus rind. The narrow green foliage is stiff with an erect structure, and new growth extends beyond the flowers. Native to the dry areas of Australia, these plants are wind- and drought-tolerant and have few insect or disease problems. Deer usually leave the plants alone because they find the stiff leaves unpalatable. Once established, these evergreen Crimson Bottlebrush shrubs need little maintenance. If you are a novice gardener and need to screen an area in a relatively short period of time, consider Crimson Bottlebrush, one of the easiest shrubs to grow. **Note:** *If you cannot find* Callistemon lanceolatus, *look for* Callistemon citrinus, *another botanical name sometimes used for the same plant. Two other varieties of C. citrinus that add interest to the landscape, but may not be readily available, are C. c. 'Burning Bush', with compact, dark-green leaves and carmine-red flowers, and C. c. 'Hannah Ray', with a semi-weeping form and bright red-orange flowers.*

Family Name / Origin Myrtaceae / Australia

Bloom Period and Color Red flowers bloom in spring and summer.

Mature Height × Spread 6 to 10 ft. × 8 ft.

When and How to Plant Select 1- or 5-gallon specimens and plant in fall or spring. Space these large plants 10 to 12 ft. apart. To maintain moisture content in porous soils, there should be 20 to 30 percent organic material such as humus mulch, planting mix, or compost mixed with the backfill. Once planted, mulch the ground's surface with 2 in. of organic material such as humus. See p. 398.

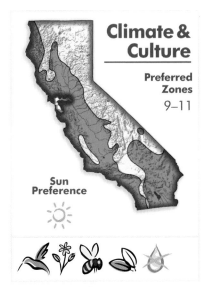

Climate & Culture

Preferred Zones 9–11

Sun Preference

Sun and Soil Preferences Make sure they are in full sun. They do well in most types of soils, and tolerate slightly alkaline soils with a pH of 6.5 to 7.0. Their root systems develop most rapidly in porous rather than clay soils.

Moisture Requirements For established Crimson Bottlebrush, water infrequently and deeply, about once every seven to ten days.

Fertilizing Fertilize twice a year, early spring and early summer, for optimum growth and blooms.

Pruning and Care There is no need to deadhead, but you can prune for shape at any time. Little pruning is necessary if you want to use these plants as large shrubs. If you prefer the form of small trees, however, train the trunks vertically to 5 ft., then allow the canopy to develop naturally.

Pests and Diseases Few pests and diseases affect Crimson Bottlebrush.

Companion Plantings and Design We particularly like these plants in xeriphitic (dry) landscapes combined with Cotoneasters, Rock Rose, and Silverberry.

Our Personal Favorite

NAME	SPECIAL CHARACTERISTICS
C. *citrinus* 'Little John'	Commonly called Dwarf Bottlebrush / grows to 3 ft. in height and width / blood-red flowers bloom most heavily in spring and sporadically through the summer / soft new growth develops into handsome, blue-green, narrow leaves

Dwarf Jade Plant

Crassula argentea 'Nana'

*Dwarf Jade Plants, smaller than Common Jade Plants, are compact and round in shape. This is one of the plants we recommend to people who do not have green thumbs because you can break off a branch, stick it in the ground, and watch it root easily. Dwarf Jade Plants also make ideal border plants as well as specimens for rock gardens. They do very well in containers because they are attractive and require little maintenance. Just as the name indicates, the foliage is light jade-green in color. Like the foliage of other succulents, the leaves have a high moisture content and are smooth in texture. Their stems have thick, delicate, star-shaped clusters of pale pink blooms that appear in the fall. Since they are native to South Africa, they are drought-, wind-, and heat-tolerant, but they cannot withstand temperatures below freezing because of their foliar structure's high moisture content. Interestingly, their leaves redden when temperatures dip or when drought conditions persist. They make ideal border or container plants as well as specimens for rock gardens. **Note:** If you cannot find Crassula argentea 'Nana', look for Crassula ovata, another botanical name sometimes used for the same plant.*

Family Name / Origin Crassulaceae /
South Africa

Bloom Period and Color Pink blooms appear
in fall.

Mature Height × Spread 1 to 2 ft. × 2 to 3 ft.

When and How to Plant Plant any time of year,
but fall or spring months are best. Space about 18
in. on center from any size container, although a 1-
gallon size is more than adequate. Make a watering
basin twice the diameter of your plant and mulch the
basin's surface with 1 to 2 in. of humus mulch or
compost. Also see Planting Techniques, p. 398.

Sun and Soil Preferences Dwarf Jade Plants in
the ground can be in full sun, partial shade, or shade. They tolerate a wide
pH range, from 6.5 to 7.2. They prefer loam soils that provide good
drainage, but survive in clay soils.

Moisture Requirements Once established, water infrequently depending
on weather conditions.

Fertilizing Fertilize in spring and fall if necessary.

Pruning and Care Pruning is unnecessary because the form of the plant is
naturally symmetrical. Cut off the spent flower clusters for a neat appearance.
Propagation is a matter of taking cuttings, air-drying them for a day or so to
allow the cut ends to callous over, tipping the ends in a rooting hormone, and
placing the cuttings halfway down into a mixture that is 50 percent sand and
50 percent coarse vermiculite. In just three weeks' time, your cuttings will
re-root and you can transplant them into containers, or directly into the landscape when new growth appears. If placed in containers, it is more convenient
to locate them in shady areas because the soil will not dry out as quickly.

Pests and Diseases Use snail bait for occasional snails and slugs.

Companion Plantings and Design Lily of the Nile, Wallflower, and
Rockspray Cotoneaster are good companions.

Our Personal Favorite

NAME	SPECIAL CHARACTERISTICS
C. ovata 'Hobbit'	Dwarf cultivar / small leaves / compact form

Glossy Abelia
Abelia × grandiflora

Glossy Abelia is a hybrid of Abelia chinensis × A. uniflora, *named for physician and author Dr. Clark Abel. I (Bruce) have observed these plants growing in landscapes in every part of California, even where temperatures dip below freezing for short periods of time. Their sweetly scented white flowers, on gracefully arching branches, can be an attractive accent in an otherwise humdrum landscape. They have an exceptionally long bloom period, from June through November in temperate climates, when few other shrubs are in flower. Plant several different varieties of Glossy Abelia en masse, such as 'Edward Goucher' and 'Prostrata', and you will have a showy display. Structurally, they make ideal dense hedges, perfect for those who think good hedges make good neighbors. They are excellent shrubs for both beginning and experienced gardeners, as they experience few pests or diseases and are drought tolerant. Their lingering sepals are a beautiful purplish or bronze hue. You can easily propagate Glossy Abelias by rooting greenwood cuttings (under glass) or rooting ripe wood cuttings taken in the fall. Whenever a client of mine requests a shrub for a low-maintenance landscape, this is one of my top suggestions.*

Family Name / Origin Caprifoliaceae / China

Bloom Period and Color White flowers bloom all summer and even early fall, with lingering purplish or bronze sepals.

Mature Height × Spread 4 to 10 ft. × 5 to 8 ft.

When and How to Plant Plant from 1- or 5-gallon containers in early spring. Consult the Planting Techniques section, p. 398.

Sun and Soil Preferences Plant in full sun. While Glossy Abelias prefer loam soils with a pH of 6.5 to 7.0, they tolerate a wide range of soil textures, as well as seaside exposures.

Climate & Culture

Preferred Zones
8–11

Sun Preference

Moisture Requirements Irrigate established Glossy Abelias every week to ten days, adjusting amount and frequency to climatic and soil conditions.

Fertilizing Use a complete fertilizer such as a 6-10-4 about three times a year: early spring, late spring, early fall.

Pruning and Care Glossy Abelias can be pruned for shape at any time, but preferably after they have finished blooming. They should be periodically laced to stimulate new growth by allowing light to reach the center of the plants. Deadheading is not necessary; as the flower petals dry, they fall to the ground.

Pests and Diseases Although largely pest-free, keep an eye out for aphid infestation. Wash off aphids with a strong stream of water; if they persist, use a Neem oil pesticide or insecticidal soap.

Companion Plantings and Design Japanese Mock Orange and Rock Rose are ideal companion plants.

Our Personal Favorites

NAME	SPECIAL CHARACTERISTICS
A. × *grandiflora* 'Edward Goucher'	Grows a little smaller and more compact than the species / lilac-pink flowers
A. × *grandiflora* 'Prostrata' (plant patent #1431)	A prostrate variety / white flowers / ground cover / bank planting / new foliar growth has striking reddish-bronze tinge / semievergreen in colder areas

Gold Dust Plant
Aucuba japonica 'Variegata'

When designing a Japanese garden, I (Bruce) like to use these plants combined with several species of bamboo as subtle accents in areas of dappled shade. The Gold Dust Plant's foliage looks as if a painter took a paintbrush and stippled the leaves with gold dust. The variegated foliage and red seeds add color and variety to shady areas of the yard and the relatively compact size makes the plant a valuable option for the small garden. A good planting site is usually on the north or east side of the house. Though it will grow well in coastal areas, be aware that the Gold Dust Plant reacts to salts in the soil; you must deep-soak the soil so the salts dissolve and leach out of the root zone. Make sure you keep mulch at least four to six inches away from the base of the plant; when mulch is too close, moisture accumulates below the bark, fungus invades, the trunk is girdled, and the plant perishes. In addition to our personal favorites listed on the following page, try the Saw-toothed Japanese Aucuba; it has long, dark-green leaves with sharply serrated edges and showy red berries in fall. The solid green species of this plant is Aucuba japonica, *and it also does well in shady environments.*

Family Name / Origin Cornaceae / E. Asia

Bloom Period and Color Grown for foliage.

Mature Height × Spread 3 to 4 ft. × 3 to 4 ft.

When and How to Plant Plant in spring, spaced at least 4 ft. on center for good air circulation. Also see Planting Techniques, p. 398.

Sun and Soil Preferences Select a location in the shade. Gold Dust plants need sandy loam soils with good drainage. The pH should be slightly on the acidic side, 6.5 to 7.0, and the planting area should have soil with 20 to 30 percent organic material.

Climate & Culture

Preferred Zones 8–11

Sun Preference

Moisture Requirements To maintain an even amount of moisture, mulch the ground's surface with 1 to 2 in. of humus mulch or compost. Since the roots of the Gold Dust plants are reactive to salt accumulation, deep-soak the soil so salts will dissolve and leach out of the root zone.

Fertilizing Use an acid food (6-10-4) in early spring and early fall.

Pruning and Care Salt accumulation damage typically starts from the outermost leaves where they will begin to brown as if they have been burned, then continue down the margins, until the leaves desiccate and fall off. Be sure to deep-soak the soil.

Pests and Diseases Look for colonies of mealybugs in the spring and summer months. Wash off the foliage once a week with a strong stream of water to suppress insect populations. If they persist, apply Neem oil. Periodically, apply snail controls to minimize their damage.

Companion Plantings and Design The bright colors of Azaleas, Camellias, and Clivia Lilies contrast beautifully with the Gold Dust Plant.

Our Personal Favorites

NAME	SPECIAL CHARACTERISTICS
A. japonica 'Mr. Goldstrike'	Grows about 4 to 6 ft. high / large, glossy, dark-green leaves with gold markings / excellent accent plant for shade gardens
A. j. 'Picturata'	Bright golden-yellow centers / deep-green leaves

Golden Mirror Plant

Coprosma repens 'Aurea'

*Golden Mirror Plants, or Looking-Glass Plants, are so called because their leaves are spatula-shaped with shiny, waxy surfaces. They are low-growing, spreading shrubs with variegated green-and-gold foliage. Many varieties produce small, colorful, clusters of seeds in hues of yellow-orange to red that are eaten and dispersed by your visiting birds. In their natural habitat they grow along the seacoast and can tolerate strong winds but not extended periods of freezing temperatures or drought conditions. As long as there is adequate humidity and moisture, Coprosma repens can withstand heat. For neighborhoods close to the ocean, I (Bruce) like to use them as low-maintenance plants—once they are established, they require very little care. Although their flowers are insignificant, their variegated foliage adds color and texture to the landscape. Since Golden Mirror Plants are dioecious, the male and female flowers are on separate plants. If you want their seeds to develop, plant male and female plants close to each other. To identify the male plants, look for flowers with stamens; if the flowers have pistils, they are female plants. **Note:** If you cannot find Coprosma repens 'Aurea', look for Coprosma baueri, another botanical name sometimes used for the same plant.*

Family Name / Origin Rubiaceae / New Zealand, Australia

Bloom Period and Color Flowers are insignificant.

Mature Height × Spread 3 to 4 ft. × 4 to 6 ft.

When and How to Plant Plant Golden Mirror Plant from 1- or 5-gallon containers in the fall, late winter, or early spring. Avoid planting in the summer months because they dislike hot, dry conditions. Space 6 to 8 ft. apart in well-drained soils. Mulch the surface of the ground out beyond the canopy of the plant with 2 to 3 in. of humus mulch or compost. See Planting Techniques, p. 398.

Climate & Culture

Preferred Zones
9–11

Sun Preferences

Sun and Soil Preferences Since they are found along the coast, they tolerate pH soil readings as high as 7.2 and do best in full-sun or partial-shade locations.

Moisture Requirements Water infrequently and thoroughly to encourage the development of deep roots.

Fertilizing If fertilizing is necessary, apply a complete fertilizer, 6-10-4, in early spring.

Pruning and Care To maintain their shape, prune back only the errant branches. Deadheading is unnecessary. Propagate in spring from semi-hardwood cuttings.

Pests and Diseases They are resistant to diseases and insects.

Companion Plantings and Design Plant several different varieties of C. *repens* together in your landscape for interesting contrast. We recommend them for mass plantings as hedges and windbreaks, providing a milder microclimate for other plants such as Ivy Geraniums, Lily of the Nile, and Impatiens.

Our Personal Favorites

NAME	SPECIAL CHARACTERISTICS
C. *repens* 'Golden Splash'	Foliage uniformly golden yellow
C. *repens* 'Marble Queen'	Light-green-and-white foliage
C. *repens* 'Pink Splendor'	Deep-green foliage with yellow margins that later turn pink

Heavenly Bamboo
Nandina domestica

It is an interesting botanical fact that N. domestica is the only species associated with the genus Nandina. Called Heavenly Bamboo because Chinese and Japanese temple gardens use them extensively, this is a misnomer, since they are really more closely related to Barberries. They are popular in temple gardens because their appearance is similar to that of bamboo, yet they have a hardier nature and colorful leaves. Their compound, lacy foliage is multicolored, in hues of red, orange, yellow, and green, and they develop from clusters of upright, cane-like stems. During the summer, white sprays of flowers are pollinated by honeybees, butterflies, and wind, but the resulting bright-red berries that form in the fall are the more spectacular feature of these plants and provide food for your resident and migratory birds. The plants are dioecious, meaning male and female flowers are borne on separate plants. Both are needed for cross-pollination for the development of berries. Heavenly Bamboo's autumn-colored leaves and red berries are wonderful seasonal additions to your cut-flower arrangements. Once established, Heavenly Bamboo tolerate drought, cold, and heat, but they prefer protection from the wind.

Family Name / Origin Berberidaceae / Asia

Bloom Period and Color White flowers bloom in summer (in addition, Heavenly Bamboo is grown for its colorful red seeds).

Mature Height × Spread 4 to 6 ft. (clumping)

When and How to Plant You can plant Heavenly Bamboo any time of year from 1- or 5-gallon containers. For accent groupings in your landscape, plant them 4 ft. on center. Make the watering basin twice the plant's diameter, create a berm 4 to 6 in. in height, and mulch the basin's surface with 2 in. of compost or humus mulch. See Planting Techniques, p. 398.

Climate & Culture

Preferred Zones
7–11

Sun Preferences

Sun and Soil Preferences Partial shade is preferred, although they will grow in full sun. Heavenly Bamboo plants tolerate pH ranges from 6.5 to 7.0. They prefer loam soil but will adapt to denser soil.

Moisture Requirements Thoroughly water after planting; thereafter, irrigate as needed. Never allow the root zone to completely dry out, because the foliage will wilt and the plant might not recover.

Fertilizing Fertilize twice a year, early spring and late summer, with a complete food such as 6-10-4.

Pruning and Care If you do not want berries to develop, deadhead the spent flowers—otherwise, leave the blossoms alone. Once the berries have dropped off, you can remove the flower stems (pedicels) if their appearance is an annoyance. If you want to emphasize the vertical beauty of their stems, remove the lower leaves from the bottom two-thirds of the plant.

Pests and Diseases Very few diseases and insects affect Heavenly Bamboo, which is also known to be deer-resistant.

Companion Plantings and Design You can plant Heavenly Bamboo *en masse* to serve as foundation plantings. They also grow well with Prostrate Natal Plum, Shore Junipers, and Pink Indian Hawthorn.

Our Personal Favorite

NAME	SPECIAL CHARACTERISTICS
N. domestica 'Gulf Stream' (Pl. Pat. #5656)	Grows to 4 ft. / bronze new growth / red fall color

Hibiscus

Hibiscus rosa-sinensis

The name Hibiscus probably comes from the fact that these plants were naturally found along the same riverbanks as the Ibis birds. Native to tropical areas of Asia, H. rosa-sinensis *plants are evergreen shrubs that produce beautiful flowers in a wide range of brilliant colors, and some of the hybrids have spectacular eight- to ten-inch-diameter blooms. There are single and double-flowered forms. While it is unfortunate that each flower lasts for only one day, the continuous and abundant bloom cycle, from late spring to fall, more than compensates for each single flower's short life span. In California landscapes they grow to ten feet high. Hibiscus have glossy-green foliage with slightly serrated edges. Since they are tropical plants, they withstand heat as long as there is plenty of humidity and moist soil, but they need protection from the wind and must be in frost-free areas. They make excellent hedge screens if allowed to reach full height. Double Hibiscus tend to be smaller than single Hibiscus varieties and make excellent container plants for patios and atriums in full sun. If you want to use Hibiscus for hedges, plant them close enough so that their mature canopies will touch each other. For example, plant the variety 'San Diego Red' six to eight feet on center—they are large plants and their canopies will merge easily when spaced properly.*

Family Name / Origin Malvaceae / India

Bloom Period and Color Red, white, pink, yellow, or orange flowers bloom late spring to fall.

Mature Height × **Spread** 4 to 10 ft. × 4 to 6 ft.

When and How to Plant The best time to plant is in spring so they will have the long summer growing period to establish their root systems. If you select 1- or 5-gallon containers, be aware they will grow much larger, and space them so that their mature canopies do not touch each other. See p. 398.

Sun and Soil Preferences They can survive in partial shade, but for maximum bloom production, full sun is best. They require an acidic pH, 6.5 to 7.0, with a rich, organic loam soil that is kept adequately moist.

Moisture Requirements Hibiscus are tropical plants and must have sufficient moisture at all times.

Fertilizing Fertilize twice a year, in spring and in early summer, with an acid food, 6-10-4.

Pruning and Care Prune for shape in the early spring and when unruly new branches appear above the canopy. Deadheading is unnecessary.

Pests and Diseases Even though Hibiscus are beautiful landscape shrubs, you must keep a vigilant eye out for disease and pests. When you see stringy strands of white cottony honeydew, resembling cotton candy, hanging from the undersides of the foliage, you can be fairly sure it is the work of the giant whitefly. One of the more effective controls is Neem oil.

Companion Plantings and Design Pink Powder Puff, Saucer Magnolia, and Lavender Starflower grow well with Hibiscus.

Climate & Culture

Preferred Zones
10–11

Sun Preferences

Our Personal Favorites

NAME	SPECIAL CHARACTERISTICS
H. rosa-sinensis 'Crown of Bohemia'	Full double blooms / golden-yellow petals / deep orange-red throat
H. rosa-sinensis 'Hula Girl'	Large single yellow blooms / a touch of bright red in its throat

Hollywood Twisted Juniper
Juniperus chinensis 'Torulosa'

J. chinensis *'Torulosa'* is a dense, tall, erect, and twisted free-form shrub. Imported from China and Japan, it has adapted easily to mild Mediterranean climates such as that found in Southern California. We suspect that its common name, Hollywood Twisted Juniper, comes from the fact that it was planted so extensively along the streets and in the gardens of Tinsel Town. Now it is used as an accent plant in areas that allow for its mature dimensions. It is often planted in pairs on opposite sides of driveways and walkways in formal landscapes. It has finely textured, matte-green foliage that, when crushed, emits a pungent smell. In summer, it forms clusters of small bluish cones that look like berries. Once established, it is extremely tolerant to wind and drought conditions, as well as temperatures down to -10 degrees Fahrenheit. If sufficient moisture is provided, it also withstands the extreme temperatures of the desert. Hollywood Twisted Junipers are often planted along coastal areas where constant prevailing winds sculpt their shapes into dramatic, twisted forms. **Note:** *If you cannot find* Juniperus chinensis *'Torulosa', look for* Juniperus chinensis *'Kaizuka', another cultivar name sometimes used for the same plant.*

Family Name / Origin Cupressaceae / Asia

Bloom Period and Color There are no flowers; the Hollywood Twisted Juniper is coniferous.

Mature Height × Spread 8 to 15 ft. × 6 to 10 ft.

When and How to Plant Spring or fall are the best seasons to plant. Choose from a variety of container sizes, even 24- to 36-in. boxed specimens, and plant at least 8 to 10 ft. on center. Create a watering basin twice the diameter of the plant's canopy; water thoroughly to collapse the air pockets in the root zone. Mulch this surface with 2 in. of compost or humus mulch. Also see p. 398.

Climate & Culture

Preferred Zones
9–11

Sun Preferences

Sun and Soil Preferences Plant in full sun or semi-shade in a well-drained, slightly acidic soil with a pH of 6.5 to 7.0.

Moisture Requirements Depending on the climatic conditions and the plant's growth rate, water deeply and thoroughly.

Fertilizing Once established, fertilize in fall and spring with a complete food, such as a 15-15-15.

Pruning and Care There is no need to prune, unless it is grown as a topiary or espalier. If you want to control their height, width, and twisted form, train these plants into topiaries or espaliers by selectively pruning for shape in late winter or early spring. Select the main vertical trunks that define the plant's form and identify the lateral branches where the growth of new foliage occurs. Next, take a picture or make a sketch of your plant, and using a pen, draw in the desired shape or design that you want. As time goes on, prune accordingly until your creative idea becomes a reality.

Pests and Diseases Few, if any, pests bother this plant.

Companion Plantings and Design For companion plants we recommend Pink Indian Hawthorn, Bird of Paradise, and Japanese Mock Orange.

Our Personal Favorite

NAME	SPECIAL CHARACTERISTICS
J. c. 'Torulosa Variegata'	Splashes of yellow variegations in the foliage

Hydrangea

Hydrangea macrophylla

*Many believe the name Hydrangea, with its origin in the word hydra, means that the plant requires massive amounts of water. Actually, the name was given because the seed capsules look like water pitchers. Hydrangeas are large, mound-shaped shrubs with long, six- to eight-inch, dark-green leaves that have coarsely serrated margins. They are used as accent plants in shady environments and are also available in flower shops as blooming potted plants. Their spectacular round clusters of blossoms can reach diameters of ten inches. Although their natural color is light pink, Hydrangeas have variable colors that depend upon their genetic history, soil chemistry, and location. Hybrids come in shades of red, pink, lavender, purple, blue, white, and whitish-green and bloom throughout the spring months. Because their inflorescences are so dramatic, they are displayed to best effect in simple vase arrangements. Although short-lived as cut flowers, their decorative beauty more than compensates for their temporary nature. They have much more longevity as dried flowers and are used to make extravagant wreaths, garlands, and many other creative designs. Just cut them in the early-morning hours, wrap wire around their ends, and hang them upside down in a cool, dark area such as a closet until completely dry. **Note:** If you cannot find Hydrangea macrophylla, look for Hydrangea hortensis, another botanical name sometimes used for the same plant.*

Family Name / Origin   Saxifragaceae / Japan

Bloom Period and Color   Pink or blue flowers bloom in spring.

Mature Height × Spread   4 to 6 ft. × 6 to 8 ft.

When and How to Plant   In the spring, after the last frost, select 1- or 5-gallon Hydrangeas and plant them 6 ft. on center. After you have a watering basin that is 4 to 6 ft. in diameter and 4 to 6 in. high, spread a blanket of humus mulch or compost that is 2 to 3 in. deep over the basin's surface. Refer to Planting Techniques, p. 398, for more information.

Climate & Culture

Preferred Zones 9–11

Sun Preferences

Sun and Soil Preferences   For best results, plant in partially shaded sites, although they will tolerate full sun as long as it is cool and humid. They prefer an acidic soil, pH 6.5 to 7.0. To ensure development of vigorous plants and facilitate good percolation, use a highly organic soil mixture of equal parts loam and planting mix.

Moisture Requirements   Successful cultivation of Hydrangeas requires an abundant supply of moisture, in an area protected from the wind and freezing temperatures. It is imperative that you water deeply, thoroughly, and regularly, keeping in mind the important variables of temperature, season, and wind activity.

Fertilizing   Fertilize with an acid food, once in early spring after the last frost and once in early summer.

Pruning and Care   In early summer, after your Hydrangeas have finished blooming, prune them back about 20 percent. Pay particular attention to any dead wood, dried inflorescences, and errant, crossing branches, and lace them out enough for sufficient air circulation and light to reach the centers of the plants. If you want a profusion of smaller-sized blossoms rather than massive, single flowers, remove the terminal buds in early spring. This stimulates the development of multiple flowers on the lower portion of the stems. To change their natural floral color from pink to blue, apply aluminum sulfate granules according to the manufacturer's instructions.

Pests and Diseases   Aphid infestations can be controlled by washing the critters off with a strong stream of water or applying Neem oil.

Companion Plantings and Design   Plant Hydrangeas with Mystery Gardenias, Camellias, and Saucer Magnolias.

Japanese Mock Orange

Pittosporum tobira

Japanese Mock Orange is considered a large shrub or small tree, and is a vigorous grower with shiny green leaves. As a tree it can reach a height of twelve to fifteen feet, but if grown as a shrub, it can be limited to six to eight feet. Even though it does not produce oranges, it bears wonderfully aromatic citrus-scented spring flowers. With blossoms resembling clusters of creamy white stars against a backdrop of green or variegated foliage, it makes an excellent hedge plant or an ideal choice for a scented garden. Once established, Japanese Mock Orange tolerates drought, wind, and even heat if enough moisture is available, but it dislikes extended periods of freezing temperatures. At our former home, in an enclosed patio we grew a magnificent Dwarf St. Mary's Magnolia Tree, a grouping of Mystery Gardenias, and variegated Japanese Mock Orange. On warm spring and summer evenings, it was so delightful to be able to sit and enjoy their fragrances wafting on the nightly breeze. Sharon used both the green and variegated foliage varieties of Japanese Mock Orange as wonderful fillers for fresh flower arrangements. During the spring months, these cuttings brought the fragrance of citrus indoors.

Family Name / Origin Pittosporaceae /
Japan, China

Bloom Period and Color Aromatic white citrus-
scented flowers bloom in spring.

Mature Height × Spread 6 to 8 ft. × 6 ft.

When and How to Plant Plant Japanese Mock
Orange from 1- or 5-gallon containers any time of
the year, but spring or fall are best. Space 6 ft. on
center if using as a hedge, 10 ft. if using as a single
focal plant. Build a watering basin 6 ft. in diameter
with an edge 4 to 6 in. high. Mulch the basin's
surface with 2 in. of humus mulch or compost as
needed. See Planting Techniques, p. 398.

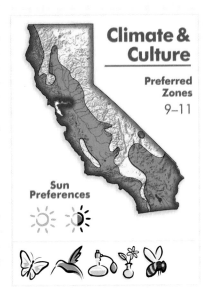

**Climate &
Culture**

Preferred
Zones
9–11

Sun
Preferences

Sun and Soil Preferences Plant in full sun or partial shade and provide a
porous soil that permits good percolation. Soil pH needs to be slightly acidic
to neutral, 6.5 to 7.0.

Moisture Requirements In loam soils, soak *P. tobira* deeply every seven
to ten days, adjusting watering frequency according to climatic and growing
conditions.

Fertilizing Fertilize with a complete food, 15-15-15, after the last frost.

Pruning and Care Prune for shape or cut back errant growth in late winter
or early spring. Deadheading the flowers is unnecessary unless you wish to
eliminate seed development.

Pests and Diseases Aphid infestations can be controlled by washing the
critters off with a strong stream of water or applying Neem oil.

Companion Plantings and Design For companion plantings we
recommend Magnolia Trees, Mystery Gardenias, Lily of the Nile, and Bird
of Paradise. Both the green- and variegated-foliage varieties of Japanese
Mock Orange make wonderful fillers for fresh flower arrangements.

Our Personal Favorite

NAME	SPECIAL CHARACTERISTICS
P. tobira 'Wheelerii'	Commonly called Wheeler's Dwarf / a very dense plant with a mounded form / no need for pruning if spaced 8 to 10 ft. on center / available as solid green or variegated

Laurustinus

Viburnum tinus

Laurustinus is a medium to large evergreen shrub with a dense branching structure that characteristically grows from its base upwards, creating a mass of foliage and flowers. Since no other Viburnum produces such a dense foliage, it makes a fine hedge, foundation planting, or even an individual focal plant. The leathery leaves are dark green above and lighter in color underneath. It blooms periodically throughout the year, but is most abundant in the late winter to early spring. The buds are initially pale pink, and then as they open, they transform into clusters of delicately fragrant white flowers. Indigo berries appear simultaneously with the flowers, creating a lovely contrast of fruits and blossoms on a single plant. Since the flowering cycle is fairly continuous throughout the year, the simultaneous appearance of buds, blooms, and berries is one of the unique features of Laurustinus. In the spring and summer months, birds, bees, and butterflies enjoy Viburnum's harvest. Although it is endemic to Mediterranean areas, the Viburnum is not drought tolerant, but it can withstand heat if you provide adequate moisture. Avoid planting in areas where there are extended periods of freezing temperatures or frigid winds.

Family Name / Origin Caprifoliaceae / SE Europe, Mediterranean

Bloom Period and Color Pink buds and white flowers are present throughout the year.

Mature Height × **Spread** 5 to 10 ft. × 6 ft.

When and How to Plant Plant in early spring or early fall from 1- or 5-gallon containers. Space 6 to 8 ft. on center if you want a hedge whose mature height is 6 to 10 ft. Build a watering basin large enough to encourage lateral root growth. If you have a hedge of Viburnums, create a long watering basin 2 ft. from the hedge line and build two parallel berms, 6 in. high. Mulch the surface of the basin with 2 in. of compost or humus mulch. Also see p. 398.

Climate & Culture

Preferred Zones
8–11

Sun Preferences

Sun and Soil Preferences This popular plant grows in just about any location, sun or shade, but full sun is preferable for flower and seed production. Make sure the soil is porous, loam, and well-drained with 20 to 30 percent organic material. Soil pH needs to be slightly acidic or neutral, 6.5 to 7.0.

Moisture Requirements Viburnums adapt to almost any site, but it is important to water adequately for continued growth. After planting, water thoroughly and deeply to collapse the air pockets in the root zone. Subsequently, monitor the soil moisture and water as necessary.

Fertilizing Feed in spring and fall with a complete fertilizer such as 15-15-15.

Pruning and Care Prune for shape and size control after spring bloom; deadhead only to prevent seed production. Since this species of *Viburnum* is such a dense grower, frequent pruning is unnecessary to maintain its form—but to encourage continued growth, lace the plant about once a year in fall, cutting out the dead wood, pruning off any errant growth, and opening the canopy.

Pests and Diseases Aphid infestations can be controlled by washing the critters off with a strong stream of water or applying Neem oil.

Companion Plantings and Design Red Clusterberry Cotoneaster, Saucer Magnolia, and Glossy Abelia make ideal companion plants.

Lavender Starflower
Grewia caffra

Lavender Starflower is a fast-growing shrub with tiered branches that makes a great espalier plant. If you have a limited space in an enclosed area that receives full sun, we recommend it as an excellent container plant. G. caffra is known for its rigid branch structure, making it easy to train as espaliers. Since every plant has a front and a back side, position your Lavender Starflower so that its foliage and blossoms are exposed to the direct sunlight and its more barren side is up against a wall, trellis, or fence. Throughout the summer, its striking one-inch lavender star-shaped flowers will be beautifully displayed against the light-green foliage. Its foliage is leathery in texture and has serrated edges. Like other established plants from South Africa, it tolerates drought, wind, and full sun but cannot tolerate extended freezing temperatures. A peaceful summertime pastime is to watch your garden butterflies, hummingbirds, and bees hover around and harvest the nectar from the Lavender Starflowers. **Note:** If you cannot find Grewia caffra, look for Grewia occidentalis, another botanical name sometimes used for the same plant.

Family Name / Origin Tiliaceae / South Africa

Bloom Period and Color Blue flowers bloom in spring, summer, and fall.

Mature Height × Spread 6 to 10 ft. × 6 to 10 ft.

When and How to Plant Plant in the spring or fall months from 1- or 5-gallon containers. Some 5-gallon container plants are already trained as espaliers. If you use them as espaliers on walls or fences, space them 8 ft. on center. If you use them as shrubs, space them 6 ft. on center. After planting, mulch the ground's surface with 2 in. of compost or humus mulch. Consult Planting Techniques, p. 398, for more definitive information.

Climate & Culture

Preferred Zones

10–11

Sun Preference

Sun and Soil Preferences Locate in full sun for maximum bloom production, in slightly acidic or neutral soil, 6.5 to 7.0 pH. Keep in mind that they prefer a porous soil.

Moisture Requirements Because it is a drought-tolerant plant, water deeply but infrequently once it is established.

Fertilizing Fertilize in the spring and fall with a complete fertilizer such as 6-10-4 and you will be rewarded with lush foliage and profuse blossoms throughout the summer season.

Pruning and Care It is unnecessary to deadhead the flowers since they fall to the ground naturally after they are spent.

Pests and Diseases Few insects or diseases bother the Lavender Starflower.

Companion Plantings and Design You can easily train it to grow upright and surround it with low-growing annual color companion plants such as Alyssum or cascading Petunias.

Mystery Gardenia

Gardenia jasminoides 'Mystery'

The genus Gardenia was assigned to the plant by botanist John Ellis (1711–1776) in honor of American naturalist Dr. Alexander Garden (1730–1791). This species is a favorite among florists, because the waxy flowers make wonderful corsages and bouquets as well as simple but elegant floating arrangements in brandy snifters. These are small shrubs with lustrous dark-green leaves and branches that spread out and up unevenly. Their dramatic, creamy white, three-inch, camellia-like, double-flowered blossoms intoxicate the passerby with their unforgettable perfumed scent. Butterflies, birds, and bees are also attracted to the fragrance. These subtropical shrubs are ideal as small patio trees, espaliers, or container plants. The bloom period is from late spring to the end of summer, provided there are adequate daylight hours and warm temperatures. Select a shaded or filtered-light location that is sheltered from prevailing winds—it can be in an area that receives morning sun and afternoon shade, such as the east side of a house or patio. Since Gardenias are native to Southern China where it is temperate and humid, they do not tolerate dry, windy, or extended cold-weather conditions. The flowers of G. jasminoides 'Mystery' bloom in succession, rather than simultaneously, which dramatically lengthens the blooming season, but you will rarely see a plant full of Gardenias at any one time.

Family Name / Origin Rubiaceae / S China, South Africa

Bloom Period and Color White flowers in summer.

Mature Height × Spread 4 × 4 ft.

When and How to Plant Plant in spring or early summer from 1- or 5-gallon containers, spacing 4 ft. on center. See Planting Techniques, p. 398.

Sun and Soil Preferences Plant in a shaded or filtered-light location. An acidic soil pH of 6.0 to 6.5 is preferred. It should be rich in organic material such as compost, humus mulch, or planting mix. Make sure its porosity allows for good percolation.

Climate & Culture

Preferred Zones 9–11

Sun Preferences

Moisture Requirements Monitor the soil moisture content. Mystery Gardenias do not like to have their roots standing in water.

Fertilizing Fertilize mid-spring with an acid food, 6-10-4. During the summer months, if you find an abundance of yellow leaves towards the lower areas of your plants, it may be due to nitrogen deficiency. Evenly apply bloodmeal, 13-0-0, as a corrective measure. Although they are susceptible to iron chlorosis, you can correct this problem by applying chelated iron in a water-soluble form directly to the foliage or soil.

Pruning and Care Prune to maintain shape or remove dead wood. As a precaution against the vectoring of diseases from plant to plant, it is a good idea to deadhead the spent flowers. Deadheading also encourages the proliferation and continuation of the bloom cycle.

Pests and Diseases Aphid infestations can be controlled by washing the critters off with a strong stream of water or applying Neem oil.

Companion Plantings and Design Yesterday-Today-and-Tomorrow, Hibiscus, and Impatiens are ideal companion plants.

Our Personal Favorite

NAME	SPECIAL CHARACTERISTICS
G. jasminoides 'Radicans'	Known as the Miniature Gardenia / spreading growth pattern / 12 in. high, 2 ft. wide / rich green petite foliage / prolific small, white, fragrant flowers in summer / used as ground cover in warmer areas

Pink Indian Hawthorn

Rhaphiolepsis indica 'Enchantress'

Rhaphiolepsis indica 'Enchantress' has a form that is known as "roundy-moundy" in the nursery trade. This term is given to plants that do not require shearing to maintain their shape because they grow so evenly and densely. Commonly called Pink Indian Hawthorn, it is an evergreen shrub with glossy, green, leathery leaves and serrated margins. It makes ideal border plants or large groupings on banks combined with other landscape plants. Because of its compact nature, it is also a popular plant with bonsai enthusiasts. From mid-spring to early summer the entire plant bursts forth with massive clusters of rose-pink flowers that make it look like a beautiful spring bouquet. In the Southern California community where we live, these plants abound en masse because of their easy maintenance and profuse flush of spring blossoms. Although they do not last long as cut flowers, they do make a lovely filler in home arrangements. After the flowers are spent, blue-black berries develop and will remain throughout the fall season, providing a feast for your mockingbirds, scrub jays, sparrows, and mourning doves. Deadhead only if you do not want the berries.

Family Name / Origin Rosaceae / S China

Bloom Period and Color Rose-pink flowers bloom mid-spring to early summer.

Mature Height × Spread 2 to 4 ft. × 3 ft.

When and How to Plant Plant in spring or fall from 1- or 5-gallon containers. For mass plantings, space 3 or 4 ft. on center in either a triangular or square pattern. After planting, build a watering basin 4 to 5 ft. in diameter and 4 to 6 in. in height; mulch the basin surface with 2 in. of compost or humus mulch. See Planting Techniques, p. 398.

Climate & Culture

Preferred Zones
10–11

Sun Preferences

Sun and Soil Preferences For optimum growth and bloom production, select a site in full sun, although these plants tolerate locations in partial shade. Make sure the soil texture for the backfill is loam with about 20 to 30 percent organic material such as planting mix or humus mulch, and that the soil is slightly acidic, with a pH of 6.5 to 7.0. A porous and friable soil is important.

Moisture Requirements Water deeply and thoroughly immediately after planting; thereafter, water as needed depending on climatic and soil moisture conditions. If you have any doubts about the moisture content, put a spade in the soil about 6 in. deep and push it back to expose the soil profile; if it is wet, wait two or three days before deep-soaking.

Fertilizing Fertilize early spring and early fall with a complete food, 6-10-4.

Pruning and Care It is wise to lace out the maturing plant. Prune back any errant growth to maintain the naturally symmetrical shape.

Pests and Diseases Aphid infestations can be controlled by washing the critters off with a strong stream of water or applying Neem oil. Control snails with a molluscicide such as iron phosphate.

Companion Plantings and Design Golden Mirror Plant, Heavenly Bamboo, and Rock Rose make good companions.

Our Personal Favorite

NAME	SPECIAL CHARACTERISTICS
Rhaphiolepsis umbellata (syn: *R. ovata*)	From Japan / commonly known as Yeddo Hawthorn / fragrant white flowers with bright pink-red stamens

Pink Powder Puff

Calliandra haematocephala

Pink Powder Puffs have large reddish-pink flowers, up to three inches in diameter, that resemble fine feather dusters or their namesake, powder puffs. The flowers are actually clusters of fine-textured stamens. One of the most interesting characteristics of Pink Powder Puffs is that their leaves fold up at night or during periods of low light intensity. If left untrained, they grow into large unruly bushes or small trees. For this reason we think they are most effective when grown as espaliers on south-facing walls or fences. You do not need a trellis to espalier them because they are self-supporting plants. Their leaves are compound, in five to ten pairs, of medium texture, light green underneath, matte green on top, and are tinged with a blush of pink when they first develop. Pink Powder Puffs do not tolerate extended freezing temperatures, and they need an even and constant amount of moisture. They also need to be pruned regularly to maintain the espalier form, or to keep them contained as shrubs. But if you are willing to take a little extra time with them, you will be rewarded with a very unusual shrub. Note: If you cannot find Calliandra haematocephala, look for Calliandra inequilatera, another botanical name sometimes used for the same plant.

Family Name / Origin Leguminosae / tropical America

Bloom Period and Color Pink flowers bloom summer and fall.

Mature Height × Spread 6 to 10 ft. × 8 ft.

When and How to Plant Plant from 1- or 5-gallon containers in spring in a frost-free location. Make watering basins 4 to 6 in. high and at least twice the diameter of the original containers. Distribute a 2-in. blanket of mulch beneath the plants, keeping it 6 in. from the bases. See p. 398.

Sun and Soil Preferences Full sun and well-drained acidic soil with a pH of 6.5 to 7.0 are necessary for optimum growth.

Moisture Requirements Provide a deep, thorough soaking once a week or as weather and growing conditions dictate.

Fertilizing Fertilize twice a year, early spring and early summer, with a complete fertilizer, 6-10-4.

Pruning and Care If growing as shrubs, prune during the formative years to maximize bloom production. When new growth reaches about 12 in., pinch back the ends at the tips. If you want to espalier, select young 1-gallon starter plants with enough branching structure. Choose two or three main stems to support future lateral growth and remove all branches behind and in front of the plants. Prune regularly because new foliage and blooms appear on current-season growth. Deadhead to extend the flowering cycle.

Pests and Diseases Aphid infestations can be controlled by washing the critters off with a strong stream of water or applying Neem oil.

Companion Plantings and Design Hibiscus, Bird of Paradise, and Saucer Magnolia are good companion plants.

Climate & Culture

Preferred Zones 10–11

Sun Preference

Our Personal Favorite

NAME	SPECIAL CHARACTERISTICS
C. *tweedii*	Known as Mexican Flame Bush / native to the southern United States / red flowers about 2 in. in diameter / foliage much finer textured than that of Pink Powder Puff / if established, very drought tolerant

Pride of Madeira

Echium candicans

While visiting the famous Hanbury Botanic Garden in La Mortola, Italy, we saw the most spectacular Echium candicans *growing in all their massive glory on steep bluffs exposed to the hot Mediterranean sun and blustery winds. It was late spring, and their dramatic spiked panicles of purplish-blue flowers looked like candles blowing in the wind against a backdrop of grayish-green leaves covered with fine hairs. The E. candicans in our yard offer a nature show with ruby-throated, iridescent green Anna hummingbirds, yellow and black bumblebees, and boldly patterned monarch and swallowtail butterflies flitting around the plants. Commonly called the Pride of Madeira, they grow tall and spread out over a wide area, so give these plants enough space. Although heat and cold will affect their rate of growth, they can easily survive such conditions as well as tolerate drought and wind. If you use them as cut flowers, make sure you remove all the foliage that might stand in water. Otherwise, the rotting foliage will increase the bacteria count of the vase water and reduce the longevity of the cut-flower arrangement.* **Note:** *If you cannot find* Echium candicans, *look for* Echium fastuosum, *another botanical name sometimes used for the same plant.*

Family Name / Origin Boraginaceae / W Europe, Canary Islands

Bloom Period and Color Blue flowers bloom in spring and summer.

Mature Height × Spread 6 to 8 ft. × 12 ft.

When and How to Plant Spring is the optimum season to plant. Plant at least 8 to 10 ft. on center from 1- or 5-gallon containers. To encourage rapid maturation of root systems, make watering basins at least 6 ft. in diameter and 6 in. high. Mulch with compost or humus. See Planting Techniques, p. 398.

Sun and Soil Preferences Plant in full sun. A pH of 6.5 is ideal, but they will tolerate pH ranges up to 7.2. They prefer porous soils to accommodate deep watering.

Climate & Culture

Preferred Zones

10–11

Sun Preference

Moisture Requirements Deeply soak your Pride of Madeira immediately after planting by filling the watering basin two or three times so that all the air pockets in the root zone will collapse.

Fertilizing When necessary, fertilize in late winter or early spring with a fertilizer such as a 16-20-0.

Pruning and Care Prune to control size and shape in fall. After the bloom cycle is complete, remove the spent panicles. If you want to propagate these plants, allow the panicles to remain until their seeds mature, then cut the panicles, shake out the seeds, sow them in starter pots, and keep moist.

Pests and Diseases Few diseases or insects affect these plants. In fact, their pubescent foliar texture discourages chewing insects.

Companion Plantings and Design In our yard we have Pride of Madeira growing beside Crape Myrtle, Butterfly Bush, and Glossy Abelia.

Our Personal Favorite

NAME	SPECIAL CHARACTERISTICS
E. wildpretii (also *E. bourgaeanum*)	Commonly known as the Tower of Jewels / long narrow leaves with spikes of funnel-shaped flowers that are salmon in color / biennial, meaning it takes two years from seed germination to death / blooms during the second year

Prostrate Natal Plum

Carissa macrocarpa 'Prostrata'

*Prostrate Natal Plums are excellent evergreen border and barrier plants because of their thorns. Due to their low-growing habit, they may also be used effectively as a ground cover. Prostrate Natal Plums have bright green foliage that contrasts nicely with delicately scented white flowers and oval-shaped red fruit. Although I (Bruce) have never tasted it, the fruits are said to make a flavorful jelly. Carissa macrocarpa comes from the southern coast of South Africa, whose climate is similar to the coastal areas of Southern California. I use Prostrate Natal Plums in landscape designs for seaside areas as well as in gardens subject to heat and wind, but I do not recommend them in frost zones. As with other members of the Apocynacae plant family, a distinctive white sap oozes when their branches are cut. Some people may suffer an allergic reaction to this sap, so wear gloves when handling these plants or wash your hands with warm water and detergent as a precautionary measure. Other plants that belong to this family are: Mandevilla, Oleanders, Plumeria, Star Jasmine, and Vinca. **Note:** If you cannot find Carissa macrocarpa 'Prostrata', look for C. grandiflora 'Prostrata', another botanical name sometimes used for the same plant.*

Family Name / Origin Apocynaceae / So. Africa

Bloom Period and Color White flowers bloom in spring; red fruit appears in summer.

Mature Height × Spread 2 to 3 ft. × 4 to 6 ft.

When and How to Plant Plant after the last frost of the season from 1- or 5-gallon containers, planting 6 ft. on center. Mix the soil from the planting pit with an equal amount of humus mulch or planting mix. See Planting Techniques, p. 398.

Sun and Soil Preferences Plant Prostrate Natal Plums in full sun. They need well-drained soils with a pH of 6.5 to 7.2.

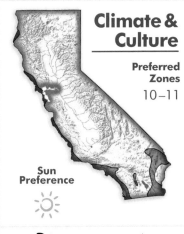

Climate & Culture

Preferred Zones
10–11

Sun Preference

Moisture Requirements Water Prostrate Natal Plums thoroughly once a week, depending on weather conditions. Since they have relatively shallow, fibrous root systems, mulching the surface area helps maintain moisture in the root zone.

Fertilizing Fertilize twice a year, once in early spring, once in early summer.

Pruning and Care There is no need to deadhead the flowers. Occasionally there are rapidly developing shoots that grow vertically, similar to water spouts on citrus trees. These should be pruned out at their base.

Pests and Diseases Since they are dense, low-growing plants, they harbor snails and slugs, but a periodic application of snail bait should keep this problem under control. The long, sharp thorns on their branches deter animals such as deer.

Companion Plantings and Design Glossy Abelias, Heavenly Bamboo, and Pink Indian Hawthorn are good companion plants.

Our Personal Favorites

NAME	SPECIAL CHARACTERISTICS
C. macrocarpa 'Tuttlei'	Commonly known as Tuttle's Natal Plum / 12 to 18 in. × 3 to 4 ft. / foliage finer texture than that of Prostrate Natal Plum, fruits not as large / flowers in spring
C. macrocarpa 'Boxwood Beauty'	Grows 2 ft. high and wide / dense, deep-green foliage on tight, short branches / mounding habit / makes excellent hedge

Red Clusterberry Cotoneaster
Cotoneaster parneyi

C. parneyi *is different from our other Cotoneaster species because it is much larger in size and looser, less dense in structure. Its foliage is dull, gray-green with a coarse texture, and the leaves are two to three inches in length. Another distinguishing characteristic is that the underside of each leaf is tomentose, meaning it is fuzzy in texture. In contrast to its evergreen foliage, the deep-red clusters of berries make an outstanding display of color from fall through winter, and often into the spring months. Its loose-growing form and size create an ideal visual screen. Once established, it is very drought tolerant and can withstand wind, heat, and cold temperatures as low as 20 degrees Fahrenheit. Birds perch and feast on its arching branches when they are laden with berries. For your home enjoyment, you can cut some of these colorful branches to create striking fresh arrangements during the fall and winter months.* **Note:** *If you cannot find Cotoneaster* parneyi, *look for Cotoneaster* lacteus, *another botanical name sometimes used for the same plant.*

Family Name / Origin Rosaceae / China

Bloom Period and Color White flowers bloom in summer.

Mature Height × Spread 6 to 8 ft. × 8 ft.

When and How to Plant Plant in the spring and fall months out of 1- or 5-gallon containers and space them about 10 to 12 ft. on center for optimum results. Mulch with compost or humus mulch 2 in. deep in a watering basin that is 4 ft. in diameter. Make sure the watering basin is twice the diameter of the plant's canopy. Refer to Planting Techniques, p. 398, for more specific planting directions.

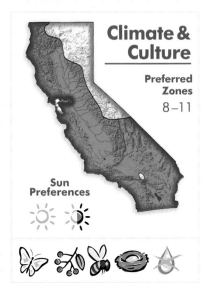

Climate & Culture

Preferred Zones
8–11

Sun Preferences

Sun and Soil Preferences Like other Cotoneaster species, Red Clusterberry Cotoneasters do best in full sun, but they can survive in partial shade. Their production of flowers and berries, however, will be much reduced in shaded areas. A neutral soil pH of 7.0 is ideal for these plants. Make sure the soil is porous enough to allow adequate percolation.

Moisture Requirements Thoroughly water the root zone immediately after planting so that all the air pockets collapse. Thereafter, irrigate depending on weather and growth demands.

Fertilizing If necessary, fertilize in late winter or early spring with a complete fertilizer, 6-10-4.

Pruning and Care Prune only for the purpose of shaping or removing dead wood. Deadheading the flowers is unnecessary. To increase bloom and berry production, pinch back the ends of the branches about 10 percent for the first and second growing seasons. This will increase the development of more branches as well as flowers and berries.

Pests and Diseases Like the other species of Cotoneasters, this one has few insect or disease problems.

Companion Plantings and Design Silverberry and Butterfly Bush make ideal plant companions.

Our Personal Favorite

NAME	SPECIAL CHARACTERISTICS
C. franchetii	Similar to Red Clusterberry Cotoneaster / grows to 10 ft. / pinkish berries

Rock Cotoneaster

Cotoneaster horizontalis

Rock Cotoneaster is so named because it is a native of hillside areas where there are rugged outcroppings of rocks. This is why I (Bruce) select it when designing rock gardens or designing a garden where there is a difference in elevation, such as a terraced area or bank. Rock Cotoneaster is a deciduous shrub with a fan-like spreading habit. With thickly intertwining prostrate branches, it is an excellent ground cover. In spring, its dark-green shiny leaves provide a lovely backdrop to its small flesh-pink spring flowers. As temperatures cool down in fall, the foliage of Rock Cotoneaster turns from a grayish-green to reddish-orange or purplish-bronze, and it produces brilliant red berries. This is an excellent choice for fall color and cold locations where temperatures drop to -10 degrees Fahrenheit. Once established, it will also tolerate drought, wind, and heat. Its abundant fall and winter berries are a source of food for quail, mockingbirds, and scrub jays as well as squirrels. In the summer months, its blooms attract butterflies, hummingbirds, and bees.

Family Name / Origin Rosaceae / China

Bloom Period and Color Small flesh-pink flowers bloom in spring.

Mature Height × **Spread** 2 to 3 ft. × 4 to 6 ft.

When and How to Plant Plant from 1- or 5-gallon containers in fall or early spring. Space about 4 to 6 ft. on center. Using 2 in. of organic material, mulch the ground's surface well beyond the plant's canopy, by at least 50 percent. This will encourage lateral root development by maintaining moisture in the root zone. Mix a preplant fertilizer, 2-10-6, at the manufacturer's recommended rate, with the backfill soil. See Planting Techniques, p. 398.

Climate & Culture

Preferred Zones
6–11

Sun Preferences

Sun and Soil Preferences Full sun is best. You can plant it in shadier areas, but it will produce fewer blooms and berries. Nevertheless, it is still an attractive plant because of its interesting branch structure and fall-colored foliage. The soil should provide even percolation and have a neutral pH, 7.0.

Moisture Requirements Immediately after planting, water thoroughly; thereafter, water as needed.

Fertilizing If necessary, fertilize in early spring with a complete fertilizer for shrubs and trees, 10-10-10.

Pruning and Care Prune only to remove the dead wood, because the form maintains itself. Do not deadhead the flowers.

Pests and Diseases Aphid infestations can be controlled by washing the critters off with a strong stream of water or applying Neem oil.

Companion Plantings and Design Other species of Cotoneaster and Silverberry are ideal plant companions.

Our Personal Favorites

NAME	SPECIAL CHARACTERISTICS
C. horizontalis 'Perpusillus'	Known as Ground Cotoneaster / intertwining branchlets with dark shiny leaves that turn orange to red in fall / red flowers in spring / semievergreen in colder areas
C. horizontalis 'Variegatus'	Another prostrate variety / green leaves edged in white

Rock Rose

Cistus × purpureus

Rock Rose comes from the Mediterranean region and the Canary Islands where annual rainfall is minimal. They are planted on our slope adjacent to our street, and although we watered them regularly during the first two years, once they established themselves, we left them alone. As shrubs, they are mound-shaped and grow to four feet high and six feet wide. Also known as Sun Roses, the leaves are ovate and green in spring, but as summer progresses, their leaves begin to desiccate and turn a dull grayish green. Flowers are single petal with the texture of crepe paper and measure about three inches in diameter. Bloom colors range from pink, to white, to purple. Their bloom period peaks in mid-spring. Once established, Rock Rose plants are extremely drought tolerant and even if their foliage wilts during the summer heat, they will revive when the rains return in fall. In addition, they tolerate cold and wind conditions. Since their bloom cycle coincides with the spring activities of butterflies, hummingbirds, and bees, you will attract lots of these visitors. It is important to select plants that are not rootbound in their containers, because the new root system needs to web into the soil that has been backfilled into the planting pit.

Family Name / Origin Cistaceae / Mediterranean, Canary Islands

Bloom Period and Color Pink, white, and purple flowers bloom in spring.

Mature Height × Spread 4 ft. × 6 ft.

When and How to Plant You can plant in fall or spring, but fall is best. Start with young 1- or 5-gallon plants that are not rootbound. To see if a plant is rootbound, carefully turn over the container and gently remove it. The rootball should not be tightly matted. Instead, you should be able to easily expose the absorbing, light-colored roots from the form of the rootball. Space 6 to 8 ft. on center and mulch the surface of the ground with 2 in. of compost or humus mulch. See Planting Techniques, p. 398, for more information.

Climate & Culture

Preferred Zones
9–11

Sun Preference

Sun and Soil Preferences Plant in full sun; if in partial shade, they will not bloom as profusely and their growth will be scraggly. They prefer a neutral pH of 7.0 and a well-drained soil so that their roots are not saturated.

Moisture Requirements Immediately after planting, give these plants a thorough and deep soaking. Once established, infrequent, deep waterings are best.

Fertilizing Fertilize with a complete fertilizer, 6-10-4, in late winter or early spring.

Pruning and Care Deadheading flowers is unnecessary, but lightly prune for shape in late winter.

Pests and Diseases Very few diseases or insects affect these plants.

Companion Plantings and Design We like to use Rock Rose plants as companions to California Lilac, Pride of Madeira, and other drought-tolerant trees, shrubs, and ground covers.

Our Personal Favorites

NAME	SPECIAL CHARACTERISTICS
C. × *purpureus* 'Brilliancy'	Clear pink flowers
C. × *purpureus* 'Betty Taudevin'	Deep reddish-pink flowers

Rockspray Cotoneaster
Cotoneaster microphyllus

C. microphyllus *plants are compact with a form that is different from that of*
C. horizontalis. *They grow in mounds and can be pruned in formal, symmetrical shapes. This particular species of Cotoneaster has a thick, dense structure that makes it ideal for pruning into formalized shapes. When pruning in this manner, make sure you lace the canopy from the inside out so that the sunlight reaches the latent buds, stimulating new growth. Commonly called Rockspray Cotoneasters, these evergreens are found growing out of clusters of rocks. Their foliage is fine-textured with a rough surface and is shiny and dark-green in color during the summer. When the weather cools, the leaves change to a reddish-green coloration. From late summer to early winter, the spent flowers give way to red berries. They are disease- and insect-resistant and tolerate wind and cold because they are native to the Himalayas. Once established, they can tolerate short periods of drought and heat.* **A Note of Caution:** *If you have clay soil, there will be insufficient amounts of oxygen exchange in the root zone, resulting in a distinctive yellowing of the foliage. This will eventually stress the plant to such an extent that the leaves will fall from their stems.*

Family Name / Origin Rosaceae / Himalayas

Bloom Period and Color White flowers bloom in late spring or early summer.

Mature Height × **Spread** 2 to 4 ft. × 4 ft.

When and How to Plant Plant in spring and fall months out of 1- or 5-gallon containers. Space about 4 ft. on center for optimum results. Mulch with compost or humus mulch 2 in. deep in a watering basin 4 ft. in diameter. Make sure the watering basin is twice the diameter of the plant's canopy. See Planting Techniques, p. 398.

Climate & Culture

Preferred Zones
6–11

Sun Preferences

Sun and Soil Preferences Like other species of Cotoneasters, they do best in full sun, but they can survive in partial shade—their production of flowers and berries, however, will be much reduced. A neutral soil pH, 7.0, is ideal. Make sure the soil is porous enough to allow adequate percolation.

Moisture Requirements Thoroughly water the root zone immediately after planting so that all the air pockets collapse. Once established, infrequent, deep waterings are best.

Fertilizing If necessary, fertilize in the late winter or early spring with a complete fertilizer, 6-10-4.

Pruning and Care Prune only for the purpose of shaping or removing dead wood. Deadheading the flowers is unnecessary.

Pests and Diseases Aphid infestations can be controlled by washing the critters off with a strong stream of water or applying Neem oil.

Companion Plantings and Design For formal landscapes, Floribunda and Shrub Roses and other species of Cotoneaster blend well with this plant.

Our Personal Favorites

NAME	SPECIAL CHARACTERISTICS
C. *microphyllus* 'Cochleatus'	An ideal ground cover / horizontal growth pattern / abundant red berries
C. *microphyllus* 'Thymifolius'	Upright growth pattern of 1½ ft. / used for hillside planting because of its dense structure

Rose of Sharon

Hibiscus syriacus

*Although H. syriacus is often thought to be from Syria, it is in fact indigenous to China and India, where it is known as the Chinese Rose. Currently, we follow the Bible's term for this plant, the Rose of Sharon. It is a densely branched, deciduous shrub that grows to about ten feet in height and is erect in form. The Rose of Sharon is used as a patio tree, an espalier against a wall or trellis, a container plant, or a hedge. Whether displayed as a singular plant or in mass plantings, H. syriacus is a wonderful addition to any garden. The somewhat small leaves are bright green with serrated margins. Flowers range in color from rich pink, dark lavender, pure white, and magenta-rose to red. Our friend's cutting has matured enough to bloom and now we know it is the magenta-rose variety. This shrub blooms from June through September with a profusion of single or double three-inch flowers that have a texture similar to crepe paper. This particular species of Hibiscus is relatively hardy in that it will tolerate freezing temperatures down to -10 Fahrenheit, as well as high temperatures if there is sufficient humidity and soil moisture. **Note:** If you cannot find Hibiscus syriacus, look for Althaea syriacus, another botanical name sometimes used for the same plant.*

Family Name / Origin Malvaceae / China, India

Bloom Period and Color White, mauve, violet-blue, and pink-red flowers bloom in summer.

Mature Height × Spread 6 to 10 ft. × 8 ft.

When and How to Plant Fall or spring are the best times to establish your Rose of Sharon. Select 1-, 5-, or 15-gallon plants. If it is your intention to allow their full, natural growth, then plant 8 to 10 ft. on center; if you want to grow a hedge, plant 6 to 8 ft. on center. When you build the watering basin, make sure it is 6 ft. in diameter and 4 to 6 in. in height, and mulch its surface with 2 in. of compost or humus mulch. See Planting Techniques, p. 398.

Climate & Culture

Preferred Zones 8–11

Sun Preferences

Sun and Soil Preferences Plant in full sun. You can plant in partial shade, but bloom production will not be as abundant. It prefers porous soil that permits good percolation, and thrives in soils that have a slightly acidic or neutral pH, 6.6 to 7.0.

Moisture Requirements Initially, give it deep, thorough soakings once a week, and adjust frequency and amount as your plant matures. Bear in mind that it requires a relatively moist soil.

Fertilizing Fertilize in late winter or early spring with a complete fertilizer, 6-10-4.

Pruning and Care For the first two or three years, prune in late winter or early spring to encourage branching structure and increase bloom production. Flowers appear on current-season (new wood) growth. It is not necessary to deadhead. As these plants age, their branching structures become less viable and their growth loses momentum. While they are still dormant, prune back their canopies 40 to 60 percent to restore their vigor. Be sure to protect the plants from harsh winds and prolonged drought.

Pests and Diseases Few diseases affect this plant, but inspect regularly for infestations of insects like giant whitefly, mealybugs, aphids, mites, and brown soft scale—use Neem oil if necessary. Use a molluscicide as needed for snails.

Companion Plantings and Design Rose of Sharon is thriving in our perennial plant area along with English Lavender, Canna Lilies, and Birds of Paradise.

Sasanqua Camellia
Camellia sasanqua

Sasanqua Camellias (like other Camellias, named for Moravian Jesuit George Joseph Kamel) are considered among the hardiest of the species. They bloom from fall to early spring and can withstand temperatures as low as 0 degrees Fahrenheit. Among the most sun-tolerant of the Camellias, they survive hot, dry climates but also thrive in light shade. Even though their flowers are smaller, usually three inches in diameter, they are more prolific bloomers than C. japonica or C. reticulata. Colors range from white to pink to light red to variegated; flowers are single, semi-double, or double. Sasanqua flowers are unique in that they are fragrant. When the blossoms are spent, their petals fall to the ground, similar to roses. They can grow in the ground or in containers as patio trees, in hanging baskets, or as low, spreading shrubs. Espalier the plants against a wall or fence for a most dramatic display—the dark, glossy, green foliage contrasts beautifully with the profuse display of flowers. I (Bruce) recommend Sasanquas for clients who love Camellias but need a more sun-tolerant species for their landscape. Other than feeding, watering, and deadheading, Camellias require very little care. Since their roots are not invasive, they are ideal choices for group plantings.

Family Name / Origin Theaceae / S Japan

Bloom Period and Color Red, white, pink, or variegated flowers bloom late winter or early spring.

Mature Height × Spread 3 ft. × 4 ft.

When and How to Plant Plant from 1- or 5-gallon containers, 4 to 6 ft. apart, in late winter or early spring. See Planting Techniques, p. 398.

Sun and Soil Preferences A semi-shady location is not as critical for this species, but the foliage might scorch if there is too much prolonged or intense sunlight or low-humidity conditions. Plant in acidic to neutral soil, pH 6.5 to 7.0.

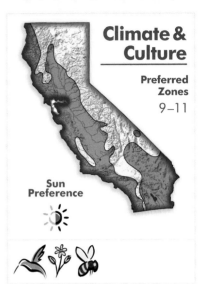

Climate & Culture

Preferred Zones
9–11

Sun Preference

Moisture Requirements It is important to avoid overwatering. If planted in loam soil, water thoroughly about once a week or as weather dictates.

Fertilizing Fertilize as the bloom season ends and the new growth begins, usually in spring, with a specially formulated food designed for Camellias. If using a granular fertilizer, make sure you distribute it evenly in the watering basin, and soak-in thoroughly.

Pruning and Care Unless the plants are overgrown, you do not normally need to hard-prune the canopies.

Pests and Diseases Inspect foliage and branches for brown soft scale and mite infestations. If left untreated, these parasites will proliferate, hinder normal foliage and stem development, and desiccate the plant. Use a suffocant like horticultural oil to control, following manufacturer's directions.

Companion Plantings and Design Plant with other shade-tolerant plants like Azaleas, Vinca Minor, and Hydrangeas.

Our Personal Favorites

NAME	SPECIAL CHARACTERISTICS
C. *sasanqua* 'Apple Blossom'	White, cerise-red edges / crowned with golden stamens / blooms midseason / grows upright / excellent for espalier
C. *s.* 'Shishi Gashira'	Low growing, spreading / semi-double, bright-red flowers / ideal for hanging baskets or for ground cover

Saucer Magnolia

Magnolia × soulangiana

The oldest major public garden in America is the lovely, historic Magnolia Plantation, ten miles from downtown Charleston and once described by Charles Kuralt as "My greatest Charleston pleasure." Among the many Southern Magnolias planted there, the deciduous Saucer Magnolias represented to us the true elegance of the South. They were grown as large shrubs or small trees with multiple trunks resembling graceful, spreading candelabras. Their abundant tulip-shaped flowers, which bloom about Easter time, are purplish pink on the outside and creamy white on the inside and are one of the main reasons these are my favorite Magnolias. Most deciduous Magnolias and their varieties bloom in early spring prior to their leafing out. Only late-flowering deciduous Magnolias like this one bloom simultaneously with the emergence of their new foliage. We also like their delicate perfume, similar to raspberries mixed with pine-apple and lilies. Their large, coarse-textured, forest-green leaves contrast beautifully with their incomparable flowers. While you can use the spectacular fragrant blossoms in cut-flower arrangements, their life span is relatively short. This species tolerates cold temperatures to -20 degrees Fahrenheit, but stresses in windy, dry, and hot conditions. Saucer Magnolia is a hybrid (M. denudata × M. liliiflora).

Family Name / Origin Magnoliaceae / Europe

Bloom Period and Color Lavender-and-white flowers bloom in spring.

Mature Height × Spread 15 to 20 ft. × 12 to 15 ft.

When and How to Plant Plant in spring and fall months from 5- or 15-gallon containers. Space about 6 to 8 ft. on center. Mulch with compost or humus mulch 2 in. deep in a watering basin 6 ft. in diameter. See Planting Techniques, p. 398.

Sun and Soil Preferences Plant in full sun or partial shade, in sandy loam soil with pH of 6.0–7.0.

Moisture Requirements Adequate soil moisture in the root zone is an important consideration. Infrequent but deep irrigation creates a reservoir of water for the root system to draw upon. As with most gardening guidelines, there are no absolutes, so remember to reduce the amount of water when your plant's leaves drop in the fall and increase your watering as it begins to grow again in the spring.

Fertilizing Fertilize with 16-20-0 fertilizer in late winter.

Pruning and Care Since Saucer Magnolias form their spring flower buds during the late summer or early fall, do not prune their branches while dormant; instead, prune after the flowers are spent. There is no need to deadhead, because the flowers fall on their own.

Pests and Diseases Saucer Magnolias have few insect or disease problems but are very sensitive to salt buildup in the soil. You can mitigate this common problem by dissolving the salts and leaching them out of the root zone with thorough and deep soakings.

Companion Plantings and Design Saucer Magnolias make ideal garden focal points.

Climate & Culture

Preferred Zones 5–11

Sun Preferences

Our Personal Favorites

NAME	SPECIAL CHARACTERISTICS
M. × s. 'Alexandrina'	Commonly known as Alexander Magnolia / vigorous grower / valued in cold climates for late blooming period
M. × s. 'Rustica Rubra'	Reddish-purple flowers / can be grown in sun or shade

Silverberry

Elaeagnus pungens

Silverberry is a large shrub known for its natural, loose-growing form. It is used for background or barrier planting as well as for a visual screen. The foliage has a medium texture with a glossy sheen on top; underneath, it is a dull silvery-white color with brown spots. In the autumn, flowers form that are silvery-white or cream in coloration and resemble tiny, elongated bells. Silverberry produces single-seeded berries, called drupes, that transform from brown to red in the late fall and early winter months. It is an excellent food source for birds and other wildlife during the cooler seasons. Once established, it tolerates drought, and its leathery-textured foliage resists moisture loss even in windy locations. Silverberry, otherwise known as Thorny Elaegnus, can survive temperature ranges from sub-zero to 100 degrees Fahrenheit for short periods of time. While in bloom, it attracts butterflies, birds, and bees. Landscape architects use it in commercial and residential designs as part of their low-maintenance palette of plants. Its silvery-green foliage contrasts nicely against a backdrop of other solid-green plants. If you shear the plant, it can be an effective addition to formal gardens as hedges. When left to grow out in its natural form, it is an equally effective visual screen.

Family Name / Origin Elaeagnaceae / Japan

Bloom Period and Color White or cream flowers appear in autumn.

Mature Height × **Spread** 6 to 8 ft. × 6 to 8 ft.

When and How to Plant Although fall and spring are best, Silverberry can be planted at any time. They grow 20 to 30 percent in a year, so a 1- or 5-gallon plant is a good choice. Plant 6 to 8 ft. on center. Create a watering basin 6 ft. in diameter and mulch its surface with 2 to 3 in. of organic material. After planting, water thoroughly. See p. 398.

Sun and Soil Preferences Plant in a sunny or shady location. It prefers a neutral pH of 7.0 with good percolation, ensuring rapid root development.

Moisture Requirements Once established, it is drought tolerant, so water deeply and infrequently.

Fertilizing Fertilize in spring and fall with a complete fertilizer such as 12-8-4.

Pruning and Care Little pruning is necessary because of its rigid stems. Errant new growth makes it look disheveled, so prune selectively for shape. Deadheading the flowers or removing the berries is unnecessary.

Pests and Diseases There are few diseases or insects that affect this plant.

Companion Plantings and Design I (Bruce) frequently use Silverberry in landscape designs as part of my palette of low-maintenance shrubs along with Rock Rose, Bottlebrush, and Glossy Abelia.

Climate & Culture

Preferred Zones
8–11

Sun Preferences

Our Personal Favorites

NAME	SPECIAL CHARACTERISTICS
E. pungens 'Fruitlandii'	Known as the Fruitland Silverberry / an average height and width of about 8 ft. / silvery scales on deep, green, round leaves with waxy edges / silvery white and brown spots on the undersides of the leaves
E. pungens 'Aurea'	Deep-yellow edges on the leaves

Yesterday-Today-and-Tomorrow
Brunfelsia australis

Popular since Victorian times, Brunfelsia australis (*named for German botanist Otto Brunfel*) *derives its common name from the fact that yesterday it bloomed, today it is at its peak, and tomorrow it will be spent. On one bush, its stunning white-eyed blooms will range from an intense, deep purple to a pale lavender to a faded white, depending on the age of the blossom. We use this delicately fragrant plant in our landscape for spring color, although it can bloom again during the summer months and even early fall depending on weather conditions. Its flowers have a delicate fragrance. Once established, Yesterday-Today-and-Tomorrow prefers a wind-protected, frost-free location. This perennial shrub, with its shiny, pale green foliage and dense growth, thrives in partial shade. As with other shade plants, they are attractive to snails and slugs, but these pests are easily controlled by a periodic application of snail bait. In addition to using the high-nitrogen fertilizer mentioned on the following page, you can prolong and enhance the bloom cycle by using a high-phosphorous fertilizer such as Super Bloom in early spring.*

Family Name / Origin Solanaceae /
South America

Bloom Period and Color Lavender flowers bloom
in spring and summer.

Mature Height × Spread 4 to 6 ft. × 4 ft.

When and How to Plant In spring, plant 1- or
5-gallon-size plants that exhibit vigorous growth but
are not rootbound. *B. australis* can be planted individually or spaced 4 ft. to 5 ft. on center. After planting,
mulch the surface of the ground. For more specific
instructions, refer to Planting Techniques, p. 398.

Sun and Soil Preferences Select a properly shaded
and protected location. Make sure the soil texture is
porous enough that the water will percolate down into the root zone evenly.
They do not do well in clay soils and require a slightly acidic pH of 6.0–7.0.

Moisture Requirements Water deeply and thoroughly at first, and then
according to climatic conditions and the plant's growth rate.

Fertilizing Brunfelsias require regular feedings of a high-nitrogen, time-
release fertilizer to maintain the vigor and dark-green coloration of the
foliage and to encourage blooms.

Pruning and Care While shaping and lacing *B. australis,* pinch off their
branch tips for more prolific bloom production. Spent flowers fall off naturally
so you do not need to cut them.

Pests and Diseases Use snail bait to control snails and slugs.

Companion Plantings and Design Yesterday-Today-and-Tomorrow
grows well with Hydrangeas, Gardenias, and Azaleas.

**Climate &
Culture**

Preferred
Zones
10–11

Sun
Preference

Our Personal Favorite

NAME	SPECIAL CHARACTERISTICS
B. pauciflora 'Macrantha'	Flowers two to three times larger than Yesterday-Today-and-Tomorrow / heavy feeder, well worth the extra effort because of stunning blooms and intense deep-purple coloration / shade, no direct sunlight / cannot tolerate poor drainage, does best as container plant / also known as Royal Purple Brunfelsia

Yew Pine

Podocarpus macrophyllus

The Yew Pine is a conifer, a densely foliated evergreen columnar in form that is used in formal landscapes. Near the entrance of the San Diego Zoo, Yew Pines are used effectively as tall, narrow hedge plants. The homeowner may plant Podocarpus between windows where tall, narrow plants offset and complement the architectural lines of the structure. It is an excellent choice for a foundation planting, visual screen, or boundary definition, where symmetry plays an important part in your landscape design. Although its form resembles the Eastern Yew (hence the common name, Yew Pine), it is in fact a Podocarpus, not a Taxus. Because it is similar in appearance, the Yew Pine is a good substitute for the Eastern Yew (Taxus) in Western gardens. Its leaves are dark green, shiny, and finely textured. Since it is a conifer, there are no blossoms. Once established, Yew Pine tolerates wind, cold temperatures down to freezing, and drought as well as heat for short periods of time. Like other conifers, male Yew Pines bear catkins that shed pollen on the seeds of the female plants. Once pollinated, small yellow cones form on the female P. macrophyllus. If cone production is not important to you, then it is not necessary to have male and female plants.

Family Name / Origin Podocarpaceae / Japan, China

Bloom Period and Color There are no blossoms.

Mature Height × Spread May grow 20 to 40 ft. × 4 to 10 ft. (normally 8 to 15 ft. × 2 to 4 ft.)

When and How to Plant Plant in fall or spring from 1-, 5-, or 15-gallon containers. If you want a more mature size, 24- or 30-in. boxed specimens are available. Space approximately 4 ft. apart if you want a cluster of three or four. If you want a hedge for visual screening, plant 3 ft. on center. Create a watering basin; mulch the basin with 2 in. of compost or humus mulch. See Planting Techniques, p. 398.

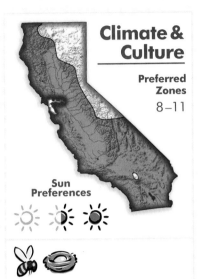

Climate & Culture

Preferred Zones
8–11

Sun Preferences

Sun and Soil Preferences *P. macrophyllus* will grow in sun or shade and prefers porous, well-drained loam soil with a neutral pH of 7.0.

Moisture Requirements Infrequent, deep, thorough watering is a must.

Fertilizing Fertilize twice a year, early spring and early fall, with a complete food such as 15-15-15.

Pruning and Care It is usually not necessary to prune Yew Pines, but they can be topped if you are growing a hedge and the top growth exceeds your height limit. Just be aware that their diameter and density will increase.

Pests and Diseases Few diseases or insects attack this plant. Aphid infestations can be controlled by washing the critters off with a strong stream of water or applying Neem oil if they persist.

Companion Plantings and Design Hollywood Twisted Junipers, Silverberry, and Lavender Starflower go well with the Yew Pine in formal landscapes.

Our Personal Favorites

NAME	SPECIAL CHARACTERISTICS
P. macrophyllus 'Maki'	Called Dwarf Yew Pine / 4 to 6 ft. high, 2 ft. wide / very slow growing / prefers sun or partial shade / popular with bonsai enthusiasts
P. henkelii	Called Henkel's Yellowwood / 8 to 10 ft. / columnar like *P. macrophyllus*, except branches and foliage droop

Trees *for California*

Surrounding us in perfect botanical harmony are splendid trees that are either native to California, or, more often than not, transplanted from all over the world. In early spring, country roads and city streets light up when the golden flowers of Bailey's Acacias burst forth and smother their branches, followed by the hazy violet glow in late spring when the Jacarandas, our welcome travelers from Australia and Brazil, are in bloom. Summer's heat opens up the pink pompon flowers of the Persian Silk Trees and the citrus-scented alabaster flowers of the Southern Magnolia. By fall, the Sweet Gums and Japanese Maples are ablaze with shades of reds, oranges, and yellows, a final energetic burst before slumbering through the winter months. As if to celebrate the winter holidays, the Incense Cedars, nature's living garlands, are particularly aromatic after the rains. And the Hong Kong Orchid Trees bear their spectacular lavender and pink flowers in defiance of cool winter and early-spring months.

Lovely Plants of Inestimable Value

No matter which season, trees are among the loveliest of living things—but they are not here as mere cosmetics, just to make our parks, streets, and gardens look nice. They help produce the air we breathe, trap and hold pollutants, offset the buildup of carbon dioxide, control and

stabilize the world's climate, and feed and shelter much of the world's wildlife. An acre of trees supplies enough oxygen each day for eighteen people.

Trees reduce water loss caused by surface runoff, soil erosion by wind and water, and the amount of harmful substances that wash into waterways. In addition to their economic value as lumber and sources of fuel, they screen unsightly views, soften harsh outlines of buildings, absorb and block noise, and define space. Where would humankind be without trees?

As gardeners and tree lovers, our own gardens should contain at least one tree, and preferably more. Trees add beauty to homes and shelter us from the harsh sun and cold winds. If planted along the eastern and western walls of a house, they will provide shade from the hot morning and afternoon sun. In winter, tall thick trees can deflect blustery winds over and around your home.

Leave a Botanical Footprint

Planting trees is a way of leaving a botanical footprint long after we are gone. They link us to past events and eras. An old, gnarled, vase-shaped Common Olive Tree with multiple trunks stood in our Grandmother Asakawa's backyard. Every fall she and her friends would patiently gather its purplish-black bounty and cure them in an alkaline

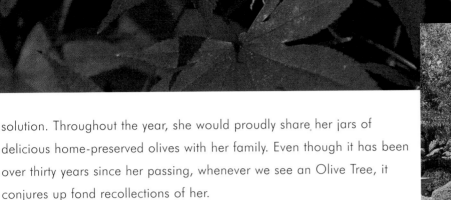

solution. Throughout the year, she would proudly share her jars of delicious home-preserved olives with her family. Even though it has been over thirty years since her passing, whenever we see an Olive Tree, it conjures up fond recollections of her.

In the spirit of our grandmother's tree as a connecting legacy from her to us, we recently planted a Crape Myrtle Tree—since they live for several hundred years, ours will probably remain to serve the next generation long after we are gone, and may still be flourishing centuries from now. There is comfort in knowing we have planted something with such beauty and longevity, connecting us to both the near and distant future.

Planning Ahead

To ensure that your trees will live long and well, give them a helping hand by planning ahead. Since trees come in a variety of shapes and sizes from a few feet tall to towering giants, choose carefully so as not to underwhelm or overwhelm the location you have in mind. Whatever function you want the tree to fulfill—shade, privacy, shelter from wind—select the one most suitable and take into careful consideration the ultimate size, both height and width. That dainty Chinese Weeping Banyan Tree, otherwise known as a *Ficus benjamina,* is often sold in a six-inch pot, but it will eventually reach forty feet in height. Madrone and Camphor Trees have been known to touch the skies at sixty feet. If trees are planted too close to each other, they will compete for space, light, food, and water, and may become deformed or stunted.

Avoid planting trees directly in front of windows and doors or close to paths, driveways, electrical wires, drainage pipes, and gas lines. Careful placement is important because once trees are established, they are difficult and often expensive to move.

Consider what the effect on both sides of the fence will be when your tree is mature. Be a considerate neighbor and think about whether or not your tree will cast unwelcome shade on the property of others, will block their view, or if there will be bothersome flowers or fruits that may drop messily in their yard. Stepping in their shoes beforehand prevents feuds later.

Trees of Life

Trees have tenaciously survived and adapted to many modern-day environmental stresses. They continue to inspire us, touch our spirits, and connect us to our past, present, and future. The phrase "tree of life" is no exaggeration, for without them, there would be no miracle of life. Although this chapter includes only a minuscule sampling of the thousands of trees available, perhaps these few will inspire you to expand your repertoire of landscape sentinels.

Bailey's Acacia

Acacia baileyana

A. baileyana, *commonly known as Bailey's Acacia or Fern Leaf Acacia, or by its aboriginal name Cootamundra Wattle, is a round-headed tree with a wide canopy composed of pendulous branches. During our travels to New South Wales, Australia, we saw many Bailey's Acacia growing in residential and park landscapes and realized this was an ideal medium-sized ornamental tree that would be easily adaptable to most California communities. Its silvery, blue-green, feathery, fine-textured leaves contrast beautifully with the fragrant clusters of small canary-yellow flowers that burst forth in early spring. Although among the hardiest of Acacias, it does not tolerate blustery winds or sustained below-freezing temperatures. In its native habitat, Acacia plants grow under the canopies in Eucalyptus forests, where they are protected from damaging overhead and lateral winds. Because they grow in temperate climates, they need adequate soil moisture to withstand extended periods of drought or heat. Once their flowers are spent, seedpods emerge; as the seedpods desiccate and split, the seeds are dispersed, providing summer morsels for birds and other wildlife. Most Acacias are relatively short-lived, and Bailey's Acacia is no exception. As a viable tree, its longevity is only about fifteen to twenty years—but sometimes it can be a positive thing to make changes in your landscape!*

Family Name / Origin Leguminosae / Australia

Mature Height × Spread 20 to 30 ft. × 25 to 40 ft.

When and How to Plant The best times to plant Acacias are in fall or early spring from 5- to 15-gallon containers. If you are planting in groups, space them 15 to 20 ft. on center. For more information, refer to the Planting Techniques section of this book, p. 398.

Sun and Soil Preferences Bailey's Acacias prefer a wind-protected, full-sun location in soils with a neutral pH of 7.0. Since the root systems of Bailey's Acacias tend to be shallow and lateral, they benefit from the good percolation of loam soils, which encourages the development of deeper root systems.

Climate & Culture

Preferred Zones 9–11

Sun Preference

Moisture Requirements Immediately after planting, build a watering basin 6 to 8 ft. in diameter by creating a berm 6 in. high, then mulching its surface with 2 to 3 in. of compost or humus mulch. Water infrequently but deeply, filling the watering basin two or three times as dictated by weather conditions and tree growth rate.

Fertilizing To maximize bloom and foliar growth, fertilize in early spring with a complete food such as 15-15-15.

Pruning and Care It is unnecessary to deadhead Acacia. To encourage new growth, prune away dead and diseased wood from its canopy.

Pests and Diseases Few pests or diseases will affect this Acacia as long as it is growing adequately.

Companion Plantings and Design We like to use it as a single tree for a focal point or on a bank with several trees. It is a perfect tree to grow with Bottlebrush, Silverberry, or Japanese Mock Orange.

Our Personal Favorite

NAME	SPECIAL CHARACTERISTICS
A. b. 'Purpurea'	New outer growth is deep burgundy, offering a lush contrast to blue-gray underfoliage

Bronze Loquat
Eriobotrya deflexa

*The genus name Eriobotrya comes from Greek words meaning "a cluster of wool."
The term probably refers to the small, lightly scented, creamy-white flowers that emerge
from fuzzy, reddish-brown stems at the ends of branches in late summer or early fall.
We like this tree's upright, bold, open canopy, which is uniquely accentuated by a
flush of rich bronze-tinted foliage that appears first at the branch tips. The tree has
stunningly colored (bronze) leaves, a vase-shaped form, medium size, and a non-
aggressive root system, allowing it to be used as an attractive shade tree in residential
landscapes. The mature foliage turns a leathery green with serrated edges, deeply
veined throughout and woolly underneath, and each leaf is about ten inches long. Its
fuzzy golden-colored fruits are quite small and, although popular with your winter bird
visitors, are not very tasty to the human palate. Because of its leathery foliage the tree
will tolerate wind, but it will not survive sustained freezing temperatures. As long as
there is sufficient humidity and soil moisture, Bronze Loquat tolerates heat and even
an occasional drought period once it is established.*

Family Name / Origin Rosaceae / E Asia

Mature Height × Spread 15 to 30 ft. × 20 ft.

When and How to Plant The best time to plant is spring, from a 5- or 15-gallon container. Space multiple plants 20 ft. on center; locate single plants at least 15 ft. from structures or paved areas. Build an 8- to 10-ft. watering basin; mulch the surface with 2 to 3 in. of compost or humus mulch. See p. 398.

Climate & Culture

Preferred Zones
10–11

Sun Preference

Sun and Soil Preferences Select a full-sun site that has well-drained soil with a neutral pH of 7.0.

Moisture Requirements Even though the Bronze Loquat is drought tolerant once it is established, infrequent and deep watering ensures continued expansion of its root system. Begin by irrigating thoroughly every week to ten days, and adjust the frequency and amount for seasonal growth and climatic conditions.

Fertilizing Fertilize in late winter or early spring with a complete granular food such as 10-10-10.

Pruning and Care Little or no pruning is necessary because the tree's canopy grows uniformly. Deadhead the flowers if you do not want fruit formation. As foliar growth emerges at the tips, it shades the older growth, causing more mature leaves to drop off. This creates a lovely, open, umbrella-like canopy but also makes a mess—instead of using the tree in a lawn area, plant in an area where its fallen leaves will blend into the ground.

Pests and Diseases It is relatively free of disease and insects, but if you see dieback among the branches after a mild winter, consult a nurseryman or University of California Cooperative Extension representative. If the problem is fireblight, you will be told to remove the affected limbs.

Companion Plantings and Design It grows well with Yew Pine, Japanese Mock Orange, and Bird of Paradise.

Our Personal Favorite

NAME	SPECIAL CHARACTERISTICS
E. deflexa 'Coppertone'	Smaller, evergreen / retains copper-colored foliage throughout most of the year / grows up to 15 ft. / also known as Coppertone Loquat

California Sycamore

Platanus racemosa

Sycamores are large, stately trees. When mature, they are admired for their graceful, twisted branches that form skyward into open, irregular crowns; their thin, mottled trunks; and their broad, light-green, maple-like leaves with three to five deep lobes covered underneath with fine, rust-colored hairs. Tiny clusters of reddish blossoms appear from April to May, followed by spherical, brown, spiky seedheads that hang down in clusters of three to ten throughout winter. In the cooler autumn months, most of their leaves turn color and fall to the ground, and their bark characteristically flakes off, revealing an attractive patchwork of grays, whites, and light browns. P. racemosa provides a scenic change from the often dull surroundings of foothills covered with chaparral and coastal shrub. In Mexico, chips of bark from the lower trunks and roots are often boiled and used as a coffee substitute, but in California landscapes I (Bruce) like to feature them as ornamental focal specimens, primarily for their crooked but picturesque branching structures. In my opinion, they are one of the best shade trees for drier soils and milder climates. They can be planted in lawns if there is excellent soil drainage. Once established, they tolerate short periods of drought, enjoy heat and wind if there is sufficient moisture, but do not survive long, freezing winters.

Family Name / Origin Platanaceae / California

Mature Height × Spread 60 ft. to 80 ft. × 60 ft.

When and How to Plant Best planting time is fall, second-best time is early spring. Plant from a 5- or 15-gallon container or a 30- to 36-in. specimen box. Space grouped trees 30 to 40 ft. on center; site a single tree at least 30 ft. from any structure or paved area. Never plant over leach lines or under power lines. Build a 10- to 15-ft. watering basin and cover with 2 to 3 in. of organic material. See p. 398.

Sun and Soil Preferences Select a full-sun site with well-drained soil, pH 7.0.

Moisture Requirements Irrigate deeply and thoroughly after planting, then twice during the first week, then according to dictates of weather and growth conditions.

Fertilizing Fertilize in late winter with a 15-15-15.

Pruning and Care Prune out dead wood while in winter dormancy. Some people develop skin irritations or sneezing reactions when handling the leaves, particularly the woolly undersides; they should handle the leaves with gloves and try to avoid contact with them during windy days.

Pests and Diseases These trees are susceptible to Sycamore Blight, a fungal disease that attacks the ends of new growth in the spring. This disease is a kind of blessing in disguise because in burning back the ends of the branches, wood growth becomes gnarled and irregular, creating artistically dramatic silhouettes.

Companion Plantings and Design Cluster them in groups of three or more as they are in nature, and combine them with shade-tolerant native or drought-resistant plants such as Glossy Abelias, California Lilacs, and Silverberry.

Climate & Culture

Preferred Zones
9–11

Sun Preference

Our Personal Favorite

NAME	SPECIAL CHARACTERISTICS
P. × acerifolia 'Bloodgood'	Broad, pyramidal form / withstands urban pollution / resistant to Sycamore Blight / also known as Bloodgood London Plane Tree

Camphor Tree
Cinnamomum camphora

Camphor Trees have adapted to most areas of California. We recommend selecting this slow-growing evergreen if you have room. Its most stunning visual feature is colorful pinkish, bronze-red new growth covering the open, airy canopy. This leathery-textured new growth changes into a light apple-green and finally deepens to a rich, dark green on top with white underneath. Masses of tiny chartreuse flowers appear in spring, followed by small, purplish-red, pea-sized berries. The essence of camphor oil is released when the leaves are rubbed. The oil was historically extracted for medicines, insecticides, and the manufacture of celluloid. Since extracting camphor has become so costly, most camphor is currently produced synthetically. Butterflies are attracted to the Camphor Tree's aromatic oil and regularly flit about the foliage, and birds enjoy the small seeds. It grows well in arid areas but can become quite a pest in tropical or subtropical conditions. It survives temperatures down to freezing for short periods of time and the strong branches withstand gusty winds. Since camphor leaves decompose slowly, they are not good for compost, but they and the dead branches make wonderful scented additions to winter fires. **Note:** *If you cannot find this tree by the name* Cinnamomum camphora, *look for* Camphora officinarum, *another botanical name sometimes given to the same plant.*

Family Name / Origin Lauraceae / China, Taiwan

Mature Height × Spread 40 to 60 ft. × 50 to 80 ft.

When and How to Plant Plant in fall or early spring from containers that are 5- or 15-gallon or larger. Site the tree 30 ft. from structural or paved areas. Never plant it over or near leach lines. Build a watering basin 12 ft. in diameter and mulch the surface with 2 to 3 in. of organic material such as humus mulch or compost. If you need more information, consult the Planting Techniques, p. 398.

Climate & Culture

Preferred Zones
9–11

Sun Preference

Sun and Soil Preferences Camphor Trees prefer full sun and soil with good percolation as well as a neutral pH of 7.0.

Moisture Requirements It is best to irrigate infrequently and deeply to encourage deep root development.

Fertilizing If fertilizing is necessary, apply in late winter or early spring with a complete food such as 10-10-10.

Pruning and Care Pruning is usually not necessary because a healthy Camphor Tree grows symmetrically and evenly.

Pests and Diseases This light-colored tree is generally insect repellent, but in the spring its new foliage is susceptible to mites and fungus infections. If you determine there is extensive damage, contact a pest-control advisor for a proper course of action.

Companion Plantings and Design Today we use Camphor Trees in parks and gardens and along streets, primarily for shade. They are compatible with Japanese Mock Orange, Yew Pine, and Laurustinus.

Our Personal Favorite

NAME	SPECIAL CHARACTERISTICS
C. camphora 'Majestic Beauty'	More uniform growth and larger, richer green foliage than the species

Canary Island Pine
Pinus canariensis

Pine trees are found throughout the world, from mountaintops to seashores, from the Arctic Circle to the steamy tropics of the Equator. There is a Pine for almost every kind of habitat, and one of the most useful in landscape design is the P. canariensis, or Canary Island Pine. It is native to the Canary Islands where rainfall is unpredictable and soil is thin, porous, and volcanic in origin. A gardener most often encounters this Pine at a nursery or florist shop where it is grown as a one- or five-gallon "cute" container plant, giving no prediction of its true magnificence as a sixty-foot-tall column. It will have tight branches covered with densely packed hunter-green needles clustered in groups of threes. I (Bruce) use them to give proportion to the house in relationship to the yard, and to give depth by planting these tall sentinels in groups in "the back forty," as well as to define property boundaries. Because of its mature height, the tree is a popular observation tower and shelter for birds. In late fall or early winter, eight-inch pine cones appear in groups of two to four. When the cones open, the seeds disperse and are eagerly gathered by squirrels and chipmunks. Once established, this conifer tolerates drought, constant wind, heat, and short episodes of freezing temperatures.

Family Name / Origin Pinaceae / Canary Islands

Mature Height × Spread 50 ft. to 70 ft. × 20 ft.

When and How to Plant Plant in the fall or spring months from 5- or 15-gallon containers or 30- to 36-in. specimen-size boxes. If planting in groups of three or more, space 15 ft. on center so branches do not compete for sunlight; plant a single tree at least 20 ft. from structures and paved areas. Avoid planting over leach lines and under power lines. Build a 10- to 12-ft. watering basin and blanket with 2 to 3 in. of organic material. Also refer to Planting Techniques on p. 398.

Climate & Culture

Preferred Zones

10–11

Sun Preference

Sun and Soil Preferences Plant in sunny locations with porous, fertile soils with a neutral pH of 7.0.

Moisture Requirements Immediately after planting, water deeply and thoroughly. During the first two weeks, soak it twice a week, then adjust the frequency and amount according to changing climatic or growth conditions.

Fertilizing Fertilize with a complete food, 10-10-10, in late winter.

Pruning and Care Clean out dead debris that accumulates in the center of the tree twice a year, in spring and fall, with a strong stream of water. Leave fallen needles to serve as nature's mulch.

Pests and Diseases Diseases are rare, but if you see dieback in the canopy with or without insect infestation, take a foliage sample to your local garden center for a diagnosis and remedy.

Companion Plantings and Design Plant with Pride of Madeira, Silverberry, and Rock Rose.

Our Personal Favorite

NAME	SPECIAL CHARACTERISTICS
P. thunbergii	Bold, irregular branching pattern / strong pyramidal form / sharp, rich green needles / rapid growing / salt tolerant / ideal focal point in formal gardens, or trained container plant such as bonsai / also known as Japanese Black Pine

Chinese Weeping Banyan
Ficus benjamina

We will never forget the stand of giant Chinese Weeping Banyan trees on the big island of Hawaii. Their trunk girths were over four feet in diameter, with towering scaffolds that cantilevered to form 100-foot-wide canopies. High buttress and aerial roots lent additional support. Although it took decades to reach their current majestic stature, they all began as wispy saplings, just like the ones we adopt as houseplants. The branches are pendulous with a weeping form and covered with pointed, glossy, bright-green leaves. Their minute flowers are never seen because of a unique characteristic common to Ficus plants: in late spring they develop inside small receptacles when pollinated by a tiny host-specific wasp. The receptacles ripen into somewhat squishy oval fruit that are popular with birds but not humans. In frost-free areas of California, F. benjamina are planted in gardens that allow for their potential massive stature and aggressive root systems. They are also used indoors, in atriums, or on patios as container plants. On the plus side, they do not succumb to many diseases. On the negative side, they do not tolerate drought, dry wind, or freezing temperatures and will quickly defoliate to display their unhappiness. If they are well established, recovery is possible when more favorable climatic conditions return.

Family Name / Origin Moraceae / Asia

Mature Height × Spread 40 ft. × 35 to 40 ft.

When and How to Plant Plant in fall or spring
from a 5-gallon, 15-gallon, or specimen-size
container. Space 20 to 30 ft. apart if grouping, and
at least 30 to 40 ft. from structures or paved areas.
Never plant near or directly over leach lines. Build a
watering basin two to three times the diameter of the
original container, and mulch the surface 2 to 3 in.
deep. If planting indoors, place a container where
there is natural light, humidity, and good air circulation. Also see Planting Techniques, p. 398.

**Climate &
Culture**

Preferred
Zones
10–11

Sun
Preference

Sun and Soil Preferences Chinese Weeping
Banyan prefer full sun and a well-drained soil with an
acidic to neutral pH of 6.5 to 7.0.

Moisture Requirements Irrigate thoroughly during the summer growing
season and less frequently during cooler months. To prevent desiccation in
Southern California, water thoroughly the evening before the predicted
arrival of Santa Ana winds.

Fertilizing Fertilize container plants with a water-soluble fertilizer once
a month or every three to four months with a timed-release 14-14-14.
Fertilize outdoor *Ficus benjamina* in early spring with ammonium phosphate,
16-20-0.

Pruning and Care Lace once a year to shape and to encourage new
growth. The cut branches contain latex, a viscous substance that can make a
mess, so prune over a protected surface or outdoors. A Chinese Weeping
Banyan thriving as a houseplant should not be moved, as it is very sensitive
to any modifications in light intensity and duration.

Pests and Diseases Control mealybugs, brown soft scale, and mites with
appropriate pesticides.

Companion Plantings and Design Some growers have developed an
interesting sculptural form by braiding the trunks of three young *Ficus* trees
while they are still pliable.

Our Personal Favorite

NAME	SPECIAL CHARACTERISTICS
F. benjamina 'Variegata'	Shiny deep-green leaves with white variegations

Crape Myrtle
Lagerstroemia indica

When we moved into our present home, there was a beautiful old flowering plum tree in our front yard. Sadly, it died suddenly from an infestation of borers . . . but sometimes change is a good thing in a garden. We began looking for a replacement and found a striking tree with large trusses of frilly magenta flower panicles. It turned out to be Lagerstroemia indica, *named for a friend of Linnaeus, Magnus von Lagerstroem. It is commonly known as Crape Myrtle because of the similarity of its crinkly textured flowers to crepe fabric. We enjoy our new garden addition, especially in late summer when it is in full bloom, but also in fall when its foliage is transformed from deep green to golden yellow. In winter, when barren of leaves, its deciduous bark reveals a smooth beige surface with maroon streaks. Since Crape Myrtles can live for several hundred years, ours will probably be in the front yard long after we are gone, and there is comfort in knowing we have planted something with such longevity. In its native homeland, China, its wood is prized for its ability to repel insects such as termites, and it is used to make furniture. Once established, it does very well in heat, wind, freezing temperatures, and even drought conditions—although it will thrive better, of course, if adequate moisture is available.*

Family Name / Origin Lythraceae / China

Mature Height × Spread 15 to 20 ft. × 20 ft.

When and How to Plant Plant in late winter or early spring, from 5-gallon, 15-gallon, or specimen-size containers. If planting in a group, space 15 ft. to 20 ft. on center; space a single specimen at least 15 ft. from a structure or paved area. Create a 10- to 12-ft. watering basin, and blanket with 2 to 3 in. of organic material. Also refer to p. 398.

Climate & Culture

Preferred Zones
9–11

Sun Preferences

Sun and Soil Preferences For optimum bloom production, plant in full sun, though it will survive partial shade. A porous, well-drained soil is essential. Slightly alkaline soils, pH 7.2, are fine, but slightly acidic soils, pH 6.7, are better.

Moisture Requirements Water thoroughly to encourage deep rooting.

Fertilizing Fertilize in late winter with a complete food, 6-10-4.

Pruning and Care Prune for shape in late winter. To encourage two bloom cycles, prune twice a year, once in late winter and once after the first blooms are spent.

Pests and Diseases Crape Myrtles in California are susceptible to mildew, but new mildew-resistant varieties have been hybridized. In the spring, sucking insects such as aphids tend to proliferate on tender emerging buds. Wash off with a strong stream of water in the early morning; if they persist, use a Neem pesticide.

Companion Plantings and Design We like to plant Crape Myrtle with Butterfly Bush, Pride of Madeira, and Shore Juniper.

Our Personal Favorites

NAME	SPECIAL CHARACTERISTICS
L. indica × faurei 'Zuni'	Dark lavender trusses of superior richness / a crown of stiff branches
L. indica 'Glendora White'	Snowy white flowers in dense, showy clusters / perfect in lawns and parkways

Deodar Cedar

Cedrus deodara

It is understandable that the Sanskrit word devadara, *meaning "tree of the gods," was given as the species name of this Cedrus—in its natural habitat, this tree can reach heights of 165 feet. Sadly, the Deodar Cedar, also known as the California Christmas Tree, is almost extinct over much of its native range in the western Himalayas. It is currently very popular in California because of its rapid growth rate and adaptability to many different growing environments. Every Christmas, we enjoy veiwing the extravagant holiday decorations at the Hotel del Coronado across the San Diego Bay, including a row of Deodar Cedars cheerfully festooned with bright lights and glittery garlands. Under average California growing conditions, these trees can reach heights of 35 to 45 feet. They have an architectural appearance because of their pyramidal shape and arching, widespread branches that bear silvery, gray-green needles. Like other coniferous plants, the California Christmas Tree produces three- to five-inch-long cones that are rounded at the top but have no depression. The cones are at first purplish in color, but as they age, they gradually turn brown. Once established, these trees are drought and wind tolerant. They withstand temperatures as low as 10 degrees Fahrenheit and as high as 100 degrees Fahrenheit, if there is adequate soil moisture.*

Family Name / Origin Pinaceae / Himalayas

Mature Height × **Spread** 60 to 80 ft. × 25 to 40 ft.

When and How to Plant Plant in early spring. Space a group 20 to 30 ft. on center; locate a single tree 20 ft. from structures or paved areas. Build a watering basin by creating a berm 6 in. high, making sure it extends to the projected drip line of a fully grown tree. Mulch the basin's surface with 2 to 3 in. of rich organic material. Also see p. 398.

Climate & Culture

Preferred Zones
8–11

Sun Preference

Sun and Soil Preferences Select a full-sun site. Well-drained soils with a neutral pH of 7.0 are best.

Moisture Requirements Thoroughly soak the Deodar Cedar's soil and root zone regularly while it is still a young tree. As the plant matures, adjust frequency and amount of watering according to climatic and growth conditions.

Fertilizing Fertilize in late winter or early spring with a complete food like 10-10-10.

Pruning and Care For best results, lace and shape it in March, and again in late August or September. This schedule will allow new growth to occur while ensuring that your tree will be perfectly shaped in time for the holidays.

Pests and Diseases Few insects and diseases affect these trees. If your trees are experiencing needle dieback, take a foliage sample to your local nursery or University of California Cooperative Extension. If your suspicion is confirmed, treat with a miticide, following the manufacturer's directions.

Companion Plantings and Design These trees make good specimens in Hybrid Tall Fescue lawns, or grouped with Red Clusterberry Cotoneaster.

Our Personal Favorites

NAME	SPECIAL CHARACTERISTICS
C. deodara 'Aurea'	Slow-growing conifer / grows up to 25 ft. / golden-colored needles throughout the year
C. atlantica 'Glauca'	Originated in the Atlas Mountains of Algeria and North Africa / common name is Blue Atlas Cedar

European White Birch

Betula alba

Whenever any transplanted Easterners or Midwesterners talk to me about how much they miss their deciduous forests, I (Bruce) suggest they consider planting Birches. These trees are graceful, open-branched, and pyramidal, and their smaller branches are pendulous, with bright-green, wedge-shaped leaves that shimmer in the slightest breeze. The bark is tough and water-resistant, and peels off in curling patches. Coleridge poetically described them as "ladies of the woods." Their bare winter branches create elegant silhouettes against an otherwise dormant landscape. Their cut branches can be used in dramatic winter arrangements. Although fast-growing, their mature height is relatively modest, and their roots are not as aggressive as other trees. Cylindrical catkins develop from insignificant flowers and fall to the ground when ripe. These catkins are a source of food for birds and deer. Because there are so many branchlets, birds love to build nests in these trees, and deer find their bark delectable. B. albas endure temperatures as low as -40 degrees Fahrenheit and as high as 100 degrees Fahrenheit as long as there is adequate moisture. Their open canopies enable them to survive strong winds, but they cannot thrive in drought conditions. **Note:** *If you cannot find this plant by the name Betula alba, look for B. pendula, another botanical name that is sometimes given to the same plant.*

Family Name / Origin Betulaceae / Europe

Mature Height × Spread 20 to 30 ft. × 15 to 20 ft.

When and How to Plant Purchase bare-root or balled-and-burlapped trees at the end of December. Space 10 to 12 ft. apart and plant far enough from structures so that canopies will attain optimum growth. To encourage vigorous lateral growth of the root systems, build watering basins 4 ft. beyond their drip lines; mulch the surface of the basins with 2 to 3 in. of organic material. See Planting Techniques section for more information, p. 398.

Soil Preferences Plant in a sunny location in well-drained soil with a pH of 6.5 to 7.0.

Climate & Culture

Preferred Zones
5–11

Sun Preference

Moisture Requirements Immediately after planting, soak thoroughly. Water twice a week for two weeks, then adjust frequency and amount according to climatic and growth factors.

Fertilizing Fertilize with ammonium phosphate, 16-20-0, in late winter or early spring, and use a potassium fertilizer in the fall.

Pruning and Care Prune for shape during winter dormancy if necessary.

Pests and Diseases When stressed from lack of moisture, Birches become susceptible to birch borers. Watch for entrance holes where the borers tunnel into the tree and sawdust-like debris called *frass* accumulates. Use a pesticide specifically for borers, following manufacturer's directions.

Companion Plantings and Design Select a tree with multiple trunks, because its silhouette will create a visually interesting focal point for your landscape. These trees are particularly beautiful when planted with Saucer Magnolias, Silverberry, and Cotoneasters.

Our Personal Favorite

NAME	SPECIAL CHARACTERISTICS
B. nigra 'Heritage'	Dark-red bark that is tinged with black as it matures / bark was gathered in strips by many Native Americans and carefully stretched on canoe frames / resistant to excessive heat, cold, moisture, and Bronze Birch Borers

Ginkgo
Ginkgo biloba

Ginkgo trees are known to grow well in serene temple areas and countryside gardens. On past trips to New York, Tokyo, and Hong Kong, we were amazed to see fresh, green Ginkgo trees flourishing in those crowded, polluted, urban environments as well. G. biloba are ancient trees that first appeared over 200 million years ago. They were saved from extinction by Chinese monks who planted them on their temple grounds. Their slender trunks are covered with reddish bark and their graceful, fan-shaped, double-lobed leaves turn from glossy green in spring to golden yellow in fall. Some call them Maidenhair Trees because their leaves are similar to Maidenhair Fern, but the Chinese refer to them in equally descriptive terms as "Duck's Foot Trees." The male Ginkgo is more upright and irregular in form, and the female is lower growing with a spreading habit. Their distinctive and richly colored foliage makes beautiful additions to cut-flower arrangements. Ginkgo trees, being deciduous, are cold hardy, but you do need to shelter them from blustery winds. They love summer heat and tolerate wet or dry conditions. For their beauty and adaptability to many adverse environmental conditions, Ginkgo trees are the perfect choice for just about any setting.

Family Name / Origin Ginkgoaceae / China

Mature Height × Spread 35 ft. to 50 ft. / 30 to 40 ft.

When and How to Plant Plant in early spring from 5-gallon, 15-gallon, or specimen-size containers. Space grouped Ginkgos 20 to 30 ft. apart; site a single plant at least 30 ft. from the nearest structure or paved area. Place Ginkgo trees in a spot sheltered from winds. Construct a watering basin 10 to 12 ft. in diameter and expand this basin to correspond with the tree's growth. Mulch the surface with 2 to 3 in. of organic material. See p. 398.

Climate & Culture

Preferred Zones
5–11

Sun Preference

Sun and Soil Preferences Ginkgos prefer full sun and a porous loam soil with a pH of 7.0.

Moisture Requirements Irrigate thoroughly and deeply to encourage deep root development.

Fertilizing Fertilize in late winter with a complete food (10-10-10) and in early fall with a 2-10-10.

Pruning and Care Prune only if shaping is necessary, in late winter while the tree is still dormant. A 20-year-old female tree planted closely to a male will produce offensive, odiferous fruit that resembles a brownish-orange, fleshy plum. It is best to avoid the female trees if possible. Unfortunately, even if you peeked at the undersides of their leaves, it would be difficult to tell the sex of the tree until it matures! Seriously, you would need to wait a few years until you could accurately observe whether it had an upright (male) or spreading (female) growth pattern.

Pests and Diseases They are relatively immune to most diseases and insect infestations.

Companion Plantings and Design They are popular trees along busy thoroughfares, in formal parks, in contemplative gardens, and as exquisite, miniaturized bonsai specimens. Heavenly Bamboo, Saucer Magnolia, and Pride of Madeira are just a few suggestions for companion plants.

Our Personal Favorite

NAME	SPECIAL CHARACTERISTICS
G. *biloba* 'Autumn Gold'	Quite symmetrical and upright / lovely deep-green, fan-like leaves turn bright gold in fall

Golden Rain Tree
Koelreuteria paniculata

Standing among Eucalyptus and Acacia trees in our neighborhood is a Golden Rain Tree that is visually prominent in summer because of its long clusters of small, bright-yellow flowers. These fragrant flowers give way to papery lantern-shaped masses of lime-green seedpods that eventually turn a brownish-buff color and persist throughout the winter. This is a medium-sized tree with an open-branched, flat-top form. It is covered with compound eighteen-inch leaves that are green in the spring and summer months, turning an autumn gold in the fall. The broad form of the Golden Rain Tree's canopy lends itself as a focal point in a tropical landscape or as a backdrop for a low growing, sweeping foreground planting. In either case, this showy tree adds an attractive silhouette to many landscapes. Golden Rain Tree is one of the few species that have yellow blossoms, and it blooms later than most other trees. Despite its delicate beauty, it is quite hardy and adaptable, able to withstand drought, heat, wind, urban air pollution, and freezing temperatures.

Family Name / Origin Sapindaceae / E Asia

Mature Height × Spread 20 to 40 ft. × 30 ft.

When and How to Plant Plant in fall or spring from 5-gallon, 15-gallon, or specimen-size containers. If planting a single tree, space 30 to 40 ft. on center; if planting a group, space 20 to 30 ft. Create a watering basin 10 ft. in diameter, and blanket with 2 to 3 in. of organic material such as humus mulch or compost. Refer to the Planting Techniques section for more information, p. 398.

Sun and Soil Preferences Although it grows best in full sun, it will do well in partial shade. This adaptive tree tolerates alkaline or acidic soils with a pH ranging from 6.5 to 7.2 and survives in clay, loam, or sandy soils.

Climate & Culture

Preferred Zones

8–11

Sun Preferences

Moisture Requirements Immediately after planting, irrigate deeply and thoroughly; then set up a watering schedule contingent upon climatic and growth conditions.

Fertilizing Fertilize in late winter with a complete food, 10-10-10.

Pruning and Care Prune only for shape or to remove dead wood. Deadhead only if you do not want the development of seedpods. Personally, we think the seedpods are very attractive and add to the fall and winter enjoyment of the tree. If you live too close to a marine environment, salt breezes will severely damage the foliage and another species should be selected.

Pests and Diseases Few disease or insect problems are associated with K. paniculata.

Companion Plantings and Design Golden Rain Tree does well in group plantings with other taller trees such as the Tulip Tree, Ginkgo, and Camphor. It is an excellent ornamental lawn tree.

Our Personal Favorite

NAME	SPECIAL CHARACTERISTICS
K. bipinnata	Finer, bipinnate leaflets give a textured fernlike appearance / common name is Chinese Flame Tree

Grecian Laurel

Laurus nobilis

I (Bruce) always have a trivia question for the audience of "The West Coast Garden Line" radio program, and so, the question today is: "What leaf is used for seasoning our food and was used to make wreaths to crown the heroes of ancient Greece and Rome?" The answer is (drum roll please), "Laurus nobilis, otherwise known as the Sweet Bay, Bay Laurel, or Grecian Laurel." This is a slow-growing tree with upright branches and a conical, slender form when young. With age it becomes a broad pyramid with dark-green, leathery leaves that are strongly aromatic when crushed. In spring it is laden with clusters of small lemon-yellow flowers. Once pollinated, these flowers become olive-like fruit, green at first and eventually turning black in the fall. Butterflies and bees are attracted to the nectar in its flowers, and we certainly enjoy using its dried leaves combined with other essential herbs in bouquet garni for stews, soups, and sauces. I like this tree for its handsome form as well as its adaptability to different soil types, wind and sun exposures, heat, and even freezing conditions for short periods of time. As a temperate zone tree, it survives in almost any climate except tropical areas.

Family Name / Origin Lauraceae / Mediterranean

Mature Height × **Spread** 20 to 30 ft. × 25 ft.

When and How to Plant Plant in fall or spring from 5- or 15-gallon containers. If planting in a group, space 10 to 15 ft. on center; site a single tree at least 15 ft. from structures or paved surfaces. Build a watering basin 10 ft. in diameter and mulch the surface with 2 to 3 in. of organic material such as humus mulch or compost. Consult the Planting Techniques section for more information, p. 398.

Sun and Soil Preferences Locate in full sun or partial shade, preferably in loam soil with a neutral pH of 7.0.

Climate & Culture

Preferred Zones
9–11

Sun Preferences

Moisture Requirements Water frequently in the beginning, about twice a week, increasing watering frequency in the summer, especially if it is hot and dry. After the tree is well established, water once every ten days to two weeks, depending on climatic and growth conditions. As a temperate-zone tree, it survives in almost any climate except tropical areas.

Fertilizing Fertilize in late winter with a complete food such as 10-10-10.

Pruning and Care Prune only for shape if necessary. This tree can also be trained as a topiary in a container or in the ground, or pruned as a hedge or shrub.

Pests and Diseases There are few diseases or insects that affect the Grecian Laurel, but brown soft scale and transient chewing insects occasionally cause damage to its foliage. Neem oil will control such infestations.

Companion Plantings and Design English Ivy, Glossy Abelias, and Prostrate Natal Plum are ideal companion plants for the Grecian Laurel.

Our Personal Favorites

NAME	SPECIAL CHARACTERISTICS
L. nobilis 'Saratoga'	A smaller variety, making an excellent container specimen for a patio
L. nobilis 'Aurea'	Leaves are tinged yellow

Hong Kong Orchid Tree
Bauhinia × blakeana

Bauhinia *was named after two sixteenth-century botanist brothers, Johann and Caspar Bauhin—an appropriate commemoration because of its unusual twin-lobed leaves. This hybrid is the floral symbol of Hong Kong. We consider it the most beautiful of all the Bauhinias, and unlike the others, it does not bear messy seedpods, because it is sterile. The spreading branches form an umbrella-shaped crown with bright-green butterfly-like leaves. From late winter through mid-spring, spectacular wine-red flowers with white-streaked petals adorn the canopy. If the tree is in a frost zone, the orchid-shaped flowers emerge prior to the flush of foliar growth; if in a temperate zone, the flowers will bloom against the backdrop of the foliage. They are excellent trees on windy slopes because their open canopies allow the wind to pass through without damaging their branching structures. In their native habitat, Hong Kong Orchid Trees withstand short periods of frost, and they thrive in heat as long as there is sufficient humidity and soil moisture. Their long bloom period and abundant large, fragrant flowers attract Mother Nature's other beautiful creatures, such as butterflies, birds, and bees.*

Family Name / Origin Leguminosae / W China

Mature Height × **Spread** 20 to 30 ft. × 25 ft.

When and How to Plant Plant in fall or spring
from containers that are 5- or 15-gallon or larger.
If planting several on a slope or in a group, space
15 ft. on center and the canopies will eventually grow
together. Plant a single ornamental at least 20 ft. from
a structure or paved area. Make sure the watering
basin is 20 percent larger in diameter than the tree's
canopy, and mulch the surface just after planting with
2 to 3 in. of compost or humus mulch. See Planting
Techniques section for more information, p. 398.

**Climate &
Culture**

**Preferred
Zones
9–11**

**Sun
Preference**

Sun and Soil Preferences To maximize bloom
production, choose a site in full sun with a neutral to
slightly acidic soil, pH 6.5 to 7.0. Like most trees, this hybrid prefers a well-
drained soil.

Moisture Requirements Water thoroughly after planting, then adjust
watering schedule and amounts according to climatic conditions and
growth cycles.

Fertilizing Fertilize with a complete food, 15-15-15, in spring and fall.

Pruning and Care Periodic pruning of errant growth maintains the tree's
shape. Deadheading is unnecessary because pods do not form on this
species. To achieve a classic tree shape, prune vigorously in December:
remove branches below 4 to 5 ft. to expose the trunk and any crossing
branches that rub against each other or grow towards the center of the tree.

Pests and Diseases These trees are not susceptible to disease and insects,
except when new foliage emerges or during times of drought.

Companion Plantings and Design Plant *en masse* as a visual screen,
or plant a single tree as an focal point amidst Rosea Iceplant, Glossy Abelias,
and Angel's Trumpet. The Hong Kong Orchid Tree is grown in landscapes for
its lavish display, often when many other trees are seasonally barren. Many
municipalities use these hybrids as street or parkway trees.

Incense Cedar
Calocedrus decurrens

*Calocedrus means "beautiful cedar," and with its dense coniferous branches covered with small bright-green scale leaves and its majestic height, this evergreen is aptly named. It has a shapely pyramidal form, neatly symmetrical, and bears small cylindrical cones. As a young tree, its foliage grows densely down to the ground; as it ages, its lower branches drop away, revealing a straight trunk that is maroon in color. C. decurrens is found on mountain slopes at 4000- to 8000-foot elevations from Baja, California, to Oregon. Commonly known as Incense Cedar, its cuttings were an important part of our retail nursery's annual "Holiday House of Christmas Magic" theme because of their highly aromatic fragrance, similar to the scent of a coniferous forest. Most of the fresh, green garlands decorating our fireplace mantles, stairway bannisters, doorways, and windows were made from these fragrant Cedar branches, and our florists enjoyed adding the cuttings to their winter floral arrangements. Incense Cedar does not do well in hot, dry, windy climates unless it has proper root development and soil moisture, but it survives in temperatures as low as -10 degrees Fahrenheit. **Note:** If you cannot find this tree by the name Calocedrus decurrens, look for Libocedrus d., another botanical name sometimes given to the same plant.*

Family Name / Origin Cupressaceae / W North America

Mature Height × Spread 60 to 70 ft. × 20 to 30 ft.

When and How to Plant The best time to plant is in fall or spring from a 1-, 5-, or 15-gallon container. Since they will eventually grow to be very tall trees, plant 30 to 50 ft. on center and at least 35 ft. from any structures or paved areas. Create an 8- to 10-ft. watering basin and cover 3 to 4 in. deep with a blanket of organic material such as humus mulch or compost. As the tree grows, expand the watering basin to encourage maximum lateral root development. Also see p. 398.

Climate & Culture

Preferred Zones
8–10

Sun Preference

Sun and Soil Preferences Incense Cedars do best in full sun in a slightly acidic soil, 6.5 to 7.0, with a porous texture.

Moisture Requirements To encourage deep rooting, water infrequently and deeply. *C. decurrens* can withstand extended periods of drought if it is watered generously for one or two years when young, facilitating the development of an extensive root system.

Fertilizing Fertilize in late winter or early spring with a complete food, 15-15-15.

Pruning and Care Pruning a coniferous tree is necessary only if the canopy needs lacing to allow sunlight to reach interior growth. As part of your routine garden maintenance program, wash out all the dead debris inside the canopy with a strong stream of water twice a year.

Pests and Diseases Though highly resistant to Oak Root Fungus, yellowing or dieback in this tree's branching structure could indicate another type of disease or insect infestation. Take a sample cutting to your local nursery or your nearest University of California Cooperative Extension for a diagnosis and remedy recommendation.

Companion Plantings and Design Incense Cedars are ideal trees for group plantings, high visual screens, and single tall accents or windbreaks in large landscapes. They blend well with other coniferous plants like Pines, Junipers, and Cedars.

Jacaranda

Jacaranda mimosifolia

*During a springtime visit to Pretoria, South Africa, the city seemed to be covered with a haze of mauve-blue trumpet flowers: thousands of Jacaranda trees were in full bloom, a breathtaking sight. (Pronounce the "J" softly, as an "H," to sound like "hak-har-an-da.") Although it is Pretoria's city tree, the Jacaranda is actually from the high, arid areas of Brazil and Paraguay, and is also known as Brazilian Rosewood. The tree's spreading branches create an umbrella-shaped, rounded crown with an open form. After the flowers are spent in late spring, large, fernlike, compound, pale-green leaves appear, along with small, woody, pancake-shaped seedpods that will ripen and split open the following year. We particularly like Jacarandas for use as handsome medium-sized shade trees in summer, and as color accents and blooms in spring. In addition to its spring and summer beauty, our Jacaranda is a haven for many songbirds and butterflies. Since they are native to dry habitats, Jacarandas tolerate drought and heat, but these brittle trees do not hold up well against strong winds, nor do they withstand freezing temperatures. If there is a cold snap in late winter, the leaves may turn yellow and drop off. **Note:** If you cannot find this plant by the name Jacaranda mimosifolia, look for J. acutifolia, another botanical name sometimes given to the same plant.*

Family Name / Origin Bignoniaceae / Brazil, Paraguay

Mature Height × Spread 25 to 40 ft. × 30 to 40 ft.

When and How to Plant Plant in spring from a 5-gallon, 15-gallon, or specimen-size container. Space 20 to 30 ft. on center. Build a watering basin 10 ft. in diameter and mulch the surface with 2 to 3 in. of organic material such as humus or compost. Consult the Planting Techniques section, p. 398, for more information.

Sun and Soil Preferences Plant in full sun, in well-drained soil with a pH of 7.0.

Climate & Culture

Preferred Zones
10–11

Sun Preference

Moisture Requirements Immediately after planting, soak deeply and thoroughly, at least twice during the first 7 to 10 days. Adjust frequency and amount thereafter according to climatic and growth conditions.

Fertilizing Fertilize in late winter or early spring with a complete food such as 15-15-15.

Pruning and Care It is only necessary to prune off the dead wood. Do not plant a Jacaranda in your lawn, because it does not like too much water. In fact, its flowering is more profuse during a dry year. Try not to locate your tree close to any paved areas, because its shallow rooting nature will cause problems as it matures.

Pests and Diseases If you see a black sooty mold or sticky honeydew, it is probably the work of aphids. Wash off the aphid colonies early in the morning; if they persist, use an insecticidal soap or a Neem oil. Other than aphids, there are few insects or diseases that affect Jacaranda trees.

Companion Plantings and Design Jacarandas work well with Butterfly Bush and Cotoneaster.

Our Personal Favorite

NAME	SPECIAL CHARACTERISTICS
J. mimosifolia 'Alba'	White trumpet-shaped flowers / common name is White Jacaranda

Japanese Maple

Acer palmatum

Japanese Maples are very desirable trees because of their delicate, open canopies; slender, artistically branched limbs; and rounded crowns. They are among our personal favorites because they can be trained as large shrubs, small trees, or even bonsai. We like to combine Japanese Maples with other plants that do well in dappled sunlight, such as Camellias, Azaleas, and Rhododendrons. Their shiny light-green leaves are sharply toothed and palmate shaped, and in the fall they are transformed into a blaze of purple, bronze, or yellow. Although their flowers are relatively nondescript, once they are spent they produce boomerang-shaped seeds called keys. Each key is composed of a pair of winged seeds known as samaras that are dispersed over long distances by the wind. The willowy branches and fine foliage are prized additions to cut-flower arrangements, particularly in highly stylized flower displays such as Ikebana. For best development, do not locate them in areas where they are exposed to extended periods of heat, drought, and wind. Because they are deciduous, they can withstand sub-freezing temperatures.

Family Name / Origin Aceracea / Japan

Mature Height × **Spread** 15 to 30 ft. × 15 to
20 ft.

When and How to Plant Fall or spring are the
best planting seasons, but bare-root or balled-and-
burlapped Maples can be planted in January or
February. Select a site protected from the wind, and
use 5-gallon plants spaced 10 to 12 ft. apart. Build
a watering basin that is 20 percent beyond the drip
lines, and mulch the basin's surface with 2 to 3 in. of
organic material. For more information, refer to the
Planting Techniques section of this book, p. 398.

**Climate &
Culture**

Preferred
Zones
10–11

Sun
Preference

Sun and Soil Preferences These plants prefer
partial shade and a slightly acidic, 6.5 to 7.0, loam
soil with a porosity high enough so that water percolates easily through the
root zones.

Moisture Requirements Water regularly, but make sure there is good
drainage.

Fertilizing Fertilize in early spring as needed, with a complete food such as
15-15-15.

Pruning and Care Prune for shape in late winter or early spring when the
trees are still dormant.

Pests and Diseases With the exception of aphids, few insects or diseases
affect these trees.

Companion Plantings and Design If you want a single Japanese Maple
as a focal point in your landscape, select a multiple-trunked specimen in a
24- to 30-in. box, for a mature tree will provide an immediate visual impact.

Our Personal Favorites

NAME	SPECIAL CHARACTERISTICS
A. *palmatum* 'Atropurpureum'	Popular for reddish foliage / grows 15 to 25 ft.
A. *palmatum* 'Dissectum'	Finest-textured foliage of the Maples / requires a humid, temperate environment / grows to 10 to 20 ft. / also known as Cutleaf Japanese Maple

Madrone
Arbutus menziesii

Madrone is the tallest of all the Arbutus, and its slender form goes well with its open canopy and airy branching structure. Large patches of its bark will shed attractively, revealing a smooth, rust-brown trunk. The glossy green leaves are elliptical in shape, with smooth margins, and they have a leathery texture. In the spring, fragrant alabaster flowers bloom in profusion, and they are followed by orange-red fruits. They are a wonderful food source for birds and other wildlife. The Madrone is often used as a dramatic focal point in commercial or residential landscapes where there is plenty of room for it to attain its mature height. A native plant, it is found along the coast from San Luis Obispo, northward, and also in certain pockets of the Sierra Nevada foothills. Since the Madrone is primarily a coastal tree, it dislikes high temperatures and arid conditions, although it can withstand wind and temperatures down to 25 degrees Fahrenheit. Its fragrant, urn-shaped flowers resemble the delicate Lily-of-the-Valley and attract butterflies, bees, and hummingbirds.

Family Name / Origin Ericaceae / British Columbia to California

Mature Height × **Spread** 60 to 80 ft. × 60 ft.

Climate & Culture

Preferred Zones
10–11

Sun Preference

When and How to Plant As with any native, the best time to plant is in the fall, from a 5- or 15-gallon container. When acquiring a Madrone, it might be advisable to spend the extra money to purchase a larger specimen in a 24- to 30-in. box. The larger size will create a more immediate visual impact. To accommodate the large mature size, you should plant at a distance of 30 to 40 ft. from any structure or paved area and never above leach lines. Mulch the ground's surface with 2 to 3 in. of compost or humus mulch, encouraging an extensive and fibrous root system. This will allow your tree to gather small amounts of moisture over a large area well beyond its drip line. The mulch will decompose, so replenish on a regular basis. Also see p. 398.

Sun and Soil Preferences Locate in full sun in soil that is acidic, pH 6.5, porous, and loam-textured.

Moisture Requirements *A. menziesii* is extremely sensitive to salt accumulation in its root zone, so be sure to irrigate sufficiently, dissolving the soluble salts and moving them away from the root system. Use water with a minimum of total dissolved salts.

Fertilizing Fertilize in the fall with a complete food such as ammonium phosphate, 16-20-0.

Pruning and Care Prune for shape as well as the removal of dead wood. There is no need to deadhead the flowers, and no need to manually remove the Madrone's reddish bark—it naturally sloughs off in large patches to expose the beautifully smooth trunk.

Pests and Diseases This tree is resistant to most diseases and insect infestations—in particular, it is highly resistant to oak root fungus.

Companion Plantings and Design Madrone is quite compatible with other native shrubs and trees that have similar cultural requirements, such as California Lilac, Silverberry, and Prostrate Manzanita.

New Zealand Christmas Tree

Metrosideros tomentosa

This tenacious, medium-sized tree with multiple trunks bursts into bloom during the Christmas season in New Zealand, which is actually summertime there. I (Bruce) use the tree extensively in coastal landscapes because of its adaptability to sandy soils, salt spray, and prevailing ocean winds. It even has a root system that can cling precariously to craggy cliff faces. This slow-growing evergreen shade tree is densely covered with elliptic leaves that are dark green on top and silvery beneath. It is an erect vase-shaped tree with many branches that form a rounded canopy. Its summer-blooming flowers look like brilliant red pincushions and are actually crimson-colored clusters of stamens that hang like rounded bottlebrush ornaments. Metrosideros means "heart of iron," a name that comes from its blood-red heartwood; many Maori, Tahitian, and Hawaiian tribes use this distinctively colored timber to make beautiful sculptures. Once established, the tree tolerates drought and withstands heat if there is enough water. While it is an excellent choice for temperate coastal regions, it is not a wise selection for inland areas that are subject to extended periods of frost or dry winds.
Note: *If you cannot find this plant by the name* Metrosideros tomentosa, *look for* M. excelsus, *another botanical name sometimes given to the same plant. Another common name is Pohutukawa.*

Family Name / Origin Myrtaceae / New Zealand, South Pacific

Mature Height × **Spread** 20 to 30 ft. × 25 ft.

When and How to Plant Plant in spring from a 5- or 15-gallon container. If planting a group, space the trees 15 to 20 ft. on center; plant a single tree at least 20 ft. from a structure or paved area. Make a watering basin 10 to 12 ft. in diameter and cover with 2 to 3 in. of rich organic material like humus mulch or compost. See the Planting Techniques section for more information, p. 398.

Sun and Soil Preferences It thrives in a full-sun location in a slightly acidic soil, pH 6.7 to 7.0, that has good percolation.

Climate & Culture

Preferred Zones

10–11

Sun Preference

Moisture Requirements Water thoroughly and deeply immediately after planting. Water twice during the first week, then water according to climatic and growth conditions.

Fertilizing Fertilize in early spring with a complete food such as 10-10-10.

Pruning and Care Deadheading is unnecessary, but prune for shape and to open up the dense canopy. Although M. *tomentosa* is most commonly grown as a tree, it can be trained into a solid hedge or visual screen as an alternative to Myoporum (*Myoporum laetum*) or Japanese Mock Orange (*Pittosporum tobira*).

Pests and Diseases There are few maladies or insects that affect the New Zealand Christmas Tree, but there is some evidence that the invasive Eugenia Psyllid and the Eucalyptus Longhorned Borer can be problems. Instead of spraying with pesticides, it is recommended that you do nothing: a parasitic wasp has been released to mitigate these infestations.

Companion Plantings and Design Rock Cotoneaster, Glossy Abelia, and Golden Mirror Plant are equally hardy companions for this tree.

Our Personal Favorite

NAME	SPECIAL CHARACTERISTICS
M. tomentosa 'Variegata'	Variegated-edged leaves

Olive Tree
Olea europaea

Whenever we see an O. europaea with its picturesque open branches, upright habit, and narrow gray-green leaves with a touch of silver on the undersides, we think of the old, gnarled, vase-shaped Common Olive Tree in Grandmother Asakawa's backyard. The Olive Tree is one of the oldest cultivated trees in the Western world. From time immemorial, the oil pressed from its fruits has been the primary reason for its popularity. In fact, the ancient Roman word for "oil" is Olea. In ancient times in the Mediterranean, the oil was used not only for cooking and seasoning, but also as a source of evening light, a lubricant, and an ingredient of soap, perfume, and cosmetics. Although it takes about ten years before the tiny off-white flowers produce fruits, or drupes, the Olive Tree more than makes up for this slow start by living for 1,500 years or more. Since it is from the Mediterranean, it loves temperate areas that have winters cool enough to allow the flowers to develop and long, hot summers that allow the olives to ripen properly. In order for olives to be edible, they must be cured or processed to neutralize their natural bitterness. Once established, the Olive Tree prefers soil kept on the dry side and can tolerate short periods of drought as well as Santa Ana winds. Hardy plants such as those listed under Companion Plantings and Design *are at home with the equally hardy Olive Tree.*

Family Name / Origin Oleaceae / Mediterranean

Mature Height × Spread 15 to 25 ft. × 20 ft.

When and How to Plant Plant in fall or spring from 5-gallon, 15-gallon, or specimen-size containers. Specimen trees in California can be successfully moved and transplanted at just about any age or size. Site a single tree 20 to 30 ft. from structures or paved areas; space grouped trees 15 to 20 ft. apart. Cover a 10- to 12-ft. watering basin with 2 to 3 in. of organic material. See Planting Techniques, p. 398, for more information.

Climate & Culture

Preferred Zones
9–11

Sun Preference

Sun and Soil Preferences Plant in full sun in a loam soil with a pH of 6.6 to 7.0.

Moisture Requirements Irrigate thoroughly after planting. Water twice again during the first week, then adjust watering amount and frequency to accommodate variable climatic and growth conditions.

Fertilizing Fertilize in late winter with a complete food such as 10-10-10.

Pruning and Care Prune for shape and to remove dead wood after harvesting the olives. For those who consider the drupes a messy nuisance, spray the tree's flowers with a plant growth regulator such as Florel™ or Olive Stop™. It may require several applications.

Pests and Diseases As new growth emerges in spring, aphids, olive scale, and black scale infestation can be a problem that is remedied with an application of horticultural oil. If the foliage begins to fade, yellow, brown, and wilt, the problem might be Verticillium wilt, a soil-dwelling fungus. Take a sample to your county agricultural department or to the University of California Cooperative Extension for verification and control recommendation. Keep in mind that in California, the label is the law, and always follow the manufacturer's directions.

Companion Plantings and Design Try 'Edward Goucher' Abelia, Bottlebrush, and Rock Rose as companions.

Our Personal Favorite

NAME	SPECIAL CHARACTERISTICS
O. europaea 'Monher'	A fruitless olive tree / also known as Majestic Beauty Olive

Persian Silk Tree

Albizia julibrissin

A. julibrissin, one of the prettiest Persian Silk Trees (named for Italian naturalist Albizzi), is popular in the Middle East, Australia, France, and California. As a landscape architect, I (Bruce) recommend this particular Albizia whenever I design a more tropical setting. It grows at a moderate pace and has a flat-topped crown with spreading branches. The feathery light-green foliage creates an attractive background for profuse clusters of pink pompon flowers that blanket the canopy during the summer months. The common name, Persian Silk Tree, comes from the silky stamens that are white to deep pink. Like other Leguminosae plants, long, green, pea-like seedpods emerge from the spent flowers and turn a deep brown in the fall, eventually splitting and providing food for visiting birds. While many cattle farmers use the leaves and seedpods for feed, those of us who do not own cattle can recycle the greenery and pods by composting and using the decomposed material to enrich our garden soils. Another interesting usage of Persian Silk Trees is that some primitive societies make soap from the powdery bark. Since these trees are deciduous, they tolerate winter temperatures as low as -10 degrees Fahrenheit. From spring through fall, their delicate foliage cannot withstand extended periods of drought, wind, or heat without adequate irrigation.

Family Name / Origin Leguminosae / Asia

Mature Height × Spread 30 ft. × 30 ft.

When and How to Plant Spring is the best season
to plant, from 15-gallon containers. Space 20 ft.
apart if planting in a group. Site a single tree at least
15 to 20 ft. from structures or paved areas, and never
plant above leach lines. Be sure to plant in a site that
is protected from wind. To encourage lateral root
development, mulch the watering basin surface with
2 to 3 in. of compost or humus mulch and maintain
the surface all year-round. Also see p. 398.

Sun and Soil Preferences Plant in full sun in
loam-textured soil with a pH of 6.5 to 7.0.

Climate & Culture

Preferred
Zones
9–11

Sun
Preference

Moisture Requirements It is important to provide an even amount of
moisture from spring through fall, but even when the trees are dormant in
the winter, continue to monitor the soil's moisture content.

Fertilizing For optimum bloom display, apply ammonium phosphate
(16-20-0) or acid food (6-10-4) in early spring.

Pruning and Care Prune for form during winter dormancy. If you dislike
the nuisance of seedpods, deadhead flowers as soon as they are spent.

Pests and Diseases Except for possible aphid infestations in the spring,
few insect or disease problems affect Persian Silk Trees.

Companion Plantings and Design Persian Silk Trees make beautiful
accents in tropical gardens. Their spreading canopies provide shade for other
tropical plants like Pink Powder Puff, Hibiscus, and Gardenias.

Our Personal Favorites

NAME	SPECIAL CHARACTERISTICS
A. j. 'Rosea'	Very deep-pink puffball flowers / slightly smaller than Persian Silk Tree
A. j. 'Alba'	Clusters of white pompon flowers

Scarlet Flowering Eucalyptus
Eucalyptus ficifolia

There are over 600 species of Australian Eucalyptus existing in an amazing array of diverse environments, from swamplands to deserts to riverbanks to mountainous forests. Their adaptability is the reason they are so common in California. I (Bruce) find them perfect for the less-manicured landscapes that have natural habitat themes. E. ficifolia has astonishingly beautiful vermilion flowers that are really clusters of stamens and anthers. Butterflies, birds, and bees are attracted to its flower-rich nectar. Following the summer bloom period, unusual woody, urn-shaped capsules appear. This relatively slow-growing tree has a spreading, dome-shaped crown. There are two features that are uniquely characteristic of most Eucalypts. One is the operculum, *a lid that covers each bud and pops off when its stamens unfold during its flowering period. The other is the* lignotuber, *a swollen portion of the root flare that is just above or below the ground. It functions as a moisture and nutrient storage reservoir during times of drought. Even after a natural disaster, such as a fire, the lignotuber allows it to regenerate. Scarlet Flowering Eucalyptus has elliptic leaves that are leathery, dark green, and stiff with light veins. Although it tolerates wind, heat, and drought conditions, it does not withstand extended periods of freezing temperatures.*

Family Name / Origin Myrtaceae / W Australia

Mature Height × Spread 15 to 30 ft. × 20 to 30 ft.

When and How to Plant Plant in spring from
5- or 15-gallon containers. Space 30 ft. apart. Build
a watering basin with a diameter of 10 ft. and mulch
the surface with 2 to 3 in. of organic material such
as humus mulch or compost. Thoroughly soak the
root zone to collapse any air pockets. Refer to the
Planting Techniques section of this book for additional
information, p. 398.

Climate & Culture

Preferred Zones
10–11

Sun Preference

Sun and Soil Preferences These trees like full
sun and an acidic soil with a pH of 6.5 to 7.0. They
prefer a loam-textured soil because it permits good
percolation.

Moisture Requirements Water twice a week for the first couple of weeks,
then modify to accommodate climatic and growth conditions.

Fertilizing Fertilize in winter with a complete food like 10-10-10.

Pruning and Care Prune only if you need to shape or remove dead wood.

Pests and Diseases *E. ficifolia* is resistant to most diseases and insects,
including the Eucalyptus Longhorned Borer.

Companion Plantings and Design These are excellent trees for xeri-
scaping or in combination with other drought-tolerant plants. They work well
with many native shrubs and ground covers that thrive in cycles of winter
rains, such as California Lilac, Dwarf Coyote Bush, and Manzanita.

Our Personal Favorites

NAME	SPECIAL CHARACTERISTICS
E. citriodora	Pungent, citrus-scented foliage / smooth, white bark / white flowers bloom in fall and winter / also known as Lemon Scented Eucalyptus
E. polyanthemos	Unusual oval, gray-green foliage that makes it popular in cut-flower arrangements / resembles an Aspen tree as it moves in the wind / deer-resistant / also known as Silver Dollar Eucalyptus

Southern Magnolia
Magnolia grandiflora

In the early 1990s, central California suffered from an unseasonably cold winter. Conifers such as Canary Island Pines, Eucalyptus, and Acacias never recovered, but the magnificent M. grandifloras *not only survived but continued to grow well. Fossilized records of Magnolias (named for French botanist Pierre Magnol), dating back over five million years, are a testament to their long genetic history. The Southern Magnolia, also known as American Bull Bay, is a favorite flowering evergreen tree because of its ability to survive many climatic conditions. Its handsome, dense, rounded canopy is covered with long, pointed, lacquered ten-inch leaves and its enormous plate-sized, citrus-scented, creamy-white, summer-blooming flowers. With the sun's warmth and soft breezes, the flowers' fragrance attracts birds, butterflies, and bees. The glossy dark-green foliage, covered beneath with a downy, rust-colored fuzz, makes elegant della Robbia–style wreaths or garlands. When the enormous cup-shaped flowers are blooming, florists use the cut branches or simply float the blossoms in glass bowls. Once the six- to twelve-petal flowers are spent, bright red seeds develop on cone-shaped heads, decorating the tree from late summer to early fall. Established Southern Magnolias love heat and humidity, and their dense branches and leathery-textured foliage allows them to withstand high winds.*

Family Name / Origin Magnoliaceae / SE North America

Mature Height × Spread 40 ft. to 60 ft. / 50 ft.

When and How to Plant The best time to plant is in fall or early spring from 5- or 15-gallon containers. Since they are large trees, space individual trees at least 40 ft. apart; space groupings at least 30 ft. apart so their canopies will touch each other. Initially, your watering basin needs to be at least 10 ft. to 15 ft. in diameter and covered and maintained with 2 to 3 in. of rich organic material such as humus mulch or compost. For more information, consult the Planting Techniques section of this book, p. 398.

Climate & Culture

Preferred Zones
8–11

Sun Preference

Sun and Soil Preferences Plant in full sun in soil with a pH range of 6.5 to 7.2, adequate moisture, and good drainage.

Moisture Requirements Immediately after planting, thoroughly soak the root zone twice the first week. Thereafter, water every seven to ten days, adjusting for climatic and weather conditions.

Fertilizing Fertilize in late winter with a complete food, 10-10-10.

Pruning and Care Prune minimally to remove dead wood.

Pests and Diseases Although they occasionally fall prey to brown soft scale or cottony cushion scale, these trees are not affected by many insects or diseases.

Companion Plantings and Design Southern Magnolia looks beautiful in a Hybrid Tall Fescue lawn with Japanese Mock Orange, Laurustinus, and Azaleas.

Our Personal Favorites

NAME	SPECIAL CHARACTERISTICS
M. grandiflora 'St. Mary'	Good when a smaller tree is desired / width: 20 ft. / common name is St. Mary Magnolia
M. grandiflora 'Little Gem'	Moderate grower / very compact / upright branches / narrow form

Sweet Gum

Liquidambar styraciflua 'Palo Alto'

Close to our home, there is a community park with many Liquidambar or Sweet Gum trees growing tall and pyramidal in its expansive lawn areas. Sweet Gums appear spindly and stunted in their native habitat because they are competing for sunlight with other more aggressive and wider-spreading trees, but when they stand alone and have a good supply of water, they grow to their full potential as strong, cone-shaped trees resembling tall sentries in the wind. In the spring, tiny clusters of greenish insignificant flowers appear at the tips of branchlets, then become spherical, spiky capsules. The trunks and branches are rough-textured, corklike, and gray. The most special quality of Sweet Gums is their foliage. The vivid green leaves are star-shaped, with five serrated lobes, and they change into a blaze of burgundies, reds, oranges, and yellows in fall. In the autumn breezes, their foliage and spiky pods fall to the ground and can be gathered up for table, floral, and wreath decorations. When mature, these trees tolerate freezing temperatures and summer heat. They also do well in coastal areas, but cannot withstand close exposure to ocean spray, drought, or blustery winds.

Family Name / Origin   Hamamelidaceae /
E North America, Mexico

Mature Height × Spread   40 to 60 ft. × 50 ft.

When and How to Plant   Plant in fall, late winter,
or early spring from a 5- or 15-gallon container.
Space at least 20 to 30 ft. on center, 30 to 40 ft. from
structures or paved areas. Build a watering basin
10 to 12 ft. in diameter and cover with 2 to 3 in. of
organic material. Also see p. 398.

Sun and Soil Preferences   Locate in full sun, in
rich loam soil with a pH of 6.7 to 7.0.

Moisture Requirements   Soak thoroughly two or
three times during the first couple of days. Water twice
a week for the next two weeks, then adjust amount and frequency according
to climatic and growth conditions.

Fertilizing   Fertilize in late winter with a complete food, 15-15-15.

Pruning and Care   Pruning is only necessary to remove precarious
branches or dead wood. If you find spiky seed capsules a nuisance, stop
their formation by using a plant growth regulator, available at a local
garden center.

Pests and Diseases   These trees are generally free of disease and insects,
but if foliage is blackened from sooty mold, look for scale infestation; if
leaves appear chewed, look for larvae of fruit tree leaf rollers or Tussock
Moths. To control these pesky critters, use *Bacillus thuringiensis*, or *B.t.*,
following label directions.

Companion Plantings and Design   Pride of Madeira, Glossy Abelia,
and Silverberry are good companions.

Climate & Culture

Preferred Zones
7–11

Sun Preference

Our Personal Favorites

NAME	SPECIAL CHARACTERISTICS
L. styraciflua 'Burgundy'	Purple-red foliage in fall that remains on the tree longer through the season / common name is Burgundy Sweet Gum
L. styraciflua 'Palo Alto'	Extra-large leaves turn a bright orange-red in fall

Tulip Tree

Liriodendron tulipifera

Elegant specimens of L. tulipifera at San Francisco's Golden Gate Park stand over 70 feet tall and have ramrod-straight trunks, strong branching structures, and broad crowns. In a residential yard, these trees normally grow to about 40 to 50 feet. The botanical name means "the tulip-bearing lily tree," and it is a poetic description. One of their unique features is four-lobed leaves that look as if they have been cut off at the top. Sometimes the trees are called Yellow Poplars because their springtime light-green leaves turn into rich buttery-yellow foliage that shimmers in the autumn breezes. In late spring, their flowers are the color of limes and have orange centers; although the tree's common name is Tulip Tree, its flowers more closely resemble Magnolia blossoms. After the blossoms are spent, clusters of cone-like seeds appear and remain on the trees long after the leaves are gone. Tulip Trees tolerate temperatures as low as -10 degrees Fahrenheit and gusty winds, but they are fast-growing, so they do not withstand drought or high temperatures without adequate moisture. During late spring when the trees are covered in blooms, butterflies, bees, and hummingbirds busily harvest their sweet nectar. In summer, birds seek sanctuary from predators and the searing rays of the sun in the cool, protective, shaded canopies.

Family Name / Origin Magnoliaceae / E North America

Mature Height × Spread 60 to 80 ft. × 60 ft.

When and How to Plant Plant in fall, from 5- or 15-gallon containers, or in December through January when bare-root trees are available. Space 40 to 60 ft. apart and at least 50 ft. from structures or paved areas. Never, ever plant above or near leach lines. To encourage rapid development of lateral root systems, provide 12- to 15-ft.-diameter watering basins and mulch the surface with 2 to 3 in. of organic material. Also see p. 398.

Sun and Soil Preferences Select a sunny location with a well-drained loam soil with a pH of 6.7 to 7.0.

Climate & Culture

Preferred Zones
6–10

Sun Preference

Moisture Requirements Water thoroughly after planting by filling the basin two or three times. Water every third day for two weeks, then adjust amount and frequency according to climatic and growing conditions. Provide moisture during drought, dry winds, and high temperatures.

Fertilizing Fertilize late winter or early spring with a complete granular food such as 11-8-4.

Pruning and Care Dead wood removal is usually all that is necessary.

Pests and Diseases As tender foliage emerges in spring, sucking and chewing insects such as aphids and leaf hoppers can cause problems. It is impractical to spray these large trees with pesticides. If a problem becomes severe, seek the help of a state-licensed pest-control advisor.

Companion Plantings and Design These are terrific shade trees for companion plants such as Japanese Mock Orange, Algerian Ivy, and Saucer Magnolia.

Our Personal Favorites

NAME	SPECIAL CHARACTERISTICS
L. tulipifera 'Arnold'	Many short, ascending branches give a compact look / also known as Arnold's Tulip Tree
L. tulipifera 'Aureo-marginatum'	Green leaves prominently edged in bright yellow

Victorian Box

Pittosporum undulatum

Victorian Boxes are dense, bushy-crowned trees growing up to thirty feet. Their trunks have gray bark that resemble coarse sandpaper. Their long, narrow leaves are glossy dark-green with undulating margins, similar to Laurel leaves. In California, the creamy bell-shaped flowers bloom in spring and early summer. The flowers are as fragrant as orange blossoms, and the seasonal warm breezes infuse the air with their perfume, attracting birds and bees. Once the flowers are spent, bright orange capsules form, containing black seeds covered with a sticky resin. This notable characteristic is the reason for the name pitta, which means "pitch," and sporus, which means "a seed." Victorian Box trees are naturally found from the tropics of Queensland to the temperate areas of Brisbane along Australia's east coast, attesting to their adaptability in high- as well as low-rainfall regions, in mild winds, and in heat if enough moisture is available. They withstand freezing temperatures for only short periods of time. P. undulatum is grown as a large shrub or a standard tree. If you grow it as a standard tree, remove its lower foliage and branches to expose its trunk and to encourage canopy growth. Victorian Box is a popular landscape tree; ours is growing under a large Jacaranda near a Cork Oak and a Mulberry.

Family Name / Origin Pittosporaceae /
E Australia

Mature Height × Spread 20 to 30 ft. × 30 ft.

When and How to Plant Plant in spring from a
1-, 5-, or 15-gallon container. Site a single tree at
least 20 ft. from buildings or paved areas; if grown in
groups, space 12 to 15 ft. on center. Build a watering
basin 10 ft. in diameter and mulch the surface with
2 to 3 in. of organic material. See p. 398.

Sun and Soil Preferences Select a full-sun or
partial-shade area and plant in a loam soil with good
drainage and a pH of 6.7 to 7.0.

Climate & Culture

Preferred Zones 9–11

Sun Preferences

Moisture Requirements Immediately after plant-
ing, water deeply and thoroughly, then twice during the following week.
Thereafter, adjust frequency and amount according to the dictates of climate
and growth.

Fertilizing Fertilize in late winter or early spring with a complete fertilizer
such as 15-15-15.

Pruning and Care Prune for shape or when unsightly suckers appear at
the bottom of the trunk, in late winter or early spring.

Pests and Diseases When their flowers and new foliage emerge in spring,
aphids and brown soft scale populations can explode quickly. These sucking
pests secrete a sticky substance called honeydew which attracts ants. If this
situation persists, a fungus known as black sooty mold will cover the leaves.
To avoid extensive damage, wash off the foliage with a strong stream of water
or use insecticidal soap, horticultural oil, or Neem oil in the early morning.

Companion Plantings and Design Plant with Japanese Mock Orange,
Pink Indian Hawthorn, and Laurustinus to make an ideal garden focal
specimen.

Our Personal Favorite

NAME	SPECIAL CHARACTERISTICS
P. undulatum 'Variegatum'	Leaves with undulating white margins

Weeping Bottlebrush

Callistemon viminalis

C. viminalis, *an evergreen with a willowlike growing habit, originated in the lowland streambeds of coastal Queensland, Australia. It is commonly called the Weeping Bottlebrush tree because of its long, downward-arching branches tipped with flower spikes that are actually masses of clustered crimson-colored stamens arranged in symmetrical rows, like bottlebrushes. Although its bloom cycle is primarily in the spring, this tree flowers periodically throughout the year, and its blossoms remain for a very long time. As a small tree, its canopy is narrow with a densely domed crown. In their native habitats, Callistemon grow in low-lying areas such as creek beds or bottoms of canyons where water tables are high. This makes them excellent choices where percolation is poor, along drainage swales or near bottoms of cut or filled banks. Since they are shallow rooted, they are also used as street, parkway, or patio trees and as visual screens. Their flowers are rich with ambrosia and attract many different species of birds, butterflies, and bees, tolerate short durations of freezing temperatures, endure wind and heat if sufficient moisture is available, and withstand brief periods of drought if the trees are mature.*

Family Name / Origin Myrtaceae / Australia

Mature Height × Spread 15 to 20 ft. × 10 to 15 ft.

When and How to Plant Plant in fall or spring from 5- or 15-gallon containers. If planting as a group, space the trees 12 to 15 ft. on center; locate a single specimen at least 15 ft. from structures or paved areas. Build a watering basin 6 in. high and 8 ft. in diameter, and mulch the surface with 2 to 3 in. of organic material. See Planting Techniques section for more information, p. 398.

Sun and Soil Preferences They do best in full sun but can adapt to partial shade. *C. viminalis* prefers porous soils with a neutral pH of 7.0, but can tolerate dense clay-to-loam soils.

Moisture Requirements Soak thoroughly immediately after planting, then begin an irrigating schedule of once a week, adjusting for weather and growth factors.

Fertilizing Fertilize in early spring with a complete food such as 10-10-10.

Pruning and Care Prune for shape at any time. Deadheading is not necessary—as the stamens drop off, woody capsules form on the stems, and new foliar and branch growth emerges at the tips. If left to grow naturally, Callistemons develop branches close to the ground. Remove all branches below 4 ft. if you want to train it into a standard-form tree. Prune off any emerging growth from the trunk's base.

Pests and Diseases They are relatively impervious to disease or insect infestation.

Companion Plantings and Design Japanese Mock Orange, Rock Rose, and Lavender Starflower plants provide lovely supportive growth when planted with the Weeping Bottlebrush.

Climate & Culture

Preferred Zones
8–11

Sun Preferences

Our Personal Favorite

NAME	SPECIAL CHARACTERISTICS
C. viminalis 'Red Cascade'	A profusion of large, rosy-red, brush-like flowers / blooms heavily in spring and sporadically at other times

Western Redbud
Cercis occidentalis

Cercis occidentalis *is sometimes known as the Judas Tree because of the ancient belief that Judas Iscariot hung himself from its limb after betraying Christ. Now this species is more familiar to gardeners as Western Redbud, and it is found throughout the southwestern United States among foothills and along rocky slopes. Back in the Dark Ages, when I (Bruce) was in college studying plant identification, I spent many hours at the Rancho Santa Ana Botanic Garden in Claremont, California. I will always remember the early spring, when the Western Redbud's abundant clusters of magenta-red flowers blanketed every bare branch. In my opinion, this fifteen-foot deciduous tree is one of the most dazzling members of the pea family. Even when it is still tightly budded, this tree creates a showy display. Once its elegant blossoms are spent, lush heart-shaped foliage that is bright-green in color bursts forth and covers all its branches. Delicate, flat seedpods dangle in the soft spring and summer breezes. Although similar in growth to the Eastern Redbud, it tends to be shrubbier in habit. There are few diseases that attack this native, and once it is established, it tolerates drought, wind, heat, and cold.*

Family Name / Origin Leguminosae / California

Mature Height × **Spread** 15 to 20 ft. × 15 to 20 ft.

When and How to Plant Fall is the best time to plant a Western Redbud because that is the season for rapid root development; the second-best time is in the spring. Select 1- or 5-gallon container plants. If planting in a group, space 12 to 15 ft. apart; locate a single tree 10 ft. from structures or paved areas. One caveat: Plan the location carefully, because Redbuds do not like to be transplanted. To encourage deep rooting, construct a watering basin with a diameter well beyond the tree's drip line and mulch its surface with 2 to 3 in. of organic material. See p. 398.

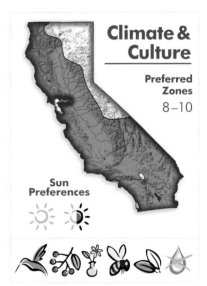

Climate & Culture

Preferred Zones
8–10

Sun Preferences

Sun and Soil Preferences Choose a full-sun site for maximum bloom production, although dappled shade will do. Western Redbuds need a porous soil with a neutral pH of 7.0.

Moisture Requirements Water infrequently but deeply.

Fertilizing Winter is the time to fertilize with a complete food such as 6-10-4.

Pruning and Care Do not deadhead. We think Western Redbud is most spectacular when grown as a multiple-trunk specimen. To create a multiple trunk, select at least three strong, main stems to be leaders, pruning away all other lateral branches below 4 ft. Bonsai enthusiasts enjoy miniaturizing this plant because of its gorgeous spring bloom and delicate foliage.

Pests and Diseases Watch out for aphids during the spring months, and keep an eye out for chewing insects such as leaf hoppers, cicadas, and grasshoppers.

Companion Plantings and Design They blend well with California Lilac, Manzanita, and California Poppies.

Our Personal Favorite

NAME	SPECIAL CHARACTERISTICS
C. occidentalis 'Claremont'	Deep-red blossoms

White Alder

Alnus rhombifolia

White Alders are useful in problem areas such as those that have poor drainage or are
nutrient-deficient. They are also appealing for their attractive, distinctive white bark,
upright shape, and contrasting deep-green, glossy foliage that covers slightly weeping
branches. In the winter, the bare appearance only enhances the delicate form; in the
warmer months, the serrated leaves quiver with the slightest breeze. These fast-growing
trees are used widely as shade trees, as windbreaks, along waterways for erosion
control, and as background trees. The pilings that have supported Venice for centuries
were made from Alder timber, which is water-repellent. In fact, Alnus is the original
Roman word for this tree. The flowers are unisexual, appearing as catkins that
blossom on the trees periodically throughout the year, with the exception of winter.
Alders are found naturally in areas where the soil is deep and constantly moist, such
as riverbanks, canyon floors, or marshes; keep this fact in mind during periods of
drought, high temperatures, and dry winds. These trees tolerate temperatures as low
as -10 degrees Fahrenheit, and they also thrive in temperate zones.

Family Name / Origin Betulaceae / W North America

Mature Height × Spread 25 to 40 ft. × 40 ft.

When and How to Plant You can plant from a container at any time, but it's best to plant in fall or early spring. Select 5- to 15-gallon containers, but make sure these fast-growing plants are not root-bound. If planting in a group, space 20 to 30 ft. apart. If planting a single tree, plant at least 30 ft. from the nearest structure or paved area, and never plant near leach lines. To establish your tree as quickly as possible, you need to encourage lateral root development by building a watering basin well beyond the tree's drip line and mulching the basin's surface with 2 to 3 in. of compost or humus mulch. Also see p. 398.

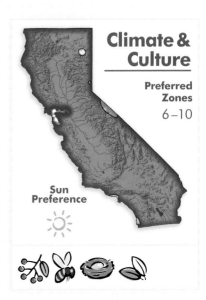

Climate & Culture

Preferred Zones
6–10

Sun Preference

Sun and Soil Preferences For optimum development, plant in full sun where the soil has adequate access to moisture and the pH is neutral, 6.5 to 7.2.

Moisture Requirements Because these trees are "water babies," it is almost impossible to overwater them, especially if there is good percolation throughout their root zones. If you water too *infrequently,* however, the trees will stress and possibly perish.

Fertilizing The most efficient time to fertilize is in early spring and fall, with a 15-15-15.

Pruning and Care If your White Alder is a focal point in your garden and you want a standard tree form, prune for shape early. Remove all but a single trunk, and remove any branches below 4 to 5 ft.

Pests and Diseases There are few diseases or insects that invade these trees, but be on the lookout in summer for migratory, chewing insects. For extensive damage, consult a professional nurseryman or pest-control advisor.

Companion Plantings and Design These trees grow well with Cotoneasters, Butterfly Bushes, and Abelias.

Vines *for California*

Whether they are casting cool shadows, creating privacy, twining up a fence, or arching over a gate, vines can be flamboyant flower factories or sedate evergreen shingles. When space is limited, think about gardening up walls, trellises, arbors, posts, or any other structure that begs for highlighting or camouflage. Rambunctious vines can even weave their way through shrubs and trees.

Training Your Vines

To keep vines from smothering their supports, other plants, or each other, pinch tender shoots about once a month during their growth cycle, saving the heavy pruning for dormancy. If you prefer a lush, more overgrown look, then relax and subscribe to a laissez-faire style of gardening.

Lavender Trumpet Vines and Clematis are easy to train in small places, but other vines such as Wisteria, Bougainvillea, Scarlet Trumpet Vine, and Passion Vine, fill larger spaces such as walls and fences. Creeping Fig and Boston Ivy are self-supporting vines with the help of holdfasts, tendrils with disc-like suction cups or rootlets that enable them to attach to just about anything. Bear in mind that even aggressive vines can be curtailed and confined with annual pruning and frequent pinching back.

Most vines have a natural tendency to grow upward, branch into a tangled mass at the top, and leave their "bottoms" bare. To prevent these growth habits, train and tie their branches horizontally until the desired width is reached. Cover a wall or trellis by laterally spreading and securing the runners, but wrap an arch by training runners upright and spreading them when they reach the top. If multiple branching or denser growth is desired, pinch back regularly, just above the buds—this also promotes more blooms, as the flowers normally emerge at the tips of branches. Once the plant's framework is established, vines can be sheared like a hedge for a dense, compact appearance, or clipped to thin out for an open look. To encourage more growth at the base, bend some shoots down and train them to fill in the gaps.

To determine how specific vines perform, check with your nearby nursery or look around your neighborhood—as a rule, the milder your climate, the wider your choices.

Cultivation and Care

Bougainvillea and Wisteria vines are not self-supporting, grow very large, develop a lot of weight, and must have a sturdy structure on which to grow. Carolina Jessamine, Madagascar Jasmine, Coral, and Passion Vines climb by twining or with tendrils, and they grow best up wires or narrow slats. If you use supporting wires, make sure they are insulated; otherwise, they might burn the tender vines in full-sun areas.

For adequate air circulation between a trellis and a wall, allow three to four inches of space, which makes pruning and tying easier and promotes healthier growth. Use insulated wire or rubber tree ties to train and support heavier vines, and stretch plastic or twist-ties for lightweight vines, but check and loosen all ties a couple times a year to prevent any girdling of the stems.

Vines serve as natural sun and wind screens, create inviting entryways, highlight special architectural features, promote privacy, and camouflage unsightly walls or fences. Some make appealing combinations, like the brilliant yellow-flowered Guinea Gold Vine and the delicately perfumed white-blossomed Star Jasmine. Once established, they forgive neglect, rebound after overzealous pruning, and often survive short bouts of drought and frost. With proper cultivation and care, they become lush havens that beckon us during glorious springs, sweltering summers, tranquil autumns, or blustery winters.

A New Zealand Memory

On our spring visit to New Zealand, few sights were more impressive than the sprawling white Clematis vines weaving their forty-foot tresses in and out among the canopies of aged trees. As we strolled by these trees, masses of star-shaped cream-white flowers released their vanilla-like fragrance in the warmth of the late-morning sun. Memories like this remind us that vines not only weave their way into landscapes, they cling to your heartstrings.

Boston Ivy
Parthenocissus tricuspidata

One memorable autumn morning we strolled around the stately grounds of Harvard
and visited their Botanical Museum. Their otherwise drab brownstone buildings were
blanketed with Boston Ivy, whose serrated, eight-inch, three-lobed leaves were morphing
from shades of shiny green, exploding into fiery fall hues of crimson, scarlet, and
aubergine. Like members of a marching band, the leaves aligned in decorative tiers,
similar to a curtain of foliage. Now we always associate fall color with our memory of
Boston Ivy and how it enlivened a staid setting with its blazing autumnal curtains. In
addition to its fall beauty, we appreciate the late-summer clusters of plum-colored
grapelike fruits attached to vermilion stems. With shoots of branched tendrils attached
to adhesive pads or suckers, deciduous Boston Ivy vines are vigorous climbers and
are excellent for covering large, unsightly structures, for growing over pergolas and
fences, and for weaving in and out of small but sturdy trees, shrubs, and hedges.
They withstand frost and, once established, short periods of drought, but they need
protection from severe wind. Heat is not a problem as long as there is adequate
moisture. **Note:** *If you cannot find* Parthenocissus tricuspidata, *look for* Ampelopsis
tricuspidata, *another botanical name sometimes used for the same plant.*

Family Name / Origin Vitaceae / China, Japan

Mature Length 30 to 60 ft.

When and How to Plant Plant in spring from rooted cuttings in flats, or from 1-gallon containers. If planting against a large structure such as a free-standing or retaining wall, space 8 to 10 ft. on center. Build a watering basin 4 ft. long and 1 ft. out from the wall's base, and mulch the surface with 2 in. of organic material such as humus mulch or compost. See Planting Techniques, p. 398, for more information.

Climate & Culture

Preferred Zones
4–11

Sun Preferences

Sun and Soil Preferences For optimum color display, grow Boston Ivy in partial shade or on free-standing structures that are exposed to dappled sunlight. They prefer well- drained soil with good moisture retention and a slightly acidic pH of 6.5 to 7.0.

Moisture Requirements Immediately after planting, soak thoroughly and deeply. Water twice during the first week; thereafter, adjust watering frequency and amount to climatic and growth conditions.

Fertilizing Fertilize in early spring with a complete food, 10-10-10.

Pruning and Care Prune at regular intervals to control rampant or errant growth or to lace out dense vines. Because of the invasive habit of its root system, make sure the free-standing structures on which you plant Boston Ivy are solidly built. Do not use Boston Ivy to cover exterior walls of wood, stucco, or brick buildings. Prune regularly to prevent the tenacious vines from grow-ing into rooftops, under eaves, or around window frames. Some people are sensitive to the fruit pulp—wear gloves as a precaution when handling or cutting the fruits.

Pests and Diseases Aside from the usual spring pests of aphids, snails, and slugs, few insects or diseases affect this vine.

Companion Plantings and Design Ginkgo, Sweet Gum, and Crape Myrtle trees are ideal companion plants for Boston Ivy.

Our Personal Favorite

NAME	SPECIAL CHARACTERISTICS
P. quinquefolia	Also known as Virginia Creeper or Woodbine / compound leaves with five leaflets

Bougainvillea

Bougainvillea spectabilis

Two blocks from our home, a dazzling bright-red Bougainvillea cascading over a brick wall seems to be in bloom all year-round. The only time it has a "bad flower day" is in winter, when days are short and mornings are frosty. Named after the first French explorer to cross the Pacific (French navigator Louis Antoine de Bougainville), Bougainvillea's intense coloration is due not to its flowers but to its bracts (three) that surround one to three clusters of tiny, tubular white flowers. The bracts of this sprawling plant range in color from white to hot pink to golden orange to brilliant red to vivid lilac. Forest-green, soft-textured, heart-shaped, ovate leaves provide a lush background. Although the Bougainvillea does not have tendrils to support itself, curved thorns located at the base of its leaves enable it to climb. It is shown off to best advantage on trellises, against a wall or fence, on pergolas or arbors, and as brambles on slopes. As a shrub, it can also be used effectively in large containers or raised planters. After about five years, it tolerates drought and heat but dislikes windy, cold locations where temperatures dip below 45 degrees Fahrenheit. Reduce watering to stress the plant in summer and fall months: this simple procedure will maximize bloom production and intensify bract color.

Family Name / Origin Nyctaginaceae / Brazil

Bloom Period and Color Red, pink, white, or orange bracts appear in summer.

Mature Length 15 to 30 ft.

When and How to Plant Plant in spring from a 1- or 5-gallon container in an area free from frost and protected from wind. It does not transplant well, so select the location carefully and do not disturb the rootball. Construct a 1 × 4-ft. watering basin and cover the surface with 2 in. of organic material such as humus mulch or compost. See Planting Techniques, p. 398.

Climate & Culture

Preferred Zones 10–11

Sun Preference

Sun and Soil Preferences Plant Bougainvillea in full sun. Although it is not particular about soil, it thrives in an area with good drainage and a pH of 6.7 to 7.2.

Moisture Requirements Immediately after planting, fill the watering basin two or three times so that all the air pockets in the root zone are collapsed. Deep-soak twice during the first week, then adjust watering frequency and amount to the climatic and growth conditions.

Fertilizing Fertilize in early spring with a complete food, 10-10-10.

Pruning and Care Prune after flowering, because the next season's bloom is on new growth. If you want to reduce the size of a mature plant, prune out all the dead wood and reduce its canopy by one-third.

Pests and Diseases Few diseases or insects affect this plant, with the exception of snails dining on its foliage.

Companion Plantings and Design This plant grows well with many other specimens, including Pride of Madeira, Bird of Paradise, and Pink Powder Puff.

Our Personal Favorites

NAME	SPECIAL CHARACTERISTICS
B. spectabilis 'San Diego Red'	A vigorous grower, reaching lengths of 30 ft. / the variety with the most brilliant red coloration
B. s. 'Monca'	Showy masses of frothy, sea-foam white bracts cascading from the branch tips

Carolina Jessamine

Gelsemium sempervirens

Charleston is a charming city, known for warm Southern hospitality, historic sites, and lovely gardens. On a walking tour through what was once its walled city district (during the seventeenth and eighteenth centuries), we noticed many decorative wrought-iron fences festooned with twining branches laden with funnel-form, sweetly fragrant, yellow flowers against a backdrop of glossy rich-green foliage. This is Charleston's native Carolina Jessamine, also known as Evening Trumpet Flower, an evergreen that blooms heavily from spring to early autumn. Despite the beauty of these plants, they had a more sinister reputation in the past. Since all parts of the vines are toxic, they were used by the villainous and the hopeless to commit nefarious deeds of murder and suicide. Fortunately, today we appreciate their ornamental value and use them on trellises, pergolas, fences, and walls, and as brambling ground covers. Once established, they survive temperatures below freezing as long as they have long, hot summers to develop hardy canes. While they prefer a wind-protected location, they tolerate wind and withstand drought, because with time, their watering needs are not as demanding as some other more tropical vines. Their perfume not only attracts our attention, but also beckons winged friends such as birds, butterflies, and bees.

Family Name / Origin Loganiaceae / SE North America

Bloom Period and Color Yellow flowers bloom spring to fall.

Mature Length 20 ft.

How to Plant Plant in early spring from a 1- or 5-gallon container. Space the plants 12 to 30 ft. on center. Construct a watering basin 1 × 6 ft. and cover with 2 in. of organic material such as humus mulch or compost. Consult Planting Techniques, p. 398, for more information.

Sun and Soil Preferences Plant in full sun to maximize flower production, in well-drained soil with a pH of 6.7 to 7.0.

Climate & Culture

Preferred Zones

7–11

Sun Preference

Moisture Requirements Immediately after planting, soak deeply and thoroughly. Water twice during the first week; thereafter, adjust watering frequency and amount according to the dictates of climatic and growth conditions. As a general rule, once the vines are established you can water moderately in the spring and summer, and sparingly in the fall and winter.

Fertilizing Fertilize in late winter with a complete food, 6-10-4.

Pruning and Care When older wood develops, in about two or three growing seasons, the vines are mature enough to prune hard after their bloom cycle. Since all parts of these vines are poisonous, wash your pruning shears carefully after use, and wear protective gloves as a precaution.

Pests and Diseases There are few diseases or insects that affect Carolina Jessamine, with the exception of mealybugs, scale insects, and whitefly during the warmer months. Neem oil is a natural pesticide that easily remedies these problems.

Companion Plantings and Design Ideal companions for Carolina Jessamine are Crape Myrtle, European Olive, and Golden Mirror Plant.

Our Personal Favorite

NAME	SPECIAL CHARACTERISTICS
G. rankinii	Smaller in stature than G. s. / grows more compactly

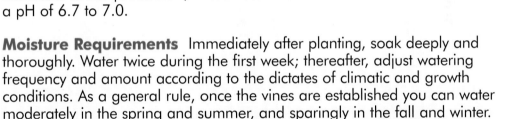

Clematis

Clematis armandii

The uses of Clematis are limited only by your imagination. They embrace fences, cover trellises, cascade over pergolas, walls, and arbors, bramble over the ground, train on supports in pots, and make lovely informal arrangements when combined with other cut flowers such as Roses, Carnations, and Lilies. Masses of star-shaped, creamy-white flowers release a vanilla-like fragrance. When new Clematis foliage emerges, it is a rich bronze color; it then transforms into a deep green with a leathery texture. These are thirsty plants that need their toes in cool, moist soil and their heads in the sun. Make sure you mitigate the damaging effects of drought, wind, and heat by providing adequate protection and moisture. This species has few disease or insect problems, but it can have a malady known as Clematis wilt, probably viral in origin. Bear in mind that the advantages of Clematis far outweigh this one small disadvantage. Although this particular species is an evergreen, it will lose a certain number of leaves as it matures, generally from the bottom upwards, giving the plant a forlornly bare appearance. To improve the look, prune the canes back four to six feet in fall or late winter so that new growth emerges from the base. You may lose a bloom cycle, but the plant will appear more vigorous.

Family Name / Origin Ranunculaceae / China

Bloom Period and Color White flowers bloom in late spring.

Mature Length 25 ft.

When and How to Plant Plant in spring from 1- or 5-gallon containers. Build watering basins 4 to 6 ft. in diameter and mulch the surface with 2 in. of organic material such as humus mulch or compost. If you plant against a south-facing wall, space the plant 18 in. away from the wall base in order to avoid damage from heat buildup and dry conditions. Consult Planting Techniques, p. 398, for more information.

Climate & Culture

Preferred Zones
8–11

Sun Preference

Sun and Soil Preferences Clematis prefer to have their root systems in a cool, moist location, but as it matures, its canopy should be in full sun for maximum bloom and fragrance. Clematis prefers a porous, well-drained soil, pH 6.5 to 7.0.

Moisture Requirements Water Clematis at least once a week in spring, adjusting frequency and amount for climatic and growth conditions.

Fertilizing Fertilize in spring with a complete food such as 6-10-4.

Pruning and Care Do not prune in late winter or you will remove the buds that appear in spring. Prune immediately after the bloom cycle.

Pests and Diseases Consult your local garden center for the varieties most resistant to Clematis wilt. These vines are also known to be deer-resistant.

Companion Plantings and Design We recommend Victorian Box, Grecian Laurel, and Climbing Roses as companions and for structural support.

Our Personal Favorites

NAME	SPECIAL CHARACTERISTICS
C. lanuginosa 'Candida'	A deciduous species / large pure-white petals with light-yellow stamens / blooms in late spring
C. l. 'Ramona'	Another deciduous species / large lavender-blue flowers with dark stamens / blooms from summer to fall

Creeping Fig

Ficus pumila

*Working with large concrete-block retaining walls in a landscape can be a challenge, to soften the massive, uninviting structure and to create a more temperate environment by deflecting some of the intense heat generated by concrete surfaces. F. pumila, or Creeping Fig, solves these dual problems very well in many landscape designs. It has two definite stages of foliar development: for the first two or three years, as a juvenile, the leaves are small, leathery, dark green, and shaped like small hearts; once established as an adult plant, larger, deep-green, oblong-shaped leaves emerge from the mat of the juvenile foliage. Its stems nimbly climb a support by means of aerial roots which appear at leaf junctures. Despite its tropical heritage, Creeping Fig is surprisingly hardy and thrives on warm, protected walls, as ground cover over a rock garden, as a houseplant, shaped as topiaries, or as trailing container plants. It will probably not, however, bear fruit in most areas of California. Similar to other species of Ficus, this vigorous vine dislikes wind, drought, and extended periods of cold temperatures, but enjoys heat if you provide enough humidity and moisture. **Note:** If you cannot find Ficus pumila, look for Ficus repens, another botanical name sometimes used for the same plant.*

Family Name / Origin Moraceae / Japan, China, SE Asia

Mature Length 20 to 30 ft.

When and How to Plant Plant in spring, after the last frost, from 1-gallon containers. If using as wall covers, space 8 to 10 ft. apart. Build a 1 × 4-ft. watering basin and mulch the surface with 2 in. of organic material such as humus mulch or compost. We do not recommend planting Creeping Fig close to wood, brick, or stucco surfaces because its invasive root system may cause damage. For additional information, see Planting Techniques, p. 398.

Climate & Culture

Preferred Zones 9–11

Sun Preferences

Sun and Soil Preferences Creeping Figs grow equally well in full sun or shade, but make sure the soil drains well and the pH is slightly acidic, 6.6 to 7.0.

Moisture Requirements Soak deeply after planting. Water twice the first week; thereafter, adjust watering frequency and amounts according to weather and growth conditions.

Fertilizing Fertilize in spring with a complete food, 10-10-10.

Pruning and Care If you see errant growth falling away from its support, prune it off. Some believe it helps to cut back a newly planted Creeping Fig in order to encourage more vigorous growth. Spray support walls with water if you want to encourage the finer and flatter immature growth. Pinch back terminal growth to increase lateral branch development.

Pests and Diseases Aside from slugs or snails, quickly controlled by a periodic application of a molluscicide, few disease or insect problems affect Creeping Fig.

Companion Plantings and Design Pink Indian Hawthorn, Bronze Loquat, and Silverberry are ideal planting companions.

Our Personal Favorites

NAME	SPECIAL CHARACTERISTICS
F. pumila 'Quercifolia'	Also known as Oak Leaf Creeping Fig / foliage shaped like lobed oak leaves
F. pumila 'Variegata'	Commonly known as Variegated Creeping Fig / leaves are marbled white to cream

Guinea Gold Vine

Hibbertia scandens

During a stay in Sydney, Australia, we took a ferry ride across the harbor to visit the Taronga Zoo. We were not really expecting too much, since past experience has shown us it is difficult to equal San Diego's Zoo. We were pleasantly surprised to discover that it was not only a world-class zoo, but it had an impressive indigenous plant collection. One plant that was particularly eye-catching was the Hibbertia scandens, *named for George Hibbert and commonly known as the Guinea Gold Vine. It has wide lance-shaped leaves that provide a verdant-green relief for brilliant-yellow five-petaled flowers. Its blossoms look like shiny gold pieces glittering in the warmth of the summer sun's rays amidst twisting vines that weave in and out of weathered rocks. Although it does not like constant wind, drought or freezing temperatures, it withstands heat if there is sufficient humidity and moisture. Since its floral fragrance is not too pleasing, plant the vine downwind—its value as a handsome ornamental and its long flowering season more than compensate for its slightly malodorous nature.*

Family Name / Origin Dilleniaceae / Australia

Bloom Period and Color Golden yellow flowers bloom in late spring.

Mature Length 10 to 15 ft.

When and How to Plant Plant in the spring from 1- or 5-gallon containers, spacing 4 to 6 ft. apart. After planting, build a watering basin 3 to 4 ft. in diameter and cover with 2 in. of organic material such as humus mulch or compost. See Planting Techniques, p. 398, for additional information.

Sun and Soil Preferences It does well in full sun or partial shade and prefers well-drained loam soils with a slightly acidic pH of 6.6 to 7.0.

Climate & Culture

Preferred Zones
10–11

Sun Preferences

Moisture Requirements Immediately after planting, soak deeply and thoroughly. During the first week, water twice; thereafter, adjust watering frequency and amounts to climatic and growth conditions. As a general rule, water generously during the spring and summer months, and taper off when daylight decreases and temperatures cool.

Fertilizing Fertilize with a water-soluble nutrient, 30-10-10, once a month during the growing season.

Pruning and Care Prune to thin out dense growth. Use plastic ties instead of wire ties to support new growth on trellises or wire supports. This will prevent any injury that results from girdling the canes.

Pests and Diseases Be on the lookout for snail invasions, but this plant is otherwise fairly free of disease and insect infestations.

Companion Plantings and Design We recommend displaying it on a wooden or wire trellis, in a hanging basket or as a ground cover. New Zealand Christmas Tree, Bottlebrush, and Pink Powder Puff are ideal planting companions. Combine with Freesia and Narcissus bulbs to expand the blooming season from early spring to late summer. If you have an old, rusty wheelbarrow, instead of throwing it away, drill a few holes at the bottom for drainage, then place a few broken shards of pottery over the holes, fill the barrow with potting soil, and plant a Guinea Gold Vine. It will form a mound of growth and spill over the sides, rewarding you with an abundance of golden yellow blooms during the warm months.

Lavender Trumpet Vine

Clytostoma callistegioides

When we go for long walks in our neighborhood during the spring and summer months, we see several residences where this exquisite vine has been used to cover arbors and walls creating areas of quiet retreat. Clytostoma is of Greek origin, from klytos, meaning "glorious," and stoma, meaning "mouth," alluding to their striking trumpet-shaped lavender flowers with purple streaks and white funnels. When the leaves first emerge they are coppery-bronze; as they mature, they are transformed into shiny-green, smooth-textured, boat-shaped foliage with smooth edges, prominent midribs, and pointed tips. Paired hooks develop at the ends of curlycue tendrils, enabling these vines to attach easily to any nearby structural support. Lavender Trumpet Vines effectively cover pergolas and arbors for summer shade and chain-link fences for floral camouflage. They also make spectacular ground covers, especially when cascading over slopes. Pollinating birds, bees, and butterflies are attracted to their brilliant and fragrant flowers. When there are extended periods of drought, blustery winds, and freezing temperatures, your Lavender Trumpet Vine might stress and defoliate, but it should recover with improved conditions and proper care. If you provide adequate moisture, this plant tolerates quite a lot of heat. **Note:** If you cannot find Clytostoma callistegioides, look for Bignonia violacea, *another botanical name sometimes used for the same plant.*

Family Name / Origin Bignoniaceae / Brazil

Bloom Period and Color Lavender flowers bloom in summer.

Mature Length 20 to 40 ft.

When and How to Plant Plant in spring from 1- or 5-gallon containers, spacing 15 to 20 ft. on center. Immediately after planting, construct a 1 × 4-ft. watering basin and mulch the surface with 2 in. of organic material such as humus mulch or compost. Refer to Planting Techniques, p. 398, for more information.

Sun and Soil Preferences Locate in full sun to maximize bloom and fragrance production. The plant needs soil that has good drainage and loam texture with a pH of 6.6 to 7.0.

Moisture Requirements After planting, water thoroughly and deeply twice during the first week; thereafter, modify watering frequency and amount according to climatic and growth conditions.

Fertilizing Fertilize in late winter or early spring with a complete food, 6-10-4.

Pruning and Care Lavender Trumpet Vines are excellent additions to scented gardens, especially when trained to grow on walls. Remove all the foliage to expose the vertical canes, allowing the lush growth and flowers to occur as ornamental capstones atop your walls.

Pests and Diseases Few diseases affect these vines, but in the spring and summer months they are susceptible to aphids, scale, and mites. The good news is that these pests are easily controlled with an appropriate pesticide such as Neem oil. If slugs or snails are damaging your plants, control with a molluscicide.

Companion Plantings and Design Bronze Loquat, Pink Powder Puff, and Bird of Paradise combine well with this vigorous and fast-growing vine. If you want to plant the Lavender Trumpet Vine in the proximity of these other tropical plants, do not select a planting location that will encourage the vine's canes to develop a canopy that will shade its companions.

Climate & Culture

Preferred Zones
10–11

Sun Preference

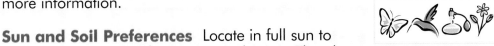

Madagascar Jasmine

Stephanotis floribunda

Bruce's parents live on the brow of a hill overlooking Mission Bay and have an atrium garden filled with many vining plants, including one of our favorites: the evergreen S. floribunda, otherwise known as Madagascar Jasmine. Now over twenty-five years old, its heavy, woody stems twine rope-like around a trellis against a wall that is shaded from the midday heat by the eaves. The dark silky sheen of the elliptic leaves enhances the elegance of the blooms. For years this vine supplied many flowers for our florists, who used them in bridal bouquets, corsages, garlands, and wreaths. Madagascar Jasmine has triple clusters of fragrant, ivory, tubular-shaped blossoms on trailing stems of deep-green leaves, and few flowers can add more joy and beauty to one of the happiest days of a family's life. In addition to being used as cut flowers, they are equally spectacular when planted on trellises or pergolas in a patio or entry-way, although they must be tied for support since their stems become quite heavy. Once established, they form seed pods that resemble bladders, but their development takes two to three years. Madagascar Jasmine appreciates cool soils and warm but shaded areas. This vine does not care for blustery winds, extended drought, or freezing temperatures.

Family Name / Origin Asclepiadaceae / Madagascar

Bloom Period and Color White flowers bloom in summer.

Mature Length 10 to 20 ft.

When and How to Plant Plant in the spring, after the last frost, from 1- or 5-gallon containers. Be very careful not to disturb the rootball, because it suffers from transplant shock easily. If growing on a trellis or fence, space the plants 10 ft. apart. Construct a watering basin 3 to 4 ft. in diameter and mulch the surface with 2 in. of organic material such as humus mulch or compost. For more information, see Planting Techniques, p. 398.

Climate & Culture

Preferred Zones 10–11

Sun Preferences

Sun and Soil Preferences Locate your vine in a partly shady or shady, frost-free location. It needs good drainage with rich, organic, loam soil and an acidic pH of 6.5-7.0.

Moisture Requirements Immediately after planting, soak deeply and thoroughly. Water three times during the first week; thereafter, adjust watering frequency and the amount according to weather and growth conditions. For example, water generously when in growth, but reduce watering in the winter months.

Fertilizing Fertilize in spring with an acid food.

Pruning and Care Prune in late winter or early spring before the growth cycle, to thin out dense vines. Tie the vines for support since it is not their nature to twist around anything that is more than 2 in. in diameter. If you want to share your plant with a neighbor, propagate by layering, cuttings, or air layering.

Pests and Diseases Few diseases or insects affect this vine, with the exception of soft scale and mealybugs. Benign remedies include washing off the leaves with water or applying Neem oil.

Companion Plantings and Design Hibiscus, Hydrangeas, and Mystery Gardenias make ideal companion plants.

Passion Vine

Passiflora × pfordtii

Our first memory of the beautiful and mysterious Passion Vine occurred many years ago while we were window-shopping in Little Tokyo right in the middle of downtown Los Angeles. In such a polluted urban environment of total neglect, you would think this vine would be struggling to survive, but it was flourishing, with lush, three-inch-long, light-green foliage and elegant, four-inch-wide, white flowers lightly tinted with pink blush. Its common name was given to it by Spanish missionaries who saw many of this vine's features as symbols of the crucifixion and passions of Christ. The purplish-blue corolla stood for the crown of thorns, the five red-tipped anthers for the five wounds, and the ten petal-like parts for the ten apostles. Even if the missionaries had never created such a rich tale of biblical proportions, the "passion" for this fragrant flower would still endure because of its exotic appearance and complex symmetry. In temperate climates the vine is evergreen, but in cooler zones it will defoliate only to vegetate again as the weather warms and the days lengthen. Our winged visitors, butterflies, bees, and hummingbirds, enjoy its sweet nectar all summer long. It does not like cold or wind, but when it is mature it blooms profusely during short periods of drought or moisture stress and loves heat, providing there is enough humidity.

Family Name / Origin Passifloraceae / Tropical South America hybrid (*P. alato* × *P. caerulea*)

Bloom Period and Color White or blue flowers bloom all summer long, but they close on overcast days and at night.

Mature Length 6 to 10 ft.

When and How to Plant Plant in spring from a 1- or 5-gallon container. Space 10 to 15 ft. apart if using on a fence or wall. Build a 1 × 4-ft. watering basin and cover with 2 in. of organic material such as humus mulch or compost. See Planting Techniques, p. 398.

Climate & Culture

Preferred Zones
10–11

Sun Preference

Sun and Soil Preferences It needs a full-sun location in well-drained, slightly acidic soil pH of 6.6 to 7.0.

Moisture Requirements Soak deeply after planting. Water three times the first week; thereafter, adjust frequency and amount to climatic and growth conditions.

Fertilizing Fertilize in spring with a complete food, 6-10-4.

Pruning and Care After the second year, prune annually in late winter or early spring to lace out and clear away dead, inner, woody vines. Root-pruning is a simple procedure to increase flower production. Sever the root system by pushing a pointed shovel 8 to 10 in. into the ground and 2 to 3 ft. from the base of the plant. Another way to increase Passion Flower blooms is to confine its roots by building an underground brick barrier 1 to 2 ft. deep and 2 ft. in diameter. This is probably why that neglected Passion Vine triumphed over such adverse conditions in downtown Los Angeles. It actually liked to be in a confined space with poor soil conditions.

Pests and Diseases Few diseases and insects affect this vine, but look for snails and aphids in spring and summer. If caterpillars are hungry enough, they will dine on Passion Flower's tender leaves. Control these chewing pests with *Bacillus thuringiensis*, or *B.t.*, a natural pesticide.

Companion Plantings and Design Passion Vine's climbing tendrils are easily supported by wires, plastic netting, or posts, and its beauty is best displayed on trellises, walls, or sunny foyers. Southern Magnolia, Hibiscus, and Bird of Paradise are ideal companions for a tropical garden.

Rosa de Montana

Antigonon leptopus

Antigonon is of Greek derivation, with anti, *meaning "against," and* gonia, *meaning "an angle." The words refer to the plant's sinuous vining characteristic, full of bends and curves. It is a fast-growing showy vine with dense, light-green, heart-shaped leaves. In fact, it is so dense it was used in the tropics during World War II as camouflage for military installations. While visiting the arroyos of Loreto, along the Sea of Cortez, we saw this vine, commonly called Rosa de Montana (Spanish for "mountain rose"), displayed in all its summer glory. We learned that long ago its seeds were gathered in October and roasted in a basket filled with hot coals until they opened, then ground and eaten. This sounds like a laborious process, so for the home gardener, we recommend using this vine as an ornamental. Also known as Coral Vine, this plant's most striking feature is its delicate coral-pink sprays of flowers that bloom in the early summer through autumn months. Rosa de Montana is extremely tolerant to drought, wind, and heat, but in lower temperatures, may be damaged or die back. As long as the root system is established, however, it will re-grow in the spring.*

Family Name / Origin Polygonaceae / Mexico and Central America

Bloom Period and Color Pink flowers bloom in summer and fall.

Mature Length 15 to 25 ft.

When and How to Plant Plant in spring or fall from a 1-gallon container. If planted as an individual espalier, space 10 to 15 ft. on center. Create a 1 × 4-ft. watering basin and mulch the surface with 2 in. of organic material such as humus mulch or compost. Once you have decided on a location for your plant, try not to move it, because it dislikes any root disturbance. For additional information, see Planting Techniques, p. 398.

Climate & Culture

Preferred Zones
10–11

Sun Preference

Sun and Soil Preferences It prefers full sun and free-draining soil with a pH of 6.7 to 7.0.

Moisture Requirements Begin by soaking the root zone once a week. Then irrigate deeply and infrequently once the vine is established, modifying the schedule according to weather and growth factors. Although it is a drought-tolerant and deciduous plant, be sure to water during the spring and summer months or its leaves will have a tendency to drop during dry periods.

Fertilizing Fertilize in late winter or early spring with a complete food, 6-10-4.

Pruning and Care Prune out any dead canes or damaged growth as needed. To control dense growth after the vine matures, prune back heavily, about 40 to 60 percent of its volume, in late winter or early spring before the flush of new growth.

Pests and Diseases Other than an occasional infestation of aphids on new growth in the spring, few diseases or insects affect Rosa de Montana.

Companion Plantings and Design We recommend planting this vine in a half-barrel as an 8-ft. trellis or espalier on a fence, pergolas, or decorative arches. When grown in this manner, it reminds us of a finer-textured version of the Bougainvillea. California Lilac, Butterfly Bush, and Angel's Trumpet are ideal planting companions.

Scarlet Trumpet Vine

Distictis buccinatoria

As a youngster, I (Bruce) enjoyed playing with my brothers in and around our family greenhouse. It was like our own secret fortress with thick-stalked vines covered with lush, green foliage that blanketed the wooden and glass structure. Throughout the warm months of spring and summer, the most spectacular feature of these dense vines was the explosions of four-inch-long, blood-red to orange-red, trumpet-shaped flowers with bright-yellow throats. Distictis *comes from the Greek words* dis, *meaning "twice,"* and stiktos, *meaning "spotted," which refers to the flattened seeds that look like two rows of spots in the capsules formed after the flowers are spent. These evergreen vines have lance-shaped, dull-green, three-inch-long compound leaves. Grasping suction cup–like appendages located at the ends of wispy three-forked tendrils enable these vines to be self-clinging as long as the support structure has a rough surface. Since they come from the tropical, moist regions of Mexico,* D. buccinatoria *love heat if there is sufficient humidity and moisture and defoliate during periods of drought, strong winds, or cold temperatures. They can, however, recover if these are temporary conditions.* **Note:** *If you cannot find* Distictis buccinatoria, *look for* Phaedranthus buccinatoria *or* Bignonia cherere, *other botanical names sometimes used for the same plant.*

Family Name / Origin Bignoniaceae / Mexico

Bloom Period and Color Red to orange-red flowers bloom in summer.

Mature Length 20 to 40 ft.

When and How to Plant Spring is the best time to plant, from 1- or 5-gallon containers, spacing 20 ft. apart. Build a watering basin that is 6 ft. in diameter and mulch the surface with 2 in. of organic material such as humus mulch or compost. Consult Planting Techniques, p. 398, for more information.

Sun and Soil Preferences If you want your vine to be covered with flowers, plant in full sun in porous, loam soil that has a pH of 6.6 to 7.0.

Climate & Culture

Preferred Zones
9–11

Sun Preference

Moisture Requirements Immediately after planting, soak deeply and thoroughly, then water twice during the first week; thereafter, adjust watering frequency and amount according to climatic and growth conditions.

Fertilizing Fertilize in spring with a complete food such as 6-10-4.

Pruning and Care As the vines mature their structures become woodier, and it may be necessary to lace out the canopies so sunlight can stimulate new growth. Otherwise, prune just to remove dead wood. Prune in the late winter or early spring, prior to the flush of new growth, because they flower from current-season growth.

Pests and Diseases Chewing insects such as caterpillars can be a problem, especially during the warmer months of the year, but they are easily controlled with applications of *Bacillus thuringiensis*, or *B.t.*, a natural larvaecide. Generally speaking, there are few diseases or insects that affect these vines.

Companion Plantings and Design For brilliant summer-long color on gazebos, arbors, walls, fences, pergolas, and in large planters with trellises, Scarlet Trumpet Vines are the *oohs* and *aaahs* of garden ornamentals. Although their floral fragrance is mild, their nectar attracts all the local bees and hummingbirds. Using these beautiful vines on free-standing supports such as trellises and arbors is recommended, but avoid planting them to cover house walls because their tenacious clinging tendrils and attaching disc-like organs can pose problems in the future. Butterfly Bush, Pride of Madeira, and Jacaranda make ideal planting companions.

Star Jasmine
Trachelospermum jasminoides

At our home we have an unsightly west-facing wall with a narrow planting strip in front of it. For years the wall remained barren of plants until we constructed a five-foot-high by fifteen-foot-long redwood trellis and put in four one-gallon containers of Star Jasmine, also known as Confederate Jasmine. Normally it is not necessary to plant so many, but we wanted the trellis to be completely covered by Jasmine in a short period of time. Two years later, from spring to early summer, we are rewarded with intensely fragrant, star-shaped, pure-white flowers that drape over vines blanketed with shiny, dark-green, oval-shaped foliage. In addition, the local honeybees, Anna hummingbirds, and monarch butterflies appreciate our Star Jasmine's spring bounty. As a landscape architect, I (Bruce) use the Star Jasmine quite often as an evergreen ground cover, slope plant, and shrub; on trellises, gazebos, pergolas, and arbors; and as hanging baskets and raised planters. Star Jasmine plants do not tolerate cold, drought, or hot, dry winds, but thrive in heat if there is sufficient humidity and water. **Note:** *If you cannot find* Trachelospermum jasminoides, *look for* Rhynchospermum jasminoides, *another botanical name sometimes used for the same plant.*

Family Name / Origin Apocynaceae / China

Bloom Period and Color White flowers bloom in summer.

Mature Length 10 to 15 ft.

When and How to Plant Plant in spring after the last frost from 1- or 5-gallon containers, spacing 4 ft. on center. Build a watering basin 3 ft. in diameter and cover with 2 in. of organic material such as humus mulch or compost. See Planting Techniques, p. 398.

Climate & Culture

Preferred Zones 9–11

Sun Preferences

Sun and Soil Preferences Star Jasmine does best in full sun but can tolerate partial shade. For optimum growing conditions, the soil should be slightly acidic, pH 6.6, but they survive in most soils, even slightly alkaline, provided the soil is rich, deep, well drained, and warmed by the sun.

Moisture Requirements Immediately after planting, soak thoroughly and deeply. Water twice the first week; thereafter, adjust frequency and amount according to weather and growth conditions.

Fertilizing Fertilize in late winter or early spring with a complete food, 10-10-10.

Pruning and Care Prune to remove dead or errant growth and to direct growth. Like many other plants that are related to the Apocynaceae family, it exudes a milky sap when the stems are cut, and can irritate your skin. Wear a long-sleeved shirt and gloves, and wash off your pruning shears.

Pests and Diseases Few diseases affect Star Jasmine, but brown soft scale and giant whitefly occasionally colonize their tender leaves in the spring and summer months. Neem oil is an excellent control for these pests. Sometimes alligator lizards seek shelter among the vines and they provide a natural solution by dining on whitefly.

Companion Plantings and Design Pink Indian Hawthorn, Golden Mirror Plant, and Lavender Starflower are ideal as companion plants.

Our Personal Favorite

NAME	SPECIAL CHARACTERISTICS
T. asiaticum	Commonly known as Yellow Star Jasmine / same growth characteristics as those of Star Jasmine / creamy-yellow flowers bloom in summer

Wisteria

Wisteria sinensis

Picture an exquisite fairy-tale castle built from quarried stones of granite and surrounded by a moat, with elegant swans gliding gracefully in its waters. Gnarled trunks laden with pendulous bluish-purple to lavender-mauve clusters of aromatic Wisteria languidly top garden walls and outline entryways. This is Chenonceau, the most beautiful castle in the Loire Valley of France, and W. sinensis can be thought of as a symbol of the enchanted life and romantic ease of this castle. Their early, spring-blooming, bunches of sweet pea–shaped flowers release a perfume like a mixture of lilacs and honey. Butterflies, bees, and hummingbirds enjoy their nectar. Once their flowers are spent, a curtain of feathery, compound, light-green, elliptic-shaped foliage blankets the twisted, bare canes. In China, Wisteria blossoms are cured with sugar, combined with flour, and made into teng lo cake, a Beijing delicacy. We have never eaten this pastry, but we must warn you that the seeds and pods of the plant are toxic. They contain a glycoside known as wisterin which causes gastroenteritis. Wisteria dislike hot, dry winds and survive short periods of drought. They thrive in heat provided there is sufficient humidity and soil moisture, and tolerate temperatures as low as 0 degrees Fahrenheit. A curious fact about W. sinensis is that it twists clockwise as it grows upwards, unlike W. floribunda, whose vines twine counterclockwise.

Family Name / Origin Leguminosae / China

Bloom Period and Color White or lavender flowers bloom in spring.

Mature Length 60 to 100 ft.

When and How to Plant Plant in late winter or early spring from bare-root stock or 5- to 15-gallon containers, spacing them 15 to 20 ft. apart. Construct a watering basin 6 ft. in diameter and cover with 2 in. of organic material such as humus mulch or compost. See Planting Techniques, p. 398, for more information.

Sun and Soil Preferences Plant in full sun. They will also survive in partial shade. They prefer well-drained, slightly acidic soils with a pH of 6.6 to 7.0.

Climate & Culture

Preferred Zones
7–11

Sun Preferences

Moisture Requirements Immediately after planting, soak twice, deeply and thoroughly. Water twice during the first week; thereafter, adjust watering frequency and amount according to weather and growth conditions.

Fertilizing Fertilize in late winter or early spring with a complete food, 6-10-4.

Pruning and Care In fall, after the vines are dormant, prune back the new, young, flexible growth, leaving two to four buds for next spring's blooms.

Pests and Diseases Few fungi and virus problems attack Wisteria, and any damage is usually cosmetic. During spring, aphids and brown soft scale may settle on tender foliage and young canes, but you can easily control them with Neem oil or insecticidal soap. Birds enjoy eating the flower buds, and they may be the cause of poor bloom production, so be on the lookout for ravenous birds.

Companion Plantings and Design As one of the most spectacular flowering vines, Wisteria can be used to cover pergolas, gazebos, shaded walkways, patios, and even pruned and miniaturized as prized bonsai container plants. Butterfly Bush, Saucer Magnolia, and European Olive make ideal planting companions.

Our Personal Favorite

NAME	SPECIAL CHARACTERISTICS
W. floribunda	Commonly known as Japanese Wisteria / pendulous flower clusters are 2 to 3 ft. in length / blooms in mid-spring

Planting Techniques for California

From talking with callers to *The West Coast Garden Line*™ and webcast programs over the years, it has become clear to us that gardening is a common denominator for folks from all walks of life and from all generations. From children to grand-parents, from physicists to students, when people get together to chat, it's about how to grow the sweetest tomatoes, or successfully graft five different apple varieties onto the same rootstock, or when to fertilize their orchids. There are as many opinions about gardening and techniques as there are people who garden, but their ideas and techniques are toward the same end: successful gardening.

Fortunately, there is never a one-and-only way to achieve this goal. A landscape is an organic, dynamic creation because plants are in a constant state of flux, encouraging us to continually experiment and learn from trial, error, and experience. Challenges and changes are the main reasons we are hooked on gardening . . . also, it is great therapy for the mind and spirit to escape the stuffy confines of indoors for the fresh air and expansiveness of the outdoors. To save you time, money, and effort, here are few Planting Techniques to keep in mind.

Planning

The Site Plan

Decide what you want from your landscape areas and the perfect master plan will unfold. Do you want it to be children- or pet-friendly? Is your preference for formal, highly stylized designs, informal cottage gardens, native or exotic plant materials, tropical or xeriphytic landscapes? A simple planning procedure will organize the spaces in your yard and keep you from over- or underplanting.

Before you lift a pencil, document the beginning, by photographing the entire site from several directions and elevations. Photographs are a visual record of capital improvements and allow you to draw up a plan without physically running back and forth to your gardening site.

Most landscape master plans are drawn at a scale of 1 inch = 8 feet (⅛ scale). If you are designing a small area such as a patio or atrium, a scale of 1 inch = 4 feet (¼ scale) would provide drawing space for more detail. Drafting paper with a fade-out, scaled, grid pattern is available from your local blueprint company. Using a semi-transparent fadeout drafting paper will permit printable copies. Note or list on the site plan all existing conditions that will affect the landscape design, including:

- Street locations, curbs, sidewalks, property lines, easements, setbacks
- Power lines/meters, water lines/meters, gas lines/meters
- Irrigation (clocks, lines, manifolds), lighting (timers, fixtures, transformers)
- Cable TV lines, telephone lines
- Wells, drain lines, sumps, surface drainage flow lines, gutter down spouts

- Septic systems and leach lines, sewer lines, sewer cleanouts
- Slopes, walls, walks, steps, ramps, fences, gates
- House floor plan (doors, windows), stoops, foyers, patios, eave lines
- Trees, shrubs, ground covers, areas where plants don't grow, vegetable growing areas
- Compass directions, view corridors, directions of the prevailing wind, limits of summer and winter shadow patterns

Other considerations are ponds, pools, hot tubs, filter equipment, play yards, storage areas, toolsheds, firewood storage, dog runs, birdfeeding stations, trash container storage, mailboxes, pergolas, gazebos, arbors, and arches.

Drawing equipment includes:

- drawing board, 20×30 in. or 30×40 in.
- T square, 30 or 40 in.
- scale/ruler, $\frac{1}{8}$ in. or $\frac{1}{10}$ in.
- 2H drawing pencils
- eraser, pink pearl
- masking tape, $\frac{3}{4}$ in.
- sheets of scaled fadeout drafting paper

When it becomes time to specify plants on the site plan, scale them to their mature rather than to their current sizes. It is much easier to erase and redraw a symbol on a sheet of graph paper than it is to dig up and replant or constantly thin and prune a would-be giant.

There is one *caveat* to landscape planning: Do not become so mired in detail that you "can't see the forest for the trees." Allow for some fluidity and seasonal changes in the big picture. Volunteer plants may pop up in serendipitous places. Or seasonal bulbs and annuals might provide just the perfect splashes of interest when the rest of the garden is quiet. Or you may discover a tree or shrub that captures your fancy and changes the entire look of your landscape. Oftentimes, change is good.

Plant Lists

Compile a list of your favorite trees, shrubs, ground covers, bulbs, annuals, fruits, and vegetables. The list should include space for the following:

- Quantities and sizes
- Common name, genus, species, variety
- Date acquired, nursery, salesperson's name, guarantee term
- Comments
- Notes about growing requirements
- Symbols drawn to scale on the site plan to represent the average mature sizes of the plants
- Notes that tell if it is all right to include plants with poisonous parts or plants that attract bees

The USDA Cold-Hardiness Zone Map

Identify the United States Department of Agriculture (USDA) cold zone for your area. The zone will approximate the minimum temperature ranges across your region. This is important information that will guide you when it is time to select plants. Most plant lists, including those in this book, are keyed to the USDA cold zone map.

The USDA cold-hardiness zone map can be found on p. 17 of this book. These zones approximate the preferred, coldest temperatures plant species will tolerate. If you are not sure what cold zone your yard is in, walk or drive around your community and list the plants that have matured by surviving several cold winters. Consult your plant list, cross-reference the plant's cold zone tolerance, and presto, you will find the applicable cold zone.

Keep in mind that every yard has many microclimates that will enhance or diminish a plant's ability to grow. For example, structures such as fences or walls provide protected areas of warmth for frost-sensitive plants; large trees with wide canopies create shaded, sun-protected environments for sun-sensitive plants; pockets of colder temperatures settle near the bottoms of slopes; and warmer temperatures are more common towards the middle and tops of slopes. About once a week during the coldest and warmest seasons of the year, record the temperature variations in your yard with a high-low thermometer, noting the dates and temperatures in your garden journal.

Soil Texture

The United States Department of Agriculture has designated twelve soil textures. Identify the soil texture in your landscape areas. Are the soils sandy, silty, or clayey? Sandy soils are porous, free-draining, and often nutrient-deficient. They permit rapid root development if amended to retain moisture and nutrients. Silty soils permit even percolation but often lack moisture-holding capacity unless amended. Clayey soils are the least desirable: they are dense, expansive, and poorly draining. Loam is the ideal soil texture, about 40 percent sand, 40 percent silt, and 20 percent clay—if the soil is moist, this composition permits you to push a shovel into it and withdraw it with relative ease. See Soil Texture Classifications on the following page.

The root zone should consist of 25 percent air, which is called soil atmosphere; 25 percent water, which is called soil solution; and 50 percent sand, silt, clay, and organic material, which is called soil structure. The root zone is not only home for absorbing, lateral, sinker, and taproots, it's also home to millions of aerobic micro-organisms, most of which are beneficial for the plant. (Anaerobic micro-organisms, such as water molds, hinder plant growth.)

In simple terms, if the soil is moist and friable enough so you can push a pointed shovel into it and not have a glob of mud stick to it as you pull it out, the soil texture should be porous enough to allow good root development. If there is a glob of mud, amend the soil with compost or humus mulch so that the organic content approaches 20 to 30 percent.

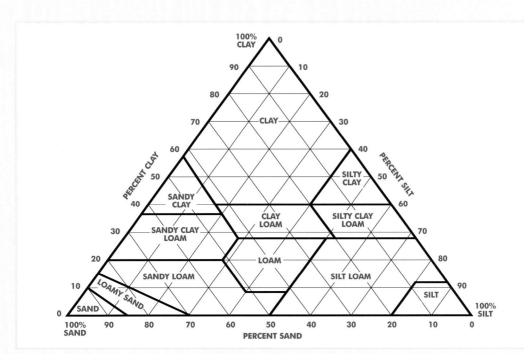

Soil Texture Classifications

Amending the soil correctly is very important. Contact the West Coast Garden Line™ (1-800-660-GROW) for more assistance.

Soil Amendment Volume and Depth Chart for Larger Areas Such as Lawns and Ground Covers

Percent of Amendment	Depth of Amended Soil in Inches (Soil and Amendments						
	3 in.	4 in.	5 in.	6 in.	7 in.	8 in.	9 in.
10	0.93	1.23	1.54	1.85	2.16	2.47	2.78
20	1.85	2.47	3.09	3.71	4.32	4.94	5.55
30	2.78	3.70	4.64	5.56	6.48	7.41	8.33
40	3.70	4.94	6.18	7.41	8.64	9.88	11.13
50	4.63	6.17	7.72	9.26	10.80	12.34	13.88

The Percolation Test

Determine the percolation rate of your soil by excavating a hole 30 inches wide by 30 inches deep. Fill the hole with water, let it drain completely, then fill it again. The second filling should drain at a rate of 1 inch per hour—in approximately a day-and-a-half, the water should be gone. If it is indeed gone after this time, drainage should not be a problem. If the hole is still half full, however, you must do one or more of the following:

1. Excavate planting pits so they are large enough to accommodate the slow percolation rate.

2. Remove excess water from the bottom of the planting pits and direct it to a lower elevation by using French drains or perforated ABS or PVC drainpipes.
3. Build a raised planting area above the planting pit.
4. Excavate to a depth where the porosity of the soil will permit free draining.
5. Terrace the land if there is a difference in elevation.

No matter which method you choose, you must adjust the frequency and volume of irrigation water to accommodate the slower percolation rate through the root zone.

The Soil Reaction (pH) Test

Before preparing the soil for planting, check the soil pH, otherwise known as soil reaction. Since California soils tend to become more alkaline over time, it is necessary to monitor the soil reaction twice a year, once in mid-spring and once in early fall. These seasonal readings are an accurate soil pH range for the entire year. Indicate on the site plan of your yard the locations where you obtained these samples, and note the date and readings in your garden journal.

Your garden soil can be acidic, neutral, or alkaline. The pH scale (0 to 14) is actually a measure of the relative concentration of hydrogen ions and hydroxyl ions in soil solution. A reading of 7 is neutral, readings below 7 indicate acid conditions, and readings above 7 indicate alkaline conditions. The scale has another peculiarity: it is logarithmic, which means each increment is ten times greater or lower than the increment before or after it. For example, a pH of 7 is 10 times greater than a pH of 6, and 100 times greater than a pH of 5.

When soils are very acidic, elements such as aluminum and manganese become overly available and may become toxic to plants. Soils that are too alkaline may limit the availability of elements such as iron, zinc, and nitrogen, leading to nutrient deficiencies.

Determining whether your garden soil is acidic, neutral, or alkaline will tell you whether or not nutrients are available to your plants. Take the test samples with a coring tool, at a depth of 10 to 12 inches, from several locations, especially where the topography and growing conditions vary. Use a pH test kit or ask your local garden center if they will test it for you. Analog and digital direct reading pH meters are also available, but they are more expensive. An overwhelming majority of plant species prefer a slightly acidic to neutral (6.5 to 7.0) soil. To lower the soil's pH (increase acidity), apply soil sulfur according to the following table.

	Pounds of Sulfur per 1000 Sq. Ft. (For Different Soil Textures)		
Change in pH Desired	**Sandy**	**Loamy**	**Clayey**
8.5 to 6.5	45.9	57.4	68.8
8.0 to 6.5	27.5	34.4	45.9
7.5 to 6.5	11.5	18.4	23.0
7.0 to 6.5	2.3	3.4	6.9

Approximate Amounts of Soil Sulfur Needed to Increase the Acidity of a 6-Inch-Deep Layer of Soil[*]

*Adapted from USDA Agricultural Handbook No. 18

To raise the soil's pH, apply dolomite lime according to the following table.

Approximate Amounts of Finely Ground Limestone Needed to Raise the pH of a 7-Inch Layer of Soil*

| | Lime Requirements lbs. / 1,000 Sq. Ft. | |
Soil Texture	From pH 4.5 to 5.5	From pH 5.5 to 6.5
Sand and loamy sand	23	28
Sandy loam	37	60
Loam	55	78
Silt laom	69	92
Clay loam	87	106
Muck	174	197

*Adapted from USDA Agricultural Handbook No. 18

There are so many variables that affect the proper amendment of soil—if you have questions on this important topic, contact the *West Coast Garden Line*™ for answers to your questions.

Planting

The Planting Pit

For decades it has been standard operating procedure to excavate circular planting pits with curved pointed shovels. Well, don't discard the curved pointed shovels (they still work), but think about changing the shape of your planting pits from circular to rectilinear (ninety-degree corners). Visualize a standard one- or five-gallon-container plant in a round pot. If you place it in a cylindrical planting pit, the roots grow through the backfill, hit the curved wall, and are deflected until they wind round and round, binding themselves in a confining space until rootbound. In a rectilinear pit, the same plant's root system would grow through the backfill to the corners, encouraging the roots to web more quickly into the native soil. (If a plant is already rootbound in its original container, it will probably never develop a proper support-ive root system, and it should not be purchased.)

Excavate a rectilinear planting pit one to one-and-a-half times the plant's original container depth and four to six times the plant's original container width. This depth-to-width proportion encourages important lateral root development. Pile the excavated earth close by so it can be amended for backfill if needed. Roughen the vertical surfaces of the planting pit with a cultivator. The rectilinear form and the roughened surface will encourage the new roots to start webbing into the native soil.

Do not place a layer of gravel or coarser rocks at the bottom of the planting pit because there is no need for it. If there is poor drainage, rocks or gravel will not solve or alleviate the problem.

The Backfill

The soil excavated from the planting pit, the backfill, should be amended to have a texture halfway between that of the native soil and that of the plant's rootball. Backfill is the material that the plant's new roots will first encounter. It is this transition zone through which your plant's root system will grow out and down, following moisture and air. When the rootball soil, the backfill, and the native soil are similar in texture, it is unnecessary to amend the backfill.

Before lowering the rootball, compress the soil in the bottom of the planting pit. Tamping the soil firm will minimize any settling of the rootball.

The rootball should be planted so that its upper surface is 1 inch higher than the finished elevation of the surrounding backfill. This 1-inch height accommodates future settling of the rootball.

Granular or tablet forms of preplanting fertilizer are useful in nutrient-poor soils. Apply so that there is no direct contact with the rootball's exposed roots—if there is a concentration of fertilizer next to the roots, they will burn.

The Watering Basin

Construct a watering basin by building a berm 4 to 6 inches high and four to six times the plant's original container diameter. It generally takes 2 inches of surface water for water to gravitate 12 inches in dense, clayey soils, so if you fill a watering basin that has a 4-inch berm, you can expect the irrigation water to soak down to 2 feet. In porous, sandy soils, it only takes 1 inch of surface water for water to gravitate the same 12 inches. Water a newly transplanted plant thoroughly enough to collapse any air pockets in the backfill.

Gallons of Water (Volume) for Different Basin Diameters

Diameter	Depth	
	4 inches	6 inches
3 ft.	17.44	26.42
4 ft.	31.00	46.97
6 ft.	69.75	105.69
8 ft.	124.01	187.39
10 ft.	193.73	293.59
12 ft.	279.03	422.77
16 ft.	496.05	751.59

Mulching

Mulching is one of the simplest and most beneficial procedures you can use in your landscape. It saves moisture, moderates soil temperature, reduces soil surface compaction, slows erosion and water runoff, improves soil structure, controls weeds, reduces evaporation, and encourages beneficial micro-organisms and earthworms. Mulch the soil surface inside the watering basin with 1 to 2 inches of humus mulch or compost.

Watering

Irrigation of landscape plants is necessary in most gardens. It takes a little under-standing and a lot of common sense to answer the question "how often should I water and for how long?" The term *evapotranspiration* describes the loss of water as it evaporates from the soil surface above a plant's root zone and as it transpires off plant surfaces. The amount of moisture lost via evapotranspiration and percolation is the volume of water that needs to be replenished. Moisture loss is greatest when soils are porous with little organic material, the air is hot, dry, and breezy, and the landscape is crowded with fast-growing, large-surfaced, shallow-rooted plants.

Fertilizing

A complete fertilizer is formulated to include all three primary elements, nitrogen, phosphorus, and potassium, in varying percentages, with the percentages listed on the container in that order. For example, a complete fertilizer formulated to promote the flowering and fruiting of plants would have an analysis high in phosphorus, like 12-55-6, which is 12 percent nitrogen, 55 percent phosphorus, and 6 percent potassium. A specialty formula for palm trees would be 6-3-6 because palms need proportionately more potassium. A formula for promoting foliar growth would have a high percentage of nitrogen (30-10-10).

There are sixteen elements required for plants to grow.

Major Elements:
- Carbon (C) combines with hydrogen and oxygen, via photosynthesis, to form carbohydrates.
- Hydrogen (H) is required in the formation of carbohydrates.
- Oxygen (O) is required in the formation of carbohydrates.

Primary Nutrients:
- Nitrogen (N) is required in the formation of amino acids, nucleic acids, enzymes, and chlorophyll.
- Phosphorus (P) is used to form DNA; it stimulates growth and root formation and promotes seed formation.
- Potassium (K) encourages root growth and disease resistance, increases the size of fruits and vegetables, and increases winter hardiness.

Secondary Nutrients:
- Calcium (Ca) is required for structural cell development.
- Magnesium (Mg) is required for photosynthesis.
- Sulfur (S) is required for protein synthesis.

Micronutrients:
- Zinc (Zn) controls the synthesis of plant growth regulators.
- Iron (Fe) is required for the formation of chlorophyll.
- Manganese (Mn) assists in chlorophyll formation.
- Copper (Cu) activates several enzymes in plants.
- Boron (B) is required in the development of meristem cells.
- Molybdenum (Mo) is required for plants to utilize nitrogen.
- Chlorine (Cl) is required for photosynthesis.

Pruning

There should be little or no pruning required if you have selected the right plant and planted it in the right place.

Pruning should be an art based on experience as much as it is a science based on research, but as our knowledge increases, it seems to be becoming less of an art form and more of an academic exercise. The following is an explanation of pruning method that tries to remain mindful of the artistry behind good technique.

The standard method once was to prune back a plant's canopy during transplanting so that it would be proportionate to the size of the excavated rootball. It seemed logical that the removed portion of the canopy would reduce moisture loss and prevent plant desiccation. But current research has found that there are plant growth hormones, called auxins, concentrated in the branch and twig tips that will stimulate new root development if there is mechanical, disease, or insect damage to the root system. Conversely, there are plant growth regulators, called cytokinins, concentrated in the plant's root system that will stimulate new canopy growth if there is damage to a plant's canopy. With this finding, we know it is not wise to prune back the plant's canopy—that would remove the auxins, slowing down new growth and hindering the reestablishment of the root system. When transplanting from ground to ground, however, it is beneficial to reduce moisture loss by pruning off 60 to 90 percent of a plant's foliage.

Any necessary pruning should enhance a plant's structural stability by creating a proportional taper to the framework. As a plant grows, the lower and inner portions should be strong and flexible enough to support the portions above or outside them. Pruning cuts should expose the least amount of surface area so they will callus over quickly and defend against disease and insect invasion.

Pruning trees can increase the quality and quantity of their fruit production. Knowing that some varieties bear on last year's wood and some bear on current season's wood will help you either enhance or eliminate next season's yield. For example, Apple trees bear on fruiting spurs, which are short, stubby branches that develop on branches that are at least one year old. This means if you heavily prune the tree in winter and remove what appear to be short, dead branches that are actually fruiting spurs, there will be no fruit the following season. When pruning an Apple tree, pay particular attention to dead, diseased, and interfering wood. Then head back the branching structure to control the canopy, and cut back all the water sprouts and suckers to the base of the trunk. Genoa Fig trees, on the other hand, bear on current-season wood and should be pruned back severely each winter to promote optimum fruit development.

Pruning to reduce a plant's size and density is relatively easy. For example, if you have an overgrown shrub that is full of dead branches, prune the plant back to 20 percent smaller than the size you want it to regrow. Selectively remove diseased, damaged, and interfering branches. Sunlight stimulates latent branch buds, so new branches and leaves will emerge if sunlight is allowed into a plant's canopy clusters.

Plants that bloom in the early spring are pruned differently. Since they set their buds in late summer or fall, prune the plants back after they finish blooming in spring, not in the winter months.

Additional Species Information

Bulbs

Dahlia (*Dahlia* × hybrid)

Propagation To successfully propagate Dahlias by tuber division, carefully dig up the tuber cluster, prune off and discard the spent growth, and sever the tuber from the cluster, with a section of the crown including one or two eyes. At planting time, place three wooden or plastic stakes tied with twine or tomato-type cages a few inches away from the center of tubers. This is particularly helpful for taller varieties, and by staking early, you avoid damaging your freshly planted tubers and future developing roots.

Design Tips Dahlias provide warm splashes of color in perennial borders, in beds by themselves, as borders for flower beds, and as charming windowbox or pot displays. Despite their sharp fragrance, they make lush summer cut-flower arrangements that last for up to a week if you use a powdered floral preservative and trim off any foliage that falls below the water line. Pick the flowers in the early morning and select only those that are fully open, because the buds will not open once they are cut. If you want dried flowers, snip them just before they are fully open and hang them upside-down in a dark, dry area with good air circulation such as a closet. As long as you have not treated your Dahlias with any pesticides, herbicides, or fungicides that have long-term residual effects, you can use their flower petals as a colorful and edible accent to salads.

Categories There are hundreds of varieties and cultivars of Dahlias. The following are the Dahlia groups designated by the Royal Horticultural Society: (1) Single-Flowered, (2) Anemone-Flowered, (3) Collerette, open-centered resembling a collar, (4) Waterlily, full double blooms, (5) Decorative, largest, full double blooms, (6) Ball, (7) Pompon, (8) Cactus-Flowered, (9) Semi-Cactus-Flowered, (10) Miscellaneous.

Freesia (*Freesia* × hybrid)

Design Tips Freesias are wonderful seasonal plants for rock gardens, in fronts of borders, along meandering paths, in containers, and as cut flowers. Pick when at least one flower on each spike is open, and to avoid premature flower wilt, keep your bouquet away from drafts, dry heat, or any source of ethylene gas such as fresh fruit or vegetables.

Gladiola (*Gladiolus* × hybrid)

Design Tips Use Gladioli as bold accent plants among other summer annuals, in perennial borders, in tall stands of grass, as patio or deck container plants if staked properly, or in cut-flower gardens. Harvest them when their spikes are tightly budded, with at least one or two showing color, and arrange them in a large vase for a simple, but dramatic decorative statement.

Categories If you become a collector of Gladioli, you will find the following are the main groupings: (1) Grandiflorus, large flowers, (2) Nanus, miniature flowers, and (3) Primulinus, small flowers.

Narcissus (*Narcissus* × hybrid)

Using a Bulb Vase If you use a special bulb vase or a container that holds 2 to 3 inches of gravel, fill with just enough water to touch the bulb base, not too deep because the bulb will rot. Place the container in a cool, dark place such as a closet until strong roots form and foliar growth reaches two to three inches. Then move it into the light, add water as needed to keep roots wet, and maintain until the flowers are spent. Then discard or plant again, but do not hold your breath waiting for them to bloom once more. It may take several years before another bloom cycle commences.

Design Tips If you select early-, mid-, and late-season varieties and plant them *en masse* in thin woodlands and grass, near deciduous shrubs, among perennial plants, packed in containers alone or with other bulbs and annuals, in rock gardens or sunny corners of borders, you can have prolific flowers for about two months. They are also grown commercially for their perfume, even though it takes about 1500 pounds of flowers to extract 2½ pounds of essence. Since this is impractical for the average gardener, simply cut a fragrant bouquet of Narcissi in the early morning, just when the flowers have begun to open. Once you cut the stems, a gooey latex that is harmful to other flowers oozes out, so wash their stems, add a drop of bleach in the water and let them stand in it all by themselves for at least twenty-four hours. Then you can combine them with other flowers.

Official Divisions There are so many Narcissus that vary in size, shape, color, habit, and bloom period that the Royal Horticultural Society in England has officially designated twelve divisions that include the traditional buttercup-yellow Trumpet Daffodils and the heavily perfumed Paper-white Narcissus. Some have large or small cups (coronas), others have two or three pendant, reflexed, or spreading flowers, while still others have up to twenty flowers on stout stems. Several stand as tall as two feet and some are miniature two-inch gems. Divisions are (1) Trumpet Daffodils, (2) Large-cupped Daffodils, (3) Small-cupped Daffodils, (4) Double Daffodils, (5) Triandrus Daffodils, (6) Cyclamineus Daffodils, (7) Jonquilla Daffodils, (8) Tazetta Daffodils, (9) Poeticus, (10) Species, (11) Split-corona Daffodils, and (12) Miscellaneous Daffodils.

Persian Buttercup (*Ranunculus asiaticus*)

Design Tips Persian Buttercups are fabulous for spring displays in borders, containers, and flower arrangements. Use them in a solid mass by themselves, or blend them with other mixed flowers. Since their bloom cycle lasts up to five weeks, you can have a bountiful supply for indoor bouquets. Cut early in the morning, selecting buds that are just showing color, add a powdered flower preservative, and change the water regularly.

Recommended Varieties *R. a.* 'Tecolote', which originated in San Diego, is composed of a group of hybrids that produce super-large, intensely colorful flowers. *R. a.* 'Picotee', a compact plant, has double flowers edged in a darker color.

Peruvian Lily (*Alstroemeria aurantiaca*)

Propagation Propagation can be done by seed or by division when the tubers are dormant. In temperate zones, the tubers can remain in the ground, but where there is frost, remove the tubers, store in a dry, cool place, and replant in spring after the last frost. Since we live in a frost-free region, we like to shake the dried seed capsules into a paper bag for storage until spring.

Cut-Flower Tips Harvest your flowers for indoor arrangements when the first buds open and the majority of the buds are showing color. Your Peruvian Lilies will last for about ten days if you make sure there are no leaves sitting in the water and you add a powdered floral preservative to your vase water.

Tuberose (*Polianthes tuberosa*)

Design Tips With their elegant beauty and delicious fragrance, they are wonderful additions to a scented garden, growing against a sunny wall, standing in front of taller summer blooms in a cottage garden, or planted by themselves in containers. As cut flowers, they provide a cool contrast to the hot, primary shades of summer blooms. Harvest them in the early morning, selecting stems that have about half their flowers open and showing color; add a powdered floral preservative to the water and they can last for up to two weeks.

Fruit Trees

Apple (*Malus sylvestris*)

Our love of apples puts us in very good company with such illustrious gardeners as John Chapman, known as Johnny Appleseed, who planted apples along the Ohio River Valley in the 1800s; Thomas Jefferson, who cultivated many apple varieties on his beloved estate, Monticello; Margaret Smith, who discovered a new seedling and called it, appropriately, the Granny Apple; and Mr. and Mrs. Robert Gordon who planted and patented the vigorous, low-to-high-chill Gordon Apple. Recently, Mrs. Gordon wrote Bruce that although her husband has passed away, his legacy, the original Gordon Apple Tree, is still viable, bearing bountiful supplies of fruits at their home in Whittier, California. It is comforting to know that our love of plants can make a difference long after we are gone.

Planting Tip Since few Apple trees are self-pollinating, plant at least two varieties for a good harvest. Purchase one- or two-year-old trees because older ones do not bear fruit any sooner and may suffer from more severe root shock than younger specimens. Consult your local retail nursery or University of California Cooperative Extensions for the latest information on the most appropriate varieties as well as the latest insect-control remedies.

Pruning At planting, prune to about three to four feet and cut away any broken or injured roots. At the end of the first season, prune new growth branches to a length of twenty-four inches and remove any weak branches. Prune back second-year growth by about 50 percent. Once established, prune to remove suckers, water sprouts, and damaged or interfering branches, and thin to keep the canopy open to sunlight and air circulation. For the plumpest, juiciest apples, thin by picking off the tiny fruit, leaving one fruit every six to eight inches along a branch.

Design Tips The trees are decorative in large containers or along patios, as hedges along driveways, as espaliers against sheltering walls, as visual screens or property boundaries, as elegant cut branches for indoor arrangements, and even as accents in mixed borders.

Recommended Varieties The Gordon Apple (Patent #4144) is self-fruitful and requires 300 to 500 winter-chill hours; the reddish-green apples with white flesh are medium to large, and taste sweet, tart, firm, crunchy, and juicy; they are excellent for fresh eating, cooking, or baking; the tree produces heavily in areas where winters are mild and ripens mid-August to mid-October. The Granny Smith Apple is self-fruitful and requires 400 winter-chill hours; the bright-green apples are sweet and firm-fleshed, good for munching, cooking, or applesauce; the tree does well in cold climates if the season has adequate length; it ripens August to September. The Pettingill is self-fruitful and requires 300 winter-chill hours (it is possibly the best red apple for low-chill areas); its large, round apples have deep-red skin with yellow stripes, taste sweet and tart, and are harvested for eating fresh, apple pies, and applesauce; it ripens August to September.

Apricot (*Prunus armeniaca*)

Harvesting Since Apricot trees bloom and bear fruit on branches one year old (last summer's growth) and on fruiting spurs, depending on the variety, they seem to cluster their fruit on the outer third, central third, or the inner third of last summer's growth. The fruit should be culled each spring when they reach the size of a dime and spaced two to three inches apart for the largest, plumpest, and tastiest fruits. The apricots ripen in just a couple of days at room temperature. Be careful not to damage the spur when picking off the fruit, or it will not bear again. Just give it a slight upward twist.

Pruning During the winter dormant period, prune for shape, cutting off any diseased or damaged branches, and removing suckers and water sprouts. To encourage foliar growth, thin lightly to keep the canopy open to sunlight and air circulation. Remove fallen fruit and dropped leaves, because a good housekeeping routine will go a long way in preventing disease and insect problems.

Winter Chill The most common complaint about Apricot trees is sporadic fruit production; for the most part, this problem is due to mild climate conditions or variety. For a good harvest, most Apricot trees require at least 500 hours of 45-degree-Fahrenheit chill during the winter, as occurs in the Central Valley. There are usually only 200 to 300 chill hours in Southern California, so select a low-chill variety for best results in this area.

Recommended Varieties 'Royal Blenheim' is self-fruitful and requires 400 to 500 winter-chill hours; its medium to large fruit is dull yellow with an orange blush, deliciously sweet and juicy, and good for eating, canning, and drying; an erratic producer, it ripens late June to early July. 'Katy' (Patent #4339) is self-fruitful and requires 300 winter-chill hours; its very large, golden-orange freestone fruit has a sweet taste and is excellent for eating, drying, or cooking; a good variety for mild-winter areas, it ripens in early June. 'Moorpark' is self-fruitful and requires 600 to

700 winter-chill hours; its large, luscious, sweet fruit has brownish-red skin, is a favorite for eating, preserves, and pies, and ripens late June to early July.

Fig *(Ficus carica)*

Pruning Wear gloves when working around the tree. At planting, prune to about thirty inches and cut away any broken or injured roots. In succeeding years, prune to remove suckers, water sprouts, interfering branches, and damaged branches, and thin out to keep canopies open to sunlight and air circulation. Since the first crop of early-summer fruit is produced on last-season's wood, only trim tip growth to maintain size and shape. The second crop develops on current-season growth, and ripens in late summer to fall. Because of the two-crop-a-year cycle, it is best to prune lightly while the trees are still dormant.

Harvesting Wear gloves when harvesting the fruit because the milky sap can irritate your skin. Pick figs when they are full-size, soft to the touch, and come off easily. If picked before its time, the stem will "bleed" a white sap.

Recommended Varieties *Ficus carica* 'Brown Turkey' has medium to large bell-shaped fruit with purplish-brown skin and light strawberry flesh; best when eaten fresh. *F. c.* 'White Genoa' has large yellow-green fruit with thin skin and yellow to light-strawberry flesh with few seeds; excellent for eating fresh and as dried fruit. *F. c.* 'White Kadota' has medium-sized lemon-yellow fruit with amber flesh and few seeds; use fresh, for canning, or for drying.

Japanese Plum *(Prunus salicina)*

We planted our Japanese Plum tree on a neglected slope that receives a minimal amount of care, and yet it is flourishing despite the lack of attention. It is living proof of the value of "planting the right tree in the right place." If you do not have another cross-pollinizing variety, place fresh bouquets of suitable pollinizers in water-filled bottles or buckets and hang them on the leeward side of your tree.

Pruning Prune to remove suckers, water sprouts, damaged branches, and dead wood, and thin to keep the canopy open to sunlight and air circulation. In early to midsummer, just after the normal fruit drop, thin more by picking off all but one of the thumbnail-size plums per spur, spacing the fruits four to six inches apart.

Harvesting Japanese Plums are usually ripe when they plop into your hand after a gentle twist. You can pick them before they are ripe because they will continue to soften and sweeten off the tree; just be sure to avoid torn skins by leaving part of the leaf stem attached.

Nectarine *(Prunus persica* 'Nectarina')

Pruning Prune annually in December or January, because fruit is produced on the shoots of previous season's growth. At planting, prune to about three to four feet and cut away any broken or injured roots. For established trees, prune enough to encourage fifteen to thirty inches of new growth each year. Remove suckers, water sprouts, and damaged branches, and thin to keep the canopy open to sunlight and air circulation.

For the plumpest, juiciest nectarines, thin by picking off the tiny fruit around April through May, leaving a single fruit every four to six inches along a branch. As a routine preventative and remedy for disease and insect infestation, clip off damaged foliage or branches as quickly as possible and dispose of any fallen fruit or leaves.

Peach (*Prunus persica*)

Pruning At planting, prune to about three to four feet and cut away any broken or injured roots. For established trees, prune enough to encourage fifteen to thirty inches of new growth each year. Remove suckers, water sprouts, and damaged branches, and thin to keep the canopy open to sunlight and air circulation. For the plumpest, juiciest peaches, thin by picking off the tiny fruit around April through May, leaving a single fruit every five to eight inches along a branch.

Harvesting For larger fruit and to prevent limb breakage, it is necessary to remove more peaches than you leave on the tree. Ripeness is determined by the skin's undercolor. At first it is greenish-yellow, but when it is ripe, the color becomes a pronounced yellow and the reddish blush brightens.

Pests and Diseases If birds and gophers damage the fruit, provide netting and traps. Peach leaf curl, peach tree borer, and brown rot are problems that may cause serious damage if left untreated. Control peach leaf curl and brown rot with a dormant spray of an appropriate fungicide. Control peach tree borer with a parasitic nematode in a squeeze bottle applicator.

Recommended Varieties *Prunus persica* 'Babcock', a heavy bearer, has medium-sized freestone fruit with red-cheeked skin and sweet, juicy white flesh; it requires 350 to 450 chill hours and ripens in early July. *P. p.* 'Ventura' has medium-large fruit with red-blushed skin and golden-yellow flesh that is sweet and mild-flavored; it is a freestone that bears very well in mild, coastal areas, has low chill requirements of 400 to 500 hours, and ripens in early July. *P. p.* 'Bonanza' has medium to large fruit with yellow skin and red blush, is yellow-fleshed and freestone, produces heavily, and ripens in early to mid-June; good for mild-winter areas, it grows five to six feet and requires 400 to 500 hours of winter chill.

Pear (*Pyrus communis*)

Some Pears are short-lived and others survive for hundreds of years, but most are not self-fruitful and need two or three trees for cross-pollination. Their hardwood is prized for musical instruments and sculptures. Winter cold is a requirement for most Pears to induce dormancy. They usually do not do well in the mild Los Angeles-San Diego regions, but there are a few low-chill varieties, such as the Asian Pear, that do fairly well. Most survive temperatures as low as -20 Fahrenheit, appreciate long, hot summers if adequate moisture is provided, and once established, tolerate short periods of drought. If they are in a bloom or growth cycle, they are sensitive to spring frosts and cold winds.

Pruning At the second year, select three or four main scaffold branches so that there is enough spread to support the weight of future crops. In succeeding years, prune lightly to maintain shape, remove suckers, water sprouts, damaged branches, and interfering limbs, and thin to keep the canopy open to sunlight and air circulation. Pear fruit buds usually have five to seven flowers and form from blooms on spurs. Thin fruit by picking off half the fruits per flower cluster four to six weeks after the blooms are spent.

Harvesting Pears are unique in that they ripen from the inside out. If you wait until a pear's outside is soft, it is overripe. It is best to harvest about a week before fully ripe and place in a paper bag until ready to eat.

Recommended Varieties *Pyrus communis* 'Winter Nelis' has medium-round, dull-green fruit that has rough skin and excellent flavor and stores well; the tree produces heavily and is a good pollinizer for the Bartlett; it requires 800 to 900 hours of winter chill and ripens in November. *P. pyrifolia* 'Shinseki', commonly referred to as Asian Pear, has rounded, apple-shaped fruit with a yellow, thick, fairly smooth skin and a sweet, mild, crispy, juicy flavor; it has a low chill requirement of 300 to 450 hours and ripens in late June to mid-August. *P. pyrifolia* 'Shinko' has medium to large fruit with brownish-green skin and excellent rich, sweet flavor; it requires 450 hours of winter chill and ripens from mid-August through mid-September.

Persimmon (*Diospyros kaki*)

Pruning For large fruits and bright color, prune to train a central leader with well-spaced laterals in summer. Prune mature trees lightly to remove suckers, water sprouts, and damaged branches, and thin to keep the canopy open to the sun and air.

Harvesting Although slow growing, the trees bear fruit two to five years after planting. If you want to get ahead of your foraging birds, pick persimmons when they are green to orange but still firm. Use clippers to avoid tearing the fruit, and snip off with a small section of their stems. Ripen indoors by placing them stem side down, leaving them at room temperature away from direct sunlight.

Pomegranate (*Punica granatum*)

Pruning If you prefer a single trunk, select one strong sucker or trunk of the original tree; encourage branch growth from that single trunk and remove all basal suckers. If a multiple trunk is your preference, select five or six vigorous suckers around the base and allow them to grow while removing all others in the summer and during dormant periods. Once established, lightly prune each winter to maintain shape, removing suckers, water sprouts, and damaged and interfering branches, and thin to keep the canopy open to sunlight and air circulation. Be careful to leave sufficient fruit-bearing wood. Thin fruit by picking off the tiny fruits, leaving one for every six to eight inches along a branch.

Gardening Tip Avoid permanently staining your clothes by cutting off the blossom end of the fruit and scoring the rind lengthwise in four to five places. Soak the fruit in cold water for a few minutes. While keeping the fruit underwater, break it apart along the scoring lines, pull back the rind, and remove the seeds from the bitter pith.

Sweet Cherry (*Prunus avium*)

When we visited Seattle in June, street vendors on every corner were selling crates of purplish-black 'Bing' and golden red-cheeked 'Rainier' cherries. As our "farmer" bagged the cherry treasures, we asked him where they were harvested, and he replied in a secretive voice that a farm in Turlock shipped them to him. To our surprise, we learned that California is the leader of the pack in the production of Sweet Cherries, closely followed by Oregon and Washington. They are usually the first summer fruits to appear in markets from late May through mid-July.

Pruning At the end of the first season, select three or four main branches that are spaced evenly around the tree, and prune off any weak branches. For succeeding years, prune to remove suckers, water sprouts, damaged branches, and shoots that grow straight up, cross, or turn towards the center. Prune to achieve a graceful and spreading canopy that opens its center to sunlight and air circulation and to control its size for ease of harvest.

Harvesting Although *Prunus avium* means "for the birds," referring to our feathered friends' food of choice, there is usually more than enough to share. The trees bear from four to five years after planting and produce as much as two-hundred pounds when they reach the age of twenty years. Most Sweet Cherries are not self-fruitful, so it is necessary to have two compatible varieties planted within fifty feet of each other for proper cross-pollination. Insects such as honeybees are the actual agents of pollen transfer. If you have the room, two Cherry trees mean twice as many delectable fruits to make juice, wine, preserves, tarts, pies, and Cherries Jubilee, as well as branches of magnificent blooms for flower arrangements. The taste test is the best determinant for the ideal harvest time. Cut while the stem is still attached to avoid any damage to the fruiting spurs.

Gardening Tip When planting and pruning, be careful not to rub off any buds along the trunk because it will hurt the potential of good lateral growth. It is preferable to purchase one-year-old trees rather than older ones, because there is little difference in bearing time, and it is easier to prune and train a younger tree.

Lawns

Bermuda Grass (*Cynodon dactylon*)

Improved Hybrid Bermudas During winter or when temperatures dip below 55 degrees Fahrenheit, Bermuda Grass can turn straw-colored and go dormant, and it does not tolerate shady conditions. Its aristocratic cousins, the hybrid Bermudas, possess the same positive strengths of heat- and drought-resistance, vigor, and freedom from serious pests and diseases, while improving on some of the weaknesses of coarseness, seed setting, and invasiveness. *Cynodon dactylon* 'Tifgreen' is an attractive cultivar that makes an excellent putting green. C. d. 'Santa Ana' tolerates smog, grows fast, and has a short dormancy.

Nut Trees

Almond (*Prunus dulcis*)

Most varieties of Almond trees are not self-fertile, and at least two varieties that bloom at the same time are needed to produce fruit. Almond trees grafted on

Peach-tree rootstock live for about twenty years and bear up to twenty-five pounds of nuts from five to seven years of age. In addition to providing roasted treats and nuts for baked delicacies, Almond trees can be used as accents in borders and among shrubs. While the buds are still closed, cut a few branches to enjoy an early breath of spring indoors.

Recommended Varieties *Prunus dulcis* 'Garden Prince' (Patent # 5146), a compact semi-dwarf tree that grows to eight to twelve feet and ripens late September to early October, is self-fruitful, requires only 250 hours of winter chill, and bears heavily while young. Thin-shelled, heavy-bearing *P. d.* 'Nonpareil', the number-one commercial Almond, needs a pollinizer, requires 400 hours of chill, adapts to most localities, blooms midseason, and ripens in September. *P. d.* 'Texas', also known as 'Mission', is semi–self-fruitful, needs 500 hours of chill, ripens in October, has a hard shell, and is the best variety for pollinating 'Nonpareil'.

English Walnut (*Juglans regia*)

Pruning Prune older trees during winter dormancy to thin out crowded or crossing branches or to remove any damaged or dead wood or limbs that are too close to the ground.

Harvesting Walnut lovers know it is time to harvest when the green husks wither and slough off, exposing their crinkled brown contents. Depending on the location, Walnuts are ready to harvest from mid-September to October. After husking, wash off the nuts and dry in full sun on shallow trays. Stir the nuts so they are evenly dry. They are completely dry when their pellicles, the papery dividers between the nut meat halves, snap rather than bend. Whole nuts can be stored in their shells for about a year. Shelled nutmeats can be stored in air-tight containers for months in the refrigerator, or for years in the freezer.

Note of Caution Although Walnut trees are excellent ornamentals for large gardens and their nuts are delicious additions to baked desserts and sauces, they have specific cultivation needs that are incompatible with lawns and flower beds. Since their fallen leaves are toxic to other plants, do not add them to a compost heap.

Recommended Varieties The nuts that *Juglans regia* 'Carmelo' bears in late September are twice the size of a normal walnut and have flavorful light-colored meat. *J. r.* 'Carpathian,' also known as 'Mesa', bears medium-sized thin-shelled nuts in early October. *J. r.* 'Chandler' (Patent # 4388) bears very heavy crops of excellent quality with well-sealed shells, ripening in mid-September. *J. r.* 'Idaho' bears very large, sweet-tasting nuts in late September; this is a good-quality, excellent eating walnut, extremely hardy, and produces well in the milder climates of Southern California. *J. r.* 'Payne' bears medium-sized nuts in early September; the tree itself is a smaller-growing tree.

Macadamia Nut (*Macadamia tetraphylla*)

Harvesting and Preparation Once the nuts fall to the ground, crack open their husks with pliers, then air-dry them on trays in a dry, shady location for up to three weeks. Continue to dry them in a food dehydrator or oven-bake them in a shallow pan at 100 to 115 degrees Fahrenheit for forty-eight hours, stirring occasionally.

After shelling, oven-bake them one final time, for fifteen to thirty minutes in a 250- to 350-degree oven. Remove when the nuts start to brown, then add salt or oil, or leave plain. Once cool, store in air-tight containers and freeze. They keep almost indefinitely when frozen. Use them for baking crumb crusts, cookies, or breads; in sauces; or as an addictive snack, smothered in chocolate.

Recommended Varieties *M. integrifolia*, commonly known as the Queensland Nut or Smooth-Shell Macadamia Nut, grows seventy feet tall, has smooth-margined leaves and creamy-white flowers, and bears throughout the year. *M.* × hybrid 'Beaumont' bears more than one crop per year; it produces more nuts than *Macadamia tetraphylla*, and grows larger and faster, but is slower to drop its crop. *M. t.* 'Cate', the only variety recommended to grow above 1500 feet, bears thin-shelled nuts.

Pecan (*Carya illinoinensis*)

Recommended Variety *Carya illinoinensis* 'Western Schley' bears large, elongated nuts that have a rich flavor and ripen in November; it is the West's leading soft-shelled variety and an excellent choice for Southern California deserts and higher altitudes.

Pistachio (*Pistacia vera*)

California Pistachio History After years of experience, we have learned that many of the surprises life offers are found just around the corner, where you least expect them. While on a promotional tour for the radio program in Chico, Bruce noticed an interesting site filled with trees down the road from the station. It was the USDA Plant Introduction Station, and this was the place where the California Pistachio industry began. In 1929, a deciduous fruit specialist named William E. Whitehouse wandered around Persian plantations, dusty village markets, and bazaars for six months, collecting distinctive Pistachio nut seeds. He came back with twenty pounds of carefully selected seeds, and germinated them in 1930 at the Chico Plant Introduction Station. Since most Pistachio trees need seven to ten years to mature, it took him about a decade to learn what he had gathered. Out of 3000 germinated trees, twenty seemed worthwhile, and three were promising enough to name, but two of those three eventually proved unsatisfactory. Although he never saw the actual tree that the one successful variety came from, he did know that he had picked it out of a pile of nuts being dried from the Agah family orchards located in Iran's central plateau, Rafsanjian. Whitehouse named the variety 'Kerman' after the famous rug-making city near the Agah orchard. Today there are over 50,000 acres of Pistachio trees in California and California is second only to Iran in production—all because of the persistence and patience of William Whitehouse, who dropped that fateful seed in his collection bag almost seventy years ago. When he visited the plant station, the Whitehouse story immediately came to mind, and thanks to life's unexpected turn, Bruce walked through a page of California agricultural history.

Pruning Develop three to five main limbs at one-foot intervals, with the first limb at least three to four feet above the ground. Once established, lightly prune off undesirable growth and thin out weak or interfering branches, but avoid heavy pruning as much as possible because the flowers are produced on previous-season's growth.

Recommended Variety *Pistacia vera* 'Peters' is a male variety that was discovered as a chance seedling in Mr. A. B. Peters' Fresno garden in the 1920s; it prolifically sheds pollen about the same time that Kermans are in bloom. 'Bronte', 'Trabonella', and 'Red Aleppo' are other female varieties that can be pollinated by 'Peters'.

Roses

Climbing Rose

Recommended Varieties (1) Climbing 'Cecile Brunner' is capable of becoming a large climber, growing as much as twenty by twenty feet, but regular pruning will restrain it. June is its peak flowering period, but there are sporadic flushes through summer and fall. Its double-shaped, fragrant, shell-pink flowers are excellent for growing into trees or covering unsightly structures. Introduced in 1894, it continues to be a favorite climber for its profuse blooms, beautifully contrasting dark-green foliage, and vigorous growth habit. (2) 'Mermaid' has striking lemon-yellow buds that open into single, pale-yellow, four-inch flowers with conspicuous golden-brown stamens. The petals overlap, and some curl at the edges, for a simple but graceful appearance. After the first bloom in June, it will continue to bloom throughout summer. Slender bright-green leaves tinged with bronze cover the new growth armed with cruel backward-pointing thorns, but their sweetly perfumed flowers and long bloom cycle more than compensate for any scratches. Unlike most climbers, it will flower in shade, but it will flower more in full sun. In all but the most temperate areas, it does best in a protected location. A vigorous grower, it is preferable to plant it alone. In fact, ours has woven its way into a tall Jacaranda tree. (3) *R. b.* 'Banksiae' or Banksia Rose has creamy-white double flowers with evergreen thornless leaves that are tinged with red. The 1½-inch flowers emerge in late April or early May and have a scent similar to that of Sweet Violets. Banksia is a healthy, vigorous climber that needs regular pruning, flowers on previous year's growth, and requires the protection of a sunny wall except in the most temperate regions. In mild-winter areas, it is evergreen and aphid- and disease-resistant. (4) *R. b.* 'Lutea' has growth habits that are similar to those of its white-flowered cousin, but the flowers are lighter in fragrance and a pale yellow in color.

Floribunda Rose

Recommended Varieties (1) 'Angel Face' bears shapely buds that are lavender-mauve, shading to deep pink at the edges, with a heady, sweet fragrance. Once fully opened, the three- to four-inch flowers have ruffled petals and golden-yellow stamens. The three-foot plant has a bushy, spreading shape covered by semi-glossy, coppery-green foliage. (2) 'Iceberg' is the most popular icy-white floribunda with two- to three-inch cup-shaped, fragrant blooms formed on sprays that flower from spring through summer. The blossoms can cover the entire four- to five-foot-tall, slightly spreading bush, making it an excellent hedge rose or specimen bush. The narrow foliage is a glossy light green. It needs extra protection from mildew and rust, but is resistant to black spot and lasts very well in cut-flower arrangements. (3) 'Pink Parfait' buds open into large, semi-double (about twenty-five to thirty petals) flowers whose petals are tinted in several shades of pink ending with a rich, cream color at their base. Although there is little or no fragrance, the flowers are excellent for cut arrangements and resistant to rain damage, and the stems are slender and practically thornless. This is a vigorous, branching plant with medium-green, leathery foliage that is fairly resistant to disease. It's one of the best choices for a rose bed or border, or for pruning as an upright specimen bush.

Grandiflora Rose

Recommended Varieties (1) 'Fame' is a true red with ruffly edges. No other rose comes close to its long vase life, which is at least twice as long as any other rose. (2) 'Gold Medal' is one of the last roses to end its bloom cycle. During particularly mild winters, some of my gardening friends have cut the tawny-edged, yellow blossoms as late as Christmas. The rose is not only a perfect example of the grandiflora class, but is my choice for one of the best yellow roses in any class. Although slightly susceptible to black spot and moderately tender in a cold climate, they are resistant to mildew and rust. The fruity or tea-like fragrance and long-lasting cut-flower quality of the large five-inch blooms more than make up for these minor flaws. (3) 'Shreveport' is named for Shreveport, Louisiana, headquarters of the American Rose Society. It has four-inch flowers with fifty petals that are color-blended in shades of orange and amber. Although its canes are covered with small, downward-facing thorns, its positive qualities include a faint tea fragrance, resistance to disease, a vigorous growth habit, and winter hardiness.

Hybrid Tea Rose

Pruning Prune back tall plants to three or four feet, and prune back small varieties to about eighteen inches. Clear the ground of all leaves and weeds and apply dormant spray to the plants and the soil. If you want the classic form of one flower bud to a stem, break away any emerging side buds. Within a few weeks of the initial disbudding, more lateral shoots will appear eight to sixteen inches below the terminal bud; they must be removed so that all the plant's energy is channeled into the development of the terminal flower, not the side shoots. Roses are at their most fragrant in the early morning before their oil evaporates from the base of their petals. When you prune back the old canes, make sure they are cut flush to the base of the plant, leaving no stubs. To shape, make cuts 1/4 inch above a growth bud that is pointed away from the center axis of the plant so that its growth is encouraged outward rather than inward.

Recommended Varieties (1) 'Double Delight' was introduced in 1976. It remains our favorite rose, with its lush, forty-petaled, creamy vanilla, 5½-inch flowers whose edges look like they have been dipped in raspberry juice. Our noses know when they inhale the spicy, fruity perfume of a 'Double Delight', and it is just as delightful to look at as it is to smell. Its semi-glossy, medium-green leaves grow on a strong three- to four-foot-tall bush. (2) 'Mister Lincoln' is one of the best red roses. It has been around since 1964 and stands tall in a large bed. Its heavily fragrant 4½- to six-inch blooms are a velvety deep red that does not fade in the sun. With its tall, unbranched stems covered with dark-green, nonglossy leaves, 'Mr. Lincoln' makes an elegant long-lasting cut flower. (3) 'Peace' was christened in 1945, on the day Berlin fell, and its spectacular five- to six-inch pink-edged, yellow blossoms is an appropriate messenger of peace. It grows up to six feet tall, needs plenty of space, and has dark-green, glossy foliage and lightly fragrant blooms in early summer. (4) 'St. Patrick' is a 1996 All-America Rose Selections winner that is yellow-gold with a chartreuse cast when tightly budded. Although its fragrance is slight, its unusual coloration, long upright stems with gray-green foliage, tolerance to all sorts of weather, and symmetrical blooms of thirty to thirty-five petals make it a very special hybrid tea. Even when other roses are wilting in the heat, these flowers remain fresh and crisp.

Miniature Rose

Indoor Care For indoor miniature rose displays, use a 2-inch tray filled with 1 inch of gravel or pebbles, and place next to a south-facing window for maximum humidity and light. Keep the bottom of the tray wet at all times, but make sure the water level is below the top of the gravel. Mist leaves frequently and water generously, but allow the pots to dry out slightly between waterings. In summer, protect the roses from the harsh midday sun.

Recommended Varieties (1) 'Cinderella' has fluffy, ½- to 1-inch blooms that are satin-white tinged with a pale flesh-pink. It stands eight to ten inches tall, and its almost thornless, upright stems are covered with light-green, shiny leaves. The fifty-five–petaled flowers have a spicy fragrance, resemble miniature hybrid teas, and last very well as cut flowers. (2) 'Magic Carrousel' has striking, shapely blossoms that are white with clearly defined reddish-pink edges. The slightly fragrant two-inch flowers are produced in small clusters amidst glossy medium-green and bronze foliage. It is one of the tallest miniature rose plants at fifteen to thirty inches, and is known for its disease resistance and winter hardiness. (3) 'Starina' was one of the first roses selected to the Miniature Rose Hall of Fame. It has perfect thimble-sized blooms that are bright vermilion with a high-centered hybrid tea form. The plant grows twelve to sixteen inches tall and has good disease resistance and fair winter hardiness. With its long-lasting flowers that cover the plant from early summer to November, it is ideal for container planting, in bedding areas, or set alone as a miniature standard.

adventitious: Describes a structure that develops in an unusual place, such as roots that develop from a trunk's base.

alkaline soil: Soil with a pH greater than 7.0.

allelopathic: Describes a plant that releases a toxic chemical that inhibits growth in other plants.

all-purpose fertilizer: Powdered, liquid, or granular fertilizer with three primary nutrients—nitrogen (N), potassium (P), and phosphorus (K). It is suitable for maintenance nutrition for most plants.

alternate bearing: Describes fruit or nut trees that produce heavily one year and little or none the next.

annual: A plant that completes its life cycle within one year.

anther: The pollen-bearing part of a stamen.

***Bacillus thuringiensis* or *B.t.*:** A bacterium, lethal to many kinds of caterpillar pests, and used to control them.

backfill: The soil mixture used to surround a rootball in a planting pit.

balled and burlapped: Describes a tree or shrub grown in the field whose rootball was wrapped with protective burlap and twine when the plant was dug up to be sold or transplanted.

bare root: Describes plants that have been packaged without any soil around their roots. (Often young shrubs and trees purchased through the mail arrive with their exposed roots covered with moist peat or sphagnum moss, sawdust, or similar material, and wrapped in plastic.)

beneficial insects: Insects or their larvae that prey on pest organisms and their eggs. They may be flying insects such as ladybugs, parasitic wasps, praying mantids, and soldier bugs, or soil dwellers such as predatory nematodes, spiders, and ants.

berm: A narrow raised ring of soil around a tree, used to hold water so it will be directed to the root zone.

biennial: A plant that completes its life cycle within two years.

bipinnate: Describes a leaf that has divisions that are themselves once or several times compound.

borer: An insect or insect larva that bores into the woody parts of plants.

bract: A modified leaf structure on a plant stem near its flower that resembles a petal. Often it is more colorful and visible than the actual flower, as in Bougainvillea.

brown rot gummosis: A disease characterized by the formation of patches of gum on a fruit tree, the result of insects, microorganisms, or weather; when left untreated, it causes bark to scale, fall off, and ooze from the infected site and will eventually lead to the tree's demise.

bud union: The place where the top of a plant was grafted to the rootstock; usually refers to roses.

bulb: A short, modified, underground stem surrounded by usually fleshy modified leaves that contain stored food for the shoot within. True bulbs have pointed tops, short underground stems on basal plates, and new growths, called bulblets, which form from offshoots of the parent bulbs. The term is used loosely to describe bulblike plants (such as corms, rhizomes, and tubers), as many plants are technically not true bulbs.

canopy: The overhead branching area of a tree, usually referring to its extent including foliage.

ciliated: Edged with hairs along the margin or edge, usually forming a fringe.

cold hardiness: The ability of a perennial plant to survive the winter cold in a particular area.

color packs: Sectioned plastic containers used for growing annuals and perennials.

compost: Organic matter that has undergone progressive decomposition by microbial and macrobial activity until it is reduced to a spongy, fluffy texture. Added to soil of any type, it improves the soil's ability to hold air and water and to drain well.

corm: A structure that grows upwards and is similar to a bulb, except that each summer a new corm grows on top of the original one. As the parent corm disappears, the roots of the new corm grow downward into the hole left by the decayed corm.

corolla: The petals of a flower considered as a group or unit.

corona: A crown-shaped, funnel-shaped, or trumpet-shaped outgrowth of certain flowers, such as the daffodil or the spider lily. Also called crown.

cultivar: A CULTIvated VARiety. It is a naturally occurring form of a plant that has been identified as special or superior and is purposely selected for propagation and production.

deadhead: To remove faded flower heads from plants to improve their appearance, abort seed production, and stimulate further flowering.

deciduous plants: Unlike evergreens, these trees and shrubs lose their leaves in the fall.

desiccation: Drying out of foliage tissues, usually due to drought or wind.

diazinon: An amber liquid, $C_{12}H_{21}N_2O_3PS$, used as an insecticide.

dimorphic: Existing or occurring in two distinct forms.

dioecious: Having the male and female reproductive organs borne on separate individuals of the same species. Both male and female plants are needed for pollination and seed production.

disbud: To take out the center flower bud shortly after the side buds emerge so that the plant's energy is directed toward the side buds.

division: The practice of splitting apart perennial plants to create several smaller-rooted segments. The practice is useful for controlling the plant's size and for acquiring more plants; it is also essential to the health and continued flowering of certain ones.

dormancy: The period, usually the winter, when perennial plants temporarily cease active growth and rest. Go dormant is the verb form, as used in this sentence: *Some plants, like spring-blooming bulbs, go dormant in the summer.*

drupe: A fleshy fruit, like a peach, plum, or cherry, with a single hard stone that encloses a seed.

drupelets: Individual bumpy, fleshy, seed-containing units that make up a whole berry.

earwig: An elongate insect of the order Dermaptera with a pair of pincerlike appendages.

epiphytes: A plant that grows on another plant upon which it depends for mechanical support but not for nutrients.

espalier: A tree or shrub that is trained to grow in a flat plane against a wall, often in a symmetrical pattern.

establishment: The point at which a newly planted tree, shrub, or flower begins to produce new growth, either foliage or stems. This is an indication that the roots have recovered from transplant shock and have begun to grow and spread.

evapotranspiration: The moving of water from the earth into the air by evaporation from soil and transpiration from plants.

evergreen: Describes perennial plants that do not lose their foliage annually with the onset of winter. Needled or broadleaf foliage will persist and continues to function on a plant through one or more winters, aging and dropping unobtrusively in cycles of three or four years or more.

floret: A tiny flower, usually one of many forming a cluster, that comprises a single blossom.

foliar: Of or about foliage.

frass: Sawdust-like debris that accumulates below the holes caused by insects or larvae that bore into the woody parts of plants.

freestone: Describes a fruit with flesh that separates easily from the stony pit.

germinate: To sprout; germination is a fertile seed's first stage of development.

graft (union): The point on the stem of a woody plant with sturdier roots where a stem from a highly ornamental plant (or plant with superior fruit quality) is inserted so that it will join with it. Roses and fruit trees are commonly grafted.

hardpan: A layer of hard subsoil or clay.

herbaceous: Describes plants having fleshy or soft stems that die back with frost.

holdfasts: Tendrils with disc-like suction cups or rootlets that enable a plant to attach to just about anything.

hybrid: A plant that is the result of intentional or natural cross-pollination between two or more plants of the same species or genus.

inflorescences: Flower clusters.

June Drop: A common citrus malady: the sudden shedding of immature fruit, nature's way of adjusting the crop size to the tree's capability to produce good fruit.

latex: The colorless or milky sap of certain plants, that coagulates on exposure to air.

leach lines: Sewer discharge lines.

lignotuber: A swollen portion of the root flare that is just above or below the ground. It functions as a moisture and nutrient storage reservoir during times of drought. Even after a natural disaster, such as a fire, the lignotuber allows it to regenerate.

molluscicide: An agent that kills mollusks, including slugs and snails.

monocarpic: Describes plants that flower and bear fruit only once.

monocotyledon: A flowering plant, like grasses, orchids, and lilies, that has a single leaf in the seed.

mulch: A layer of material over bare soil to protect it from erosion and compaction by rain, and to discourage weeds. It may be inorganic (gravel, fabric) or organic (wood chips, bark, pine needles, chopped leaves).

naturalize: (a) To plant seeds, bulbs, or plants in a random, informal pattern as they would appear in their natural habitat; (b) to adapt to and spread throughout adopted habitats (a tendency of some nonnative plants).

nectar: The sweet fluid produced by glands on flowers that attract pollinators such as hummingbirds and honeybees.

offset: A shoot that develops at the base of a plant and may root to form a new plant.

operculum: A lid that covers each bud and pops off when its stamens unfold during its flowering period.

organic material, organic matter: Any material or debris that is derived from plants. It is carbon-based material capable of undergoing decomposition and decay.

palmate: Describes fronds that are round or semicircular in outline.

peat moss: Organic matter from peat sedges (United States) or sphagnum mosses (Canada), often used to improve soil texture.

pedicel: In a cluster of flowers, a stem bearing a single flower.

pellicle: The papery divider between nut meat halves.

percolation: Passing or oozing through porous material, as in water passing through soil.

perennial: A flowering plant that completes its life cycle in more than two years. Many die back with frost, but their roots survive the winter and generate new shoots in spring.

petiole: The stalk by which a leaf is attached to a stem.

pH: a measurement of the relative acidity (low pH) or alkalinity (high pH) of soil or water based on a scale of 1 to 14, 7 being neutral. Individual plants require soil to be within a certain range so that nutrients can dissolve in moisture and be available to them.

pinnate: Describes fronds that are linear or oblong in outline with segments arranged like the pattern of a feather.

pollen: The yellow, powdery grains in the center of a flower. A plant's male sex cells, they are transferred to the female plant parts by means of wind or animal pollinators to fertilize them and create seeds.

pollinator: The (male) plant that supplies the pollen to fertilize the female plant of a dioecious pair; also called pollinizer.

pollinizer: Pollinator.

pony packs: Sectioned plastic containers used for growing annuals and perennials.

rectilinear: A shape bound by four straight lines and with 90-degree corners.

rhizome: A specialized stem that spreads horizontally underground or on the surface with adventitious roots and sprouts stems, leaves, and flowers from the rhizome's upper sections.

rhizome: A swollen energy-storing stem structure, similar to a bulb, that lies horizontally in the soil.

rootbound (or potbound): The condition of a plant that has been confined in a container too long, its roots having been forced to wrap around themselves and even swell out of the container.

rootstock: The lower part of a grafted tree or rose.

russeting (or silvering): A blemishing of the rind on lemon trees, caused by mite infestations.

scion: The top part of a tree or rose that has been grafted onto a rootstock.

self-fruitful: Describes a fruit tree that pollinates itself.

semi-evergreen: Tending to be evergreen in a mild climate but deciduous in a rigorous one.

shearing: The pruning technique whereby plant stems and branches are cut uniformly with long-bladed pruning shears (hedge shears) or powered hedge trimmers. It is used when creating and maintaining hedges and topiary.

slow-acting fertilizer: Fertilizer that is water insoluble and therefore releases its nutrients gradually as a function of soil temperature, moisture, and related microbial activity. Typically granular, it may be organic or synthetic.

sow bug: A small terrestrial crustacean; also known as wood louse.

spathe: A leaf or bract subtending a flower grouping.

spray: A cluster of flowers in different stages of development on a single stem.

stamen: The pollen-producing reproductive organ of a flower.

stolon: A specialized above-the-ground stem that produces roots and shoots at the nodes.

stomata: Leaf pores.

sucker: A new growing shoot. Underground plant roots produce suckers to form new stems and spread by means of these suckering roots to form large plantings, or colonies. Some plants produce root suckers or branch suckers as a result of pruning or wounding.

tillering: Sending forth shoots from its base (as grass does).

tomentose: Fuzzy in texture.

tuber: A swollen rhizome that produces pulpy, instead of scaly, stems. Tubers normally grow just below the surface of the soil and, like bulbs, store food for the plants. The buds on tubers become stems, leaves, and flowers, and clusters of roots form at the base. They multiply by division, and as they divide, the parent tuber deteriorates.

umbel: A flat-topped or rounded flower cluster; the flower stalks rise from about the same point.

variegated: Having various colors or color patterns. The term usually refers to plant foliage that is streaked, edged, blotched, or mottled with a contrasting color, often green with yellow, cream, or white.

vectoring: Carrying (diseases from plant to plant).

xeriphytic: Having to do with water-conserving landscaping.

xeriscape: A landscape system designed to conserve water.

Bibliography

Bailey, L. H. *A Standard Cyclopedia of Horticulture*. 3 volumes. New York, New York: The Macmillan Company, 1958.

Condit, Ira J. *Ficus: The Exotic Species*. Berkeley, California: University of California Division of Agricultural Sciences, 1969.

Graf, Alfred Byrd. *Exotica Series 3: Pictorial Cyclopedia of Exotic Plants from Tropical and Near-tropic Regions*. East Rutherford, New Jersey: Roehrs Company, Inc., 1973.

Griffiths, Mark. *Index of Garden Plants*. Portland, Oregon: Timber Press, Inc., 1994.

Pizzetti, Ippolito and Henry Cocker. *Flowers: A Guide for Your Garden*. 2 volumes. New York, New York: Harry N. Abrams, Inc., 1975.

Smiley, Beth and Ray Rogers, editors. *Ultimate Rose*. New York, New York: Dorling Kindersley Publishing, Inc., 2000.

Vavilov, N. I. *Origin and Geography of Cultivated Plants*. New York, New York: Press Syndicate of the University of Cambridge, 1994.

Photography Credits

Sources for photographs in this book are as follows:

Thomas Eltzroth
   Pages: Front cover, 5, 6, 7, 9, 10, 12, 14, 15, 18, 24, 28, 32, 40, 41, 42, 44, 46, 50, 52, 53, 56, 60, 62, 66, 68, 70, 72, 74, 75, 76, 77, 80, 82, 84, 86, 88, 90, 94, 96, 99, 104, 108, 118, 119, 120, 121, 124, 126, 130, 134, 136, 138, 140, 141, 142, 146, 148, 160, 164, 166, 172, 173, 174, 176, 184, 186, 188, 192, 196, 197, 198, 202, 212, 218, 220, 222, 226, 228, (lower), 229, 230, 231, 234, 236, 240, 242, 243, 246, 256, 258, 260, 266, 268, 274, 278, 280, 284, 286, 288, 290, 292, 296, 302, 306, 308, 310, 312, 313 (lower), 314, 318, 320, 322, 330, 336, 342, 346, 350, 352, 354, 358, 360, 364, 366, 370, 372, 376, 382, 386, 388, 392

Lorenzo Gunn
   Pages: 13, 22, 26, 78, 92, 100, 102, 106, 110, 112, 116, 122, 132, 143, 144, 150, 152, 154, 156, 158, 161, 178, 180, 182, 185, 190, 194, 206, 214, 228 (upper), 264, 270, 272, 276, 282, 316, 324, 326, 338, 348, 356, 362, 368, 371, 374, 378, 380, 384, 394, About the Authors, Back cover

Liz Ball and Rick Ray
   Pages: 8, 19, 20, 30, 34, 36, 38, 48, 54, 58, 64, 98, 114, 128, 162, 170, 200, 204, 208, 210, 216, 224, 232, 244, 250, 254, 262, 294, 298, 300, 304, 313 (upper), 328, 332, 334, 340, 344, 390, 396

Bruce Asakawa
   Pages: 11, 168, 238, 248, 252

Chart Credits

Charts on pages 401, 402, and 403 are reproduced from *Western Fertilizer Handbook—Horticulture Edition* © 1990 by the California Fertilizer Association and Interstate Publishers, Inc.

Meet Bruce and Sharon Asakawa

Bruce and Sharon Asakawa

Bruce Asakawa has been active in the green industry, landscape design, and gardening communication most of his life. His parents started Presidio Garden Center in 1950, which became one of the premier retail nurseries on the West Coast. Their nursery business was one of the first to diversify into landscape architectural planning, landscape contracting, FTD floral designing, and koi/tropical fish importing . . . and it got Bruce himself started in the gardening industry.

In college at Cal Poly, Pomona, Bruce majored in landscape architecture, a field that combined his interest and talents in horticulture, art, design, and nature. He developed and taught classes for the University of California, San Diego, Extension Program. During the early nineties, Bruce was asked by Bert Wahlen Jr. of CPMI to syndicate his popular garden show, and that was the beginning of the the *West Coast Garden Line*™. This very popular radio call-in program is now heard by 1.2 million listeners every week.

Sharon Asakawa began working in the family garden center business after marrying Bruce in the early 1960s. Ultimately, Sharon managed the florist department, gaining much practical experience. Today Sharon co-hosts and is the content producer for the *West Coast Garden Line*™ and the live interactive webcast **OvertheHedge.net**. She also coordinates the programs' horticultural tours.

Bruce and Sharon live in Bonita, California, and have a daughter and a son, Tasia and Eric.

Contact Bruce and Sharon at **basa@gardencompass.com** with your gardening questions.

If you enjoyed this book and would like to receive
gardening and lifestyle information from
Bruce and Sharon all year long, then subsribe
to their bi-monthly magazine,
Garden Compass.

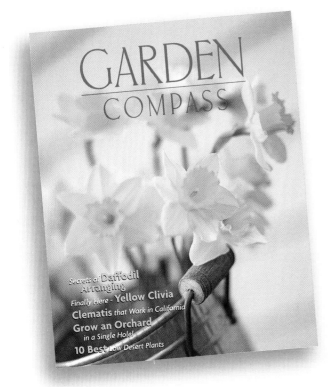

Garden Compass features articles and advice on all of the latest gardening tips and techniques. It is tailored to the California gardener. You'll find answers to many of your gardening questions and subscribers are invited to ask questions of their own. You'll find recipes that might include vegetables, fruits or herbs from your garden. Enjoy the thoughful advice of Bruce and Sharon all year long and/or give a gift subscription to a fellow gardener.

It's easy to subscribe – Simply call 800-566-3622

SPECIAL OFFER

for purchasers of this book

One year subsription price now $15.00 (normally $18.50)

2 years for $29.00 (normally $34.00) • 3 years for $42.00 (normally $49.95)

Please mention "Guide Book Special Offer" when calling